Divine Dynamics:

Exploring Ancient Mesopotamian Mythology, Rivalries, and Spiritual Legacies

M. L. Ruscsak

Divine Dynamics

Trient Press
3375 S Rainbow Blvd
#81710, SMB 13135
Las Vegas,NV 89180

Ordering Information:
Quantity sales. Special discounts are available on quantity purchases by corporations, associations, and others. For details, contact the publisher at the address above.
Orders by U.S. trade bookstores and wholesalers. Please contact Trient Press: Tel: (775) 996-3844; or visit www.trientpress.com.

Printed in the United States of America

Publisher's Cataloging-in-Publication data
Ruscsak, M.L.
A title of a book : Divine Dynamics: Exploring Ancient Mesopotamian Mythology, Rivalries, and Spiritual Legacies volume 1

ISBN
Hard Cover   979-8-88990-103-7

Paper Back   979-8-88990-104-4

Ebook   979-8-88990-105-1

Exploring Ancient Mesopotamian Mythology, Rivalries, and Spiritual Legacies

Divine Dynamics

CANCER RESEARCH UK

St Andrews
143 South Street
St Andrews
01334 474175
Vat #: GB788138678

Date: 18 October 2024 12:09
Transaction Ref: 1067-2410-223163928
Served by:

Sales		

19642	1	£1.00
Books All		

TOTAL	
SUB TOTAL	£1.00
VAT	£0.00
TOTAL	£1.00

TENDER	
Cash	£1.00

If you are a UK Taxpayer your kindly donated items could
be worth 25% more with Gift Aid, with no additional cos
t to you as a donor. Please ask a member of staff for mo
re information.If you change your mind about your purcha
se, please return the item within 14 days with the valid
price ticket attached and your receipt, and we will eit
her offer you an exchange or a refund at the manager's d
iscretion. We do not refund or exchange Books, Videos, C
Ds, DVDs or Lottery Tickets. Your legal right to a refun
d is not affected where the item is faulty. Registered C
harity in England and Wales (1089464), Scotland (SC04166
6) and the Isle of Man (1103).VAT #: GB788138678

Exploring Ancient Mesopotamian Mythology, Rivalries, and Spiritual Legacies

Chapter 1: Introduction to Ancient Mesopotamia: An Overview of the Region and its Significance

Understanding Ancient Mesopotamia: Unveiling the Cradle of Civilization

The study of ancient Mesopotamia holds immense importance in unraveling the origins of human civilization and the development of complex societies. As we embark on this journey through time, Chapter 1 aims to provide a comprehensive introduction to the region of Mesopotamia and its enduring significance. By delving into the rich tapestry of Mesopotamian history, culture, and spirituality, we can gain valuable insights into the foundations of our modern world.

Goals and Objectives of the Chapter

The primary goal of this chapter is to familiarize students with the historical and geographical context of ancient Mesopotamia and its impact on the course of human history. Through a meticulous exploration of key topics and themes, students will develop a deep appreciation for the region's contributions to various fields of study, including witchcraft, divination, herbalism, shamanism, ecospirituality, and even magic in ancient Mesopotamia.

Furthermore, this chapter aims to:

Provide a chronological overview: By examining the timeline of ancient Mesopotamia, students will gain a foundational understanding of the major periods and civilizations that flourished in the region. This includes the Sumerians, Akkadians, Babylonians, and Assyrians, among others.

Explore the geography and environment: Mesopotamia, nestled between the Tigris and Euphrates rivers, played a pivotal role in shaping the region's cultural and social dynamics. Students will delve into the unique geographic features, climate, and natural resources that influenced the development of early civilizations.

Uncover the cultural and religious diversity: Mesopotamia was a melting pot of different peoples, each contributing their own beliefs, practices, and systems of worship. By examining the religious and spiritual traditions of Mesopotamia, students will gain insights into the cosmologies, mythologies, and rituals that underpinned ancient Mesopotamian society.

Preview of Key Topics and Themes

Throughout this chapter, students will encounter a variety of key topics and themes, including:

➢ Mesopotamian geography and its impact on civilization

➢ Chronological overview of ancient Mesopotamian civilizations

➢ Social and cultural aspects of Mesopotamian life

➢ Religious and spiritual beliefs and practices

➢ Influence of ancient Mesopotamia on later civilizations

➢ Critical analysis of available evidence and interpretation

By engaging with these topics, students will develop a solid foundation for further exploration of ancient Mesopotamia's rich history and its enduring impact on modern societies.

In order to enhance student learning and foster critical thinking, each section of this chapter will include examples, problems, and exercises, along with classroom activities that encourage students to reflect, discuss, and analyze the subject matter in a rigorous and engaging manner.

As we embark on this sacred journey into the depths of ancient Mesopotamia, let us embrace the opportunity to unravel the mysteries and unravel the tapestry of this remarkable civilization.

Geographical and Historical Context

In order to fully grasp the significance of ancient Mesopotamia, it is crucial to delve into its geographical and historical context. Chapter 1 sets the stage by providing an in-depth overview of the region's location, geography, and the development of civilization within its boundaries. By exploring these key aspects,

Exploring Ancient Mesopotamian Mythology, Rivalries, and Spiritual Legacies

students will gain a comprehensive understanding of the unique factors that contributed to the rise and flourishing of ancient Mesopotamian societies.

Geographical Features and Location of Mesopotamia

Mesopotamia, meaning "land between the rivers" in Greek, is situated in the fertile crescent of the Near East. It encompasses the vast region between the Tigris and Euphrates rivers, which flow through what is now modern-day Iraq, southeastern Turkey, northeastern Syria, and southwestern Iran. The strategic location of Mesopotamia, characterized by its abundant water supply and fertile soil, played a pivotal role in the development of agricultural practices and the emergence of early human settlements.

The Development of Civilization in the Region

Mesopotamia holds the distinction of being one of the cradles of human civilization, where remarkable advancements in various fields transformed the course of history. Over several millennia, this region witnessed the evolution of complex societies, the birth of written language, the establishment of legal systems, the development of mathematics and astronomy, and the creation of monumental architecture.

Key Historical Periods and Empires

Sumerians (c. 4000 BCE - 2000 BCE): The Sumerian civilization, regarded as the earliest known civilization in Mesopotamia, laid the groundwork for subsequent cultures. They established city-states, invented cuneiform writing, built impressive ziggurats, and contributed to the development of religious and mythological beliefs.

Akkadians (c. 2334 BCE - 2154 BCE): Led by Sargon of Akkad, the Akkadian Empire rose to prominence and became the first known empire in history. Their conquests and centralized administration greatly influenced subsequent Mesopotamian societies.

Babylonians (c. 1894 BCE - 539 BCE): The Babylonian Empire, with Hammurabi as its renowned ruler, introduced one of the world's first comprehensive legal codes, the Code of Hammurabi. They also made notable advancements in astronomy, mathematics, and literature.

Assyrians (c. 2025 BCE - 609 BCE): The Assyrian Empire expanded its territory through military conquests, employing advanced military tactics and infrastructure. They developed an efficient administrative system and left behind impressive architectural wonders.

Neo-Babylonians (c. 626 BCE - 539 BCE): Under Nebuchadnezzar II, the Neo-Babylonians rebuilt the city of Babylon, creating one of the ancient world's most splendid cities. They were known for their astronomical observations and the famous Hanging Gardens of Babylon.

As we embark on this journey through the cradle of civilization, let us explore the geographical and historical foundations of ancient Mesopotamia, unraveling the complexities and marvels that have left an indelible mark on human history.

Cultural and Societal Characteristics

Diversity of Ancient Mesopotamian Cultures

Ancient Mesopotamia was a mosaic of diverse cultures, each contributing its unique customs, languages, and traditions. Various civilizations, such as the Sumerians, Akkadians, Babylonians, and Assyrians, flourished within the region throughout different periods. Despite their differences, these cultures shared common features, such as a polytheistic religious worldview, reliance on agriculture, and a keen interest in literature and the arts.

By examining the diverse cultural characteristics of each civilization, students will gain a deeper understanding of the complexities and shared heritage of ancient Mesopotamia.

Social Structure and Hierarchies

Social structure in ancient Mesopotamia was marked by distinct hierarchies and divisions. At the top of the societal pyramid stood the ruling elite, including kings, nobles, and high-ranking priests who held significant political and religious power. They were responsible for maintaining order, overseeing the administration of laws, and leading military campaigns.

Beneath the ruling class, there existed a middle class consisting of merchants, artisans, and scribes who played vital roles in economic activities, trade, and record-keeping. The majority of the population comprised farmers, laborers, and slaves who toiled to sustain the agricultural and urban sectors.

Exploring Ancient Mesopotamian Mythology, Rivalries, and Spiritual Legacies

By examining the social structure and hierarchies of ancient Mesopotamia, students will gain insights into the dynamics of power, social mobility, and the complex relationships that characterized Mesopotamian society.

Economic Systems and Trade Networks

Ancient Mesopotamia boasted a thriving economy that relied on diverse economic systems and extensive trade networks. Agriculture formed the foundation of the economy, with farmers cultivating crops such as barley, wheat, dates, and vegetables. Irrigation systems, such as canals and dikes, were developed to harness the waters of the Tigris and Euphrates rivers, ensuring a steady food supply.

Trade played a crucial role in Mesopotamia's economic prosperity. The region's strategic location facilitated trade routes connecting various civilizations across the ancient world. Students will explore the significance of trade, including the exchange of goods, such as textiles, metals, spices, and luxury items, and the establishment of trade colonies in distant lands.

Through the examination of economic systems and trade networks, students will gain a holistic understanding of the interconnectedness of ancient Mesopotamia with the broader world and the economic mechanisms that sustained its societies.

In order to engage students in critical thinking and discussion, this chapter will incorporate examples, problems, and exercises that prompt students to reflect on the cultural and societal characteristics of ancient Mesopotamia. Classroom activities will encourage students to analyze primary sources, engage in group discussions, and explore case studies that shed light on the complexities of ancient Mesopotamian culture and society.

As we unravel the cultural tapestry and societal dynamics of ancient Mesopotamia, let us appreciate the multifaceted nature of this civilization, recognizing its enduring influence and contributions to human history.

Religion in Ancient Mesopotamia

Significance of Religion in Ancient Mesopotamian Society

Religion held a paramount significance in the lives of ancient Mesopotamians. It was intricately woven into the fabric of their society, influencing their worldview, moral values, and social structures. Understanding the profound influence of religion is crucial for comprehending the motivations and actions of the people who inhabited this ancient land.

In this section, students will delve into the multifaceted significance of religion in ancient Mesopotamian society. They will explore how religion provided a sense of meaning and purpose, offering explanations for natural phenomena, the origins of the world, and the complexities of human existence. Through a deep analysis of primary sources and archaeological evidence, students will uncover the religious underpinnings of Mesopotamian art, literature, law, and social organization.

Polytheistic Beliefs and Pantheon of Deities

Ancient Mesopotamia was characterized by a polytheistic belief system, in which numerous gods and goddesses held sway over different aspects of life and the natural world. Students will embark on a journey through the diverse pantheon of Mesopotamian deities, encountering powerful entities such as Enki, Enlil, Inanna/Ishtar, Marduk, and others.

Through a meticulous examination of religious texts, students will uncover the unique characteristics, roles, and mythological narratives associated with these deities. They will gain insights into how these gods and goddesses were revered, invoked, and worshiped by the Mesopotamians, and how their influence extended into various realms of human existence, including agriculture, fertility, war, and wisdom.

Role of Temples, Priests, and Religious Rituals

Temples stood as magnificent structures dotting the Mesopotamian landscape, serving as focal points for religious worship and community activities. Students will explore the architecture and symbolism of these temples, such as ziggurats, and the integral role they played in the religious and social life of the ancient Mesopotamians.

The role of priests, as intermediaries between the human and divine realms, will be examined in detail. Students will learn about the training, rituals, and responsibilities of these religious functionaries, as well as their close association with political power and governance. Through the study of religious rituals and ceremonies, students will gain insights into the methods employed by the Mesopotamians to communicate with the gods, seek their favor, and ensure the well-being of their communities.

Exploring Ancient Mesopotamian Mythology, Rivalries, and Spiritual Legacies

Incorporating Classroom Activities:

To foster student engagement and critical thinking, this chapter will include a range of activities and exercises. Students may analyze primary sources, such as hymns, prayers, and mythological texts, to gain a deeper understanding of Mesopotamian religious beliefs and practices. They may also participate in discussions and debates on the role of religion in shaping ancient Mesopotamian society and its impact on various aspects of life. Additionally, problem-solving exercises and case studies will challenge students to think analytically and apply their knowledge to real-world scenarios.

By exploring the significance of religion, the polytheistic beliefs, and the role of temples, priests, and religious rituals in ancient Mesopotamia, students will develop a comprehensive understanding of this vibrant and influential aspect of Mesopotamian civilization. This knowledge

Writing and Literature

In ancient Mesopotamia, the invention of writing systems revolutionized human communication, enabling the recording and preservation of knowledge, stories, and religious texts. Chapter 3 delves into the fascinating world of Mesopotamian writing and literature, exploring the invention of writing systems, the importance of literature and epic tales, and the preservation and decipherment of ancient texts.

Invention of Writing Systems: Unveiling Cuneiform

The invention of writing systems marked a pivotal moment in human history. Ancient Mesopotamia boasts one of the earliest known writing systems, known as cuneiform. In this section, students will embark on a journey to understand the origins and development of cuneiform, a complex system of wedge-shaped symbols impressed onto clay tablets.

Through an examination of archaeological discoveries and linguistic analysis, students will explore the evolution of cuneiform from its early pictographic origins to a sophisticated system capable of recording various aspects of life, including religion, law, commerce, and literature. They will gain insights into the role of scribes, the training they underwent, and the materials and tools used in the process of writing.

Importance of Literature and Epic Tales: The Power of Words

Literature held a central place in Mesopotamian society, serving as a means of entertainment, education, and cultural preservation. The Epic of Gilgamesh, an ancient Mesopotamian literary masterpiece, stands as a testament to the enduring power of storytelling. In this section, students will explore the significance of literature and epic tales in Mesopotamia.

By delving into the Epic of Gilgamesh, students will analyze the themes, motifs, and narrative structure of this renowned work. They will grapple with the complexities of the hero's journey, the search for immortality, and the exploration of human nature. Through close reading and textual analysis, students will appreciate the timeless wisdom and profound insights encapsulated in ancient Mesopotamian literature.

Preservation and Decipherment of Ancient Texts: Unlocking the Past

The preservation and decipherment of ancient texts have played a crucial role in unlocking the secrets of Mesopotamian civilization. Students will delve into the challenges and triumphs faced by scholars in deciphering cuneiform and deciphering the messages contained within ancient clay tablets.

Through a case study approach, students will explore the work of notable scholars and their contributions to the decipherment of cuneiform script, such as Henry Rawlinson and George Smith. They will examine the methods employed, including comparative linguistics and the use of bilingual texts, to unravel the meanings and messages hidden within these ancient texts.

Incorporating Classroom Activities:

To engage students actively, this chapter will include various activities and exercises. Students may have the opportunity to practice writing cuneiform symbols using clay or interactive digital tools, gaining a hands-on understanding of the complexities of this ancient writing system. They may also participate in group discussions and presentations, analyzing excerpts from the Epic of Gilgamesh and exploring the universal themes and moral dilemmas found within.

Contributions to Science and Technology

Mesopotamian Advancements in Mathematics and Astronomy: Unveiling the Cosmic Order

Ancient Mesopotamia stands as a cradle of mathematical and astronomical knowledge, where scholars and scribes made groundbreaking discoveries that laid the foundation for future scientific developments. In this section, students will uncover the mathematical prowess of Mesopotamian thinkers and their profound impact on ancient and modern numerical systems.

By examining clay tablets and cuneiform texts, students will explore Mesopotamian mathematical concepts, including the base-60 numeral system and the development of mathematical operations such as addition, subtraction, multiplication, and division. They will encounter mathematical problems and exercises, demonstrating how ancient Mesopotamian scholars used their knowledge in practical applications, such as measuring land, calculating areas, and solving geometric puzzles.

Furthermore, students will delve into the field of Mesopotamian astronomy, understanding the connection between celestial observations and religious beliefs. They will analyze the astronomical knowledge recorded on clay tablets, including the tracking of celestial bodies, the development of calendars, and the understanding of celestial events. Through these examples, students will appreciate the sophisticated understanding of the cosmos achieved by Mesopotamian astronomers.

Innovations in Agriculture and Irrigation Systems: Cultivating the Land

Mesopotamia's fertile lands owed much of their productivity to the innovative agricultural and irrigation practices developed by its ancient inhabitants. In this section, students will examine the ingenuity of Mesopotamian farmers and the systems they employed to ensure sustainable food production in an arid environment.

Students will explore the advancements in irrigation technology, such as the development of canals, levees, and reservoirs. They will understand how these systems allowed for efficient water management, ensuring the continuous cultivation of crops and the sustenance of urban centers. Through case studies and examples, students will gain insights into the societal and economic impacts of these agricultural innovations.

Engineering Achievements: Building the Mesopotamian Landscape

Mesopotamian cities were renowned for their impressive architectural and engineering achievements, which transformed the physical landscape of the region. This section will highlight the notable engineering feats of ancient Mesopotamia, including the construction of ziggurats and the planning of cities.

Students will analyze the purpose and symbolism behind ziggurats, monumental structures that served as religious centers and focal points of worship. They will examine the architectural elements and the mathematical precision employed in their construction, illustrating the integration of religious beliefs and engineering knowledge.

Additionally, students will explore the urban planning and city layout of ancient Mesopotamian settlements. They will understand the principles of city design, including the organization of streets, the construction of defensive walls, and the establishment of public infrastructure. By examining the ruins of ancient cities such as Babylon and Ur, students will gain a comprehensive understanding of the urban environments created by Mesopotamian architects and city planners.

Class Exercise: Exploring Ancient Mesopotamia's Scientific and Technological Advancements

In this chapter, we will not only delve into the fascinating scientific and technological achievements of ancient Mesopotamia but also actively engage in hands-on activities and research projects to deepen our understanding. These exercises will provide you with an opportunity to experience the ingenuity of this ancient civilization firsthand.

Hands-on Experiment: Designing a Mesopotamian Irrigation System
Step into the shoes of ancient Mesopotamian farmers and engineers by designing and constructing a model of a Mesopotamian irrigation system. You will explore the innovative methods used to cultivate the land in this arid region. Consider factors such as the terrain, water sources, and efficient water distribution. Collaborate in groups to brainstorm and build your irrigation system, and then test its effectiveness by simulating water flow and observing its impact on crop growth. Through this activity, you will gain insight into the challenges faced by ancient Mesopotamian farmers and appreciate their inventive solutions.

Simulating Mathematical Calculations: Creating Clay Tablets
Experience the numerical system of ancient Mesopotamia by creating your own clay tablets with mathematical calculations using the base-60 numeral system. This hands-on exercise will give you a practical understanding of the numerical concepts used by Mesopotamian scholars. Using clay or modeling material, inscribe the cuneiform symbols representing numbers and perform basic mathematical operations, such as addition, subtraction, multiplication, and division. Discuss your findings with your peers and reflect on the advantages and limitations of the Mesopotamian numerical system. This activity will provide a unique insight into the mathematical prowess of ancient Mesopotamians.[

Exploring Ancient Mesopotamian Mythology, Rivalries, and Spiritual Legacies

Research Project: Unveiling Mesopotamian Scientific and Technological Marvels

Embark on a research project exploring specific areas of scientific and technological advancements in Mesopotamia. Select a topic of interest, such as Mesopotamian astronomy, the development of agricultural practices, or the engineering marvels of ancient Mesopotamian cities. Conduct in-depth research, consult primary and secondary sources, and present your findings and analysis to the class. This project will enhance your research and critical thinking skills while allowing you to delve deeper into a particular aspect of Mesopotamian contributions to science and technology.

Through these engaging activities and research projects, you will develop a profound appreciation for the scientific and technological acumen of ancient Mesopotamia. By exploring their advancements in mathematics and astronomy, innovations in agriculture and irrigation systems, and the engineering achievements that shaped their cities, you will gain insight into the enduring legacy of this civilization. You will recognize how their contributions have shaped subsequent scientific and technological advancements throughout history.

Art, Architecture, and Material Culture

Characteristics of Mesopotamian Art and Architecture

Mesopotamian art and architecture offer a fascinating glimpse into the cultural and aesthetic expressions of this ancient civilization. The art of Mesopotamia is characterized by its intricate details, meticulous craftsmanship, and the diverse range of materials used. From monumental sculptures to vibrant ceramics and intricately carved reliefs, Mesopotamian art showcases the creativity and technical prowess of its artisans.

> Monumental Architecture: Ziggurats and Palaces

One of the most distinctive architectural features of Mesopotamia is the ziggurat, a massive stepped pyramid-like structure that served as a religious center and symbol of divine connection. These towering structures, such as the famous ziggurat of Ur, were constructed with baked bricks and adorned with colorful glazed tiles, reflecting the grandeur and spiritual significance of the Mesopotamian religion.

In addition to ziggurats, palaces played a vital role in Mesopotamian society. These palatial complexes, such as the Palace of Sargon II at Dur Sharrukin, featured elaborate courtyards, impressive facades, and intricate wall reliefs depicting scenes of royal power, religious ceremonies, and mythological narratives. The architectural design of these palaces emphasized both functionality and symbolism, serving as a testament to the wealth and authority of the ruling elite.

>   Relief Sculpture and Cylinder Seals

Mesopotamian artists excelled in the art of relief sculpture, which adorned palace walls and public buildings. These relief sculptures, typically carved into stone or gypsum slabs, depicted a wide range of subjects, including deities, rulers, battles, and everyday life. The intricate details and precise execution of these reliefs provide invaluable insights into Mesopotamian cultural practices, social hierarchies, and religious beliefs.

Cylinder seals were another significant artistic medium in Mesopotamia. These small, cylindrical objects made of stone or clay were intricately engraved with scenes and symbols. When rolled onto clay or wax, they served as personal signatures, official marks, and protective amulets. The imagery on cylinder seals often depicted mythological narratives, religious rituals, and historical events, providing a glimpse into the beliefs and customs of the time.

II. Symbolism and Motifs in Artistic Representations

Mesopotamian art is replete with symbolism and recurring motifs that reflect the cultural and religious beliefs of the civilization. These artistic expressions were often imbued with divine, cosmic, and ritualistic significance, conveying the complex worldview and spiritual practices of the ancient Mesopotamians.

>   Divine Figures and Symbolic Beings

Mesopotamian art prominently featured representations of gods, goddesses, and other divine beings. The divine figures were depicted in human or anthropomorphic form, often with elaborate headdresses, regal attire, and symbolic attributes. The portrayal of these deities served to communicate their power, attributes, and roles within the divine pantheon. Additionally, mythical creatures, such as winged bulls and lions, were commonly depicted, symbolizing protection and divine authority.

>   Narrative Scenes and Mythological Motifs

Narrative scenes and mythological motifs were integral to Mesopotamian art. These visual narratives depicted episodes from epic tales, religious myths, and historical events. The relief sculptures on palace walls and cylinder seals often portrayed heroic exploits, religious rituals, and cosmic battles. These artistic representations served not only as a means of storytelling but also as a means of conveying moral and ethical messages, reinforcing cultural values, and legitimizing the power of rulers.

III. Influence of Mesopotamian Art on Subsequent Civilizations

The artistic achievements of ancient Mesopotamia had a profound influence on subsequent civilizations, both geographically neighboring and distant. The legacy of Mesopotamian art can be observed in various aspects of later artistic traditions, demonstrating the enduring impact of this ancient civilization.

> Influence on Near Eastern and Egyptian Art

The artistic traditions of the Near Eastern civilizations, including the Hittites, Assyrians, and Persians, were heavily influenced by Mesopotamian art. This influence is evident in architectural forms, decorative motifs, and the use of relief sculptures to communicate power and authority. Similarly, Egyptian art, although distinct in its style and religious symbolism, shows evidence of cross-cultural exchanges with Mesopotamia, particularly during periods of political and cultural interactions.

> Impact on Western Art and Architecture

Mesopotamian art and architecture also left an indelible mark on the development of Western art. As trade routes expanded and cultural exchange took place, elements of Mesopotamian art began to permeate the artistic traditions of ancient Greece and Rome. Greek and Roman architecture, for instance, drew inspiration from the monumental structures and engineering prowess of Mesopotamia. The influence of Mesopotamian motifs and iconography can also be seen in later European art movements, such as neoclassicism and art nouveau.

In conclusion, the art, architecture, and material culture of ancient Mesopotamia offer a rich tapestry of creative expressions, intricate symbolism, and enduring influences. By studying Mesopotamian art, we gain valuable insights into the cultural, religious, and social aspects of this civilization. The legacy of Mesopotamian art not only shaped subsequent artistic traditions but also serves as a testament to the creativity and artistic ingenuity of humanity throughout the ages.

Conclusion

In conclusion, this chapter has provided a comprehensive overview of the significance of ancient Mesopotamia in the study of spirituality and religions. We have explored the diverse religious beliefs, practices, and deities of this ancient civilization, highlighting the polytheistic nature of their faith and the central role of temples, priests, and religious rituals.

Ancient Mesopotamia holds immense importance for understanding the development of human spirituality and religious thought. It serves as a gateway to exploring the roots of various spiritual traditions, including witchcraft, divination, herbalism, shamanism, and magic. By examining the religious institutions and beliefs of ancient Mesopotamia, we gain insights into the complex and interconnected nature of human spirituality throughout history.

Furthermore, we have examined the geographical and historical context of Mesopotamia, emphasizing its strategic location between the Tigris and Euphrates rivers and its pivotal role in the development of early civilizations. We have delved into the cultural and societal characteristics of this region, highlighting the diversity of ancient Mesopotamian cultures, the social structures and hierarchies that governed their societies, and the economic systems and trade networks that sustained their civilization.

Looking ahead, the next chapter will explore Mesopotamian cosmology and creation myths. We will delve into the ancient Mesopotamian understanding of the universe, the creation of the world, and the divine beings responsible for these cosmic processes. By examining their cosmological beliefs, we will gain a deeper understanding of how ancient Mesopotamians perceived the origins of existence and the interplay between the divine and the earthly realms.

As we continue our journey through the fascinating world of ancient Mesopotamia, it is crucial to approach the study of spirituality and religions with an open mind and a willingness to explore diverse perspectives. The rich tapestry of ancient Mesopotamian spirituality offers us valuable lessons, insights, and connections to the human quest for meaning and transcendence. Let us embark on this exploration with curiosity, respect, and a commitment to critical thinking, as we unravel the mysteries of Mesopotamian cosmology and creation myths in the next chapter.

Chapter 2: Mesopotamian Cosmology: Creation Myths and the Origins of the Universe

Mesopotamian cosmology, the study of the origins and structure of the universe as perceived by ancient Mesopotamians, holds significant importance in understanding their ancient beliefs and spiritual traditions. In this chapter, we will embark on a journey through Mesopotamian cosmology, exploring the ancient Mesopotamian worldview and their understanding of the cosmos. By delving into their cosmological beliefs, we aim to unravel the intricate tapestry of ancient Mesopotamian spirituality and shed light on the foundations of their religious and philosophical thought.

The objectives of this chapter are twofold. Firstly, we seek to provide a comprehensive analysis of Mesopotamian cosmology, examining its key elements, underlying principles, and cosmological narratives. Through a detailed exploration of ancient texts, including creation myths and cosmological accounts, we will unravel the intricate layers of the Mesopotamian worldview, offering insights into their understanding of the origins of the universe, the nature of divine beings, and the relationship between humans and the cosmos.

Secondly, we aim to highlight the significance of Mesopotamian cosmology in the broader context of ancient beliefs and spirituality. By understanding the cosmological framework within which ancient Mesopotamian religious practices and rituals were conducted, we can grasp the profound impact of cosmology on their religious and philosophical thought. Furthermore, we will examine the ways in which Mesopotamian cosmology influenced and interacted with other aspects of their culture, such as art, literature, and social structures, providing a holistic understanding of ancient Mesopotamian civilization.

The structure of this chapter will guide us through the key topics and themes of Mesopotamian cosmology. We will begin by exploring the Mesopotamian creation myths, which offer profound insights into their cosmological beliefs and the origins of the universe. Through a detailed analysis of these narratives, we will examine the role of divine beings, the creation of the world, and the intricate interplay between the divine and the earthly realms.

Next, we will delve into the cosmological concepts and principles that shaped the Mesopotamian worldview. This will involve an exploration of their understanding of celestial bodies, such as the sun, moon, and stars, and their interpretation of celestial events as divine messages or omens. We will also investigate the concept of cosmic order and the notion of divine governance of the universe.

Throughout the chapter, we will present various interpretations, counterarguments, and dissenting opinions to foster critical thinking and encourage students to engage in scholarly discourse. By examining different scholarly perspectives and engaging with diverse viewpoints, students will develop a nuanced understanding of Mesopotamian cosmology and its complexities.

In conclusion, this chapter aims to provide a thorough and in-depth analysis of Mesopotamian cosmology, its significance in understanding ancient beliefs, and its broader implications for ancient Mesopotamian culture. By delving into the cosmological narratives, concepts, and principles of this ancient civilization, we will gain valuable insights into the interconnectedness of their spiritual, philosophical, and social frameworks. Let us embark on this exploration with an open mind and a commitment to intellectual inquiry as we unravel the mysteries of Mesopotamian cosmology and its enduring relevance in ancient beliefs and spirituality.

Theoretical Framework: Exploring Mesopotamian Worldviews

Cosmology, the study of the universe and its organization, held immense significance in ancient societies. It provided a comprehensive framework through which individuals and communities interpreted their existence and sought to understand the mysteries of the cosmos. In ancient Mesopotamia, cosmology served as the bedrock of their belief systems, shaping their perception of the world, their relationship with the divine, and their understanding of their place within the greater cosmic order.

Cosmology in ancient societies went beyond a purely scientific inquiry into the physical properties of the universe. It encompassed metaphysical and philosophical dimensions, seeking to address fundamental questions about the origins of life, the nature of divinity, and the purpose of human existence. It formed the basis for religious practices, social structures, and cultural expressions, permeating every aspect of ancient life.

By studying Mesopotamian cosmology, we gain valuable insights into the cultural, religious, and philosophical fabric of this ancient civilization. The cosmological beliefs of the Mesopotamians were deeply intertwined with their understanding of creation, the divine hierarchy, and the interplay between celestial and earthly realms. They believed in the existence of a pantheon of gods, each with specific roles and powers, who governed different aspects of the universe and influenced human affairs. These beliefs guided their religious rituals, such as temple worship and divination, as well as their moral and ethical principles.

Comparative analysis of Mesopotamian cosmology with other ancient cosmological frameworks enables us to discern both shared and distinct characteristics among different cultures. By examining the cosmological beliefs of ancient Egypt, Greece, India, and other civilizations, we uncover common themes and patterns that reflect the universal human quest to comprehend the mysteries of the cosmos. These include the presence of divine hierarchies, celestial symbolism, and the association of natural phenomena with divine forces.

At the same time, delving into the unique features of Mesopotamian cosmology allows us to appreciate the specific contributions of this civilization. Mesopotamian cosmology emphasized the interdependence between gods and humans, with gods intervening in human affairs and humans fulfilling their religious obligations to maintain cosmic harmony. Divination and the interpretation of celestial omens played a prominent role in Mesopotamian cosmology, with celestial events believed to carry important messages and indications of divine will.

By situating Mesopotamian cosmology within a broader cross-cultural context, we gain a deeper understanding of its significance and influence. Comparative analysis enriches our exploration of Mesopotamian cosmology by shedding light on both the shared human yearning for cosmic understanding and the unique cultural and intellectual perspectives of this ancient civilization.

In conclusion, cosmology held immense relevance in ancient societies, including Mesopotamia. It provided a comprehensive framework for understanding the universe, one's place within it, and the nature of the divine. By studying Mesopotamian cosmology and conducting comparative analysis with other ancient cosmological frameworks, we unravel the rich tapestry of human beliefs, perceptions, and aspirations that shaped the cultural, religious, and philosophical landscape of ancient civilizations.

Comparative analysis of Mesopotamian cosmology with other ancient cosmological frameworks

Comparative analysis of Mesopotamian cosmology with other ancient cosmological frameworks unveils intriguing similarities and intriguing differences, offering valuable insights into the diversity of human thought and belief systems. By examining the cosmological beliefs of civilizations such as ancient Egypt, Greece, and

India, we can identify shared themes that transcend geographical and cultural boundaries.

One common theme that emerges is the presence of a divine hierarchy. In both Mesopotamian and Egyptian cosmologies, the gods occupy distinct positions within a hierarchical structure, with certain deities holding supreme power and authority. This hierarchical framework reflects the human inclination to organize and comprehend the divine realm in a structured manner. Similarly, Greek and Indian cosmologies feature pantheons of gods and goddesses, each with their own domain of influence and responsibility.

Another shared characteristic is the use of celestial symbolism. Ancient cultures often associated celestial bodies, such as the sun, moon, and stars, with divine forces and cosmic principles. In Mesopotamia, for instance, the movements of celestial bodies were interpreted as signs and omens from the gods, influencing human affairs and offering glimpses into the cosmic order. This association between celestial phenomena and the divine can also be observed in Egyptian and Greek cosmologies, where celestial bodies were revered as representations of gods and cosmic powers.

Furthermore, the association of natural phenomena with divine forces is another common feature. In Mesopotamian cosmology, natural elements such as rivers, mountains, and storms were imbued with divine significance and seen as expressions of the gods' power and influence. Similarly, in ancient Egypt, natural features like the Nile River held immense religious and symbolic value, believed to be interconnected with the gods and their divine plan. The Greek cosmology also attributed divine attributes to natural phenomena, with gods and goddesses associated with various aspects of the natural world, such as the sea, forests, and fertility.

Despite these shared elements, each cosmological framework possesses unique characteristics that reflect the specific cultural and intellectual context of the civilization. Mesopotamian cosmology, for instance, places significant emphasis on the concept of divine governance. The gods in Mesopotamian belief systems actively intervened in human affairs, shaping the course of events and influencing human destiny. This close interplay between gods and humans highlights the dynamic and reciprocal relationship between the divine and the earthly realms in Mesopotamian cosmology.

Moreover, divination and the interpretation of celestial omens played a prominent role in Mesopotamian cosmology. The Mesopotamians believed that celestial events and natural phenomena carried important messages and indications of divine will. They meticulously observed celestial bodies and natural occurrences, seeking to decipher the gods' intentions and gain insight into the future. This focus on divination as a means of understanding the cosmic order distinguishes Mesopotamian cosmology from other ancient cosmologies, revealing the unique intellectual and spiritual landscape of the region.

In conclusion, comparative analysis of Mesopotamian cosmology with other ancient cosmological frameworks provides a deeper understanding of the diversity of human thought and belief systems. While shared elements such as the presence of divine hierarchies, celestial symbolism, and the association of natural phenomena with divine forces can be observed across various ancient civilizations, the unique characteristics of Mesopotamian cosmology, such as its emphasis on divine governance and the role of divination, highlight the distinct cultural and intellectual contributions of this civilization. By situating Mesopotamian cosmology within a broader cross-cultural context, we gain a more comprehensive understanding of its significance and enrich our exploration of ancient beliefs and worldviews.

Influence of cosmological beliefs on religious, social, and cultural aspects of Mesopotamian life

Cosmological beliefs had a profound impact on various aspects of Mesopotamian life, including religious practices, social structures, and cultural expressions. The Mesopotamian pantheon of deities, with its intricate hierarchies and diverse functions, reflected the cosmological understanding of divine order and the interconnectedness between the celestial and earthly realms. The religious rituals and practices, such as temple worship, divination, and astrology, were deeply rooted in cosmological concepts and aimed to maintain harmony between the divine and human spheres.

Furthermore, cosmological beliefs influenced social hierarchies and power structures in Mesopotamian society. The association of kingship with divine authority and the concept of divine favor and divine punishment shaped the political and social landscape. The alignment of human actions with cosmic principles and the belief in cosmic justice underscored the moral and ethical dimensions of Mesopotamian society.

Moreover, cosmological concepts permeated Mesopotamian culture, finding expression in various artistic forms, literature, and architecture. Artistic representations, such as cylinder seals and reliefs, often incorporated celestial motifs and symbolism, reflecting the cosmological understanding of the interconnectedness between the celestial and earthly realms. Epic tales, such as the Epic of Gilgamesh, embedded cosmological themes, providing narratives that explored the human condition in light of the cosmic order.

Additionally, Mesopotamian architecture was influenced by cosmological beliefs, as seen in the construction of ziggurats, towering temple complexes that symbolized the connection between heaven and earth. These monumental structures served as physical manifestations of the cosmic hierarchy, with the temple's elevated position representing the divine realm. The planning and layout of cities and sacred spaces also adhered to cosmological principles, aligning structures with celestial orientations and creating sacred landscapes that mirrored the cosmic order.

Cosmological beliefs had implications for daily life as well. The Mesopotamians perceived the natural world as an interconnected web of cosmic forces, where every aspect of existence was imbued with divine presence. This worldview fostered a deep reverence for nature and the environment, influencing agricultural practices, resource management, and the understanding of humans' relationship with the natural world. It emphasized the importance of maintaining harmony with the cosmic rhythms and respecting the gods' creation.

Furthermore, the cosmological framework shaped the Mesopotamians' perception of time. They believed in cyclical patterns and recurring cosmic cycles, influencing their understanding of history, destiny, and the eternal nature of the universe. Time was perceived as a cosmic phenomenon, intricately woven into the fabric of existence and governed by divine order. This cosmological understanding of time influenced concepts of fate, divination, and the cyclic rise and fall of civilizations.

In conclusion, cosmological beliefs had a far-reaching influence on religious, social, and cultural aspects of Mesopotamian life. They provided a foundation for religious practices, shaped social hierarchies, and influenced the construction of sacred spaces and monumental architecture. Cosmological themes found expression in artistic representations and epic literature, while the understanding of nature and time as intertwined with the cosmic order impacted daily life and shaped the Mesopotamians' relationship with the world around them. By exploring the influence of cosmological beliefs, we gain a deeper appreciation for the interconnectedness of various facets of Mesopotamian civilization and the enduring legacy of their cosmological worldview.

Enuma Elish: The Babylonian Creation Epic

The Enuma Elish, translated as "When on High" or "When in the Heights," begins by introducing the primeval chaos of the universe. It describes the existence of two primary gods: Apsu, the freshwater deity, and Tiamat, the saltwater goddess.

Exploring Ancient Mesopotamian Mythology, Rivalries, and Spiritual Legacies

These primordial forces, representing male and female principles, mingle and give birth to a generation of younger gods.

As the younger gods multiply, they become noisy and disruptive, disturbing the sleep of Apsu and Tiamat. Apsu, driven to silence the clamor, plans to destroy his offspring. However, Ea, the god of wisdom and magic, learns of Apsu's intentions and takes action to protect the younger gods. Ea uses his powers to kill Apsu and establishes his own dwelling place atop Apsu's lifeless body.

After Apsu's demise, Tiamat, grief-stricken and enraged, becomes the primary antagonist in the epic. She unleashes chaos upon the cosmos, creating a fearsome army of monstrous creatures and seeks vengeance for the death of Apsu. Tiamat's fury prompts the remaining gods to seek a champion who can confront her and restore order to the universe.

Marduk, the god of Babylon, emerges as the heroic figure chosen to face Tiamat. The gods agree to elevate Marduk to the highest rank among them and provide him with extraordinary powers and weapons. Marduk accepts the challenge and confronts Tiamat, engaging in a fierce battle. With his superior strength and weaponry, Marduk defeats Tiamat, splitting her body in two and using her remains to fashion the heavens and the earth.

The epic continues with Marduk establishing his rule as the supreme god and creating the cosmos and its various features. Marduk assigns roles and responsibilities to the other gods, establishing the divine order and hierarchy. Finally, Marduk fashions human beings from the blood of a slain god and the bones of a defeated monster. Thus, humanity is created to serve the gods and fulfill their needs.

The Enuma Elish is not only a creation myth but also a tale of the triumph of order over chaos and the establishment of divine kingship. It reflects the Babylonians' understanding of the cosmological forces and their desire to justify the rule of their own patron deity, Marduk. The epic reinforces the belief in the divine right of kings and the significance of Babylon as the center of religious and political power.

Comparisons can be drawn between the Enuma Elish and other creation myths from different cultures. For example, the Enuma Elish shares similarities with the earlier Sumerian creation myth, the Atrahasis Epic, and exhibits parallels with the creation narratives found in other ancient Near Eastern civilizations, such as the Hebrew Bible's Book of Genesis and the Hittite creation myth, the Kumarbi Cycle.

Divine Dynamics

The Enuma Elish has had a lasting influence on later cultures and literature. Its themes of creation, conflict, and divine power have resonated across time, and echoes of its narrative can be found in subsequent mythologies and religious texts. Its influence on Babylonian religion and subsequent Mesopotamian cultures cannot be overstated, as it shaped their understanding of the divine, cosmology, and the origins of the world. Analysis of key themes and symbols in the epic

The Enuma Elish explores several key themes and symbols that are central to the Mesopotamian cosmological framework. One prominent theme is the primordial chaos that precedes the creation of the world. The epic describes a conflict between the gods Tiamat, the personification of chaos, and Marduk, the champion of the younger generation of gods. This conflict culminates in Marduk's victory over Tiamat, leading to the establishment of order and the subsequent creation of the cosmos.

Another significant theme in the Enuma Elish is the concept of divine kingship. The epic portrays Marduk as the supreme deity who assumes kingship over the gods and entrusts him with the task of organizing the universe. This theme reflects the Babylonians' belief in the divine authority vested in their kings, who were seen as the earthly representatives of the gods.

Symbolism is also prevalent in the Enuma Elish. For instance, the use of water imagery symbolizes the primordial state of chaos, while the act of separating the waters represents the establishment of order. Additionally, the epic employs celestial imagery, such as the positioning of the stars and the planets, to convey the divine design of the universe and the interplay between the celestial and earthly realms.

Interpretations and implications of the creation narrative

The creation narrative in the Enuma Elish has been the subject of various interpretations and has significant implications for understanding ancient Mesopotamian beliefs. One interpretation views the epic as a reflection of the Babylonian political and religious context, with Marduk's triumph over chaos symbolizing the ascendancy of Babylon as a dominant power. It underscores the close connection between political power and divine favor in Mesopotamian society.

Another interpretation considers the Enuma Elish as a symbolic representation of natural phenomena and cosmic processes. The conflict between Tiamat and Marduk can be seen as a metaphorical portrayal of the forces at work in the natural world, with chaos representing the untamed elements and Marduk symbolizing the divine power that brings order and stability.

Exploring Ancient Mesopotamian Mythology, Rivalries, and Spiritual Legacies

The creation narrative in the Enuma Elish raises philosophical questions about the origins of the universe, the nature of divinity, and the purpose of human existence. It prompts us to contemplate the relationship between chaos and order, the role of gods and humans in shaping the world, and the moral implications of divine authority. By studying and interpreting the Enuma Elish, we gain a deeper understanding of the complexity and depth of Mesopotamian cosmology, and we can appreciate the enduring legacy of this creation epic on subsequent mythological and religious traditions.

Atrahasis: The Epic of Creation and the Great Flood

The Atrahasis epic holds a central place in the ancient Mesopotamian literary tradition and provides us with a captivating narrative that intertwines creation mythology and the Great Flood. Composed during the Old Babylonian period, which spanned from the 20th to the 16th centuries BCE, this epic reflects the cultural and religious beliefs of the Mesopotamian civilization, particularly in relation to their understanding of the origins of the world and humanity.

At the heart of the Atrahasis epic lies the story of the creation of the cosmos and the emergence of humankind. The Mesopotamians perceived the universe as a carefully orchestrated realm governed by powerful deities who shaped and controlled every aspect of existence. In their cosmology, the gods were seen as active participants in the creation process, with each deity assigned specific roles and responsibilities. The epic provides valuable insights into the Mesopotamian understanding of divine order and the intricate connections between the celestial and earthly realms.

Through the Atrahasis epic, we gain a deeper understanding of the Mesopotamian worldview, revealing their beliefs about the purpose of human existence and the dynamic interactions between gods and mortals. The epic explores themes of divine favor, obedience, and the consequences of human actions. It emphasizes the interconnectedness of the divine and mortal spheres, suggesting that human conduct has a direct impact on the harmony or disharmony between the realms. By studying this epic, we gain valuable insights into the religious and ethical frameworks that guided Mesopotamian society.

Furthermore, the Atrahasis epic sheds light on the origins of cultural and religious practices within ancient Mesopotamia. Many rituals and ceremonies observed in this civilization can be traced back to the narratives and themes presented in the epic. The beliefs and values embedded within the text served as a foundation for societal norms and moral codes. By examining the Atrahasis epic, we unravel the origins of Mesopotamian cultural and religious practices, such as temple worship, divination, and the veneration of deities.

The Atrahasis epic's connection to creation mythology highlights the significance of this ancient text in understanding the broader scope of Mesopotamian cosmology and religious beliefs. It offers a comprehensive narrative that explores the origins of the world, the creation of humanity, and the complex relationships between gods and mortals. By delving into the Atrahasis epic, we embark on a journey to uncover the ancient Mesopotamian worldview, unravel their cosmological beliefs, and appreciate the rich tapestry of their cultural and religious heritage.

Examination of the Creation Account and Flood Narrative in Atrahasis

The examination of the creation account in the Atrahasis epic allows us to delve into the Mesopotamian cosmology and their beliefs about the origins of the world and humanity. The epic depicts a hierarchy of gods, each with their own roles and responsibilities in the creation process. We witness the gods engaging in complex interactions, engaging in acts of divine craftsmanship to shape the cosmos and establish the foundations of the earthly realm.

In the creation account, the gods mold humanity from clay, imbuing them with the breath of life. However, they also bestow limitations upon humans, setting boundaries and establishing societal roles. This narrative highlights the concept of divine favor, as the gods grant certain privileges and gifts to humanity, while also placing restrictions to maintain divine order. The Atrahasis epic explores the dynamics between gods and humans, emphasizing the reciprocal relationship between obedience and divine blessings.

Moving to the flood narrative within the Atrahasis epic, we encounter a cataclysmic event that serves as a form of divine punishment for human transgressions. This flood narrative bears resemblance to flood stories found in various cultures, such as the Epic of Gilgamesh and the biblical story of Noah's Ark. The similarities among these narratives suggest shared cultural and mythological motifs, reflecting the universality of the flood as a symbol of destruction and rebirth.

In the Atrahasis flood narrative, the gods resolve to wipe out humanity due to their growing noise and defiance. However, one god, Enki, who sympathizes with humanity, warns the protagonist, Atrahasis, about the impending catastrophe and advises him on how to survive the flood. Atrahasis constructs a massive boat, fills it with animals and provisions, and rides out the deluge. After the flood recedes, the gods acknowledge the survival of Atrahasis and his role in preserving humanity, thus leading to the reestablishment of order and the continuation of life.

Exploring Ancient Mesopotamian Mythology, Rivalries, and Spiritual Legacies

The flood narrative in the Atrahasis epic explores themes of divine justice, human fallibility, and the importance of obedience to the gods. It portrays the gods as agents of both destruction and renewal, underscoring the cyclical nature of existence. The flood serves as a transformative event, purging the world of corruption and paving the way for a new beginning.

By analyzing the creation account and flood narrative in the Atrahasis epic, we gain a deeper understanding of the Mesopotamian cosmology and their beliefs about the relationship between gods and humans. These narratives provide insights into the moral and ethical dimensions of Mesopotamian society, emphasizing the consequences of human actions and the role of divine intervention in shaping the course of human history. Through critical analysis of these narratives, we unravel the complex layers of Mesopotamian myth and gain valuable insights into the cultural and religious fabric of this ancient civilization.

Comparisons with Other Flood Narratives in Different Cultural Contexts

Exploring the flood narrative in the Atrahasis epic prompts us to embark on a comparative analysis, examining similar stories from diverse cultural contexts. By delving into flood narratives found in other ancient cultures, such as the biblical account of Noah's Ark, the flood myth in the Epic of Gilgamesh, and flood stories from ancient India and China, we can discern both shared elements and distinctive features.

The flood narrative holds a significant place in the mythologies of numerous civilizations, indicating a common human fascination with the themes of cataclysm, survival, and renewal. By comparing these narratives, we can identify overarching motifs that transcend cultural boundaries. One such motif is the concept of divine punishment, where a flood is used as a means to cleanse the world of human corruption and restore order. This notion can be found in both the Atrahasis epic and the biblical story of Noah's Ark, where humanity's transgressions lead to divine retribution through a catastrophic flood.

Another shared element among flood narratives is the theme of human survival against all odds. In the Atrahasis epic, Atrahasis constructs a boat to escape the impending flood and ensures the continuation of human life. Similarly, in the biblical account of Noah's Ark, Noah builds an ark to save himself, his family, and a selection of animals from the floodwaters. These stories emphasize the resilience and resourcefulness of human beings in the face of overwhelming adversity.

Divine Dynamics

Despite these shared elements, each flood narrative also exhibits distinct features that reflect the cultural and theological contexts from which they originate. For example, the Epic of Gilgamesh offers a flood narrative with nuanced complexities, where the flood is unleashed as a response to the gods' disapproval of humanity's noise and hubris. The flood story in ancient Indian and Chinese mythologies reflects their unique cosmological and cultural beliefs, often involving the intervention of deities and the preservation of knowledge or virtuous individuals.

By engaging in a comparative analysis of flood narratives, we not only recognize the commonalities but also appreciate the distinctive aspects of each cultural expression. Through this exploration, we gain insights into the diverse ways in which different societies have grappled with questions of creation, destruction, and rebirth. These flood narratives serve as repositories of cultural values, moral teachings, and theological perspectives, offering profound insights into the human condition and our relationship with the divine.

Through careful analysis and reflection, we develop a nuanced understanding of the Atrahasis epic, its significance within Mesopotamian cosmology, and its connections to broader cross-cultural narratives. This comparative exploration enriches our appreciation of ancient mythologies, fostering a deeper comprehension of human thought, belief systems, and the enduring themes that transcend time and geography.

Mythological Cosmologies

In delving into the rich tapestry of mythological cosmologies, it is essential to begin by exploring the various creation myths that emerged in ancient Mesopotamia. These myths provide valuable insights into the cultural, religious, and philosophical fabric of this civilization, offering glimpses into the ancient Mesopotamians' understanding of the origins and organization of the cosmos.

One prominent Mesopotamian creation myth is the Enuma Elish, also known as the "Babylonian Creation Epic." This epic narrative unfolds a complex cosmological account, depicting a cosmic struggle between primordial forces and the emergence of the world and humanity. Through the story of the battle between the god Marduk and the chaotic dragon Tiamat, we witness the formation of the universe, the establishment of celestial bodies, and the creation of humankind. The Enuma Elish explores themes of divine hierarchy, cosmic order, and the divine right of kingship, offering a comprehensive cosmological framework that shaped Mesopotamian beliefs and societal structures.

Exploring Ancient Mesopotamian Mythology, Rivalries, and Spiritual Legacies

The Enuma Elish serves as a powerful example of how creation myths in ancient Mesopotamia conveyed not only the origins of the cosmos but also the establishment of political and social systems. The narrative presents Marduk's victory over Tiamat as a symbol of the divine right of kingship, legitimizing the rule of Babylonian kings and asserting their authority as representatives of the gods on Earth. This connection between cosmic creation and human governance highlights the close interplay between cosmology, religious belief, and political power in ancient Mesopotamia.

Another significant Mesopotamian creation myth is the Atrahasis epic, which not only encompasses creation mythology but also contains a captivating flood narrative. The Atrahasis epic explores the divine creation of the world, the allocation of responsibilities to gods and humans, and the delicate balance between the divine and mortal realms. It provides insights into the Mesopotamian understanding of the divine order, the purpose of human existence, and the consequences of human transgressions.

The flood narrative within the Atrahasis epic shares similarities with other flood stories from various cultures, highlighting universal themes of divine punishment, human survival, and the renewal of life after catastrophe. This narrative serves as a testament to the enduring human fascination with floods as transformative events that shape the destiny of humanity. The Mesopotamian flood myth, like its counterparts in other cultures, emphasizes the moral implications of human behavior, underscoring the need for obedience to divine commands and the consequences of disobedience.

The Atrahasis epic also raises profound questions about the relationship between gods and humans and the moral responsibility of humanity in maintaining cosmic order. The gods in the Atrahasis epic allocate specific duties and limitations to humans, emphasizing their role as both co-creators and caretakers of the Earth. This highlights the Mesopotamian belief in the interconnectedness between the divine and human realms and the shared responsibility for maintaining harmony within the cosmos.

By exploring these Mesopotamian creation myths, we gain valuable insights into the ancient Mesopotamians' worldview, their understanding of the origins and organization of the cosmos, and the moral and ethical dimensions of human existence. These myths serve as windows into the cultural and religious practices of this civilization, inviting us to contemplate the profound questions of creation, existence, and human purpose that have intrigued humanity since time immemorial.

Divine Dynamics

Analysis of Different Cosmological Concepts and Their Symbolic Meanings

The analysis of different cosmological concepts and their symbolic meanings allows for a deeper understanding of the intricate tapestry of ancient Mesopotamian cosmology. These concepts offer insights into the ways in which the ancient Mesopotamians perceived and interpreted the cosmos, the natural world, and the interplay between the divine and mortal realms.

One fundamental concept is that of divine hierarchy, where gods and goddesses occupy distinct positions within a complex cosmic order. The Mesopotamians attributed specific roles and responsibilities to different deities, reflecting their understanding of the organization and functioning of the universe. For example, Enlil was associated with wind, storms, and kingship, while Inanna represented love, fertility, and war. The celestial bodies, such as the sun, moon, and stars, were also associated with deities and held symbolic significance within the cosmological framework.

The notion of divine hierarchy underscores the Mesopotamian belief in the divine authority and power that governed the cosmos. Each deity possessed unique qualities and domain, contributing to the overall harmony and functioning of the universe. This concept of hierarchy also extended to the human realm, where rulers and leaders were seen as representatives of the gods on Earth, responsible for upholding cosmic order and ensuring the welfare of their subjects.

Another significant cosmological concept is the symbolism of sacred geography. The ancient Mesopotamians believed that certain locations held divine significance and were considered the dwelling places of deities. Cities and temples were constructed to honor and worship specific gods and goddesses, forming sacred landscapes that reflected the cosmological order. For instance, the city of Babylon was closely associated with Marduk, the patron deity of the city, and its temple, the Esagila, was believed to be the earthly abode of Marduk.

The symbolism of sacred geography not only emphasized the Mesopotamian belief in the divine presence within the physical world but also served as a means to establish a connection between the human and divine realms. Pilgrimages to these sacred sites were undertaken as acts of devotion and reverence, allowing individuals to access the divine presence and seek divine blessings. The construction and maintenance of temples and sacred spaces were seen as essential in maintaining cosmic harmony and reinforcing the reciprocal relationship between the gods and humans.

Exploring Ancient Mesopotamian Mythology, Rivalries, and Spiritual Legacies

Furthermore, the Mesopotamians interpreted natural phenomena as manifestations of divine forces. They believed that celestial events, such as eclipses and comets, were celestial omens sent by the gods, providing insights into their will and foretelling future events. This association between cosmic occurrences and divine intentions underscores the profound interconnectedness between the celestial and earthly realms in Mesopotamian cosmology.

The Mesopotamians' interpretation of celestial phenomena as divine messages highlights their belief in a participatory universe, where humans and gods coexisted and interacted. By observing and interpreting these natural signs, the Mesopotamians sought to understand and align themselves with the divine will, enabling them to navigate the complexities of life and make decisions guided by divine guidance.

In conclusion, the analysis of different cosmological concepts in ancient Mesopotamia reveals a complex web of symbolic meanings and interconnected beliefs. The concepts of divine hierarchy, sacred geography, and the interpretation of natural phenomena as divine signs contribute to the rich tapestry of Mesopotamian cosmology, reflecting the ancient Mesopotamians' profound understanding of the cosmos and their place within it. Through the exploration of these cosmological concepts, we gain a deeper appreciation for the intricate interplay between the divine and mortal realms and the ways in which these beliefs shaped the worldview and cultural practices of ancient Mesopotamia.

Understanding the Roles of Gods and Goddesses in the Creation Process

The roles of gods and goddesses in the creation process were central to Mesopotamian cosmology and mythology. These deities played active roles in the formation and organization of the cosmos, shaping the natural world and establishing the order of existence.

In Mesopotamian cosmogony, the primeval waters, represented by Tiamat, symbolized the chaotic and formless state that preceded creation. The emergence of the gods marked the transformation of this primordial chaos into a structured and ordered universe. Through their actions, the gods engaged in cosmic battles, established celestial bodies, and assigned roles and responsibilities to various natural elements.

For instance, Marduk, the chief deity of Babylon, played a central role in the Enuma Elish. He defeated Tiamat and her forces, demonstrating his power and establishing his authority as the supreme god. Marduk's actions, such as dividing Tiamat's body to create the heavens and the earth, exemplify the active participation of the gods in the creation process. Other deities, such as Enki, the god of wisdom and water, contributed their divine attributes to the formation and sustenance of the natural world.

Understanding the roles of gods and goddesses in the creation process provides valuable insights into Mesopotamian cosmological beliefs. These deities represented cosmic forces, embodying the powers and principles that governed the universe. Their actions and interactions shaped the natural world, established the order of existence, and influenced human destinies. Exploring these roles fosters a comprehensive comprehension of the ancient Mesopotamian worldview and the integral relationship between the divine and mortal realms.

Interpretations and Variations

Mesopotamian creation myths have been the subject of extensive scholarly analysis, leading to a wide range of interpretations and perspectives. Scholars from various disciplines, such as archaeology, anthropology, history, and religious studies, have delved into the rich tapestry of Mesopotamian cosmology, offering diverse insights into the complexities of these ancient myths.

One interpretation posits that the Mesopotamian creation myths, including the Enuma Elish and the Atrahasis epic, reflect an inherent struggle for power and authority among deities. This perspective emphasizes the political and sociocultural dynamics of ancient Mesopotamian society, where the rise and fall of empires and city-states influenced the portrayal of gods and their roles within the cosmic order. Scholars argue that the creation myths were not merely religious narratives but also served as tools for legitimizing rulership and establishing political hierarchies.

Another interpretation focuses on the ecological and environmental dimensions of Mesopotamian creation myths. Scholars explore the symbolism of natural elements, such as water, earth, and sky, in relation to agricultural practices, irrigation systems, and the cyclical patterns of nature. They suggest that the myths encapsulated the ancient Mesopotamians' understanding of their ecological surroundings and the fundamental role of agriculture in sustaining their civilization.

Furthermore, psychological interpretations of Mesopotamian creation myths have gained prominence. Scholars draw on concepts from psychology, such as Carl Jung's collective unconscious and archetypes, to analyze the symbolic motifs and characters within the myths. They argue that these narratives reflect universal human experiences and psychological processes, providing insights into the human psyche and the quest for meaning and identity.

Exploring Ancient Mesopotamian Mythology, Rivalries, and Spiritual Legacies

Examination of the Influence of Socio-cultural Factors on Mythological Interpretations

The interpretation of Mesopotamian creation myths is a dynamic and evolving process that is heavily influenced by socio-cultural factors. It is essential to recognize that interpretations are not fixed or objective, but rather shaped by the historical and intellectual contexts in which scholars operate.

One influential factor in the interpretation of Mesopotamian creation myths is the scholar's own background, biases, and theoretical frameworks. Scholars with religious affiliations may approach the myths from a faith-based perspective, seeking to validate or reconcile the narratives with their own religious beliefs. Their interpretations may be influenced by theological considerations and a desire to find theological coherence within the myths. Conversely, scholars who adopt a more secular or agnostic stance may approach the myths with a focus on cultural, literary, or historical analysis, emphasizing the societal and literary functions of the narratives.

In recent years, there has been a shift towards multidisciplinary approaches in the interpretation of Mesopotamian creation myths. Scholars draw from a range of disciplines, including anthropology, comparative mythology, and literary analysis, to explore the cultural and literary dimensions of the myths. This interdisciplinary approach allows for a more comprehensive understanding of the myths by considering their social, historical, and literary contexts. It enables scholars to delve into the symbolic meanings, narrative structures, and cultural functions of the myths, going beyond simplistic religious or historical interpretations.

Furthermore, the cultural and linguistic context of the scholars themselves plays a significant role in interpreting Mesopotamian creation myths. Different languages, such as Sumerian and Akkadian, present unique challenges in translation and interpretation. Nuanced translations of key terms and concepts are crucial in capturing the subtleties and nuances of the original texts. Moreover, scholars from diverse cultural backgrounds bring their own cultural lenses and assumptions to the interpretation process. Their cultural perspectives and experiences can shape their understanding of the myths, influencing their interpretations and introducing variations in their analysis.

In conclusion, the interpretation of Mesopotamian creation myths is a complex undertaking influenced by socio-cultural factors, the scholar's background, biases, and theoretical frameworks. The historical and intellectual contexts in which scholars operate shape their interpretations of the myths. The shift towards multidisciplinary approaches and the consideration of cultural and linguistic contexts have enriched our understanding of these myths. It is important to approach the interpretation of these ancient narratives with an awareness of these influences and to engage in critical analysis that recognizes the dynamic and evolving nature of mythological scholarship.

Comparison of Mesopotamian Cosmology with Other Ancient and Modern Cosmological Frameworks

To gain a broader perspective on Mesopotamian cosmology, it is valuable to compare it with other ancient and modern cosmological frameworks. By examining the similarities and differences, we can discern universal themes and patterns across cultures and deepen our understanding of the human quest to comprehend the cosmos.

One comparative approach is to explore the cosmologies of neighboring ancient civilizations, such as ancient Egypt and ancient Greece. By examining their creation myths and cosmological concepts, we can identify shared motifs and narratives, as well as distinctive cultural expressions and theological perspectives. These comparisons shed light on the interconnectedness of ancient civilizations and their collective human experiences.

Furthermore, a comparative analysis can extend beyond the ancient world to include modern cosmological frameworks, such as scientific cosmology and contemporary spiritual and ecological perspectives. By juxtaposing ancient Mesopotamian cosmology with these modern frameworks, we engage in a dialogue between ancient wisdom and modern scientific understanding, opening up avenues for interdisciplinary exploration and dialogue.

For instance, we can examine the similarities and divergences between Mesopotamian cosmology and scientific cosmology in terms of their explanations of the origins and structure of the universe. We can also explore how contemporary spiritual and ecological perspectives, such as eco-spirituality and deep ecology, resonate with or diverge from the ancient Mesopotamian understanding of the interconnections between the natural world, humanity, and the divine.

In conclusion, interpretations and variations in Mesopotamian creation myths reflect the diverse perspectives of scholars from different disciplines and cultural backgrounds. By exploring the influence of socio-cultural factors on mythological interpretations, we gain insight into the dynamic nature of mythological scholarship. Additionally, by comparing Mesopotamian cosmology with other ancient and modern cosmological frameworks, we deepen our understanding of universal themes and the ways in which different cultures have grappled with questions of creation, existence, and the interplay between the divine and mortal realms. This comparative approach encourages critical thinking and fosters a deeper appreciation for the richness and complexity of mythological cosmologies.

Critical Perspectives and Counterarguments

In exploring the realm of Mesopotamian cosmology, it is crucial to acknowledge and examine alternative viewpoints and dissenting opinions that challenge prevailing interpretations. While scholarly consensus often emerges around certain interpretations, it is essential to consider alternative perspectives that offer different insights and raise pertinent questions about Mesopotamian cosmology.

For instance, some scholars argue that Mesopotamian creation myths should not be seen as literal accounts of historical events, but rather as symbolic narratives that convey deeper philosophical or psychological truths. They propose that these myths functioned as metaphors or allegories, providing a framework for understanding the human condition, societal dynamics, or natural phenomena. This perspective challenges the traditional understanding of the myths as straightforward explanations of cosmological events, inviting a more nuanced and symbolic interpretation.

Additionally, dissenting opinions may arise regarding the influence of external cultural and religious factors on Mesopotamian cosmology. Some scholars argue that the cosmological ideas in Mesopotamia were not solely products of indigenous thought, but rather influenced by interactions with neighboring cultures, such as Egypt or Canaan. These scholars emphasize the need to consider the broader cultural and historical context, examining the potential cross-cultural exchanges and adaptations that may have shaped Mesopotamian cosmology.

Alongside the exploration of alternative viewpoints, it is essential to engage in a critical analysis of existing interpretations and consider the criticisms and limitations that have been raised by scholars. By examining these critiques, students can develop a more comprehensive understanding of the complexities and challenges involved in interpreting Mesopotamian cosmology.

One criticism pertains to the fragmentary nature of the available textual and archaeological evidence. Scholars must grapple with incomplete or damaged texts, making it challenging to reconstruct a cohesive and comprehensive cosmological framework. This limitation requires caution in drawing definitive conclusions and invites ongoing dialogue and reinterpretation as new evidence emerges.

Another criticism relates to the biases and assumptions inherent in the interpretive process. Scholars may bring their own cultural, religious, or theoretical perspectives to the analysis, potentially influencing their interpretations and limiting the objectivity of their conclusions. It is crucial for students to critically examine these biases and engage in self-reflection, recognizing the limitations that subjective perspectives may introduce into scholarly discourse.

Critical thinking and engagement with diverse perspectives are essential components of studying Mesopotamian cosmology. By encouraging students to think critically, question prevailing interpretations, and engage with alternative viewpoints, educators can foster intellectual growth and open the door to new insights.

Classroom activities can involve structured debates or panel discussions, where students are assigned roles representing different interpretations or dissenting opinions on Mesopotamian cosmology. This encourages students to thoroughly research and articulate their assigned positions, while also actively listening to and respectfully engaging with opposing viewpoints. By engaging in constructive dialogue, students can develop skills in critical analysis, effective communication, and the ability to consider multiple perspectives.

Problem-based exercises can also be employed, where students are presented with hypothetical scenarios or conflicting evidence related to Mesopotamian cosmology. Students can be tasked with critically evaluating the available information, identifying biases or gaps in knowledge, and proposing alternative interpretations or lines of inquiry. These exercises encourage students to think independently, apply their knowledge, and develop their own analytical frameworks.

In conclusion, critical perspectives and counterarguments play a vital role in the study of Mesopotamian cosmology. By examining alternative viewpoints, critically analyzing existing interpretations, and fostering engagement with diverse perspectives, students can develop their critical thinking skills and cultivate a deeper understanding of the complexities of Mesopotamian cosmology.

Conclusion

In conclusion, this chapter has delved into the rich tapestry of Mesopotamian cosmology, exploring various creation myths, analyzing cosmological concepts and their symbolic meanings, and examining the roles of gods and goddesses in the creation process. Through the exploration of creation myths such as the Enuma Elish and the Atrahasis epic, we have gained valuable insights into the Mesopotamians' understanding of the origins and organization of the cosmos. The symbolism of divine hierarchy, sacred geography, and natural phenomena has provided us with a deeper understanding of their cosmological framework.

Mesopotamian cosmology holds significant importance in understanding the spiritual beliefs of ancient civilizations. It offers a window into the worldview and religious practices of the Mesopotamians, shedding light on their perceptions of the divine, the natural world, and the interconnectedness between humans and gods. By studying their cosmological beliefs, we gain a broader understanding of the cultural and intellectual context in which ancient Mesopotamian societies thrived. Mesopotamian cosmology influenced various aspects of their lives, from religious rituals and social structures to political systems and artistic expressions.

Moreover, Mesopotamian cosmology provides a foundation for the exploration of spirituality and belief systems across different cultures and time periods. It offers a point of comparison with other mythological and cosmological frameworks, facilitating cross-cultural analysis and the identification of universal themes and patterns in human spiritual expression. Understanding Mesopotamian cosmology enhances our appreciation for the diversity of human experiences and the myriad ways in which societies have sought to comprehend the cosmos and their place within it.

In the next chapter, we will shift our focus to the pantheon of gods and goddesses in Mesopotamia. We will explore the diverse deities that populated the Mesopotamian religious landscape, their characteristics, roles, and relationships with humans. By examining the pantheon, we will gain insights into the complex interplay between the divine and mortal realms, the divine hierarchy, and the ways in which the Mesopotamians worshipped and interacted with their gods and goddesses. The pantheon of gods and goddesses in Mesopotamia offers a fascinating glimpse into the spiritual and religious practices of this ancient civilization, enriching our understanding of their cosmology and worldview.

To engage students in critical thinking and discussion, classroom activities can involve group discussions on the significance of cosmology in understanding ancient beliefs, where students are encouraged to share their reflections and insights. Problem-solving exercises can revolve around analyzing different cosmological concepts and their symbolic meanings, encouraging students to explore the cultural and philosophical implications embedded within these concepts. Additionally, exercises can be designed to facilitate comparative analysis between Mesopotamian cosmology and other ancient or contemporary cosmological frameworks, fostering critical thinking and encouraging students to identify commonalities and differences.

Divine Dynamics

In conclusion, the study of Mesopotamian cosmology provides a captivating exploration of ancient spiritual beliefs. By recapitulating the key points discussed in this chapter, recognizing the importance of Mesopotamian cosmology in understanding ancient beliefs, and previewing the next chapter on the pantheon of gods and goddesses, students are poised to continue their journey into the rich tapestry of ancient Mesopotamian spirituality.

Chapter 3: Pantheon of Gods and Goddesses: Exploring the Deities of Mesopotamia

Welcome to the fascinating world of the Mesopotamian pantheon! In ancient Mesopotamia, the pantheon of gods and goddesses held a central place in religious practices and beliefs. In this chapter, we will embark on a journey to explore the characteristics, roles, and relationships of these deities, providing us with valuable insights into the religious and spiritual landscape of this ancient civilization.

Our objectives for this chapter are two-fold: first, to introduce you to the major gods and goddesses of Mesopotamia and their significance within the religious framework; and second, to analyze the interplay between the divine and mortal realms, the divine hierarchy, and how the Mesopotamians worshipped and interacted with their deities. Through a comprehensive exploration of the pantheon, we aim to deepen our understanding of the complexities and nuances of Mesopotamian religious beliefs.

This chapter will cover various key topics and themes related to the pantheon of gods and goddesses in Mesopotamia. We will examine the unique characteristics and attributes of prominent deities, their roles in shaping the cosmos, their interactions with humans, and the religious rituals associated with their worship. Additionally, we will analyze the concept of divine hierarchy and how the pantheon influenced different aspects of ancient Mesopotamian society, including social structures, political systems, and cultural practices. By exploring these topics, we will gain a holistic understanding of the significance of the pantheon within the broader religious and cultural context of ancient Mesopotamia.

To ensure an engaging learning experience, we will incorporate examples, problems, and exercises throughout the chapter. In the classroom, we will encourage group discussions on the role of deities in shaping ancient Mesopotamian society, allowing you to explore the influence of the pantheon on various aspects of daily life. We will also provide problem-solving exercises that focus on analyzing the characteristics and roles of specific deities, helping you develop critical thinking skills and make connections between the divine realm and human experiences. Furthermore, you will be encouraged to reflect on the similarities and differences between the Mesopotamian pantheon and other pantheons from different cultures and time periods.

Divine Dynamics

By the end of this chapter, you will have gained a comprehensive understanding of the pantheon of gods and goddesses in Mesopotamia, their significance within ancient religious practices, and their impact on the cultural and social fabric of the civilization. Equipped with this knowledge and critical thinking skills, you will be ready to explore the intricate world of ancient Mesopotamian spirituality and engage in meaningful discussions about the profound role of deities in shaping human beliefs and experiences

Understanding the Mesopotamian Pantheon

In our exploration of ancient spiritual beliefs and practices, it is essential to understand the concept of a pantheon. A pantheon refers to a collective group of gods and goddesses worshipped within a particular religious system or culture. This chapter aims to provide a comprehensive definition of a pantheon, explore its characteristics, and examine its significance within various spiritual traditions.

Definition of a Pantheon

A pantheon typically consists of a hierarchy of gods and goddesses who govern various aspects of the universe and human existence. Each deity within the pantheon often possesses distinct personalities, domains, and responsibilities. They may represent natural forces, celestial bodies, abstract concepts, or specific areas of human life, such as fertility, war, wisdom, love, or death.

Pantheons can be found in various mythological and religious traditions throughout history and across different cultures. For example, the Greek pantheon includes deities such as Zeus, Hera, Poseidon, Athena, Apollo, and Aphrodite, among many others. In Norse mythology, the Norse pantheon consists of gods like Odin, Thor, Freya, Loki, and Tyr. Hinduism, with its rich and diverse mythology, features a vast pantheon of gods and goddesses, including Brahma, Vishnu, Shiva, Lakshmi, Saraswati, and Durga, among countless others.

Pantheons serve several purposes within religious and mythological systems. They provide a framework for understanding and explaining the supernatural world and its interaction with the human realm. Deities in the pantheon often embody archetypal qualities and represent human virtues, vices, or natural phenomena. They become central figures in myths and legends, serving as sources of inspiration, moral guidance, and models of behavior for the followers of the respective religion.

Moreover, pantheons can reflect the social, cultural, and historical context in which they arise. They often mirror the values, beliefs, and concerns of the society that reveres them. The relationships and interactions among the deities within the pantheon can shed light on power dynamics, social hierarchies, and the collective aspirations and fears of a civilization. Pantheons can also foster a sense of community and shared identity among believers, as they provide a common mythological framework and set of rituals.

It is important to note that pantheons are not static entities. They can evolve and change over time as religious beliefs and practices transform. New deities may be incorporated into existing pantheons, while others may lose prominence or be replaced. Pantheons can also adapt to cultural encounters and syncretism, where deities from different traditions are merged or incorporated into a new pantheon.

Overall, pantheons play a crucial role in shaping the religious, cultural, and mythological landscapes of various civilizations. They provide a complex and interconnected network of divine beings, offering a framework for understanding the supernatural and exploring the relationship between the divine and the human.

Characteristics of a Pantheon

Hierarchy: Pantheons often exhibit a hierarchical structure, with certain deities holding more significant positions and powers than others. This hierarchy is based on factors such as cosmic functions, domains of influence, or historical narratives. For example, in the Mesopotamian pantheon, the supreme gods, such as Anu and Enlil, occupy the highest positions of authority.

Interconnectedness: The deities within a pantheon are interconnected through complex relationships and interactions. They may be portrayed as family members, allies, rivals, or even enemies. These connections contribute to the overall dynamics and narratives within the pantheon. For instance, in Greek mythology, the interactions between Zeus, Poseidon, and Hades shape the power dynamics within the Olympian pantheon.

Specializations: Pantheons often exhibit specialization, with individual deities governing specific aspects of the natural world, human experiences, or societal domains. For instance, in the Norse pantheon, Odin is associated with wisdom and war, Thor with thunder and strength, and Freya with love and fertility. Each deity possesses unique attributes and responsibilities.

Symbolism: Pantheons are often accompanied by symbols and representations that encapsulate the essence and attributes of the deities. These symbols serve as visual or conceptual cues, aiding in the recognition and worship of specific gods and goddesses. For example, the ankh symbolizes life and fertility in ancient Egyptian religion and represents the goddess Isis.

Divine Dynamics

Significance of Pantheons

One of the key significance of pantheons is their role in providing a sense of order and meaning to the world. By ascribing specific deities to different aspects of nature, human experiences, and cosmic forces, pantheons offer explanations for the mysteries of existence. They provide narratives and mythologies that help individuals and communities make sense of the origins of the universe, the purpose of human life, and the workings of the natural world. Pantheons create a comprehensive framework that allows believers to navigate the complexities of existence and find their place within the larger cosmic order.

Pantheons also play a crucial role in shaping religious practices and rituals. They provide a basis for worship, prayer, and offerings, as well as guidelines for moral behavior and ethical conduct. By venerating the various deities within the pantheon, individuals seek to establish and maintain a harmonious relationship with the divine. Rituals and ceremonies associated with specific gods and goddesses become important avenues for expressing devotion, seeking blessings, and seeking divine intervention.

Moreover, pantheons foster a sense of communal identity and unity among believers. The shared belief in a pantheon and the rituals associated with it create a sense of belonging and solidarity within a religious community. The pantheon becomes a central focus of religious life, with temples, shrines, and festivals dedicated to the worship and celebration of the deities. This communal aspect strengthens social bonds, reinforces cultural values, and provides a source of collective identity and cohesion.

Pantheons also have a significant impact on art, literature, and cultural expression. The myths, stories, and symbols associated with the deities inspire artistic creations, such as sculptures, paintings, and poetry, that depict and celebrate the divine beings. These artistic representations not only serve aesthetic purposes but also serve as vehicles for conveying religious and philosophical concepts, preserving cultural heritage, and transmitting moral and spiritual teachings across generations.

Furthermore, pantheons can exert influence on political and social structures. In some civilizations, the rulers and political elite claim divine legitimacy by aligning themselves with specific deities within the pantheon. The pantheon becomes intertwined with the power structures of society, reinforcing hierarchical systems and justifying the authority of rulers. The religious institutions associated with the pantheon often hold significant political and economic influence, further solidifying their role in shaping societal norms and governance.

Exploring Ancient Mesopotamian Mythology, Rivalries, and Spiritual Legacies

It is worth noting that the significance of pantheons extends beyond the specific cultures in which they originate. As human civilizations interact and exchange ideas, pantheons can influence and be influenced by other religious traditions. Syncretism, the merging of deities or religious practices from different pantheons, can occur, resulting in the formation of new pantheons or the adaptation of existing ones. This dynamic nature of pantheons highlights their capacity to evolve and adapt to changing cultural and religious landscapes.

Overall, pantheons hold immense significance in human culture and religion. They provide a framework for understanding the divine, offer guidance for moral and ethical living, foster communal identity and cohesion, inspire artistic expression, and influence societal structures. By studying and exploring pantheons, we gain insights into the beliefs, values, and aspirations of civilizations throughout history, and we deepen our understanding of the complex relationship between the human and the divine.

Exercises and Classroom Activities

To enhance your critical thinking and foster engaging discussions, we have included exercises and activities throughout this chapter. These activities will encourage you to delve deeper into the concept of a pantheon and its significance within different cultures. Get ready to explore and analyze the complexities of pantheons!

Research and Compare Pantheons: Take the opportunity to research and compare pantheons from diverse cultures. Choose two or more pantheons that interest you, and investigate their characteristics and functions. Consider the deities, their roles, and any unique aspects of worship. Then, create a comparative analysis that highlights both the similarities and differences between the pantheons. Discuss your findings with your peers, sharing your insights and interpretations.

Group Discussions: Engage in group discussions to explore the significance of pantheons in shaping cultural identity and societal structures. Form small groups and select a pantheon to focus on. Discuss how the pantheon influenced religious practices, social organization, and power dynamics within the culture. Consider the impact of the pantheon on the daily lives of individuals and the collective beliefs and values of the society. Be prepared to present your group's findings and engage in thoughtful dialogue with the class.

Role-Playing Activity: Imagine you are a member of an ancient society that worships a specific pantheon. In small groups, assign roles to each member representing different deities within the pantheon. Conduct a role-playing activity where each group member embodies their assigned deity and discusses their role, attributes, and relationships with other deities. Engage in a dialogue that explores how these deities interact and influence human affairs. Reflect on the broader implications of these interactions for the society as a whole.

Written Reflection: Write a reflective essay discussing the impact of pantheons on religious practices and the organization of power. Consider how pantheons shape belief systems, rituals, and the social hierarchy within a culture. Analyze the ways in which pantheons influence the authority and roles of individuals, as well as the relationship between divine beings and mortals. Support your arguments with evidence and examples from different pantheons and ancient civilizations.

These exercises and activities are designed to deepen your understanding of pantheons and their significance in shaping cultural identity and societal structures. Through research, discussion, role-playing, and reflection, you will gain a comprehensive perspective on the complexities and impact of pantheons across various civilizations. Enjoy exploring the world of pantheons and engaging in meaningful discussions with your peers!

Conclusion

In conclusion, a pantheon is a central element of many ancient spiritual traditions. It is a structured collection of gods and goddesses, exhibiting characteristics such as hierarchy, interconnectedness, specialization, and symbolism. Understanding the definition and characteristics of a pantheon enables us to explore the cultural, religious, and social dimensions of ancient civilizations, deepening our understanding of their spiritual beliefs and practices.

The Mesopotamian pantheon, consisting of a rich and diverse array of gods and goddesses, holds a central position in the religious and spiritual beliefs of ancient Mesopotamia. Understanding the intricacies of this pantheon is essential for comprehending the complex religious landscape of this ancient civilization. This chapter aims to provide a comprehensive understanding of the Mesopotamian pantheon, exploring its structure, major deities, and their roles within the divine hierarchy.

Exploring Ancient Mesopotamian Mythology, Rivalries, and Spiritual Legacies

The Structure of the Pantheon:

The hierarchical structure of the Mesopotamian pantheon reflects the division of labor and specialization found in human societies. Just as individuals in a society have different roles and responsibilities based on their skills and abilities, the gods and goddesses in the pantheon have specific areas of expertise and influence.

At the top of the pantheon are the supreme gods, who hold the highest authority and power. Anu, the god of the heavens, is often considered the head of the pantheon. He represents the celestial realm and is associated with the divine council. Enlil, the god of wind, storms, and the earth, is considered the ruler of the gods and the enforcer of divine justice. Enki, the god of wisdom, water, and creation, possesses great knowledge and is often depicted as a benevolent figure who aids humanity.

Below the supreme gods, there are several tiers of deities, each associated with specific domains or functions. For example, Inanna/Ishtar, the goddess of love, beauty, and war, holds a prominent position in the pantheon. She represents both the passionate and destructive aspects of human nature and plays a significant role in mythological narratives and religious rituals. Nanna/Sin, the moon god, is associated with fertility, timekeeping, and divination. Utu/Shamash, the sun god, is the divine judge who dispenses justice and illuminates the world with his light.

Other gods and goddesses in the pantheon include Ninurta, the warrior god who defends humanity against chaos and evil; Ninhursag, the mother goddess associated with fertility and the earth; and Ea, the god of wisdom and magic. Each deity has a distinct personality, symbols, and cult centers where they are worshipped.

The hierarchical structure of the pantheon reflects the interplay between gods and mortals. The supreme gods govern the universe and determine the fate of humanity, while the lesser deities have more direct interactions with humans, mediating between the divine and the mortal realms. The worship and offerings to these deities are believed to influence the gods' decisions and bring blessings, protection, and favor to individuals and communities.

It is important to note that the structure of pantheons can vary across different mythological traditions. For example, in the Greek pantheon, the Olympian gods occupy the highest positions, with Zeus as the king of the gods. The Hindu pantheon, on the other hand, has a complex hierarchical structure with a trinity of gods—Brahma, Vishnu, and Shiva—holding supreme positions, while a multitude of other gods and goddesses fulfill specific roles and responsibilities.

Divine Dynamics

The hierarchical structure of pantheons serves multiple purposes. It provides order and organization to the divine realm, reflecting the perceived cosmic order. It also allows individuals to identify and interact with specific deities according to their needs and concerns. The hierarchical structure facilitates a sense of specialization and expertise among the gods, ensuring that different aspects of human life and the natural world are overseen and governed by appropriate deities.

Overall, the structure of the pantheon reflects the complexities of human existence and the attempt to comprehend and navigate the divine forces at work in the world. It highlights the diverse roles and responsibilities of the gods and goddesses and their significance in shaping the beliefs, values, and rituals of ancient Mesopotamian society.

Major Deities and their Roles:

In this section, we will explore the characteristics and attributes of some of the major deities within the Mesopotamian pantheon. Let's delve into a few examples:

Enlil: Enlil, the god of wind and storms, holds a prominent position within the pantheon. He is highly revered and associated with kingship and the maintenance of order. Enlil plays a crucial role in ensuring the prosperity of the land, protecting the people from harm, and guiding the affairs of the state. His worship is closely linked to the well-being and success of the kingdom, and rituals and offerings are dedicated to him to seek his favor.

Inanna: Inanna, the goddess of love, fertility, and war, embodies both nurturing and destructive aspects. She is a multifaceted deity revered for her powers of creation and destruction. Inanna's worship involves rituals and celebrations aimed at ensuring bountiful harvests, successful warfare, and fertility. As the goddess of love, she is also associated with matters of passion and desire.

Nanna/Sin: Nanna, also known as Sin, is the moon god and one of the most significant deities in the Mesopotamian pantheon. He is associated with wisdom, divination, and fertility. As the moon god, Nanna/Sin is believed to have a deep understanding of the cycles of time and the cosmic order. His worship involves observing and interpreting the phases of the moon as a means of divination and guidance. Nanna/Sin's influence extends to agriculture and fertility, as the moon's phases were thought to affect the growth of crops and the reproductive cycles of humans and animals.

Enki: Enki, the god of wisdom, water, and creation, plays a vital role in the pantheon. He is associated with fresh water, which is essential for sustaining life in the arid Mesopotamian region. Enki is revered as a benevolent deity who brings knowledge, wisdom, and civilization to humanity. He is credited with creating the first humans and imparting them with the arts of civilization, such as agriculture, writing, and craftsmanship. Enki is also known for his ability to heal and provide solutions to problems. His worship involves rituals dedicated to seeking his wisdom, guidance, and blessings.

Ishtar: Ishtar, also known as Inanna, is a prominent goddess in the Mesopotamian pantheon. She embodies the dualities of love and war, passion and destruction. Ishtar is associated with fertility, sexuality, and the powers of attraction. She is believed to bring about the renewal and flourishing of life, both in the natural world and in human relationships. Ishtar's worship involves rituals and ceremonies that celebrate her role in ensuring the continuity of life and the well-being of society. As a warrior goddess, she is also invoked for protection and victory in times of conflict.

Shamash: Shamash, the sun god, is the divine judge and the provider of justice. He is associated with truth, law, and order. Shamash's role involves upholding moral principles, ensuring the fair treatment of individuals, and maintaining social harmony. As the sun god, Shamash illuminates the world and brings light to darkness, symbolizing the dispelling of ignorance and the revelation of truth. His worship involves offerings and prayers for guidance, justice, and the protection of laws.

These examples highlight the diverse roles and attributes of the major deities within the Mesopotamian pantheon. Each god and goddess holds a distinct position and domain, and their worship and rituals reflect the specific needs and concerns of the people. The major deities embody various aspects of human experience, from the forces of nature to the complexities of emotions and social structures. Their roles in the pantheon are integral to the functioning of the cosmos and the well-being of humanity within ancient Mesopotamian society.

Interactions between Gods and Humans:

The Mesopotamians firmly believed in the active involvement of gods and goddesses in human affairs. They perceived the pantheon as intermediaries between the mortal realm and the divine. To establish a connection with the gods and seek their favor, individuals engaged in various religious rituals and offerings. The purpose of these practices was to gain blessings, protection, guidance, and assistance from specific deities.

For instance, kings, who held a special relationship with the gods due to their divine appointment, often sought guidance from the pantheon. They consulted diviners or priests who possessed the knowledge and skills to interpret divine will and provide counsel on important matters. These consultations were crucial for making significant decisions that impacted the kingdom and its people.

In addition to seeking guidance, individuals would also express their gratitude, devotion, and supplication through prayers, hymns, and offerings. Temples and sacred spaces were dedicated to specific deities, where rituals and ceremonies were conducted to honor and invoke their presence.

By actively engaging with the pantheon, the Mesopotamians sought to establish a harmonious relationship with the gods, ensuring their well-being, protection, and prosperity in both individual and communal contexts.

Through the exploration of the structure of the pantheon and the interactions between gods and humans, we gain valuable insights into the religious beliefs and practices of ancient Mesopotamia. These aspects not only shape our understanding of the culture and spirituality of this ancient civilization but also shed light on the intricate relationship between the divine realm and human experiences.

Religious Rituals and Worship:

Religious rituals and worship practices held great significance in Mesopotamian culture, serving as a means to honor and appease the gods. Central to these practices were the ziggurats, towering temple structures that served as sacred spaces and physical manifestations of the divine presence. These monumental edifices symbolized the connection between heaven and earth, acting as portals through which mortals could commune with the gods.

Worship in Mesopotamia involved a wide array of rituals, ceremonies, and offerings dedicated to specific deities. These acts of devotion were performed with the aim of maintaining cosmic balance, securing divine blessings, and ensuring the well-being of the community. Offerings of food, drink, and other valuables were presented to the gods, symbolizing gratitude, supplication, and the establishment of a reciprocal relationship between mortals and the divine. Sacrifices, both animal and occasionally human, were also carried out to express devotion and seek divine favor.

Prayers and hymns formed an integral part of Mesopotamian worship, serving as a means of communication with the gods. These invocations expressed praise, gratitude, and requests for guidance or assistance. Rituals and ceremonies were often accompanied by music, dance, and processions, creating a vibrant and immersive experience that engaged the senses and fostered a collective sense of religious identity.

Exploring Ancient Mesopotamian Mythology, Rivalries, and Spiritual Legacies

The Pantheon in Mythology and Literature:

The gods and goddesses of the Mesopotamian pantheon played prominent roles in the rich mythological narratives and literature of the ancient civilization. Epic tales, such as the Epic of Gilgamesh, featured divine characters and explored profound themes of heroism, mortality, and the nature of the divine. These myths and legends provided cultural and moral lessons, addressing fundamental questions about the human condition and the relationship between mortals and the gods.

The interactions between gods and mortals depicted in Mesopotamian mythology revealed the complexities of these relationships. Divine beings often intervened in human affairs, shaping destinies, rewarding virtue, and punishing transgressions. The narratives showcased the gods' diverse personalities, motivations, and emotions, presenting them as multidimensional characters with their own desires and conflicts. Through these stories, the Mesopotamians sought to understand the nature of the divine, grapple with existential questions, and derive meaning from the world around them.

In addition to Mesopotamian mythology, the concept of a pantheon and its divine characters have been integral to numerous other mythological and literary traditions throughout history. Let's explore some examples:

Greek Mythology: The Greek pantheon, led by Zeus, consisted of gods and goddesses who presided over various aspects of the world. Each deity had distinct powers and responsibilities. For instance, Athena was the goddess of wisdom and warfare, Poseidon ruled over the seas, and Aphrodite was the goddess of love and beauty. Greek mythology featured epic tales of heroism, such as the adventures of Hercules and the Odyssey of Odysseus, where gods and goddesses often played significant roles, intervening in mortal affairs and shaping the outcomes of events.

Norse Mythology: The Norse pantheon, headed by Odin, included gods and goddesses associated with war, fertility, wisdom, and other domains. The gods in Norse mythology, such as Thor, Loki, and Freyja, were portrayed as powerful beings engaged in battles against giants and other mythical creatures. Norse mythology featured legends like the Ragnarok, the great battle between gods and giants, and the tales of heroic figures like Sigurd and Beowulf.

Hindu Mythology: The Hindu pantheon is vast and encompasses a multitude of gods and goddesses with diverse attributes and roles. Deities such as Brahma, Vishnu, and Shiva are regarded as the supreme forces of creation, preservation, and destruction, respectively. Hindu mythology includes epic texts like the Mahabharata and the Ramayana, which feature gods and demigods intervening in mortal affairs and imparting profound teachings and moral lessons.

Egyptian Mythology: The Egyptian pantheon consisted of numerous gods and goddesses, each associated with specific aspects of life and nature. For example, Ra was the sun god, Osiris governed the afterlife, and Isis was the goddess of magic and fertility. Egyptian mythology featured tales of creation, the struggles of gods and mortals, and the journey of the soul through the realms of the afterlife.

Literary Works: Pantheons and divine characters have also influenced various works of literature outside of mythological contexts. For instance, John Milton's "Paradise Lost" draws upon Christian theology to depict the fall of angels and the struggle between God and Satan. J.R.R. Tolkien's "The Lord of the Rings" includes a pantheon of deities known as the Valar and the Maiar, who shape the events of Middle-earth. These literary examples showcase the enduring fascination with divine characters and their impact on human stories and narratives.

Across different mythological and literary traditions, the pantheon and its divine characters serve as sources of inspiration, embodying aspects of human experience, and exploring fundamental questions about existence, morality, and the nature of divinity. They provide a rich tapestry of narratives that continue to captivate and resonate with audiences, offering insights into the complexities of the human condition and our relationship with the divine.

The Legacy of the Pantheon:

The influence of the Mesopotamian pantheon extends far beyond the boundaries of ancient Mesopotamia. The concepts, symbols, and narratives associated with these deities have left an indelible mark on subsequent cultures and religions. Elements of the Mesopotamian pantheon can be found in various belief systems, such as the ancient Canaanite and Egyptian religions, which shared trade and cultural connections with Mesopotamia. Additionally, the pantheon's legacy can be seen in the symbolism and motifs adopted by later civilizations, including the Assyrians, Babylonians, Persians, and Greeks.

Moreover, the themes and archetypes present in Mesopotamian mythology continue to resonate in contemporary spiritual practices. Modern interpretations and revivals of ancient wisdom draw inspiration from the rich tapestry of Mesopotamian cosmology, offering insights into human spirituality, ethics, and the relationship between humanity and the natural world.

Exploring Ancient Mesopotamian Mythology, Rivalries, and Spiritual Legacies

By exploring the rituals, mythology, and legacy of the Mesopotamian pantheon, we gain a deeper understanding of the enduring impact of these ancient deities. Their worship and narratives provide a window into the religious and cultural landscape of ancient Mesopotamia and serve as a testament to the human fascination with the divine and the eternal quest for meaning.

The influence and legacy of the Mesopotamian pantheon are indeed profound and far-reaching. Here are some key aspects of its legacy:

Cultural Exchange and Borrowing: The ancient civilizations of the Near East, including the Canaanites, Egyptians, and Persians, had contact and trade with Mesopotamia, leading to the exchange of religious ideas and the adoption of certain deities and motifs. For example, the Canaanite god Baal shares similarities with the Mesopotamian storm god Enlil, while the Egyptian goddess Isis exhibits parallels with the Mesopotamian goddess Ishtar. These exchanges highlight the interconnectivity and cross-pollination of religious concepts in the ancient world.

Influence on Later Civilizations: The Assyrians and Babylonians, who succeeded the Sumerians and Akkadians in Mesopotamia, inherited and built upon the pantheon and religious practices of their predecessors. Their cultural and religious achievements, including the construction of grand temples and the preservation of mythological texts, helped disseminate Mesopotamian religious concepts throughout the region. The Persian Empire, influenced by Mesopotamian traditions, incorporated elements of the pantheon into their own religious practices.

Greek and Hellenistic Period: The conquests of Alexander the Great and the subsequent Hellenistic period brought Greek culture into contact with the Near East, including Mesopotamia. The Greeks, already familiar with their own pantheon, encountered Mesopotamian deities and mythologies. This interaction influenced the syncretism of Greek and Mesopotamian religious concepts, resulting in the identification of Mesopotamian deities with Greek counterparts. For example, the Greek deity Zeus was equated with the Mesopotamian god Enlil.

Literary and Cultural Impact: The literary legacy of Mesopotamian mythology, including the Epic of Gilgamesh and the Enuma Elish, has had a lasting impact on subsequent literary traditions. These ancient works continue to inspire and inform modern literature, art, and popular culture. The themes of heroism, mortality, the quest for immortality, and the interplay between gods and mortals resonate with universal human experiences and have been reimagined and reinterpreted in various forms throughout history.

Divine Dynamics

Contemporary Revivals: In recent times, there has been a resurgence of interest in Mesopotamian spirituality and mythology. Scholars, practitioners of modern paganism, and enthusiasts of ancient wisdom have delved into the pantheon's rich symbolism, rituals, and cosmology. By studying and reconstructing ancient Mesopotamian religious practices, individuals seek to reconnect with ancestral roots, explore alternative spiritual paths, and gain insights into the human experience.

The legacy of the Mesopotamian pantheon extends across centuries and continents, shaping the religious, cultural, and artistic landscape of diverse civilizations. Its enduring influence underscores the universal human fascination with the divine, the search for meaning, and the ongoing dialogue between humanity and the mysteries of the cosmos.

Exercises and Classroom Activities

To engage students in critical thinking and discussion, various exercises and activities can be incorporated into the chapter. Students can be encouraged to create their own pantheon, drawing inspiration from the Mesopotamian gods and goddesses, and discuss the roles and attributes of each deity. Classroom activities can involve group discussions on the impact of the pantheon on societal structures, such as kingship and social hierarchies. Problem-solving exercises can focus on analyzing mythological narratives and identifying the underlying cultural and moral values conveyed through these stories.

Conclusion

In conclusion, understanding the Mesopotamian pantheon is crucial for comprehending the religious and spiritual beliefs of ancient Mesopotamia. The hierarchical structure, major deities, and their roles within the pantheon shed light on the ancient Mesopotamians' worldview and their interactions with the divine. Exploring the rituals, mythology, and legacy of the pantheon allows us to appreciate the enduring significance of these deities and their impact on subsequent cultures and religious traditions.

Anu, Enlil, and Enki: The Divine Triad

Introduction to the Three Major Deities and Their Significance:

In the vast pantheon of Mesopotamian gods and goddesses, three deities stand out as central figures: Anu, Enlil, and Enki. Revered and worshipped throughout ancient Mesopotamia, these divine beings held immense power and played pivotal roles in shaping the cosmic order and the fate of humanity. Understanding the attributes, domains, and interactions of this divine triad is crucial to unraveling the complex tapestry of Mesopotamian religious beliefs.

Analysis of the Attributes and Domains of Anu, Enlil, and Enki:

Anu, often referred to as the supreme god, holds a position of paramount importance in the Mesopotamian pantheon. He is associated with the heavens and is considered the ruler of the gods. Anu embodies concepts of transcendence, cosmic order, and divine authority. As the overseer of the celestial realm, he governs the movement of the stars, the cycles of time, and the unfolding of cosmic events. Anu is often depicted as wise and just, embodying the ideals of kingship and providing a divine model for earthly rulers.

Enlil, the god of wind and storms, holds a prominent position within the divine triad. He is recognized as the supreme deity of the earthly realm and possesses immense power over natural forces. Enlil is associated with fertility, agriculture, and the protection of cities and their inhabitants. He is often depicted as a warrior, wielding thunderbolts and storms to maintain order and safeguard the well-being of the land. Enlil's domain encompasses the forces of nature, and his authority extends over both gods and humans.

Enki, also known as Ea, complements the roles of Anu and Enlil with his unique attributes and domains. He is revered as the god of wisdom, intellect, and craftsmanship. Enki possesses vast knowledge and creative abilities, which he employs to benefit humanity. He is the patron of artisans, scientists, and those seeking spiritual insight. Enki is associated with the vitalizing and life-giving waters, which symbolize both physical and spiritual nourishment. His domain encompasses rivers, canals, and subterranean waters, as well as the domains of knowledge, magic, and healing.

Interactions and Relationships among the Divine Triad:

The interactions and relationships among Anu, Enlil, and Enki form a dynamic interplay within the Mesopotamian pantheon. While Anu holds the highest position, Enlil and Enki play crucial roles in executing divine will and maintaining the balance of power. Enlil, as the supreme deity of the earthly realm, acts as an intermediary between Anu and humanity, implementing divine decrees and ensuring the well-being of mortals. Enki, on the other hand, serves as a bridge between the divine and human realms, bestowing wisdom, knowledge, and protection upon humanity.

The divine triad also displays complex relationships with one another. Enlil, as the son of Anu, enjoys a close bond with his father and often seeks his counsel and approval. Enki, as the half-brother of Enlil, shares a more nuanced relationship characterized by both cooperation and rivalry. Their interactions shape the course of events in Mesopotamian mythology and literature, as they navigate conflicts, alliances, and the intricate dynamics of power.

Understanding the attributes, domains, and interactions of Anu, Enlil, and Enki provides valuable insights into the religious and cosmological framework of ancient Mesopotamia. As we delve further into the Mesopotamian pantheon, we will explore the roles and significance of these deities in greater detail, unraveling the complexities of their mythologies, rituals, and their influence on the lives of both gods and mortals.

Exercise:

Research and compare the attributes and domains of Anu, Enlil, and Enki. Discuss how their roles complemented and interacted with one another within the divine triad. Consider their influence on human affairs and the broader cosmic order.

Problem:
2. Imagine you are a priest or priestess in ancient Mesopotamia. Write a prayer or invocation addressing either Anu, Enlil, or Enki, focusing on their specific attributes and domains. Reflect on how your prayer seeks to establish a connection and seek favor from the divine being.

Classroom Activity:
3. Divide into small groups and discuss the divine triad in the context of other pantheons from different cultures. Compare and contrast the hierarchical structures, attributes, and interactions of the deities in these pantheons. Explore the similarities and differences in the roles of the divine triad compared to other prominent divine groups.

Ishtar, Inanna, and Ninhursag: Goddesses of Power and Fertility

In the vast pantheon of Mesopotamian gods and goddesses, three deities stand out as central figures: Anu, Enlil, and Enki. Revered and worshipped throughout ancient Mesopotamia, these divine beings held immense power and played pivotal roles in shaping the cosmic order and the fate of humanity. Understanding the attributes, domains, and interactions of this divine triad is crucial to unraveling the complex tapestry of Mesopotamian religious beliefs.

Exploring Ancient Mesopotamian Mythology, Rivalries, and Spiritual Legacies

Analysis of the Attributes and Domains of Anu, Enlil, and Enki:

Anu, often referred to as the supreme god, holds a position of paramount importance in the Mesopotamian pantheon. He is associated with the heavens and is considered the ruler of the gods. Anu embodies concepts of transcendence, cosmic order, and divine authority. As the overseer of the celestial realm, he governs the movement of the stars, the cycles of time, and the unfolding of cosmic events. Anu is often depicted as wise and just, embodying the ideals of kingship and providing a divine model for earthly rulers.

Enlil, the god of wind and storms, holds a prominent position within the divine triad. He is recognized as the supreme deity of the earthly realm and possesses immense power over natural forces. Enlil is associated with fertility, agriculture, and the protection of cities and their inhabitants. He is often depicted as a warrior, wielding thunderbolts and storms to maintain order and safeguard the well-being of the land. Enlil's domain encompasses the forces of nature, and his authority extends over both gods and humans.

Enki, also known as Ea, complements the roles of Anu and Enlil with his unique attributes and domains. He is revered as the god of wisdom, intellect, and craftsmanship. Enki possesses vast knowledge and creative abilities, which he employs to benefit humanity. He is the patron of artisans, scientists, and those seeking spiritual insight. Enki is associated with the vitalizing and life-giving waters, which symbolize both physical and spiritual nourishment. His domain encompasses rivers, canals, and subterranean waters, as well as the domains of knowledge, magic, and healing.

Interactions and Relationships among the Divine Triad:

The interactions and relationships among Anu, Enlil, and Enki form a dynamic interplay within the Mesopotamian pantheon. While Anu holds the highest position, Enlil and Enki play crucial roles in executing divine will and maintaining the balance of power. Enlil, as the supreme deity of the earthly realm, acts as an intermediary between Anu and humanity, implementing divine decrees and ensuring the well-being of mortals. Enki, on the other hand, serves as a bridge between the divine and human realms, bestowing wisdom, knowledge, and protection upon humanity.

The divine triad also displays complex relationships with one another. Enlil, as the son of Anu, enjoys a close bond with his father and often seeks his counsel and approval. Enki, as the half-brother of Enlil, shares a more nuanced relationship characterized by both cooperation and rivalry. Their interactions shape the course of events in Mesopotamian mythology and literature, as they navigate conflicts, alliances, and the intricate dynamics of power.

Understanding the attributes, domains, and interactions of Anu, Enlil, and Enki provides valuable insights into the religious and cosmological framework of ancient Mesopotamia. As we delve further into the Mesopotamian pantheon, we will explore the roles and significance of these deities in greater detail, unraveling the complexities of their mythologies, rituals, and their influence on the lives of both gods and mortals.

Exercise:

Research and compare the attributes and domains of Anu, Enlil, and Enki. Discuss how their roles complemented and interacted with one another within the divine triad. Consider their influence on human affairs and the broader cosmic order.

Problem:

2. Imagine you are a priest or priestess in ancient Mesopotamia. Write a prayer or invocation addressing either Anu, Enlil, or Enki, focusing on their specific attributes and domains. Reflect on how your prayer seeks to establish a connection and seek favor from the divine being.

Classroom Activity:

3.Divide into small groups and discuss the divine triad in the context of other pantheons from different cultures. Compare and contrast the hierarchical structures, attributes, and interactions of the deities in these pantheons. Explore the similarities and differences in the roles of the divine triad compared to other prominent divine groups.

Nergal, Marduk, and Shamash: Gods of Justice and Power

In the vibrant tapestry of the Mesopotamian pantheon, the gods Nergal, Marduk, and Shamash stand as powerful figures representing justice, power, and the enforcement of divine order. These deities played significant roles in Mesopotamian mythology and held sway over aspects of life relating to law, governance, and the dispensation of justice. Exploring their attributes, domains, and mythological narratives offers insights into the societal and cultural dynamics surrounding the concepts of justice and power in ancient Mesopotamia.

Exploring Ancient Mesopotamian Mythology, Rivalries, and Spiritual Legacies

Nergal, the god of war, plague, and the underworld, represents the primal force of destruction and the embodiment of necessary violence. Often depicted as a fearsome warrior, Nergal wields power over life and death, symbolizing the inherent duality of justice. While his association with war and plague might seem contradictory, Nergal's domain also extends to the concept of necessary retribution and the restoration of cosmic balance. His mythological narratives often highlight the consequences of wrongdoing and the need for just consequences to maintain societal order.

Marduk, the patron deity of Babylon and the preeminent god of the Babylonian pantheon, assumes a central role in Mesopotamian mythology. Marduk embodies the qualities of kingship, power, and justice. He is often portrayed as a wise and strategic deity, known for his triumph over the primordial chaos and the establishment of cosmic order. Marduk's mythological narratives depict him as a champion of justice and protector of the gods and humanity. His ascension to supremacy within the pantheon reflects the evolving political and religious landscape of ancient Mesopotamia.

Shamash, the god of the sun and justice, holds a vital place in the Mesopotamian pantheon. As the divine judge and dispenser of justice, Shamash illuminates truth and exposes falsehood. He represents the embodiment of fairness, impartiality, and divine law. Shamash's radiance symbolizes the revelation of hidden knowledge and the uncovering of the truth in legal proceedings. His mythological narratives often feature his role as a mediator and the ultimate arbiter of disputes among gods and mortals, emphasizing the significance of justice in maintaining societal harmony.

These gods of justice and power played crucial roles in the religious and social fabric of ancient Mesopotamia. Their worship involved rituals, prayers, and offerings dedicated to upholding justice and seeking their guidance in matters of governance and law. The rituals sought to establish a connection with these deities, invoke their wisdom, and ensure the fair and equitable functioning of society.

Exercise:

Research the mythological narratives of Nergal, Marduk, and Shamash. Compare and contrast their roles as gods of justice and power. Analyze how their attributes and actions reflect the concept of justice in ancient Mesopotamia and its implications for societal order.
Problem:

2. Imagine you are a judge presiding over a court case in ancient Mesopotamia. Write a statement invoking the presence and guidance of Shamash in ensuring a just and fair resolution to the dispute. Consider the principles of fairness, impartiality, and the revelation of truth in your statement.

Classroom Activity:

3. Engage in a mock trial activity, where students take on the roles of judges, plaintiffs, defendants, and advocates in a simulated legal proceeding. Use the principles of justice embodied by Nergal, Marduk, and Shamash as a framework for assessing the cases and reaching fair judgments. Reflect on the challenges and complexities of dispens

Lesser Deities and Demons

Within the intricate tapestry of the Mesopotamian pantheon, a multitude of lesser deities and demons play essential roles in the divine order and the lives of mortals. These entities, occupying a vast spectrum of characteristics and domains, bring forth a complex web of supernatural influences and forces that shape various aspects of existence. Exploring the attributes, roles, and interactions of these lesser deities and demons offers insights into the multifaceted nature of the Mesopotamian cosmology and the interplay between the divine and the mortal realms.

The lesser deities, often referred to as the "Anunnaki," encompass a diverse array of divine beings that serve specific functions and preside over distinct domains. For example, Nanshe, the goddess of social justice and divination, holds sway over matters of law, prophecy, and dreams. She acts as a guardian of societal ethics and delivers judgments that ensure fairness and equity. Nisaba, the goddess of writing and wisdom, governs the realms of knowledge, education, and the arts. She is revered as a patroness of scribes and teachers, bestowing her blessings upon those who seek intellectual pursuits.

In contrast to the benevolent nature of the lesser deities, the realm of demons in Mesopotamian mythology comprises entities that embody malevolent or chaotic forces. These demons, often known as "Lamashtu" or "Utukku," manifest in various forms and exhibit destructive tendencies. Lamashtu, a fearsome demoness, is believed to cause harm to newborns and expectant mothers, while Utukku, a group of malevolent spirits, are associated with diseases and misfortune. These demonic entities challenge the natural order and are often invoked in protective rituals and amulets to ward off their harmful influences.

Exploring Ancient Mesopotamian Mythology, Rivalries, and Spiritual Legacies

The interactions between humans and these lesser deities and demons are characterized by a complex web of rituals, offerings, and invocations. Ancient Mesopotamians sought to establish connections with these entities through prayers and dedicatory rituals, seeking their favor, protection, and guidance. They believed that maintaining a harmonious relationship with the supernatural realm was crucial for personal well-being, societal prosperity, and the prevention of misfortune.

Exercise:

Choose a lesser deity or demon from the Mesopotamian pantheon and conduct research on their attributes, roles, and interactions with humans. Write a comparative analysis discussing the differences and similarities between the divine and demonic entities in Mesopotamian mythology. Reflect on the significance of these entities in the lives of ancient Mesopotamians.

Problem:

2. Imagine you are a Mesopotamian priest or priestess entrusted with performing rituals and invocations to a specific lesser deity or demon. Write a step-by-step guide outlining the ritual procedures, offerings, and prayers that would be employed to establish a connection and seek the entity's blessings or protection. Consider the specific attributes and domains associated with the chosen entity.

Classroom Activity:

3. Engage in a group discussion on the role of lesser deities and demons in different cultural and spiritual belief systems. Compare and contrast the representations of such entities in Mesopotamian mythology with those found in other mythologies, such as Greek, Egyptian, or Norse. Analyze the common themes and archetypes present in the various pantheons, and discuss the cultural significance of these supernatural beings in shaping human belief systems.

By delving into the intricacies of lesser deities and demons, students can deepen their understanding of the complex tapestry of the Mesopotamian cosmology and the diverse roles played by these entities in the lives of ancient Mesopotamians. It invites contemplation on the nature of the divine, the interplay between the mortal and the supernatural realms, and the dynamics of belief systems in different cultural contexts.

Interactions and Conflict among Deities

Within the vast and intricate tapestry of the Mesopotamian pantheon, interactions and conflicts among the deities serve as a fascinating reflection of the complex relationships and dynamics within the divine realm. These interactions shed light on the diverse attributes, powers, and agendas of the gods and goddesses, offering insights into the intricacies of ancient Mesopotamian cosmology and belief systems. Examining these interactions fosters a deeper understanding of the multifaceted nature of the divine pantheon and the intricate web of influence that governs both the mortal and supernatural realms.

In the Mesopotamian pantheon, conflicts and rivalries often arise due to differences in domains, powers, and personal agendas among the deities. For instance, the Epic of Enuma Elish, a Babylonian creation myth, recounts the epic battle between Marduk, the patron deity of Babylon, and the primordial goddess Tiamat. This conflict represents the struggle for power and supremacy within the divine hierarchy. Marduk emerges victorious, establishing his dominance and becoming the supreme god of the Babylonian pantheon. This narrative exemplifies the underlying theme of power struggles and the establishment of order amidst chaos.

Furthermore, conflicts may arise due to the diverse roles and responsibilities of the deities. For example, Ishtar, the goddess of love, fertility, and war, often clashes with other deities due to her multifaceted nature and influence over various aspects of life. Her romantic entanglements with other deities, such as the shepherd god Tammuz, frequently lead to tensions and conflicts within the pantheon. These conflicts reflect the complexities of divine relationships and the intertwining of personal and cosmic forces.

The interactions among deities are not solely characterized by conflict but also encompass collaboration, alliances, and shared responsibilities. For instance, Enlil, the god of wind and storms, collaborates with other deities to maintain cosmic order and fulfill his role as a guardian and sustainer of the land. In the myth of Enki and Ninmah, Enki, the god of water and wisdom, forms a partnership with the goddess Ninmah to create humanity. This collaboration highlights the harmonious cooperation among deities in shaping the mortal realm.

Exercise:

Choose two conflicting deities from the Mesopotamian pantheon and analyze the factors that contribute to their conflicts. Compare and contrast their attributes, domains, and roles, and consider how these differences contribute to their clashes.

Exploring Ancient Mesopotamian Mythology, Rivalries, and Spiritual Legacies

Write a reflective essay discussing the implications of these conflicts on the divine hierarchy and the mortal world.

Problem:

2. Imagine you are a scholar tasked with mediating a conflict among deities in the Mesopotamian pantheon. Write a proposal outlining strategies for conflict resolution and maintaining balance within the divine realm. Consider the potential consequences of the conflict on the mortal world and propose measures to mitigate any negative impacts.

Worship and Rituals

In the realm of spirituality, worship and rituals have long been regarded as powerful vehicles for establishing connections with the divine and expressing profound reverence, gratitude, and devotion. Throughout history, these practices have played a central role in various spiritual traditions, including Witchcraft, Divination, Herbalism, Shamanism, Ecospirituality, and even ancient Mesopotamian magic. In this chapter, we will embark on a comprehensive exploration of the significance of worship and rituals, analyzing their underlying principles, common elements, and diverse practices. By delving into these topics, we aim to provide students with a thorough understanding of the transformative power inherent in these practices.

I. The Purpose and Importance of Worship and Rituals

Within spiritual practices, the concept of the sacred represents a realm that transcends ordinary human perception and encompasses the numinous and divine. It is a realm that elicits awe, reverence, and a sense of profound mystery. Worship and rituals serve as powerful tools through which individuals can explore and connect with the sacred, allowing them to transcend the limitations of everyday existence and immerse themselves in the divine realm.

Through worship, practitioners enter a state of heightened consciousness and attunement. By engaging in ritualistic practices, they create a sacred space and time that is separate from the mundane world. This intentional separation allows individuals to focus their attention, energy, and intentions on connecting with the sacred. Whether it is through chanting, meditation, prayer, dance, or other ritual acts, practitioners open themselves up to receiving spiritual experiences and insights that go beyond the confines of ordinary human perception.

Divine Dynamics

In these moments of connection with the sacred, individuals may experience a profound sense of unity, a dissolution of boundaries between self and other, and a deep recognition of the interconnection of all things. They may encounter a sense of awe, beauty, and transcendence that inspires and uplifts their spirit. Through worship, practitioners embark on a transformative journey that allows them to transcend the limitations of their individual selves and touch something greater, something that transcends the human condition.

B. Establishing Relationships: Worship as a Means of Communication

Worship is not merely a one-sided act; it is a means of establishing relationships and engaging in communication with the divine. Through rituals and acts of devotion, individuals seek to establish a connection and dialogue with the spiritual realms. They express their reverence, gratitude, and longing to connect with the sacred forces that exist beyond the material realm.

Rituals provide a structured framework through which practitioners can express their intentions, desires, and aspirations to the divine. They offer a platform for individuals to voice their prayers, offer their gratitude, seek guidance, and ask for blessings. By engaging in these acts of communication, practitioners create a space for dialogue with the divine, fostering a reciprocal relationship built on trust, respect, and mutual exchange.

Within this dialogue, individuals may experience a sense of being heard, seen, and understood by the divine. They may receive guidance, insights, and signs that provide them with a deeper understanding of their spiritual path and the challenges they face. Worship rituals become a vehicle through which practitioners can express their deepest longings, share their joys and sorrows, and seek solace and guidance from the sacred realms.

C. Cultivating Devotion: Worship as an Expression of Faith

Worship rituals also serve as a means of cultivating devotion and expressing faith. Through these practices, individuals demonstrate their unwavering commitment to their spiritual path and their chosen deities. Worship becomes an act of devotion, an expression of love, loyalty, and dedication to the divine forces that they revere.

Practitioners engage in various forms of worship to deepen their connection and devotion. They may offer prayers, chant sacred mantras, perform rituals, create and maintain sacred spaces, make offerings, or engage in acts of service. These acts of devotion allow individuals to express their heartfelt commitment and devotion to the divine, reinforcing their spiritual bonds and fostering a sense of intimacy and belonging within their respective traditions.

By engaging in worship rituals, individuals not only express their devotion but also reaffirm their faith in the presence and power of the divine. These rituals provide a tangible means of connecting with the ineffable and formulating a personal relationship with the divine. Through their acts of devotion, practitioners find solace, inspiration, and strength, deepening their spiritual connection and shaping their worldview.

In conclusion, worship and rituals serve a multifaceted purpose within spiritual practices. They provide a path to transcendence, allowing practitioners to explore the sacred and experience profound spiritual insights. These practices also facilitate the establishment of relationships with the divine, providing a means of communication and connection with the spiritual realms. Additionally, worship rituals cultivate devotion, enabling individuals to express their faith, love, and dedication to the divine forces they revere. Through the study and engagement with worship and rituals, students gain a deeper understanding of the transformative potential of these practices and their significance within diverse spiritual traditions.

II. Ritual Elements and Practices in Worship

In worship rituals, the creation of sacred spaces holds great significance. These spaces serve as physical manifestations of the sacred, acting as gateways that bridge the gap between the mundane and the divine. Altars and designated ritual areas are meticulously prepared and arranged to evoke a sense of reverence and spiritual presence. They are adorned with sacred objects, symbols, and tools that hold deep symbolism within the specific spiritual tradition. For instance, in Wicca, the creation of a sacred circle is a central element, symbolizing the sacred space where rituals take place and creating a boundary between the mundane world and the realm of the divine. In Shamanic practices, sacred groves or natural landscapes are designated as ritual spaces, serving as places of connection with the spiritual realms. In ancient Mesopotamia, temples were constructed with intricate precision and dedicated to specific deities, providing a physical space where worshippers could engage in rituals and commune with the divine.

B. Symbolic Actions: Gestures, Movements, and Offerings

Symbolic actions are an integral part of worship rituals, encompassing gestures, movements, and offerings that carry deep spiritual significance. These actions are performed with intention and purpose, infusing the rituals with energy and symbolism. Gestures and movements serve as conduits for the practitioner's intentions and focus their energy toward the divine. They may include raising hands in prayer, bowing, circumambulation (walking in a circle), or specific dance movements. Each gesture and movement holds specific meanings within the cultural and spiritual context, serving as a means to express devotion, gratitude, and reverence.

Offerings, another form of symbolic action, represent acts of giving and reciprocity. They can take various forms depending on the tradition, such as offering food, drink, flowers, herbs, or sacred objects. These offerings symbolize the practitioner's willingness to share and establish a reciprocal relationship with the divine. By presenting these gifts, practitioners express their gratitude, devotion, and desire for a deeper connection with the sacred. The act of offering becomes a tangible manifestation of their spiritual commitment and a means to honor the divine presence.

C. Sacred Time: Rituals for Celestial and Seasonal Alignments

Time holds a sacred quality within worship rituals, with specific celestial and seasonal alignments being honored and celebrated. Rituals are often conducted during significant celestial events such as solstices, equinoxes, and other planetary alignments. These moments mark important transitions and shifts in cosmic energies, and by aligning with them, practitioners synchronize themselves with the larger rhythms of the universe.

Seasonal rituals are also observed, reflecting the cyclical nature of the natural world. These rituals honor the changing seasons, such as the arrival of spring or the harvest season. By acknowledging and participating in these rituals, practitioners deepen their connection with the cycles of nature and the interconnected web of life. They recognize their place within the grand tapestry of existence and cultivate a sense of harmony with the natural world.

The observation of sacred time in rituals not only serves as a means to attune with cosmic and seasonal cycles but also provides an opportunity for reflection, introspection, and renewal. It invites practitioners to pause and connect with the profound forces at play in the universe, fostering a deeper understanding of their place within the divine order.

In conclusion, the elements and practices in worship rituals encompass the creation of sacred spaces, engagement in symbolic actions, and the observance of sacred time. These elements work together to facilitate spiritual connection, foster reverence, and deepen the practitioner's relationship with the divine. By understanding and engaging with these ritual elements, students gain insight into the profound symbolism and transformative power of worship rituals within various spiritual traditions.

III. The Role of Divination and Prophecy in Worship

A. Divination as a Sacred Practice

Divination is deeply rooted in the belief that the universe is interconnected, and that divine forces or higher powers can influence and guide human affairs. Across cultures and throughout history, various forms of divination have emerged, each with its own symbolism, rituals, and practices. Divination can be seen as a sacred act, as it involves the seeker reaching out to the divine, surrendering to its wisdom, and placing trust in the messages received.

In ancient Mesopotamia, divination played a significant role in religious and societal life. The Mesopotamians believed that the gods communicated with mortals through signs and omens, and divination was the means by which humans could interpret and understand these messages. The practice encompassed a wide range of methods, such as observing the movements of celestial bodies, interpreting the flight patterns of birds, examining the entrails of sacrificial animals, or analyzing patterns in oil or wax.

Divination was not only used for personal guidance but also for matters of great importance, such as the outcomes of battles, the success of agricultural endeavors, or the establishment of new cities. Expert diviners, known as baru or bārû, were highly respected and sought after for their ability to interpret the signs and provide insights into the will of the gods. Divination was considered a sacred act that bridged the gap between mortals and the divine, allowing individuals and communities to align their actions with the greater cosmic forces.

The significance of divination lies in its potential to offer guidance, reassurance, and a sense of connection to something greater than oneself. It provides a means for individuals to seek answers to pressing questions, gain clarity during times of uncertainty, and navigate life's challenges. Divination can offer solace, validation, and empowerment by affirming that one is not alone in their journey and that there is guidance available from the spiritual realms.

Moreover, divination serves as a reminder of the interconnectedness of all things and the belief that there is a greater plan or purpose at work in the universe. It encourages individuals to cultivate a sense of trust, surrender, and openness to the divine, allowing them to tap into the deeper wisdom that lies beyond the rational mind.

While divination practices may vary across cultures and time periods, the underlying principle remains the same—to access divine knowledge and gain insight into the mysteries of existence. By engaging in divination, individuals can forge a deeper connection with the sacred, discover hidden truths, and navigate their spiritual journey with greater clarity and purpose.

B. Prophecy: The Voice of the Divine

The voice of the divine, expressed through prophecy, is a powerful and mysterious phenomenon found in various religious and spiritual traditions. Prophets, seers, and oracles are believed to have a direct line of communication with the divine realm, enabling them to receive and convey messages from higher powers. These messages may encompass a wide range of topics, including guidance for individuals or communities, warnings of impending events, or revelations about the nature of reality.

The act of prophecy often involves a transcendent experience in which the prophet enters an altered state of consciousness, allowing them to connect with divine energies or entities. This connection grants them access to knowledge beyond ordinary human perception, granting them insights into hidden truths and future events. The language and symbols used in prophecy are often metaphorical or symbolic, requiring interpretation to fully understand their meaning.

Prophecy serves several purposes within spiritual practices. Firstly, it offers guidance and direction to individuals and communities, helping them navigate challenges, make decisions, and align their actions with divine will. The prophetic messages can serve as a moral compass, providing insights into ethical choices and offering a framework for personal and collective growth.

Secondly, prophecy can act as a means of validation and affirmation, reassuring individuals of their connection to the divine and providing a sense of comfort and purpose. By hearing the voice of the divine, people can feel seen, heard, and supported on their spiritual journeys.

However, the authenticity and interpretation of prophecy have been subjects of debate and controversy throughout history. It is essential to approach prophetic messages with discernment and critical thinking. The motivations and biases of prophets must be taken into account, as personal beliefs, cultural influences, and societal pressures can shape the messages they convey. Furthermore, prophecies may be subject to misinterpretation or distortion, and the fallibility of human perception should be acknowledged.

Engaging with prophecy requires a balance between openness and skepticism. While being receptive to the potential wisdom and insights offered by prophetic messages, it is also important to maintain a critical mindset and engage in thoughtful analysis. This approach allows individuals to extract valuable teachings while recognizing the limitations and complexities inherent in prophetic practices.

The voice of the divine, expressed through prophecy, continues to captivate and inspire individuals seeking spiritual guidance and connection. It represents an ongoing exploration of the mysteries of the universe and offers a glimpse into the profound interplay between the mortal and divine realms. Through discernment and thoughtful engagement, individuals can navigate the realm of prophecy and uncover the profound wisdom it may hold.

Chapter 4: Inanna/Ishtar: The Queen of Heaven and Goddess of Love and War

Significance of Inanna/Ishtar in Mesopotamian Mythology and Religion

Inanna, also known as Ishtar, is indeed a fascinating and influential deity in Mesopotamian mythology and religion. Her diverse roles and attributes reflect the complexities of human existence and the multifaceted nature of the divine. By exploring the significance of Inanna/Ishtar, we gain a deeper understanding of the beliefs, values, and societal dynamics of ancient Mesopotamia.

As the goddess of love and fertility, Inanna/Ishtar played a vital role in ensuring the prosperity and continuity of life. She was associated with the sacred marriage between the king and the land, symbolizing the union of heaven and earth. Through her divine influence, she blessed couples with fertility, promoting the growth of crops and animals. Inanna/Ishtar's worship involved rituals and ceremonies aimed at invoking her blessings for bountiful harvests and successful reproduction.

However, Inanna/Ishtar's sphere of influence extended beyond love and fertility. She was also associated with war and sovereignty, representing the fierce and protective aspects of femininity. In this role, she demonstrated her power and authority in the face of conflict and played a crucial role in the military and political affairs of ancient Mesopotamia. As the embodiment of sovereignty, Inanna/Ishtar empowered rulers, granting them legitimacy and divine guidance.

Inanna/Ishtar's mythology is rich with narratives that highlight her prowess and complex personality. One of the most famous myths is the Descent of Inanna, where she undertakes a journey to the underworld, facing trials and challenges along the way. This myth symbolizes the cyclical nature of life, death, and rebirth and underscores Inanna/Ishtar's ability to traverse different realms and embody contrasting roles.

Inanna/Ishtar's cultic practices were vibrant and influential. Temples dedicated to her worship, such as the magnificent Eanna temple in Uruk, were centers of religious and social activities. Priestesses, known as the "hierodules," played a significant role in these rituals, embodying the presence of Inanna/Ishtar and participating in sacred sexual rites that symbolized fertility and renewal.

Exploring Ancient Mesopotamian Mythology, Rivalries, and Spiritual Legacies

The influence of Inanna/Ishtar extended beyond the boundaries of religious practices. She permeated various aspects of Mesopotamian society, including art, literature, and legal codes. Images of Inanna/Ishtar adorned seals, statues, and other artifacts, emphasizing her status and power. In literature, she was often depicted as a powerful and assertive figure, challenging gender norms and societal expectations.

Inanna/Ishtar's significance in Mesopotamian mythology and religion cannot be overstated. Her diverse and complex nature encapsulates the human experience and reflects the aspirations, fears, and desires of ancient Mesopotamians. Through her worship and mythology, she provided a framework for understanding the divine and offered inspiration and guidance for navigating the challenges of life. By studying Inanna/Ishtar, we gain valuable insights into the rich tapestry of ancient Mesopotamian beliefs and the role of powerful and influential female deities in shaping the cultural and social dynamics of the time.

Objectives and Structure of the Chapter

The primary objectives of this chapter are to explore the significance of Inanna/Ishtar in Mesopotamian mythology and religion, and to examine the various aspects of her worship, rituals, and symbolism. By delving into the myths, cultic practices, and historical context surrounding Inanna/Ishtar, we aim to deepen our understanding of her role and significance within the pantheon and the broader religious landscape of ancient Mesopotamia.

To achieve these objectives, this chapter will be structured as follows:

Overview of Mesopotamian Mythology and Religion: We will provide a brief introduction to the religious beliefs and practices of ancient Mesopotamia, highlighting the pantheon and the cosmological framework within which Inanna/Ishtar operates.

Mythology of Inanna/Ishtar: We will explore key myths and narratives that feature Inanna/Ishtar as a central figure, shedding light on her relationships with other deities, her exploits, and her interactions with mortal beings.

Cult of Inanna/Ishtar: We will examine the cultic practices associated with Inanna/Ishtar, including worship rituals, festivals, and the role of priests and priestesses in her service. We will also explore the symbolism and iconography associated with her cult.

Sociopolitical Significance: We will discuss the sociopolitical implications of Inanna/Ishtar's worship, exploring her connections to kingship, the divine feminine, and the power dynamics within ancient Mesopotamian society.

Preview of Key Topics and Themes

Throughout this chapter, we will delve into a range of topics and themes related to Inanna/Ishtar, providing a comprehensive understanding of her significance within Mesopotamian mythology and religion. Some of the key topics and themes that we will explore include:

Inanna/Ishtar as a goddess of love, fertility, and war: We will analyze the different facets of her divine persona, examining her roles as a patroness of love and sexuality, a bestower of fertility, and a fierce warrior goddess.

Inanna/Ishtar's descent to the Underworld: We will delve into the famous myth of Inanna's descent to the Underworld, exploring its symbolism, themes of death and rebirth, and its parallels with other mythological narratives from different cultures.

Inanna/Ishtar's relationships with other deities: We will investigate Inanna/Ishtar's interactions and relationships with other deities, such as her brother Utu/Shamash and her lover Dumuzid/Tammuz, unraveling the complex dynamics and the divine hierarchy within the pantheon.

Gender and power in Inanna/Ishtar's cult: We will examine the ways in which Inanna/Ishtar challenges traditional gender roles and norms, exploring the implications of her divine femininity and her impact on gender dynamics in ancient Mesopotamian society.

By delving into these key topics and themes, we aim to provide students with a comprehensive and nuanced understanding of Inanna/Ishtar and her significance within the realm of Mesopotamian mythology and religion. Through critical analysis and engagement with primary sources, students will develop a deeper appreciation for the cultural, social, and religious complexities of ancient Mesopotamia.

Inanna/Ishtar: An Overview

In the vast pantheon of ancient Mesopotamia, one deity shines with remarkable significance and complexity: Inanna, also known as Ishtar. As a goddess of unparalleled power and influence, Inanna/Ishtar occupies a central place in the religious and mythological traditions of this ancient civilization. Understanding the essence and attributes of Inanna/Ishtar is essential for comprehending the spiritual landscape of ancient Mesopotamia.

Understanding Her Multifaceted Nature and Domains of Influence

Inanna/Ishtar encompasses a diverse range of roles and attributes, making her a deity of extraordinary complexity. She embodies various domains of influence, each with its unique symbolism and significance. To truly appreciate Inanna/Ishtar, we must explore her multifaceted nature and delve into the diverse aspects of her divine persona.

Love and Sexuality: Inanna/Ishtar is revered as the goddess of love and sexuality, representing the sacred embodiment of desire, passion, and romantic connections. She is often depicted as a sensual and alluring figure, evoking both the joys and challenges that accompany matters of the heart.

Fertility and Motherhood: Inanna/Ishtar also holds sway over the realm of fertility and motherhood. She blesses mortals with abundant harvests, grants fertility to women, and ensures the continuation of life. As the divine nurturer, she embodies the life-giving forces of nature and the cyclical rhythms of creation.

War and Sovereignty: In a striking contrast to her roles as a lover and a mother, Inanna/Ishtar manifests as a fierce warrior goddess. She is associated with the defense of cities, the protection of boundaries, and the assertion of sovereignty. In this aspect, she represents the strength and determination needed to confront and overcome obstacles.

Wisdom and Divine Order: Inanna/Ishtar is also revered as a bestower of wisdom and a bringer of divine order. She is associated with justice, law, and the establishment of societal harmony. Through her wisdom and guidance, she helps maintain cosmic balance and fosters human civilization.

By comprehending the various domains of influence within Inanna/Ishtar's divine essence, students gain a deeper understanding of the complexity and diversity of ancient Mesopotamian beliefs and values.

Cultural and Historical Contexts of Inanna/Ishtar Worship

To fully grasp the significance of Inanna/Ishtar, we must explore the cultural and historical contexts in which her worship flourished. The worship of Inanna/Ishtar was deeply embedded in the social fabric of ancient Mesopotamia, reflecting the beliefs, values, and aspirations of its people.

Mesopotamian Cosmology and Pantheon: The cosmological framework of ancient Mesopotamia revolved around a pantheon of gods and goddesses, with Inanna/Ishtar occupying a prominent position within this divine hierarchy. Understanding the broader context of Mesopotamian mythology and the relationships between deities enhances our comprehension of Inanna/Ishtar's place in the religious landscape.

Roles and Rituals of Inanna/Ishtar's Cult: Inanna/Ishtar's worship was marked by a rich array of rituals, ceremonies, and festivals. These practices were led by priests and priestesses who played vital roles in maintaining the connection between mortals and the divine. Exploring the specific rituals associated with Inanna/Ishtar's cult provides students with insights into the ancient Mesopotamian religious experience.

Sociopolitical Dimensions: Inanna/Ishtar's worship was not confined solely to matters of spirituality. It intersected with sociopolitical structures, including the realms of governance, royalty, and social hierarchies. The influence of Inanna/Ishtar extended beyond the temples, shaping the very fabric of Mesopotamian society.

By examining the cultural and historical contexts of Inanna/Ishtar worship, students gain a comprehensive understanding of the interplay between religion, culture, and power dynamics in ancient Mesopotamia.

In the following chapters, we will delve deeper into the mythological narratives, rituals, and symbolism associated with Inanna/Ishtar, allowing students to explore the intricacies of this remarkable deity and her enduring impact on the spiritual and cultural heritage of ancient Mesopotamia. Through engaging examples, thought-provoking problems, and stimulating exercises, students will embark on a journey of critical thinking and scholarly exploration.

Inanna/Ishtar in Mythology and Epic Literature

The Mythological Tapestry: Exploring Inanna/Ishtar's Narrative Presence

Inanna/Ishtar, the revered goddess of ancient Mesopotamia, graces the mythological tapestry with her compelling presence. Through an exploration of mythological narratives and epic literature, students can gain deeper insights into the significance and symbolism surrounding this multifaceted deity. By examining the tales and legends associated with Inanna/Ishtar, we unravel the layers of her divine persona and the enduring impact she had on the collective consciousness of the ancient Mesopotamian people.

The Descent of Inanna: The most renowned myth featuring Inanna/Ishtar is the epic tale known as "The Descent of Inanna." In this narrative, Inanna undertakes a perilous journey to the underworld, a realm ruled by her sister, Ereshkigal. The myth explores themes of death, rebirth, and the cyclical nature of existence. Through her descent, Inanna undergoes a transformative ordeal, shedding aspects of her divine power to gain profound wisdom and empathy.

Inanna and Dumuzid: Another prominent myth highlights Inanna/Ishtar's romantic relationship with Dumuzid, the shepherd-king. This narrative explores the themes of love, sacrifice, and the cycle of life and death. It delves into the challenges faced by mortal and immortal beings in their pursuit of love and the inevitability of loss and renewal.

Inanna's Divine Authority: In the mythological narratives, Inanna/Ishtar embodies aspects of divine authority and sovereignty. Through her actions, she asserts her power and influence over the mortal realm, while also navigating complex relationships with other deities. These stories provide insights into the intricate dynamics of divine hierarchy, power struggles, and the delicate balance between the human and divine realms.

Symbolism and Archetypes: Unveiling Deeper Meanings

Beyond the narrative aspects, the mythological stories surrounding Inanna/Ishtar are rich in symbolism and archetypal motifs. By delving into these symbols and archetypes, students can uncover deeper layers of meaning and explore the universality of Inanna/Ishtar's themes within the broader context of human experience.

The Sacred Marriage: The symbol of the sacred marriage appears frequently in Inanna/Ishtar's myths, representing the union of the divine masculine and feminine principles. This union symbolizes the harmony of opposites, the balance of power, and the potential for creative manifestation.

The Hero's Journey: Inanna/Ishtar's descent into the underworld and subsequent return can be viewed as a symbolic representation of the hero's journey. This archetypal motif, found in various mythologies worldwide, encompasses the protagonist's transformation, trials, and ultimate attainment of wisdom or enlightenment. By analyzing Inanna/Ishtar's journey, students can identify parallels with other hero's journeys and explore the universal themes of personal growth and self-discovery.

Comparative Perspectives: Inanna/Ishtar in the Context of World Mythology

Inanna/Ishtar's myths and archetypes resonate beyond the boundaries of ancient Mesopotamia. Comparative analysis of her narratives allows us to discern parallels and shared motifs with other mythological traditions, fostering a broader understanding of the human quest for meaning and transcendence.

Love and Passion: Inanna/Ishtar's role as a goddess of love and passion finds resonance in numerous mythologies, such as the Greek goddess Aphrodite or the Hindu goddess Parvati. Exploring these parallels expands our understanding of the human longing for connection, desire, and the complexities of love.

Death and Rebirth: The theme of death and rebirth, central to Inanna/Ishtar's descent narrative, can be found in various mythologies, including the Egyptian myth of Osiris and the Greek myth of Persephone. Comparing these myths enables students to recognize shared motifs and underlying cultural and psychological themes.

Exercises:

Analyze the narrative structure and symbolism in "The Descent of Inanna" and compare it with a myth from a different cultural tradition that features a journey to the underworld.

Identify archetypal motifs in the mythological stories of Inanna/Ishtar and discuss their significance in relation to human psychology and the collective unconscious.

Research and present a comparative analysis of Inanna/Ishtar's myths and their counterparts in Greek, Egyptian, or Hindu mythology, highlighting shared themes and cultural variations.

Through an in-depth exploration of Inanna/Ishtar's presence in mythology and epic literature, students will uncover the timeless wisdom and universal truths embedded within these narratives. By critically engaging with the text, reflecting on the symbolism, and drawing connections to other mythological traditions, students develop a nuanced understanding of the cultural, psychological, and spiritual dimensions of Inanna/Ishtar's significance.

Analysis of key myths and stories involving Inanna/Ishtar

Inanna/Ishtar, the multifaceted goddess of ancient Mesopotamia, assumes various roles within the mythological narratives, showcasing her prowess as a divine lover, warrior, and bringer of justice. In this chapter, we delve into the exploration of key myths and stories that shed light on these aspects of her divine persona. Through a comprehensive analysis of her relationships, we uncover the symbolism, cultural significance, and psychological insights embedded within Inanna/Ishtar's divine unions.

Dumuzid, the Shepherd-King: One of the central narratives surrounding Inanna/Ishtar involves her passionate and tumultuous relationship with Dumuzid, the shepherd-king. This myth symbolizes the cyclical nature of life, the interplay between love and loss, and the profound transformations that occur through sacrifice. By examining the dynamics of their relationship and the consequences that unfold, students gain a deeper understanding of the complexities of love, power dynamics, and the intricate connections between the divine and mortal realms.

Gilgamesh and Inanna: In the epic of Gilgamesh, the legendary hero encounters Inanna/Ishtar, resulting in a powerful and transformative interaction. This myth explores themes of divine intervention, the limitations of mortal desire, and the consequences of challenging divine authority. By analyzing the nuances of this encounter, students reflect on the intricate relationships between gods and mortals, the temptations of power, and the potential for personal growth through divine encounters.

The Warrior Goddess: Unleashing Inanna/Ishtar's Power and Ferocity

In addition to her role as a divine lover, Inanna/Ishtar embodies the archetype of the warrior goddess, representing strength, courage, and fierce determination. This section focuses on myths and stories that highlight Inanna/Ishtar's martial aspects, enabling students to delve into the symbolism, cultural context, and psychological dimensions of her warrior persona.

The Battle with Kur: One of the prominent narratives features Inanna/Ishtar's encounter with the monstrous serpent Kur. This myth explores themes of cosmic battles, the triumph of order over chaos, and the goddess's role as a protector of divine order and justice. Through the analysis of this myth, students gain insights into the significance of cosmic battles within mythologies and the archetypal dynamics of order and chaos.

Divine Dynamics

The Weapons of Inanna/Ishtar: Inanna/Ishtar is often depicted wielding powerful weapons such as the bow and arrow, the mace, or the spear. These symbols of warfare and defense further illustrate her martial prowess and her role as a guardian of the divine realm. By examining the symbolism and cultural context of these weapons, students explore the role of weaponry in mythological narratives and its representation of power and protection.

The Descent of Inanna: While primarily known for her warlike attributes, Inanna/Ishtar's journey to the underworld in the myth known as the Descent of Inanna reveals another facet of her warrior persona. In this story, Inanna/Ishtar descends to the realm of the dead, facing various challenges and trials along the way. This myth explores themes of death, rebirth, and the courage required to confront the darkest aspects of existence. By analyzing the Descent of Inanna, students can explore the psychological and spiritual significance of the warrior goddess's journey and the transformative power of facing and overcoming adversity.

Inanna/Ishtar as a Symbol of Female Empowerment: Inanna/Ishtar's role as a warrior goddess also carries implications for gender dynamics and female empowerment in ancient Mesopotamia. Her ability to navigate both the realms of love and war challenges traditional gender roles and expectations. This section will delve into the cultural and societal implications of Inanna/Ishtar's warrior persona, exploring how she may have served as an empowering figure for women in ancient Mesopotamian society. It will also examine the ways in which her archetype continues to resonate with contemporary notions of feminine strength and empowerment.

Cultic Practices and Rituals: The worship and rituals dedicated to Inanna/Ishtar as a warrior goddess will be explored in this section. Students will learn about the rituals performed to invoke her protection, courage, and victory in battle. These rituals may have included offerings, prayers, and enactments of martial feats. Understanding the cultic practices associated with Inanna/Ishtar as a warrior goddess provides valuable insights into the cultural and religious context in which she was revered.

Inanna/Ishtar's influence on Ancient Warfare: This section will discuss the potential influence of Inanna/Ishtar on ancient warfare and military strategies in Mesopotamia. It will explore the concept of divine intervention in battles and how warriors may have sought the favor and protection of the warrior goddess before engaging in warfare. By examining historical and textual evidence, students can gain a deeper understanding of the interplay between mythology, religion, and military practices in ancient Mesopotamia.

Exploring Ancient Mesopotamian Mythology, Rivalries, and Spiritual Legacies

By exploring the power and ferocity of Inanna/Ishtar as a warrior goddess, students can engage with the psychological, cultural, and historical dimensions of her mythology. This section provides a comprehensive analysis of her martial aspects, revealing her complex and multifaceted nature as a divine figure in ancient Mesopotamian beliefs and practices.

The Bringer of Justice: Inanna/Ishtar as a Dispenser of Divine Law

Inanna/Ishtar's mythological stories also highlight her role as a bringer of justice and divine law. Through the exploration of these narratives, students gain insight into the cultural and societal functions of the goddess, as well as the ethical implications associated with her dispensation of justice.

The Huluppu Tree: The myth of the Huluppu Tree illustrates Inanna/Ishtar's role as a restorer of balance and order. In this narrative, she rescues the sacred tree from chaos, reclaiming its rightful place in the divine realm. This myth highlights the goddess's commitment to upholding justice, preserving cosmic harmony, and ensuring the stability of the world.

Inanna/Ishtar's Decree: In certain myths, Inanna/Ishtar pronounces decrees and laws that govern the behavior of gods and mortals alike. These pronouncements emphasize her role as a moral authority and a dispenser of justice. By examining these stories, students reflect on the nature of divine law, the concept of ethical responsibility, and the relationship between divine authority and human conduct.

The Judgment of Inanna/Ishtar: In the myth known as the Judgment of Inanna/Ishtar, the goddess holds court and passes judgment on various individuals who have violated social and moral norms. This narrative showcases Inanna/Ishtar's role as a divine arbiter, examining the concepts of justice, accountability, and the consequences of one's actions. Through the analysis of this myth, students explore the intricacies of divine judgment and the moral framework established by the goddess.

Inanna/Ishtar's Code of Ethics: In addition to her role as a dispenser of justice, Inanna/Ishtar is associated with a code of ethics that guides human behavior. These ethical principles, embodied in her myths and teachings, offer guidance on matters such as truthfulness, loyalty, and compassion. Students will delve into these ethical teachings, examining their relevance in ancient Mesopotamian society and reflecting on their potential applications in contemporary ethical frameworks.

The Symbolism of Inanna/Ishtar's Scepter: Inanna/Ishtar is often depicted holding a scepter, a symbol of her authority and power as a dispenser of justice. This section will explore the symbolism and cultural significance of the scepter in Mesopotamian society, shedding light on the goddess's role as a lawgiver and enforcer. Students will analyze the artistic representations of Inanna/Ishtar with her scepter and explore its implications in terms of divine authority and the administration of justice.

The Legal and Judicial System in Ancient Mesopotamia: To provide a broader context, this section will examine the legal and judicial system of ancient Mesopotamia, with a focus on how it intersected with the myths and cultic practices associated with Inanna/Ishtar. Students will gain an understanding of the societal structures, legal codes, and the role of religious beliefs in shaping the legal framework of the civilization. The discussion will highlight the ways in which Inanna/Ishtar's mythology and teachings may have influenced the legal system and notions of justice in ancient Mesopotamia.

By exploring Inanna/Ishtar as a dispenser of divine law, students gain insights into the ethical and moral dimensions of her mythology, as well as the cultural and societal implications of her role as a bringer of justice. This section provides a comprehensive analysis of her position as a moral authority, deepening our understanding of the complexities and dynamics of ancient Mesopotamian belief systems.

Exercises:

Analyze the myth of Inanna/Ishtar and Dumuzid, exploring the themes of love, sacrifice, and transformation. Discuss the cultural and psychological implications of their relationship.

Compare and contrast Inanna/Ishtar's encounter with Gilgamesh and its consequences with her encounters with other mortal heroes in different mythologies. What common themes and lessons emerge from these encounters?

Reflect on the symbolism of Inanna/Ishtar's weapons and their significance in relation to her warrior persona. How do these symbols reflect cultural values and perceptions of power?

Discuss the ethical implications of Inanna/Ishtar's role as a bringer of justice. How does her dispensation of divine law impact human behavior and societal order?

By engaging with the key myths and stories involving Inanna/Ishtar, students develop a comprehensive understanding of her multifaceted nature as a divine lover, warrior, and bringer of justice. Through critical analysis, students gain insights into the psychological, cultural, and ethical dimensions of these narratives, fostering a deeper appreciation for the complex tapestry of ancient Mesopotamian mythology and its enduring relevance.

Love and Sexuality: Inanna/Ishtar as the Goddess of Desire

Inanna/Ishtar, the ancient Mesopotamian goddess, holds a prominent position as the embodiment of desire, love, and sensuality. In this chapter, we explore the multifaceted aspects of her divine persona related to love and sexuality. By delving into the myths, symbols, and rituals associated with Inanna/Ishtar, students will gain a deeper understanding of the cultural, psychological, and spiritual significance of the goddess's connection to desire.

Cultural and Historical Context of Love and Sexuality

Before delving into the specific aspects of Inanna/Ishtar's role as the goddess of desire, it is essential to examine the cultural and historical context in which she was worshipped. Mesopotamian society held a complex relationship with love and sexuality, which influenced the understanding and reverence of Inanna/Ishtar. By studying the social norms, religious practices, and gender dynamics of ancient Mesopotamia, students will develop a comprehensive understanding of the broader cultural framework within which Inanna/Ishtar's divine role as the goddess of desire emerged.

Ancient Mesopotamian society had a multifaceted approach to love and sexuality. The understanding and expression of these concepts were influenced by various factors, including religious beliefs, societal norms, and the roles of men and women in the civilization. Love and sexuality were seen as integral aspects of human existence and were celebrated and explored through a range of cultural practices.

In Mesopotamian religious beliefs, fertility was highly valued, and the procreation of children was considered a vital duty. This emphasis on fertility led to the worship of deities associated with love, sexuality, and reproduction, with Inanna/Ishtar being one of the most prominent among them. The rituals and cultic practices dedicated to Inanna/Ishtar often involved acts of sacred sexuality, symbolizing the union of divine and human energies and the promotion of fertility in both the natural and human realms.

Mesopotamian society recognized the importance of sexual desire and its expression within the boundaries of marriage. Marriage was a significant institution, primarily for the purpose of procreation and the continuation of family lines. While monogamy was the ideal, polygamy and concubinage were also practiced, particularly among the elite. The institution of marriage provided a framework for regulating sexual relationships and establishing social and familial bonds.

Gender dynamics played a crucial role in shaping the understanding of love and sexuality in ancient Mesopotamia. Women were often seen as objects of desire and beauty, and their sexuality was celebrated in certain contexts. However, societal norms and legal codes placed greater restrictions on women's behavior and sexual autonomy compared to men. Women were expected to maintain fidelity within marriage and adhere to societal expectations of modesty and chastity.

Literature, such as the love poetry of ancient Mesopotamia, offers further insights into the cultural understanding of love and desire. These poems, often composed by male authors, depict passionate and sometimes illicit love affairs, expressing a range of emotions and desires. The exploration of love in literature provided an outlet for the expression of human emotions and offered a glimpse into the complexities of human relationships.

By examining the cultural and historical context of love and sexuality in ancient Mesopotamia, students gain a nuanced understanding of the societal norms, religious beliefs, and gender dynamics that influenced the worship of Inanna/Ishtar as the goddess of desire. This contextual knowledge enriches the interpretation of her myths and rituals, shedding light on the cultural dynamics and the significance of love and sexuality within ancient Mesopotamian society.

Love and Passion: Inanna/Ishtar's Divine Unions

The Descent of Inanna/Ishtar myth is a powerful and symbolic narrative that explores the themes of love, desire, and the transformative nature of human experience. In this myth, Inanna/Ishtar descends into the realm of the Underworld, leaving behind her status as a powerful goddess, and faces a series of trials and challenges orchestrated by her sister, Ereshkigal, the Queen of the Underworld.

The stages of Inanna/Ishtar's descent and ascent hold deep symbolic meaning. As she travels through the seven gates of the Underworld, she is required to remove her divine garments and ornaments, stripping away her worldly identity and power. This act symbolizes the vulnerability and surrender required to embark on a journey of self-discovery and transformation. Inanna/Ishtar's willingness to undergo this process demonstrates the depths of her desire and her quest for a profound connection with the divine.

Exploring Ancient Mesopotamian Mythology, Rivalries, and Spiritual Legacies

During her time in the Underworld, Inanna/Ishtar confronts the shadow aspects of her own being and experiences death and rebirth. Ereshkigal, representing the darker aspects of existence, inflicts punishments upon Inanna/Ishtar, and the goddess experiences a symbolic death. This descent into darkness represents the necessary confrontation with one's own fears, pain, and limitations to achieve personal growth and spiritual enlightenment.

Inanna/Ishtar's ultimate resurrection and return to the realm of the living symbolize the transformative power of love and desire. The myth portrays the cyclical nature of love and the potential for renewal and growth that can arise from embracing the full spectrum of human experience, including both light and shadow aspects. It highlights the interconnectedness of life and death and the inherent power of desire to challenge and transform one's perception of reality.

The concept of sacred unions and hieros gamos is closely associated with Inanna/Ishtar and her worship. The sacred marriage represents the union of masculine and feminine energies, the integration of opposites, and the pursuit of harmony and wholeness. Through rituals and myths, Inanna/Ishtar embodies the divine feminine, while her lovers or consorts, such as Dumuzid or Tammuz, represent the divine masculine. The hieros gamos symbolizes the sacred balance and integration of these forces, emphasizing the importance of embracing and integrating all aspects of one's self to achieve spiritual completeness.

By studying the Descent of Inanna/Ishtar myth and the concepts of sacred unions and hieros gamos, students gain a deeper understanding of the transformative power of love and desire. They explore the archetypal dynamics at play in relationships, the significance of embracing the shadow aspects of the self, and the potential for personal growth and spiritual evolution through the integration of opposing forces. These insights provide valuable lessons for navigating the complexities of human relationships and the pursuit of spiritual wholeness.

Erotic Power and Empowerment

Inanna/Ishtar's association with erotic power and empowerment is a significant aspect of her divine role and mythology. As the goddess of desire and love, she embodies the transformative and liberating potential of embracing one's sexuality and sensuality. Studying her symbolism, rituals, and practices related to erotic power allows students to explore the cultural and societal attitudes toward sexuality and reflect on the interplay between personal empowerment and sexual expression.

Inanna/Ishtar serves as a symbol of erotic power, challenging conventional norms and societal expectations surrounding sexuality. Her worship in ancient

Divine Dynamics

Mesopotamia included rituals and practices that celebrated sensuality and desire. Sacred dances were performed in her honor, often involving rhythmic movements and gestures that embodied the expression of desire and pleasure. These rituals aimed to connect worshippers with the divine through the exploration of their own erotic energy and power.

By delving into the rituals and practices associated with Inanna/Ishtar's erotic aspect, students can reflect on the ethical considerations and personal agency involved in the exploration of erotic power. Discussions may revolve around topics such as consent, boundaries, and the empowerment that comes from embracing one's authentic sexual expression. These explorations provide an opportunity for students to examine the intersection of spirituality, personal empowerment, and sexual identity.

Furthermore, studying Inanna/Ishtar's association with erotic power allows students to critically analyze the cultural and historical context in which she was worshipped. They can explore the gender dynamics, societal attitudes, and power structures prevalent in ancient Mesopotamia, and how these influenced the understanding and reverence of erotic power within the religious and social spheres.

By engaging in these discussions and exercises, students gain a deeper understanding of the transformative potential of embracing and celebrating one's sexuality. They develop a broader perspective on the significance of erotic power as a source of personal empowerment and spiritual connection. These insights provide a platform for examining and redefining societal narratives surrounding sexuality, gender, and personal agency in contemporary contexts.

Exercises:

Reflect on the significance of the Descent of Inanna/Ishtar into the Underworld and its symbolism in relation to love and desire. Discuss the transformative power of desire and the role of passion in personal growth and spiritual evolution.

Compare and contrast the concept of hieros gamos in Mesopotamian mythology with similar concepts in other spiritual traditions, such as the union of Shiva and Shakti in Hinduism or the alchemical marriage in Western esotericism. Discuss the common themes and symbolism associated with sacred unions.

Analyze the representation of erotic power in different mythological narratives, such as the story of Aphrodite in Greek mythology or the tales of the sacred courtesans in ancient India. Discuss the cultural and social implications of these representations and their relevance to contemporary discussions on sexuality and empowerment.

Create a personal ritual or practice inspired by Inanna/Ishtar's role as the goddess of desire. Reflect on the intentions, symbols, and ethical considerations that shape your practice and discuss how it contributes to your personal growth and connection to the divine.

By exploring Inanna/Ishtar's role as the goddess of desire, students will gain a comprehensive understanding of the cultural, psychological, and spiritual dimensions of love and sexuality in ancient Mesopotamian mythology and its relevance to contemporary spiritual practices and personal empowerment. Through critical analysis and reflective exercises, students will deepen their appreciation for the diverse expressions of desire and the transformative potential of embracing and celebrating their own erotic power.

Seeking Inanna/Ishtar's Blessings in Matters of Love

Rituals for Love and Relationships: Within ancient Mesopotamian culture, rituals dedicated to Inanna/Ishtar played a significant role in seeking her blessings and guidance in matters of love. These rituals aimed to establish a direct connection with the goddess and invoke her divine presence to intervene in the realm of human relationships. Students studying this chapter will have the opportunity to explore the various rituals and practices associated with seeking Inanna/Ishtar's blessings in matters of love. These may include offerings, prayers, and sacred invocations performed in temples or private spaces.

Invoking Inanna/Ishtar's Divine Presence: Inanna/Ishtar was believed to be accessible to those who sought her favor and guidance. Students will delve into the ways in which individuals sought to invoke her presence through specific words, gestures, or actions. They will learn about the importance of creating sacred spaces, establishing a connection through prayer or meditation, and engaging in acts of devotion to open themselves to the goddess's influence and wisdom. By understanding the rituals and practices associated with invoking Inanna/Ishtar's presence, students gain insights into the ancient Mesopotamian belief system surrounding love and relationships.

The Power of Symbols: Symbols played a vital role in seeking Inanna/Ishtar's blessings in matters of love. The chapter will explore the significance of symbols such as the eight-pointed star, the lion, the dove, and the lapis lazuli, which were associated with the goddess and used in rituals and offerings. Students will learn about the symbolic meanings of these objects and how they were incorporated into rituals and practices as a means of connecting with Inanna/Ishtar's energy and invoking her blessings.

Transformative Love and Personal Growth: Inanna/Ishtar's blessings extended beyond the realm of romantic love. The goddess was also associated with personal transformation, empowerment, and self-discovery. Students will explore the concept of transformative love, examining how seeking Inanna/Ishtar's blessings in matters of love and relationships can facilitate personal growth, healing, and the expansion of consciousness. Through the study of myths and stories, students will gain insights into the goddess's role as a catalyst for personal and spiritual evolution.

By delving into the rituals, symbols, and transformative aspects of seeking Inanna/Ishtar's blessings in matters of love, students can apply these insights to their own lives. They will explore how ancient Mesopotamian practices can be adapted and integrated into contemporary contexts, offering new perspectives and approaches to navigating relationships, cultivating self-love, and experiencing personal transformation through the power of love.

Historical and Cultural Context of Love in Mesopotamia

In ancient Mesopotamia, love and sexuality held a complex and multifaceted role within society. The cultural and historical context greatly influenced the understanding and expression of love, romance, and sexuality, and this context provides a foundation for understanding the rituals and practices associated with seeking Inanna/Ishtar's blessings.

Love in Relationships: Love within relationships was considered essential for the stability and harmony of society. Marriage was primarily viewed as an institution for procreation and the preservation of social order rather than solely for romantic love. While arranged marriages were common, there was still room for personal affection and emotional bonds to develop between spouses. Love poems and romantic literature from the time highlight the longing, desire, and emotional connection experienced by individuals in their relationships.

Gender Dynamics and Roles: Gender dynamics in ancient Mesopotamia were heavily influenced by societal norms and cultural expectations. Men held dominant positions within the social hierarchy, and marriage was often seen as a way to establish alliances and maintain family lineage. Women were expected to fulfill their roles as wives, mothers, and caretakers. However, there were instances where women held positions of power and influence, such as the priestesses of Inanna/Ishtar's temples. Inanna/Ishtar's association with love and sexuality provided a space for the expression and empowerment of female desires and agency.

Exploring Ancient Mesopotamian Mythology, Rivalries, and Spiritual Legacies

Divine Influence on Love: The worship of Inanna/Ishtar and other love goddesses played a significant role in shaping the cultural understanding of love and desire. These goddesses were seen as embodying the ideal of love and passion, and their cults and rituals allowed individuals to seek divine intervention in matters of the heart. The belief in the power of these goddesses to bless relationships, ensure fertility, and protect against heartbreak provided a spiritual framework for understanding and navigating love and romance.

Cultural Expressions of Love: Love and romance were often celebrated through poetry, songs, and literature in ancient Mesopotamia. Love poems, known as "desire" or "courtship" songs, expressed the longing, attraction, and emotional experiences associated with love. These poetic expressions served as a way for individuals to convey their feelings and connect with others on a deep emotional level.

By understanding the historical and cultural context of love in Mesopotamia, students can contextualize the rituals and practices associated with seeking Inanna/Ishtar's blessings. They will gain a greater appreciation for the role of love in society, the dynamics of gender and power, and the influence of divine figures in shaping the understanding and expression of love and desire.

Creating Sacred Space and Preparation

Setting up an Inanna/Ishtar shrine provides a dedicated space for individuals to establish a personal connection with the goddess and seek her blessings in matters of love. Creating such a shrine involves careful selection of symbols, images, and offerings that evoke Inanna/Ishtar's presence and create a sacred atmosphere conducive to deepening one's connection with her.

Choosing a Sacred Space: The first step in setting up an Inanna/Ishtar shrine is to select an appropriate location. It can be a corner of a room, a table, or any space that can be designated solely for this purpose. It is essential to choose a space where one can focus and feel a sense of sacredness.

Altar or Shrine Construction: Students will learn how to construct an altar or shrine that reflects the essence of Inanna/Ishtar. This can include a small table or surface covered with a cloth in a color associated with the goddess, such as red or gold. The cloth may be adorned with symbols or patterns that represent love, fertility, or empowerment.

Symbols and Images: Selecting appropriate symbols and images is crucial in creating a visual representation of Inanna/Ishtar's energy. These may include statues, figurines, or artwork depicting the goddess or related symbols such as lions, stars, or the eight-pointed star of Ishtar. Students will explore the significance of these symbols and how they relate to Inanna/Ishtar's mythology and attributes.

Offerings and Ritual Items: Offerings play a significant role in shrine rituals as a way to honor and connect with the divine. Students will learn about traditional offerings associated with Inanna/Ishtar, such as flowers, incense, fruits, or libations. They will also explore the meaning and symbolism behind these offerings and how they can enhance the connection with the goddess. Additionally, ritual items such as candles, crystals, or oracle cards may be incorporated to create an ambiance conducive to invoking Inanna/Ishtar's presence.

Purification and Invocation: Before engaging in the shrine rituals, it is customary to perform purification rituals. This can involve taking a cleansing bath, smudging the space with sacred herbs, or reciting purification prayers or invocations. These practices help students prepare themselves energetically and spiritually, creating a focused and sacred atmosphere for their connection with Inanna/Ishtar.

Invoking Inanna/Ishtar's Presence: Students will explore various invocations, prayers, or chants specifically dedicated to Inanna/Ishtar. These invocations serve as a means to call upon her, invite her presence into the shrine, and establish a sacred connection. Through these practices, students can cultivate a deep sense of connection with the goddess and open themselves to her blessings and guidance in matters of love.

By setting up an Inanna/Ishtar shrine and engaging in purification rituals and invocations, students create a sacred space where they can connect with the goddess and seek her blessings. The careful selection of symbols, images, offerings, and invocations allows individuals to create a focused and powerful atmosphere that facilitates a profound connection with Inanna/Ishtar's divine energy and guidance.

Rituals for Seeking Inanna/Ishtar's Blessings in Matters of Love

Love Offering Ritual: This ritual focuses on expressing gratitude and offering devotion to Inanna/Ishtar for her blessings in matters of love. Students will learn how to prepare a meaningful offering, such as flowers, love poems, or personal tokens, and perform a ritual act of offering as a symbolic gesture of reverence and appreciation.

Exploring Ancient Mesopotamian Mythology, Rivalries, and Spiritual Legacies

Love Offering Ritual:

Preparation:

Create a sacred space: Find a quiet and undisturbed area where you can set up your Inanna/Ishtar shrine or altar. Clear the space of any clutter and create a serene atmosphere.
Select meaningful offerings: Choose items that symbolize love, beauty, and devotion. Some suggestions include fresh flowers, fragrant incense, love poems written on beautiful paper, or personal tokens that hold sentimental value.
Cleansing and Grounding:

Take a few moments to center yourself and let go of any distractions or negative energies. You can do this by taking deep breaths, visualizing a bright light surrounding you, or using a grounding technique such as imagining roots extending from your feet into the earth.
Invocation:

Light a candle or burn some incense to set the ambiance and invoke the presence of Inanna/Ishtar. You can recite a simple invocation or prayer to invite her energy and blessings into the space. For example:
"Goddess Inanna/Ishtar, divine embodiment of love,
I invite your presence and blessings into this sacred space.
With gratitude and reverence, I offer my devotion to you."
Offering:

Hold the items you have chosen for the offering in your hands and infuse them with your love and intention. Feel the energy and emotions flowing through you as you connect with the essence of Inanna/Ishtar.
Approach your shrine or altar and place the offerings in a respectful manner. You may arrange the flowers in a vase, light the love poems with a candle, or position the personal tokens with care. As you do so, express your gratitude and appreciation for the blessings of love in your life and your desire for further guidance and support.
Take a moment to silently or verbally express your heartfelt intentions and wishes to Inanna/Ishtar, trusting that she will hear and respond to your sincere devotion.

Closing:

Offer a final expression of gratitude to Inanna/Ishtar for her presence and blessings. You may choose to recite a closing prayer or simply take a few moments of silence to feel the energy of the ritual and the connection you have established.

Extinguish the candle or incense, marking the end of the ritual. Take a deep breath, feeling the energy of love and gratitude filling your being.

After completing the Love Offering Ritual, take time to reflect on your experience. Consider journaling about any insights, emotions, or sensations that arose during the ritual. Pay attention to any shifts in your perception of love and your connection with Inanna/Ishtar. You may also choose to repeat this ritual periodically to maintain your relationship with the goddess of love and deepen your understanding of her blessings in matters of the heart.

Love Spell Ritual: This ritual aims to harness Inanna/Ishtar's energy and assistance in attracting or deepening love in one's life. Students will explore different elements of spellcraft, such as candle magic, affirmations, or visualization techniques, and learn how to structure a love spell ritual that aligns with their intentions and ethical considerations.

Love Spell Ritual:

Preparation:

Find a quiet and undisturbed space where you can perform the ritual without interruptions. Create a sacred atmosphere by cleansing the area with incense, smudging, or your preferred method.

Gather the necessary materials: You will need a red or pink candle, a small piece of paper, a pen, and any additional items that resonate with love for you, such as rose petals, essential oils, or crystals.

Setting Intentions:

Take a few moments to clarify your intentions for the love spell. Reflect on what you desire in your love life, whether it's attracting a new partner, deepening an existing relationship, or cultivating self-love and acceptance. Formulate your intention in a clear and positive statement.

Candle Preparation:

Dress the candle with an appropriate oil or simply cleanse it with your intention. As you anoint the candle, visualize it being infused with the energy of love and the assistance of Inanna/Ishtar.

Affirmations and Visualization:

Sit comfortably in front of the candle and close your eyes. Take a few deep breaths to center yourself.

Begin reciting affirmations that align with your intention. For example:

"I am open to receiving love in my life."
"I attract a loving and supportive partner."
"I embody love and radiate it to others."

Visualize your desired outcome as vividly as possible. Imagine yourself in a loving relationship, feeling cherished, or experiencing the qualities of love you desire. Hold this image in your mind and allow yourself to fully immerse in the emotions associated with it.

Spell Casting:

Light the candle and place it in a safe holder or dish. As you do so, state your intention aloud or silently, calling upon Inanna/Ishtar for her assistance and guidance. For example:
"Inanna/Ishtar, goddess of love,
I seek your aid in manifesting love in my life.
With gratitude and respect, I ask for your blessings."

Write your intention on the small piece of paper. Fold the paper and hold it over the candle flame (be cautious of fire safety) while visualizing the energy of your intention being infused into the paper.

Once the paper has caught fire, place it in a fireproof dish and let it burn completely, symbolizing the release of your intention to the universe.

Gratitude and Closing:

Express your gratitude to Inanna/Ishtar for her assistance and the love that exists in your life. Thank her for her presence and support.
Safely extinguish the candle, acknowledging the completion of the ritual.
Take a few moments to ground yourself, allowing the energy of the ritual to settle within you. Reflect on the love you have invoked and embrace a sense of openness and receptivity to its manifestation.
Remember to approach love spell rituals with ethical considerations and respect for the free will of others. It is important to focus on attracting love that aligns with the highest good and respects the autonomy of all individuals involved. Regularly evaluate your intentions and adapt your rituals accordingly to maintain a responsible and conscious approach to love spellwork.

Sacred Dance or Movement:

Preparation:

Find a quiet and spacious area where you can move freely and without distractions. Clear the space to create a sacred and safe environment for your practice. You may choose to play soft instrumental or rhythmic music to enhance the ambiance.

Dress in comfortable clothing that allows for unrestricted movement and makes you feel connected to your body. You may also choose to adorn yourself with symbols or colors associated with Inanna/Ishtar, such as red or gold.

Centering and Intention Setting:

Stand tall with your feet grounded, take a few deep breaths, and close your eyes. Allow your body to relax and release any tension.

Set your intention for the sacred dance or movement practice. Consider what aspect of love, sensuality, or embodiment you wish to explore or invoke. Formulate a clear and positive intention statement in your mind or speak it aloud.

Warm-up and Body Awareness:

Begin with gentle warm-up exercises to prepare your body for movement. Start by stretching your limbs, rolling your shoulders, and loosening your joints. Pay attention to any sensations or areas of tension in your body.

Take a few moments to engage in body awareness exercises. Stand still and bring your attention to each part of your body, from head to toe. Notice any physical sensations, emotions, or thoughts that arise.

Exploratory Movement:

Allow yourself to move freely and intuitively, guided by your own body's impulses and the energy of Inanna/Ishtar. There are no right or wrong movements in this practice; simply let your body express itself authentically.

Experiment with different types of movement, such as flowing, sensual, rhythmic, or expansive movements. Explore the entire space, using gestures and postures that feel natural to you. You can incorporate elements of dance, yoga, or other movement practices that resonate with you.

Exploring Ancient Mesopotamian Mythology, Rivalries, and Spiritual Legacies

Connecting with Inanna/Ishtar:

As you move, envision Inanna/Ishtar's energy flowing through you. Imagine her sensuality, confidence, and embodiment infusing your movements. Allow yourself to embody her qualities and embrace the divine feminine essence within you.

If it feels appropriate, speak or silently invoke Inanna/Ishtar, inviting her presence to guide and inspire your dance. You may use words such as:

"Inanna/Ishtar, goddess of love and embodiment,

I welcome your energy and grace into my movement.

May I express my desires and honor the sacredness of my body through this dance."

Expressing Desires and Intentions:

Use the sacred dance or movement as a means of expressing your desires, intentions, and emotions related to love, sensuality, or embodiment. Allow your body to communicate and release any suppressed or unexpressed emotions or desires.

Engage in movements that evoke the qualities you wish to cultivate or experience. For example, you may incorporate flowing, sensual movements to awaken your sensuality or strong, expansive movements to embody confidence and empowerment.

Closing and Integration:

Gradually bring your movements to a slower pace, allowing your body to naturally come to rest. Stand still and take a few deep breaths, feeling the energy of your dance settling within you.

Express gratitude to Inanna/Ishtar for her presence and guidance throughout the practice. Thank her for the opportunity to connect with your body, desires, and the divine feminine energy.

Take a moment of stillness and reflection, acknowledging the insights, emotions, or sensations that arose during the sacred dance or movement. Consider journaling or meditating on your experience to deepen your understanding and integration.

Engaging in regular sacred dance or movement practices inspired by Inanna/Ishtar can foster a deeper connection with your body, sensuality, and desires. Remember that each person's experience will be unique, and it is essential to honor your own boundaries and comfort levels throughout the practice.

Divine Dynamics

Integration and Reflection

Integration and reflection are integral parts of the journey with Inanna/Ishtar and seeking her blessings in matters of love. Through journaling and reflection, students have the opportunity to deepen their understanding of the rituals, explore their experiences, and gain insights into their relationship with love and the divine.

Journaling and reflective practices provide a space for students to document their thoughts, emotions, and experiences before, during, and after each ritual. They can write about their intentions, the symbols and offerings used, their sensations and feelings during the ritual, any messages or guidance they received, and their overall experience of connecting with Inanna/Ishtar's energy. This process allows for personal exploration and self-expression, helping students to uncover and process their thoughts and emotions related to love and their connection with the goddess.

Engaging in self-reflection after each ritual enables students to gain deeper insights into themselves and their relationship with love. They can explore any shifts in their perception, beliefs, or patterns in relationships that may have emerged during the rituals. They can also reflect on the guidance received from Inanna/Ishtar and how it resonates with their personal experiences and aspirations in matters of love. This reflective practice cultivates self-awareness and a greater understanding of the transformative potential of working with Inanna/Ishtar's energy.

Integration exercises further support the integration of the rituals' lessons and insights into students' daily lives. These exercises provide practical applications for the wisdom gained from the rituals, allowing students to embody the qualities of love, empowerment, and divine connection in their interactions and relationships. Examples of integration exercises may include practicing self-love and self-care, expressing gratitude for the presence of love in their lives, setting healthy boundaries in relationships, or consciously engaging in acts of kindness and compassion towards others. These exercises help students bridge the gap between the ritualistic experiences and their everyday lives, fostering a deeper connection with Inanna/Ishtar's blessings and guidance in matters of love.

By engaging in journaling, reflection, and integration exercises, students can enhance their understanding of the rituals, deepen their connection with Inanna/Ishtar, and integrate the wisdom gained into their daily lives. These practices facilitate personal growth, self-awareness, and a more profound alignment with the energies of love and the divine.

Exploring Ancient Mesopotamian Mythology, Rivalries, and Spiritual Legacies

Exercises:

Design and perform your own love offering ritual to Inanna/Ishtar. Consider the symbols, objects, and actions that hold personal meaning to you.

Write a love poem or create a piece of artwork inspired by Inanna/Ishtar's energy. Reflect on how the creative process can deepen your connection with the goddess of love.

Explore different forms of sacred movement or dance that embody the essence of Inanna/Ishtar. Practice a dance routine or movement sequence that expresses your desires and invokes the goddess's energy.

By engaging in these rituals and practices, students will not only deepen their connection with Inanna/Ishtar but also cultivate a more profound understanding of love, desire, and relationships within the context of ancient Mesopotamian culture. The integration exercises and reflective practices will empower students to incorporate the wisdom and blessings of Inanna/Ishtar into their own lives, fostering personal growth and transformation in matters of the heart.

War and Power: Inanna/Ishtar as the Warrior Goddess

Inanna/Ishtar, the ancient Mesopotamian goddess, embodies not only love and desire but also power and warfare. This chapter delves into the multifaceted aspects of Inanna/Ishtar's persona as the warrior goddess. By examining the myths, symbols, and historical context surrounding her role as a warrior, students will gain a deeper understanding of the complex interplay between power, femininity, and the pursuit of justice within the ancient Mesopotamian worldview.

Cultural and Historical Context of Warfare

Cultural and historical context is essential for understanding the role of warfare in ancient Mesopotamia and its connection to Inanna/Ishtar as a warrior goddess. Warfare held a prominent place in the cultural, political, and social dynamics of the region, shaping the beliefs, values, and practices of the ancient Mesopotamians.

Ancient Mesopotamia was a land marked by city-states that often engaged in territorial disputes, power struggles, and conflicts. These city-states, such as Sumer, Akkad, and Babylon, were constantly vying for dominance and control over resources. Warfare was not only a means of expansion and territorial gain but also a mechanism for asserting political authority and maintaining societal order.

Divine Dynamics

In the ancient Mesopotamian worldview, gods and goddesses were intimately involved in the affairs of humans, including warfare. Deities were believed to actively participate in battles, favoring certain city-states or individuals and providing divine guidance and protection. It was common for rulers and warriors to invoke the aid of deities before engaging in warfare, seeking their blessings and support.

Understanding the role of gods and goddesses in warfare provides insight into Inanna/Ishtar's association with power and war. Inanna/Ishtar's attributes as a warrior goddess reflected the societal values placed on courage, strength, and victory in battle. Her role as a protector of divine order and justice extended to the realm of warfare, where she was believed to empower warriors, ensure victory, and mete out divine justice on the battlefield.

Moreover, the social implications of warfare in ancient Mesopotamia cannot be overlooked. Military campaigns and conflicts affected not only the rulers and warriors but also the entire society. Warfare had economic repercussions, impacting trade, agriculture, and the overall stability of the city-states. It also had social implications, including the recruitment of soldiers, the displacement of populations, and the disruption of daily life.

Studying the cultural and historical context of warfare in ancient Mesopotamia provides a deeper understanding of the motivations, values, and societal impact of conflicts. It sheds light on the significance of Inanna/Ishtar as a warrior goddess within this context, showcasing her role in empowering warriors, maintaining cosmic balance, and embodying the ideals and aspirations of ancient Mesopotamian society.

By examining the military practices, the involvement of deities in warfare, and the social consequences of conflicts, students can gain a comprehensive understanding of the complexities surrounding warfare in ancient Mesopotamia and its connection to the worship and veneration of Inanna/Ishtar as a warrior goddess.

Inanna/Ishtar as a Divine Warrior

The myth of Inanna and the Mountain is a significant narrative that showcases Inanna/Ishtar's role as a warrior goddess and highlights her ability to triumph over challenges and adversity. In this myth, Inanna/Ishtar confronts a formidable mountain, representing chaos and obstacles, and emerges victorious, symbolizing the triumph of divine power over the forces of disorder.

By analyzing the symbolic elements within the myth, students can gain deeper insights into the transformative potential of harnessing inner strength and courage.

Exploring Ancient Mesopotamian Mythology, Rivalries, and Spiritual Legacies

The mountain represents the challenges and struggles that individuals and societies face in their journey towards growth and transformation. Inanna/Ishtar's victory over the mountain illustrates the power of resilience, determination, and the ability to overcome obstacles on the path to personal and spiritual development.

In addition to the myth itself, exploring the weapons and symbols associated with Inanna/Ishtar further elucidates her role as a warrior goddess. She is often depicted with a bow and arrow, symbolizing her skill in battle and her ability to strike down enemies from a distance. The bow and arrow also represent precision and focus, emphasizing the importance of strategic thinking and careful planning in times of conflict.

The lion is another powerful symbol associated with Inanna/Ishtar. It represents her ferocity, courage, and dominance. Lions were often seen as symbols of strength and royalty in ancient Mesopotamia, and Inanna/Ishtar's association with the lion highlights her regal and commanding presence as a warrior goddess.

The thunderbolt is another symbol connected to Inanna/Ishtar's martial aspect. It represents her ability to harness the forces of nature and unleash devastating power. The thunderbolt embodies the awe-inspiring and destructive aspects of her warrior persona, underscoring her ability to vanquish enemies and maintain order.

By examining the symbolic meanings behind these weapons and symbols, students can delve into deeper philosophical and ethical questions surrounding power, violence, and the pursuit of justice. They can reflect on the potential for power to be used responsibly and the complexities involved in engaging in warfare and conflicts. This exploration encourages students to consider the role of courage, strength, and determination in facing personal and collective challenges, and the transformative potential that can arise from harnessing one's inner warrior spirit.

Overall, the myth of Inanna and the Mountain and the symbolism associated with Inanna/Ishtar's weapons and symbols provide rich material for students to explore the themes of triumph, resilience, power, and the complexities of warfare. These narratives and symbols offer valuable insights into the human experience and can inspire individuals to cultivate their inner strength and face life's obstacles with courage and determination.

Justice and the Warrior Ethos

Inanna/Ishtar's role as the bringer of justice is a significant aspect of her mythology and highlights her authority in ensuring the establishment of cosmic order. Alongside her warrior persona, she assumes the responsibility of dispensing justice and maintaining a balance of power. By studying the myths and rituals associated with Inanna/Ishtar's role as a bringer of justice, students can delve into the ethical dimensions of power and contemplate the responsibilities that accompany it.

While Inanna/Ishtar's warrior aspect is often associated with physical combat and the triumph over adversaries, it also encompasses the ethical and moral responsibilities of wielding power. This notion of warrior ethics goes beyond the use of force and emphasizes the importance of integrity, honor, and the protection of the vulnerable. By exploring the concept of warrior ethics within the context of Inanna/Ishtar's mythology, students can reflect on the ethical implications of power and the challenges faced by individuals in positions of authority.

Through critical analysis and discussions, students can examine the intersection of power, social responsibility, and personal integrity. They can explore the ethical dilemmas that arise when one wields power and the complex decisions that need to be made to ensure justice and maintain a harmonious society. By drawing insights from Inanna/Ishtar's mythological narratives, students can consider the broader implications of power dynamics in their own lives and society at large.

Furthermore, the exploration of warrior ethics and social responsibility invites students to reflect on the interconnectedness between personal integrity and the well-being of the community. They can contemplate the importance of upholding moral principles, acting with fairness and compassion, and using power to protect and uplift others. By examining Inanna/Ishtar's role as a bringer of justice, students can gain a deeper understanding of the ethical dimensions of power and the impact that individuals in positions of authority can have on society.

In conclusion, studying Inanna/Ishtar as the bringer of justice allows students to explore the ethical dimensions of power and the responsibilities that come with it. By examining the concept of warrior ethics and reflecting on the intersection of power, social responsibility, and personal integrity, students can develop a greater understanding of the complexities involved in maintaining justice and cosmic order. This exploration encourages students to contemplate their own ethical decision-making and the impact they can have in promoting justice and fairness in their own lives and communities.

Exercises:

Reflect on the myth of Inanna and the Mountain and its symbolic significance in relation to personal challenges and the pursuit of power. Discuss the lessons learned from the myth and how they can be applied to personal growth and empowerment.

Exploring Ancient Mesopotamian Mythology, Rivalries, and Spiritual Legacies

Analyze the symbolic meanings behind Inanna/Ishtar's weapons and symbols of warfare. Discuss the potential positive and negative interpretations of these symbols and their implications for power dynamics and justice.

Engage in a role-playing exercise where students embody the archetype of the warrior and explore the ethical dilemmas and moral responsibilities associated with wielding power. Discuss the challenges and considerations that arise during the exercise.

Research and present a comparative analysis of warrior goddesses or female warriors from different mythological and historical contexts. Explore the similarities and differences in their representations and discuss the cultural and social significance of these figures.

Through the exploration of Inanna/Ishtar as the warrior goddess, students will gain a comprehensive understanding of the complexities of power, war, and justice in ancient Mesopotamian culture. By engaging in critical analysis, reflection, and experiential exercises, students will develop a nuanced perspective on the interplay between power, femininity, and social responsibility, and its relevance to contemporary discussions on power dynamics, gender, and ethics.

Rituals and ceremonies honoring Inanna/Ishtar in times of conflict

Inanna/Ishtar, the Mesopotamian goddess associated with love, sensuality, and war, offers a complex and multifaceted archetype for navigating times of conflict. Her presence in ancient mythology and religious practices provides inspiration for modern rituals and ceremonies aimed at seeking guidance, healing, and resolution in the midst of strife. In this section, we will explore various rituals and ceremonies that can be employed to honor Inanna/Ishtar and draw upon her energies to navigate and transform conflicts.

Conflict Acknowledgment Ritual:

Objective: To acknowledge and bring awareness to the conflicts present within oneself and in the external world.

Procedure:

a) Find a quiet and sacred space where you can reflect without distractions.
b) Light a candle or create a small altar with symbols representing Inanna/Ishtar.
c) Take a few deep breaths to center yourself and bring your attention to the conflicts you wish to address.

d) Use visualization or written reflection to identify the conflicts within yourself and any external conflicts that you are currently experiencing.

e) Offer a prayer or invocation to Inanna/Ishtar, asking for her guidance and support in navigating these conflicts with wisdom and grace.

f) Spend a few moments in quiet reflection, allowing any emotions or insights to arise.

g) Conclude the ritual with a gesture of gratitude and extinguish the candle or leave the altar undisturbed.

Mediation and Reconciliation Ceremony:

Objective: To seek resolution and harmony in conflicts between individuals or groups.

Procedure:

a) Gather the parties involved in the conflict in a neutral and safe space.

b) Create an altar or focal point that includes symbols of Inanna/Ishtar, as well as objects that represent the conflicting parties or their intentions.

c) Begin with a grounding meditation or a moment of silence to establish a peaceful and receptive atmosphere.

d) Encourage each person to express their perspectives and feelings without interruption, using active listening techniques to ensure everyone feels heard.

e) Invoke the presence and guidance of Inanna/Ishtar, inviting her energy of love and justice to infuse the space.

f) Facilitate a dialogue where the conflicting parties are encouraged to find common ground, explore solutions, and work towards reconciliation.

g) Encourage the use of rituals such as sharing and receiving symbolic objects or gestures of forgiveness to foster healing and closure.

h) Close the ceremony with a collective affirmation or prayer for harmony and resolution.

i) Follow up with individual or group reflections to deepen the integration of the ceremony's insights and experiences.

Peace-Building Ritual:

Objective: To cultivate peace and harmony in communities or within oneself during times of conflict.

Procedure:

a) Choose a peaceful outdoor location or create a sacred space indoors.

b) Set up an altar or focal point with elements representing Inanna/Ishtar and symbols of peace.

c) Begin with a grounding practice or meditation to center yourself and connect with the intention of peace.

d) Perform a ritual act, such as lighting candles, offering flowers, or reciting peace-affirming chants or mantras.

e) Engage in a collective meditation or visualization, envisioning a world free from conflict and filled with love and understanding.

f) Invite participants to share their personal commitments to peace and non-violence.

g) Encourage individuals to take practical actions towards peace, such as volunteering, engaging in dialogue, or supporting peace-building initiatives.

h) Close the ritual with a circle of gratitude, expressing thanks to Inanna/Ishtar and to each other for their presence and participation.

i) Provide resources and suggestions for ongoing practices that promote peace and harmony.

Note: It is essential to approach conflicts with sensitivity and respect for all parties involved. These rituals and ceremonies are intended as tools for personal and collective transformation, fostering understanding, and seeking peaceful resolutions. It is recommended to adapt and modify these practices to suit specific contexts and cultural sensitivities.

Examples for Critical Thinking and Discussion:

Reflect on the potential benefits and limitations of incorporating ancient deities, such as Inanna/Ishtar, in modern rituals for conflict resolution. Discuss how the archetypal energies associated with these deities can contribute to the transformation of conflicts.

Explore different ethical considerations when designing and facilitating rituals or ceremonies involving conflicts. Discuss the importance of consent, inclusivity, and cultural sensitivity in such practices.

Research and compare rituals or ceremonies from different spiritual traditions that address conflict resolution. Analyze the similarities and differences in their approaches and the underlying philosophical foundations.

Exercises:

Design a conflict resolution ritual inspired by Inanna/Ishtar that incorporates elements from your own cultural or spiritual background. Explain the symbolism and intentions behind each step of the ritual.

Write a reflective essay on the role of ritual and ceremony in promoting peace and healing in times of conflict. Support your arguments with examples from historical or contemporary contexts.

Engage in a group discussion on the challenges and potential benefits of using rituals as a means of conflict transformation. Explore alternative approaches to conflict resolution and analyze their strengths and weaknesses.

By engaging in these rituals, discussions, and exercises, students can deepen their understanding of the transformative potential of ritual practices and develop critical thinking skills regarding conflicts, their resolution, and the role of spirituality in these processes.

Sacred Prostitution and the Sacred Marriage Ritual

Within the context of ancient Mesopotamian cultures, the practice of sacred prostitution and the associated ritual of sacred marriage held significant religious and cultural importance. In this section, we will explore the concept of sacred prostitution, its historical and cultural contexts, and its association with the sacred marriage ritual. We will delve into the scholarly debates surrounding this topic and examine the various perspectives that have emerged.

Sacred Prostitution: Historical and Cultural Contexts

a) Historical Evidence: The practice of sacred prostitution in ancient Mesopotamia is supported by archaeological and textual evidence. Cuneiform tablets, which were used to record various aspects of Mesopotamian life, contain references to the roles and functions of temple prostitutes. These texts provide insights into the organization and administration of temples, including the management of sacred prostitution.

Additionally, reliefs and depictions found in Mesopotamian art showcase scenes related to sacred prostitution. These visual representations often portray temple prostitutes engaging in sexual acts or performing rituals within the sacred precincts of the temple. Such archaeological evidence offers tangible proof of the existence of sacred prostitution and its significance within the religious and cultural practices of ancient Mesopotamia.

b) Cultural Significance: Sacred prostitution held deep cultural and religious significance in ancient Mesopotamia. It was believed that the sexual union between a temple prostitute and a worshiper served as a symbolic representation of the union between the divine and human realms. This union was seen as vital for maintaining fertility, prosperity, and the overall harmonious functioning of the cosmos.

The act of engaging in sexual acts within the temple was considered a sacred ritual, wherein the temple prostitute served as a conduit for divine blessings. It was believed that through these encounters, the worshiper would gain favor from the gods or goddesses associated with the temple, particularly those connected with fertility and sexuality, such as Inanna/Ishtar.

Sacred prostitution was also tied to the concept of sacred marriage or hieros gamos, the symbolic union between a deity and a human representative. The temple prostitute, acting as a representative of the goddess, engaged in sexual acts as part of this sacred union. This ritualistic practice aimed to ensure the continuity of life, fertility of the land, and the well-being of the community.

Furthermore, sacred prostitution played a social role within ancient Mesopotamian societies. It provided economic support for the temples, as the fees paid by the worshipers for engaging in sexual acts with the temple prostitutes served as a form of offering. The income generated from these practices contributed to the maintenance and functioning of the religious institutions.

However, it is important to note that our understanding of sacred prostitution in ancient Mesopotamia is limited, and there are debates among scholars regarding its exact nature and extent. The interpretation of textual and archaeological evidence is still subject to ongoing research and scholarly discourse.

In conclusion, the historical and cultural evidence supports the existence of sacred prostitution in ancient Mesopotamia. This practice held religious significance, symbolizing the union between the divine and human realms, and played a role in facilitating fertility, prosperity, and the harmonious functioning of the cosmos. The practice also had social and economic implications, providing support for the temples and contributing to their maintenance.

Divine Dynamics

The Sacred Marriage Ritual: Symbolism and Function

a) Symbolism: The sacred marriage ritual held profound symbolic meaning in ancient Mesopotamia. It was viewed as a reenactment of the divine union between a goddess, often Inanna/Ishtar, and a mortal king who symbolized the god. The sexual union between the goddess and the king represented the harmonious integration of masculine and feminine energies, mirroring the cosmic principles of creation, fertility, and abundance.

The ritual was believed to have a direct impact on the fertility of the land and the well-being of the community. By engaging in the sacred marriage, the king and the goddess would bestow their blessings upon the earth, ensuring a prosperous harvest, abundant livestock, and overall fertility in nature. The ritual was seen as a vital link between the divine realm and the earthly realm, bridging the gap and facilitating the continuous flow of life-sustaining energies.

b) Roles and Participants: The sacred marriage ritual involved several key participants. The central figures were the king and the priestess or temple prostitute who embodied the goddess. The king, acting as the representative of the god, would engage in sexual intercourse with the priestess or temple prostitute, who portrayed the goddess herself. This union symbolized the divine marriage and served as a means of connecting the earthly and divine realms.

The ritual was witnessed by the community, including priests, priestesses, and other individuals present in the temple. The priests and priestesses played an officiating role, overseeing the ceremonial proceedings and ensuring the proper conduct of the ritual. They would guide and facilitate the sacred marriage, invoking the blessings of the gods and goddesses associated with fertility and abundance.

It is worth noting that the sacred marriage ritual varied in its specific practices and participants across different Mesopotamian city-states and time periods. The details of the ritual might have differed in various regions, reflecting the unique traditions and beliefs of each city-state.

The sacred marriage ritual held immense significance for ancient Mesopotamian societies, as it was believed to directly influence the well-being and prosperity of the community. By invoking the powers of the goddess and uniting them with the mortal realm through the king, the ritual aimed to ensure the continuation of life, fertility, and abundance in the land. It symbolized the interconnection between the divine and human realms, reinforcing the fundamental principles of creation and sustenance within the cosmological worldview of ancient Mesopotamia.

Exploring Ancient Mesopotamian Mythology, Rivalries, and Spiritual Legacies

Scholarly Perspectives and Debates

a) Ritualistic Interpretation: The sacred prostitution and sacred marriage ritual were deeply rooted in the religious and symbolic aspects of ancient Mesopotamian culture. Scholars argue that these practices were primarily performed for their ritualistic and spiritual significance rather than solely for sexual pleasure. The sexual union between the goddess and the mortal king represented the divine union and the integration of masculine and feminine energies. It was believed to bring about blessings of fertility, abundance, and the harmonious functioning of the cosmos. The ritual was a way of connecting the earthly realm with the divine realm, and its symbolism played a vital role in the religious beliefs and practices of the time.

b) Economic Interpretation: Another perspective proposes an economic motivation behind sacred prostitution. It suggests that the practice served as a means of generating revenue for the temples and providing financial support for the maintenance of religious institutions. The temple prostitutes, as intermediaries between the divine and human realms, attracted worshippers who sought to engage in sexual acts as part of their religious devotion. Donations and offerings made by these worshippers contributed to the economic sustenance of the temples and the support of the religious infrastructure. From this perspective, sacred prostitution can be seen as an economic strategy employed by the temples to ensure their financial stability.

c) Empowerment or Exploitation: The question of agency and autonomy of temple prostitutes remains a topic of debate. Some argue that sacred prostitution empowered women in ancient Mesopotamian society. These women held positions of influence and economic independence within the temple precincts. They were revered as embodiments of the goddess and had significant roles in religious ceremonies. In this view, the practice provided women with a degree of agency and social standing.

However, counterarguments highlight the potential for exploitation and objectification of women within the context of sacred prostitution. Critics argue that the system may have subjected women to sexual objectification and commodification, reducing them to instruments of religious and economic transactions. The exact extent of agency and control that temple prostitutes had over their lives and bodies is difficult to ascertain due to the limited historical records and the inherent biases of the sources.

It is important to note that the understanding of sacred prostitution and its implications is complex and multifaceted. Various interpretations and perspectives exist, and the reality likely encompassed a combination of ritualistic, economic, and social factors. Further research and examination of available evidence contribute to ongoing discussions and a deeper understanding of the practice and its implications in ancient Mesopotamia.

Critical Thinking and Discussion:

a) Analyze the cultural and religious significance of sacred prostitution within the context of ancient Mesopotamia:

The practice of sacred prostitution held significant cultural and religious significance in ancient Mesopotamia. It was intricately woven into the fabric of religious beliefs, social customs, and cosmological understandings of the time. By interpreting it as a religious ritual, we can explore its potential benefits and drawbacks:

Benefits:

Symbolic Representation: Sacred prostitution symbolically represented the union between the divine and human realms. It embodied the cosmic principles of creation, fertility, and abundance. This symbolic union was believed to ensure the well-being of the community, the fertility of the land, and the continuation of life.

Ritualistic and Spiritual Significance: Sacred prostitution was viewed as a sacred act that brought worshippers closer to the divine. It was seen as a means of participating in the divine order and receiving blessings. The ritualistic nature of the practice fostered a sense of connection with the gods and provided a religious experience for both the participants and the community.

Economic Support: Interpreting sacred prostitution as a religious ritual acknowledges its role in providing economic support to the temples. The financial contributions made by worshippers who engaged in the practice helped sustain the religious institutions and their activities, ensuring the continuation of religious practices and the upkeep of the temples.

Drawbacks:

Potential Exploitation: Interpreting sacred prostitution as a religious ritual does not negate the potential for exploitation. Women engaged in this practice might have faced societal pressures, economic necessity, or limited options that compelled them to participate. The power dynamics within the system might have created an environment where women's agency and autonomy were compromised.

Exploring Ancient Mesopotamian Mythology, Rivalries, and Spiritual Legacies

Objectification: The practice of sacred prostitution could have objectified women, reducing them to mere vessels for religious and economic transactions. This objectification may have reinforced gender inequalities and perpetuated harmful societal norms regarding the role of women.

b) Compare the practice of sacred prostitution in ancient Mesopotamia with similar practices in other cultures throughout history:

Sacred prostitution or similar practices existed in various cultures across different time periods. While there may be similarities, there are also notable differences in their cultural contexts, functions, and social implications. Some examples include:

Temples of Aphrodite in Ancient Greece: The ancient Greek practice of temple prostitution, particularly in the temples of Aphrodite, had similarities to sacred prostitution in Mesopotamia. It involved sexual acts performed by priestesses or dedicated women as acts of devotion. However, the social and cultural contexts in Greece differed from Mesopotamia, and the religious significance and societal attitudes towards sexuality varied.

Devadasis in Ancient India: The devadasi system in ancient India involved the dedication of young girls to temples and their service as sacred prostitutes. While there were religious elements involved, the system also had social and cultural dimensions. Devadasis had specific roles in temple rituals and cultural performances but were often subject to exploitation and societal marginalization.

Oiran in Edo Period Japan: The Oiran, highly skilled courtesans in Edo period Japan, were sometimes associated with religious practices and rituals. They entertained clients through conversation, arts, and sexual companionship. Although there were elements of ceremony and ritual in their profession, it primarily served as a form of entertainment and pleasure for the upper class.

Each of these examples demonstrates how similar practices existed in different cultural contexts and had varying social implications. The specific religious, cultural, and social dynamics of each society shaped the nature and significance of these practices.

c) Engage in a discussion about the ethical considerations surrounding the practice of sacred prostitution:

The practice of sacred prostitution raises important ethical considerations, including consent, agency, and power dynamics. Here are some points to consider:

Consent: It is crucial to evaluate whether the participants in sacred prostitution had the capacity to give informed and voluntary consent. Factors such as social pressures, economic necessity, and limited options may have influenced their involvement. Exploring historical sources and accounts, although limited, can provide insights into the degree of agency and choice available to those participating in the practice.

Agency: Analyzing the agency of women involved in sacred prostitution requires careful consideration. While some argue that it empowered women by providing them with economic independence and influential roles within the temple, others emphasize the potential for exploitation and the constraints imposed by societal norms. It is necessary to consider the broader social context and the options available to women in ancient Mesopotamia to assess the true extent of agency within the practice.

Power Dynamics: Power dynamics within the system of sacred prostitution should be critically examined. The involvement of priests, temple officials, and the wider community raises questions about the balance of power and the potential for abuse. Recognizing and understanding these power dynamics is essential for evaluating the ethical implications of the practice.

Engaging in discussions about the ethical considerations surrounding sacred prostitution helps shed light on the complexities of the practice and challenges us to critically assess its implications within its historical and cultural context.

Exercises:

Write a research paper exploring the evidence and interpretations of sacred prostitution in ancient Mesopotamia. Evaluate different scholarly perspectives and present a well-supported argument.

Conduct a group debate on the societal and cultural implications of sacred prostitution. Assign different roles, such as historians, anthropologists, or religious scholars, and engage in a critical analysis of the practice.

Imagine you are an ancient Mesopotamian community member. Write a reflective journal entry discussing your thoughts and feelings about witnessing the sacred marriage ritual. Consider the spiritual, social, and personal significance of the ceremony.

By engaging in critical thinking and discussion, as well as completing the suggested exercises, students will gain a comprehensive understanding of the historical, cultural, and religious aspects of sacred prostitution and the sacred marriage ritual in ancient Mesopotamia. They will also develop analytical and research skills, enabling them to evaluate different perspectives and engage in nuanced discussions on complex topics.

Inanna/Ishtar and the Underworld: Descent and Resurrection

The mythological tale of Inanna's descent into the Underworld and subsequent resurrection is one of the most captivating and profound narratives in ancient Mesopotamian mythology. In this section, we will explore the significance of Inanna/Ishtar's journey to the Underworld, analyze its symbolic and psychological implications, and discuss the themes of death, rebirth, and transformation that emerge from this myth.

The Myth of Inanna's Descent:

The myth of Inanna's descent recounts the goddess's decision to visit the realm of the Underworld, ruled by her sister, Ereshkigal. Inanna undertakes this perilous journey, facing various trials and challenges, ultimately leading to her death and subsequent resurrection.

a) Symbolism of the Underworld: The Underworld symbolizes the realm of death, darkness, and the unconscious. It represents a liminal space where transformative experiences occur and the potential for rebirth and spiritual growth resides.

b) Trials and Challenges: Inanna encounters several gatekeepers and obstacles during her descent, each representing psychological and spiritual tests that she must overcome. These trials highlight the transformative nature of the journey and the necessity of confronting inner demons and shadows.

c) Death and Rebirth: Inanna's death in the Underworld symbolizes the dissolution of the ego and the surrender of old patterns and attachments. It represents a metaphorical death and the opportunity for rebirth and renewal. In the depths of the Underworld, Inanna undergoes a process of self-transformation, shedding her old identity and emerging transformed and renewed.

d) Psychological Implications: The myth of Inanna's descent holds psychological significance, reflecting the individuation process and the integration of the shadow self. Inanna's journey represents the descent into the depths of the psyche, confronting the unconscious aspects of the self, and embracing the totality of one's being. It emphasizes the importance of acknowledging and integrating the shadow aspects for personal growth and psychological wholeness.

e) Archetypal Themes: The myth of Inanna's descent resonates with archetypal themes found across cultures, such as the hero's journey, the descent into the underworld, and the transformative cycle of death and rebirth. These themes tap into universal human experiences and provide a framework for understanding the human psyche and the transformative potential of facing challenges and embracing change.

f) Spiritual and Mystical Dimensions: In addition to its psychological implications, the myth of Inanna's descent also carries spiritual and mystical dimensions. It explores the cyclical nature of life and death, the interconnectedness of all things, and the mysteries of the divine. It offers insights into the transformative power of surrender, sacrifice, and transcendence.

Studying the myth of Inanna's descent allows for a deeper exploration of profound existential and psychological themes. It invites contemplation on the human experience of confronting darkness, undergoing transformation, and experiencing the cycles of life, death, and rebirth. The myth provides a rich tapestry of symbolism and narrative that continues to resonate with individuals seeking personal growth, spiritual awakening, and a deeper understanding of the human journey.

Psychological Interpretations:

a) Jungian Perspective: The myth of Inanna's descent can be analyzed through a Jungian lens, exploring the individuation process and the integration of the shadow self. Inanna's journey symbolizes the descent into the depths of the psyche, the exploration of repressed aspects, and the subsequent integration of those elements into consciousness.

b) Mythic Archetypes: The myth reflects universal archetypal themes, such as the hero's journey, the dark night of the soul, and the transformative power of death and rebirth. Inanna's descent represents the archetype of the goddess descending into the underworld, a motif present in various mythologies across cultures.

c) Symbolic Transformation: The myth of Inanna's descent holds symbolic significance for personal growth and transformation. Inanna's trials and challenges symbolize the inner obstacles and psychological barriers that individuals encounter on their own journeys. By confronting and overcoming these challenges, individuals can experience personal growth, self-realization, and a deeper understanding of their own psyche.

d) Integration of the Shadow: Inanna's descent into the Underworld represents the confrontation and integration of the shadow self, the unconscious aspects of the psyche that are often repressed or denied. The myth highlights the importance of acknowledging and embracing these shadow elements in order to achieve psychological wholeness and self-acceptance.

e) Archetypal Patterns: The myth of Inanna's descent follows the pattern of the hero's journey, a narrative structure found in many myths and stories worldwide. This archetype involves the protagonist venturing into the unknown, facing challenges, undergoing transformation, and returning with newfound wisdom and growth. Inanna's journey embodies this archetypal pattern, making the myth relatable and meaningful to individuals seeking personal growth and self-discovery.

f) Personal and Collective Significance: The myth of Inanna's descent holds personal and collective significance. On a personal level, it invites individuals to reflect on their own inner journeys, confront their fears and limitations, and embrace change and transformation. On a collective level, the myth reflects the universal human experience of facing darkness, undergoing trials, and seeking renewal, providing a shared narrative that resonates across cultures and generations.

By studying the psychological interpretations of the myth of Inanna's descent, students can gain a deeper understanding of the human psyche, the transformative power of myth and symbolism, and the universal themes and patterns that shape our personal and collective journeys. This exploration offers valuable insights into personal growth, self-discovery, and the pursuit of psychological wholeness.

The Resurrection and Return:

a) Ereshkigal's Bargain: In the Underworld, Inanna is stripped of her divine attributes and hung on a hook, experiencing death and the dissolution of her identity. However, with the help of divine intervention and the cleverness of her loyal servant, she is eventually resurrected and allowed to return to the realm of the living.

b) Symbolic Meanings: Inanna's resurrection signifies the triumph of life over death, the renewal of vitality and creative power. It emphasizes the cyclical nature of existence and the transformative potential that arises from facing and embracing the darker aspects of oneself.

c) Psychological Rebirth: Inanna's resurrection can be interpreted as a metaphorical representation of psychological rebirth and transformation. Her descent into the Underworld represents a symbolic death, a journey into the depths of the unconscious and the exploration of the shadow self. Through this process, Inanna confronts her fears, undergoes a symbolic death, and emerges renewed and transformed. This mirrors the psychological process of confronting one's inner demons, integrating repressed aspects, and experiencing personal growth and self-actualization.

d) The Power of Divine Intervention: Inanna's resurrection is not solely achieved through her own efforts but also involves divine intervention. This highlights the importance of external support, guidance, and the presence of higher powers in one's personal journey of transformation. It suggests that seeking assistance and relying on spiritual or psychological resources can facilitate the process of resurrection and renewal.

e) Lessons of Resilience and Perseverance: Inanna's journey and subsequent resurrection convey the importance of resilience and perseverance in the face of adversity. Despite the challenges and trials she encounters, Inanna demonstrates determination and resourcefulness, ultimately achieving rebirth and returning to the realm of the living. This serves as a powerful message for individuals facing their own hardships and encourages them to persist in their personal growth and transformation.

f) Collective Symbolism: Inanna's resurrection also holds collective symbolism. It reflects the cyclical nature of life, death, and rebirth that is present in many cultural and religious traditions worldwide. The myth reminds individuals of the universal human experience of facing challenges, undergoing transformation, and finding renewal. It offers hope and inspiration, emphasizing that even in the darkest moments, there is the potential for resurrection, growth, and the restoration of life's vitality.

By studying the resurrection and return of Inanna, students can explore themes of renewal, resilience, and transformation. They can gain insights into the psychological and symbolic dimensions of the myth, discovering parallels with their own journeys of self-discovery and personal growth. This exploration encourages a deeper understanding of the complexities of the human experience and the transformative power of embracing the full spectrum of life's challenges and triumphs.

Exploring Ancient Mesopotamian Mythology, Rivalries, and Spiritual Legacies

Practical Application and Personal Reflection:

a) Reflect on a personal experience of facing a metaphorical descent into your own "Underworld." Consider the challenges you encountered, the lessons learned, and the growth that resulted from the experience.

b) Engage in a group discussion about the psychological and symbolic significance of death and rebirth in various spiritual and mythological traditions. Compare and contrast the themes present in the myth of Inanna's descent with those found in other cultural narratives.

c) Explore the concept of the shadow self in relation to personal growth and self-acceptance. Reflect on aspects of yourself that you may have repressed or denied, and consider the potential transformative power of integrating these shadow aspects into your conscious awareness.

d) Create a symbolic representation of your own journey of transformation and rebirth. This could take the form of artwork, poetry, or a written narrative. Reflect on the symbols and imagery you choose and what they represent in relation to your personal growth and the lessons learned from your own "descent."

e) Consider the role of support systems and external resources in times of personal transformation. Reflect on the importance of seeking guidance, whether it be from trusted mentors, therapists, or spiritual practices. Share experiences and insights with classmates to deepen understanding of the role of external support in the process of resurrection and personal growth.

f) Discuss the relevance of the myth of Inanna's descent in contemporary society. Explore how the themes of death, rebirth, and transformation can be applied to challenges individuals face in the modern world. Consider how embracing the transformative power of personal growth can lead to resilience, self-empowerment, and the ability to navigate life's complexities with greater wisdom and understanding.

Engaging in practical applications and personal reflection allows students to connect the myth of Inanna's descent to their own lives and experiences. It encourages self-awareness, empathy, and a deeper understanding of the universal themes of transformation and resilience. By examining the myth's relevance across cultures and exploring its psychological and symbolic dimensions, students gain a broader perspective on the human journey and the potential for personal growth and self-transformation.

Exercises:

Write a reflective essay on the significance of Inanna's descent and resurrection in your personal spiritual journey. Explore the parallels between your own experiences and the mythic elements of the story.

Create a visual representation, such as a collage or artwork, depicting the transformative journey of Inanna/Ishtar's descent into the Underworld. Explain the symbolism and elements you have incorporated.

Engage in a guided meditation or visualization exercise where you imagine yourself descending into your own symbolic Underworld. Reflect on the emotions, insights, and potential for growth that arise during this inner exploration.

Through critical thinking and engaging with the suggested exercises, students will deepen their understanding of the myth of Inanna's descent and resurrection, explore its psychological implications, and contemplate its relevance in their own lives. They will develop analytical skills and expand their capacity for personal reflection, fostering a deeper appreciation for the transformative power of myths and narratives.

Analysis of the themes of death, rebirth, and transformation in the myth

The myth of Inanna's descent into the Underworld is rich with symbolism and profound themes that resonate across cultures and throughout human history. In this section, we will explore the themes of death, rebirth, and transformation as they manifest in the myth, examining their significance in the context of personal growth, spiritual evolution, and the human experience.

Death as a Catalyst for Transformation:

a) Inanna's Death: In the myth, Inanna undergoes a symbolic death, representing the dissolution of her ego and identity. This death serves as a catalyst for profound transformation and rebirth, enabling her to gain new insights and wisdom.

b) Psychological Interpretation: From a psychological perspective, the death of Inanna can be seen as a metaphor for the ego death or the shedding of old patterns and beliefs. It represents a necessary step in the process of personal growth and the integration of the shadow self.

c) The Role of Loss and Grief: Inanna's death highlights the role of loss and grief as catalysts for transformation. Just as Inanna had to confront her own mortality and face the loss of her former self, individuals often experience significant personal growth and transformation following periods of loss, grief, or life-altering events. Reflecting on personal experiences of loss and the subsequent transformative journey can provide valuable insights and understanding.

d) Embracing the Unknown: Inanna's descent into the Underworld represents a journey into the unknown, where she confronts her fears, vulnerabilities, and the mysteries of existence. This aspect of the myth emphasizes the importance of embracing uncertainty and the unfamiliar as a means of personal transformation. Students can explore their own relationship with the unknown, discussing how they navigate uncertainty and the potential for growth that arises from stepping outside their comfort zones.

e) Applying the Myth to Personal Growth: Encourage students to reflect on their own experiences of personal transformation and growth. They can identify moments of metaphorical death and rebirth in their lives, considering the challenges faced, the lessons learned, and the resulting personal transformation. Students can explore the parallels between their experiences and the myth of Inanna's death, drawing connections between their own journeys and the universal themes of transformation and renewal.

f) Cultivating Resilience: The myth of Inanna's death and rebirth illustrates the resilience inherent in the human spirit. Students can explore the qualities and strategies that contribute to resilience, such as adaptability, self-reflection, seeking support, and embracing change. Through personal reflection and group discussions, students can identify ways to cultivate resilience in their own lives and navigate future challenges with greater strength and adaptability.

By delving into the symbolism and psychological interpretations of Inanna's death, students gain a deeper understanding of the transformative power of loss, the significance of embracing the unknown, and the role of resilience in personal growth. Applying the myth to personal experiences fosters self-reflection, empathy, and a broader perspective on the universal journey of transformation.

Rebirth and Resurrection:

a) Inanna's Resurrection: After her death, Inanna is resurrected and returns to the world of the living. Her resurrection signifies the renewal of life, vitality, and creative power. It emphasizes the cyclical nature of existence and the transformative potential that arises from facing the depths of one's being.

b) Symbolism of Resurrection: The theme of resurrection in the myth reflects the universal human desire for renewal and the belief in the possibility of transformation. It speaks to the inherent capacity for growth and change within each individual.

c) Comparing Inanna's Resurrection to the Bible: The theme of resurrection in the myth of Inanna can be compared to the concept of resurrection in the Bible, particularly in the story of Jesus. Both narratives involve a figure experiencing death and subsequently being brought back to life, symbolizing renewal and the triumph over mortality. While the specific details and religious contexts may differ, the overarching themes of transformation, redemption, and the victory of life over death resonate in both stories.

The comparison between Inanna's resurrection in Mesopotamian mythology and the resurrection of Jesus in the Bible reveals several shared themes and symbolic meanings. While there are notable differences in the specific details and religious contexts of these narratives, the overarching themes of transformation, redemption, and victory over death are present in both stories.

Symbolism of Renewal: In both narratives, the theme of resurrection represents a profound renewal of life and a triumph over mortality. Inanna's resurrection signifies the renewal of life and vitality after her descent into the Underworld, while Jesus' resurrection represents the victory over sin and death, offering eternal life to believers.

Sacrifice and Redemption: In both stories, the figures of Inanna and Jesus undergo a sacrificial death that leads to redemption. Inanna's descent into the Underworld and subsequent resurrection serve as a form of atonement, bringing about the restoration of balance and harmony. Similarly, Jesus' crucifixion and resurrection are seen as a sacrificial act that offers salvation and redemption to humanity.

Transformation and Spiritual Growth: Both narratives emphasize the transformative power of death and resurrection. Inanna's journey to the Underworld and subsequent return symbolize personal growth, wisdom gained from the experience, and the integration of shadow aspects. Likewise, Jesus' resurrection represents a transformational event that brings about spiritual growth, forgiveness, and the potential for believers to experience a new life in Christ.

Cosmic Significance: The resurrection narratives in both Inanna and Jesus' stories hold cosmic implications. Inanna's resurrection ensures the continuation of life and the well-being of the community, while Jesus' resurrection is seen as the fulfillment of divine prophecy and the establishment of a new covenant between God and humanity.

Cultural and Religious Context: It is important to note that the cultural and religious contexts of these narratives differ significantly. Inanna's story originates from ancient Mesopotamian mythology, where she was revered as a powerful goddess associated with various aspects of life. On the other hand, the resurrection of Jesus holds central significance in Christian theology and is considered a cornerstone of the faith.

In comparing Inanna's resurrection to the biblical narrative of Jesus' resurrection, students can explore the common themes and symbolic meanings present in both stories. This comparison highlights the universal human longing for transformation, redemption, and victory over death. It also invites students to appreciate the diverse cultural and religious expressions of these themes while recognizing the shared human quest for renewal and spiritual growth.

d) Personal Reflection: Encourage students to reflect on the theme of resurrection in their own lives. They can consider moments of personal renewal and transformation, times when they have experienced a "rebirth" or a renewed sense of purpose and vitality. Students can explore the factors that contributed to their own resurrection experiences, such as personal growth, inner strength, or external support.

e) Resurrection as a Metaphor: Discuss with students the metaphorical aspect of resurrection in various contexts. Explore how the theme of resurrection extends beyond literal physical resurrection and can be applied to symbolic, psychological, or spiritual rebirth. Students can reflect on areas of their lives where they seek renewal or transformation and consider the potential for their own "resurrections" in these areas.

f) Cultivating Resilience and Renewal: Building on the concept of resurrection, discuss with students the importance of cultivating resilience and creating opportunities for personal renewal. Explore practices and strategies that support growth and transformation, such as self-care, self-reflection, setting goals, and seeking support. Encourage students to identify areas in their lives where they desire renewal and to develop action plans for fostering their own personal resurrection.

By exploring the theme of resurrection in the myth of Inanna and making connections to personal experiences and other cultural narratives, students develop a deeper understanding of the universal human longing for renewal and transformation. This exploration fosters self-reflection, empathy, and a recognition of the inherent capacity for growth and change within each individual.

Divine Dynamics

Transformation and Personal Growth:

a) Symbolic Journey: Inanna's descent into the Underworld and her subsequent resurrection serve as a powerful metaphor for the transformative journeys we experience in our own lives. The myth illustrates that personal growth and self-discovery often involve delving into the depths of our being, confronting our shadow aspects, and embracing the unknown.

Inanna's descent can be seen as a symbolic representation of the inner journey towards self-realization. It reflects the process of exploring the hidden realms of our psyche, confronting our fears, and facing the aspects of ourselves that we may have repressed or neglected. This symbolic journey invites us to go beyond our comfort zones, to venture into the unknown territories of our own consciousness, and to embrace the transformative potential that lies within.

b) Lessons and Insights: The challenges and trials faced by Inanna during her descent carry valuable lessons for our own journeys of personal transformation. Each gatekeeper and obstacle encountered along her path represents psychological and spiritual tests that she must overcome. These challenges teach us about the importance of resilience, courage, and self-reflection in the face of adversity.

Inanna's journey reminds us that personal growth is often accompanied by challenges and discomfort. It is through facing these obstacles that we gain deeper insights into ourselves and acquire the tools necessary for transformation. The myth highlights the significance of acknowledging and integrating our shadow aspects—the parts of ourselves that we may have rejected or denied—in order to achieve wholeness and personal growth.

By examining the trials faced by Inanna, students can reflect on their own experiences of overcoming obstacles and gaining personal insights. They can identify the lessons learned during times of difficulty and explore how those lessons have contributed to their own personal growth and transformation. Additionally, the myth invites students to consider the importance of embracing the unknown and stepping out of their comfort zones in order to fully embrace the transformative journey of self-discovery.

Cultural and Spiritual Significance:

a) Cross-Cultural Parallels: The myth of Inanna's descent carries a cultural and spiritual significance that extends beyond its original context. The themes of death, rebirth, and transformation found in this myth resonate with similar motifs found in mythologies and spiritual traditions across different cultures and time periods. The universal human experience of grappling with the mysteries of life, death, and the quest for meaning is reflected in these shared themes.

In various mythologies, there are stories of gods and goddesses undergoing journeys to the underworld or experiencing symbolic deaths and subsequent rebirths. These narratives often serve as metaphors for the cycles of life, the transformative power of adversity, and the potential for personal growth and spiritual awakening. Examples include the myth of Persephone in Greek mythology, the story of Osiris in Egyptian mythology, and the concept of the bardo states in Tibetan Buddhism.

The presence of these cross-cultural parallels suggests a common human longing for understanding and transcendence. Exploring the similarities and differences in these narratives can deepen our appreciation for the collective wisdom encoded within different cultures and provide insights into the universal themes that resonate with the human psyche.

b) Ritual and Symbolic Practices: The myth of Inanna's descent has inspired various ritual practices and symbolic ceremonies aimed at personal transformation and spiritual growth. These practices often draw upon the themes of death and rebirth, allowing individuals to engage in symbolic acts that mirror the transformative journey undertaken by Inanna.

For example, meditation practices may involve visualizations or guided journeys that guide participants through their own symbolic descent into the depths of their psyche. They may explore their fears, confront their shadows, and ultimately experience a metaphorical death and rebirth, emerging with new insights and a sense of renewed purpose.

Ritual purification is another common practice inspired by the myth of Inanna's descent. It involves symbolic acts of cleansing, such as bathing or smudging, to release old patterns and energies associated with the past. This purging process creates space for new growth and transformation, aligning with the mythological themes of letting go and embracing the unknown.

Additionally, symbolic acts of releasing and embracing new beginnings are prevalent in rituals inspired by the myth. These acts may involve writing down old beliefs or patterns and burning them, symbolizing the release of what no longer serves, followed by setting intentions or planting seeds to symbolize the initiation of new possibilities.

By engaging in these ritual and symbolic practices, individuals can tap into the cultural and spiritual significance of the myth, drawing inspiration from Inanna's journey and applying its transformative themes to their own lives. These practices offer pathways for personal growth, self-reflection, and the cultivation of a deeper connection with the cycles of life and the transformative potential within each individual.

Exercises:

Reflect on a personal experience of transformation or rebirth in your own life. Write a journal entry discussing the challenges faced, the lessons learned, and the growth that resulted from the experience.

Engage in a group discussion exploring the ways in which the themes of death, rebirth, and transformation manifest in different mythologies and spiritual traditions. Compare and contrast the symbolic elements and cultural variations.

Create a visual representation, such as a collage or artwork, depicting the themes of death, rebirth, and transformation inspired by the myth of Inanna's descent. Explain the symbolism and elements you have incorporated.

By engaging in critical analysis and reflective exercises, students will deepen their understanding of the themes of death, rebirth, and transformation in the myth of Inanna's descent. They will develop their capacity for introspection, broaden their cultural knowledge, and cultivate a greater appreciation for the transformative power of myths in our lives.

Interpretations and symbolic meanings associated with Inanna/Ishtar's journey

The myth of Inanna's journey to the Underworld holds a multitude of interpretations and symbolic meanings that have been explored by scholars and practitioners across various fields. In this section, we will delve into some of the key interpretations and symbolic associations associated with Inanna/Ishtar's journey, shedding light on their broader significance in personal, cultural, and spiritual contexts.

Psychological Interpretations:

a) Individuation and Self-Integration: The myth of Inanna's descent into the Underworld and subsequent return can be analyzed from a psychological perspective, particularly through the lens of Carl Jung's concept of individuation. Individuation refers to the process of self-realization and the integration of all aspects of the psyche, including both conscious and unconscious elements.

Exploring Ancient Mesopotamian Mythology, Rivalries, and Spiritual Legacies

In the myth, Inanna's journey represents a symbolic exploration of the depths of the psyche, mirroring the individuation process. Her descent into the Underworld signifies a willingness to confront the unconscious, represented by the shadow aspects and repressed elements of the self. By facing these hidden aspects, Inanna engages in a transformative process of self-discovery and self-integration.

The trials and challenges she encounters during her descent can be seen as psychological tests that mirror the difficulties and obstacles encountered in the individuation process. These challenges force Inanna to confront her fears, vulnerabilities, and illusions, facilitating a deep exploration of her true nature and an integration of previously unrecognized aspects of herself.

The myth emphasizes the importance of embracing the shadow and acknowledging the unconscious elements within us. Through the integration of these aspects, individuals can achieve a greater sense of wholeness and authenticity. Inanna's return from the Underworld signifies the successful integration of the unconscious into consciousness, representing a significant step in the individuation process.

b) Ego Dissolution and Transformation: Inanna's death and resurrection can be interpreted as a psychological journey of ego dissolution and transformation. The death of Inanna symbolizes the dissolution of her ego and the shedding of old identities, beliefs, and patterns. This death is a necessary step for transformation and personal growth to occur.

The myth highlights the importance of letting go of rigid ego attachments and identifying with something greater than the limited self. Inanna's willingness to surrender and undergo this symbolic death allows for the emergence of a more authentic and expanded self.

Through the process of ego dissolution, individuals can experience profound transformation and undergo a redefinition of their identities. The death of old patterns and beliefs creates space for new possibilities and a renewed sense of self. Inanna's resurrection represents the triumph of life and vitality over the ego's limitations, signifying the transformative potential that arises from embracing the depths of one's being.

By engaging with the psychological interpretations of the myth, individuals can gain insight into their own journeys of self-discovery, personal growth, and the integration of unconscious elements. It invites reflection on the shadow aspects of the self, the willingness to confront challenges, and the transformative power of letting go and embracing new identities and possibilities.

Divine Dynamics

Feminine Empowerment and Divine Feminine:

a) Feminine Archetypes: The myth of Inanna/Ishtar celebrates and embodies various powerful feminine archetypes, allowing for the exploration and appreciation of the multifaceted nature of femininity. Inanna is depicted as a warrior goddess, demonstrating strength, courage, and assertiveness. She also embodies the archetype of the lover, representing passion, sensuality, and the pursuit of desire. Additionally, Inanna exhibits nurturing qualities, highlighting her role as a caregiver and protector. These archetypes showcase the diverse capabilities and strengths of women, challenging traditional gender roles and promoting gender equality.

The myth encourages women to embrace their inherent power and agency, encouraging them to recognize and express their own unique blend of feminine qualities. By embracing the various archetypes embodied by Inanna, women can reclaim their personal power, celebrate their individuality, and challenge societal expectations that limit their potential.

b) Sacred Marriage: The myth of Inanna/Ishtar includes the sacred marriage ritual, often interpreted as a symbolic union between the masculine and feminine principles. In this ritual, Inanna/Ishtar engages in a sacred union with Dumuzi/Tammuz, representing the integration and harmonization of polarities within and outside ourselves.

The sacred marriage signifies the recognition and acceptance of both the masculine and feminine energies within individuals. It emphasizes the importance of balancing and integrating these energies to achieve wholeness and spiritual growth. The myth invites individuals, regardless of gender, to embrace and honor both their masculine and feminine qualities, acknowledging the inherent value and significance of each.

Furthermore, the sacred marriage ritual symbolizes the profound connection between the divine and human realms. It highlights the divine feminine principle and its role in shaping the cosmos and influencing the human experience. By honoring and embracing the divine feminine, individuals can tap into a source of inner wisdom, creativity, and empowerment.

The myth of Inanna/Ishtar and the concept of the sacred marriage encourage individuals to cultivate a deep reverence for the feminine, both within themselves and in the world around them. This reverence extends beyond gender and promotes a greater understanding and appreciation of the diverse expressions of femininity. It invites individuals to honor and embrace the power, beauty, and transformative potential of the divine feminine archetype.

Exploring Ancient Mesopotamian Mythology, Rivalries, and Spiritual Legacies

Life, Death, and Rebirth:

a) Cycle of Life: The myth of Inanna/Ishtar delves into the profound and universal theme of the cycle of life, death, and rebirth. Inanna's journey reflects the natural rhythms and patterns observed in the world around us. Just as nature goes through seasons of growth, decay, and renewal, so does the human experience.

The descent into the Underworld represents the metaphorical death or dissolution of the old self, where aspects of our identity, beliefs, or relationships may need to be shed or released. This stage of the journey can be challenging and confrontational, as we confront our fears, face our shadows, and confront the aspects of ourselves that no longer serve us.

However, Inanna's resurrection symbolizes the transformative power of renewal and the potential for rebirth. It signifies the emergence of a revitalized self, infused with new insights, wisdom, and a deeper understanding of oneself and the world. This phase of the journey represents personal growth, self-discovery, and the integration of previously unrecognized aspects of ourselves.

The myth invites individuals to recognize the cyclical nature of existence and to embrace the inevitability of change. By acknowledging and accepting the cycles of life, death, and rebirth, individuals can navigate their own transformative journeys with greater resilience, adaptability, and a sense of purpose.

b) Agricultural Symbolism: Inanna/Ishtar's descent and resurrection in the myth also hold profound agricultural symbolism. The story has been interpreted as a reflection of the agricultural cycles observed in ancient Mesopotamia and other agrarian societies.

In this interpretation, Inanna's death is associated with the barrenness and dormancy of the land during the winter season. It represents a period of scarcity, where the earth is depleted, and life appears to have withdrawn. This agricultural symbolism echoes the challenges and hardships faced by agricultural communities during periods of drought or unfavorable conditions.

On the other hand, Inanna's resurrection symbolizes the return of fertility and abundance in the land. It represents the arrival of spring, where new life emerges, crops begin to grow, and the promise of a bountiful harvest is restored. This agricultural symbolism underscores the vital connection between the natural world, human life, and spiritual forces. It highlights the dependence of human societies on the cycles of nature and the profound impact of seasonal changes on their well-being and prosperity.

By drawing parallels between the myth's agricultural symbolism and the human experience, individuals can develop a deeper appreciation for the interconnectedness of life and the importance of living in harmony with the natural world. It encourages us to recognize and honor the cycles of growth, decay, and renewal that shape our lives and the world around us.

Cosmic and Cosmic Balance:

a) Cosmic Descent: Inanna/Ishtar's journey to the Underworld carries profound cosmic symbolism, reflecting the descent of consciousness into the depths of the cosmos or the underworld realms of the psyche. This cosmic descent represents a quest for knowledge, wisdom, and a deeper understanding of the mysteries that lie beyond the realm of everyday experience.

In this interpretation, the Underworld symbolizes the hidden dimensions of existence, the realm of the unconscious, and the collective unconscious, as proposed by Carl Jung. It represents the vast reservoir of knowledge, emotions, and archetypal patterns that influence human behavior and shape the fabric of reality.

By undertaking the cosmic descent, Inanna/Ishtar embarks on a journey of self-discovery and exploration, seeking to integrate the hidden aspects of her being and unravel the secrets of the cosmos. This symbolic descent emphasizes the human longing to connect with something greater than oneself, to transcend the limitations of individual existence, and to uncover profound truths that hold cosmic significance.

b) Balance of Power: The myth of Inanna/Ishtar's journey also delves into the balance of power between the divine and mortal realms, shedding light on the importance of maintaining equilibrium and respecting cosmic order. It explores the themes of authority, sovereignty, and the consequences of overstepping boundaries.

In the story, Inanna, as a powerful goddess, ventures into the realm of her sister, Ereshkigal, who is the ruler of the Underworld. This journey challenges the delicate balance between the divine and mortal realms, highlighting the potential repercussions when one seeks to exert control or manipulate forces beyond their rightful domain.

The myth underscores the significance of maintaining cosmic balance and acknowledging the inherent limits and responsibilities associated with power. It serves as a reminder that disrupting the natural order can have far-reaching consequences, both on an individual level and within the larger cosmic framework.

Exploring Ancient Mesopotamian Mythology, Rivalries, and Spiritual Legacies

By reflecting on the myth's exploration of power dynamics and the consequences of imbalances, individuals are prompted to consider their own roles and responsibilities in maintaining harmony and cosmic equilibrium. It encourages the cultivation of humility, respect for boundaries, and a deeper understanding of the intricate interplay between the forces at work in the universe.

Overall, the myth's cosmic descent and the exploration of power dynamics offer valuable insights into the human quest for cosmic balance and the profound impact of maintaining harmony within oneself, relationships, and the larger cosmos.

Exercises:

Reflect on a personal journey or transformative experience in your life. Identify the symbolic elements and archetypes present in your journey. Write a reflective essay discussing the parallels between your experience and the myth of Inanna's journey.

Conduct a comparative analysis of the myth of Inanna's journey and other myths or stories from different cultures that explore similar themes of transformation and rebirth. Discuss the similarities and differences in the symbolism and interpretations.

Engage in a group discussion exploring the relevance of Inanna/Ishtar's journey in modern contexts. How can the myth be applied to personal growth, social change, or ecological restoration? Discuss practical ways in which the themes and symbols from the myth can be integrated into contemporary rituals or practices.

By engaging in these exercises, students will deepen their understanding of the interpretations and symbolic meanings associated with Inanna/Ishtar's journey. They will develop critical thinking skills, expand their cultural and psychological knowledge, and gain insight into the transformative power of myths in personal and collective narratives.

Inanna/Ishtar in Modern Contexts

The ancient goddess Inanna/Ishtar continues to captivate and inspire individuals in modern times, transcending the boundaries of time and culture. In this section, we will explore the ways in which Inanna/Ishtar is understood, revered, and invoked in contemporary contexts, including witchcraft, divination, herbalism, shamanism, ecospirituality, and magic in Ancient Mesopotamia. By examining her relevance in these diverse fields, we can gain a deeper understanding of her enduring significance and her potential for personal and collective transformation.

Divine Dynamics

Witchcraft:

In contemporary witchcraft and Wiccan traditions, Inanna/Ishtar holds a significant place as a revered deity and symbol of feminine power, sexuality, and sovereignty. Drawing inspiration from her mythic journey and archetypal qualities, practitioners incorporate her energies into their rituals, spellwork, and spiritual practices.

One aspect of Inanna/Ishtar's significance in witchcraft lies in her embodiment of feminine power and sensuality. As a goddess associated with love, sexuality, and fertility, she represents the potent force of feminine desire and the celebration of one's authentic self. Practitioners may invoke her during rituals focused on love spells, sensuality, and self-empowerment, seeking her guidance and blessings in matters of the heart and personal growth.

Inanna/Ishtar's journey also serves as a source of inspiration for practitioners seeking to explore their own inner strength and navigate transformative experiences. Her descent into the Underworld and subsequent resurrection symbolize the process of facing and embracing the shadow self, undergoing personal transformation, and emerging stronger and wiser. Practitioners may draw on this mythic narrative as a metaphorical framework for their own journeys of self-discovery, healing, and empowerment.

Furthermore, Inanna/Ishtar's embodiment of sovereignty resonates with witches and Wiccans who embrace their own autonomy and personal power. She symbolizes the ability to assert oneself, make choices aligned with one's true nature, and embody a sense of personal authority. Practitioners may invoke her to cultivate a deeper connection to their own sovereignty and to invoke her qualities of confidence, assertiveness, and self-determination.

Within witchcraft and Wiccan practices, the invocation of Inanna/Ishtar is not limited to rituals or spellwork focused on love and sensuality. Her energy and archetypal qualities can be invoked in various aspects of magical and spiritual work. For instance, she may be called upon for rituals related to abundance, creativity, personal growth, and empowerment. She is seen as a source of inspiration and guidance in embracing one's desires, embracing personal power, and embodying the authentic self.

In summary, within contemporary witchcraft and Wiccan traditions, Inanna/Ishtar holds a revered position as a symbol of feminine power, sensuality, and sovereignty. Her mythic journey and archetypal qualities inspire practitioners to embrace their desires, explore their inner strength, and embody their authentic selves.

Through rituals, spellwork, and invocations, practitioners seek her blessings and guidance in matters of love, personal growth, and empowerment. By connecting with Inanna/Ishtar's energies, practitioners aim to cultivate a deeper understanding of themselves, their desires, and their personal power within the framework of their spiritual and magical practices.

Divination:

In divination practices, Inanna/Ishtar serves as a powerful and revered deity who can be called upon for guidance, wisdom, and insight. Her archetypal qualities and mythic journey provide a rich source of inspiration for tarot readings, oracle readings, and other divinatory methods.

Tarot or oracle decks may feature cards that are directly inspired by Inanna/Ishtar or embody themes associated with her energy. These cards often symbolize love, passion, transformation, and the exploration of the subconscious. They may depict images such as a sensuous figure, a divine union, or a descent into the depths, representing the various aspects of Inanna/Ishtar's myth and archetypal symbolism.

When seeking guidance or answers in divination, practitioners may invoke Inanna/Ishtar's energy and presence. They may set up a sacred space, light candles, and create an atmosphere conducive to connecting with her essence. Through focused intention and invocation, diviners aim to establish a connection with Inanna/Ishtar, inviting her wisdom and guidance into the divination session.

The presence of Inanna/Ishtar in divination can enhance the intuitive abilities of the practitioner. By invoking her energy, diviners seek to amplify their own intuition and open themselves to receiving messages and insights from higher realms. They may ask specific questions or seek general guidance on matters of the heart, personal growth, or spiritual development.

Inanna/Ishtar's energy in divination is particularly suited for exploring matters related to love, relationships, and personal transformation. Diviners may turn to her for insights into romantic partnerships, deepening connections, or resolving relationship challenges. Her energy can also shed light on inner transformation and the exploration of subconscious patterns, inviting diviners to delve into the depths of their psyche and uncover hidden aspects of themselves.

During a divination session, practitioners may interpret the cards in the context of Inanna/Ishtar's mythology and archetypal qualities. They may draw upon the themes of her descent, resurrection, and personal empowerment to provide insights and guidance to the querent. The cards inspired by Inanna/Ishtar can serve as potent symbols and archetypal gateways, allowing diviners to access deeper layers of meaning and wisdom.

In summary, Inanna/Ishtar's presence in divination practices offers a channel for seeking guidance, wisdom, and insight. Tarot or oracle cards inspired by her mythic journey and archetypal qualities provide a means of exploring themes of love, passion, transformation, and the exploration of the subconscious. By invoking her energy and connecting with her essence, diviners aim to enhance their intuition, receive messages from higher realms, and gain deeper insights into personal and spiritual inquiries.

Herbalism:

Herbalists and practitioners of plant-based healing arts have a deep appreciation for the energetic properties of plants and their ability to support healing on physical, emotional, and spiritual levels. In the context of Inanna/Ishtar's energy, certain herbs and plants are often associated with her qualities of love, sensuality, and emotional healing. Incorporating these herbs into their work allows practitioners to tap into the essence of Inanna/Ishtar and harness the specific energies they represent.

One herb commonly associated with Inanna/Ishtar is rose. Known for its enchanting fragrance and symbolism of love and passion, rose is often used in herbal remedies and rituals aimed at invoking the blessings of Inanna/Ishtar. Rose petals or rose essential oil may be utilized in preparations such as love potions, sensual bath blends, or aromatherapy blends designed to enhance sensuality and emotional healing. The use of rose in these practices is seen as a way to connect with the essence of Inanna/Ishtar and draw upon her energies of love, beauty, and emotional transformation.

Another herb linked to Inanna/Ishtar is damiana. With a reputation as an aphrodisiac and mood enhancer, damiana is often associated with sensual and passionate energies. It is believed to stimulate the sacral chakra, promoting feelings of pleasure, desire, and emotional connection. Herbalists and practitioners may incorporate damiana into herbal formulas or rituals intended to support love, intimacy, or emotional healing. This could include creating damiana-infused oils, teas, or bath blends to evoke the essence of Inanna/Ishtar and enhance the desired energetic qualities.

Yarrow is yet another botanical ally associated with Inanna/Ishtar. Known for its protective and healing properties, yarrow has a long history of use in folk medicine and spiritual practices. It is believed to have a strong connection to the emotional realm and can aid in emotional healing, releasing past wounds, and promoting inner strength. Yarrow may be used in herbal remedies, such as teas or tinctures, to support emotional well-being and resilience. In rituals, dried yarrow flowers or leaves may be burned as an offering or used as part of an energetic cleansing practice. Its inclusion in herbal work associated with Inanna/Ishtar signifies the intention to invoke her energies of healing, emotional balance, and protection.

Incorporating Inanna/Ishtar's energy into herbal practices extends beyond the use of specific herbs. It involves cultivating a deep reverence for nature, acknowledging the sacredness of the plant kingdom, and working in harmony with the energetic qualities that resonate with Inanna/Ishtar's archetype. Herbalists and plant-based practitioners who connect with Inanna/Ishtar's energy may also infuse their work with rituals, invocations, or meditations to deepen their connection with her essence and the healing energies she represents.

In summary, herbalists and practitioners of plant-based healing arts may incorporate Inanna/Ishtar's energy into their work by associating her with specific herbs or plants known for their properties related to love, sensuality, and emotional healing. The use of herbs such as rose, damiana, and yarrow allows practitioners to tap into the essence of Inanna/Ishtar and harness the specific energies they embody. By infusing their herbal remedies or rituals with these herbs, practitioners aim to invoke Inanna/Ishtar's blessings and channel her energies of love, sensuality, emotional healing, and transformation.

Shamanism:

Shamanic practitioners, who engage in ancient spiritual practices aimed at connecting with the spirit world and facilitating healing and transformation, may invoke Inanna/Ishtar as a guide or ally in their journeys. Inanna/Ishtar's archetype holds deep symbolic significance, representing aspects of power, transformation, and the exploration of the unconscious realms. Shamanic practitioners may seek her assistance in traversing these realms, retrieving lost aspects of the self, and undergoing personal growth and transformation.

Shamanic journeys often involve entering altered states of consciousness, such as through rhythmic drumming, chanting, or the use of entheogenic plants. In this altered state, practitioners connect with the spirit realm and seek guidance from various spiritual entities, including Inanna/Ishtar. Through focused intention and ritual practices, shamanic practitioners may call upon Inanna/Ishtar as a source of wisdom, power, and inspiration.

Divine Dynamics

During shamanic rituals and healing ceremonies, Inanna/Ishtar's archetype may be invoked to facilitate the transformative aspects of the journey. Shamanic practitioners may embody the qualities and energies associated with Inanna/Ishtar, drawing upon her strength, sensuality, and connection to the unconscious. This invocation serves to enhance the practitioner's own power and create a sacred space where healing and transformation can take place.

Inanna/Ishtar's archetype provides shamanic practitioners with a framework through which they can explore their own personal growth and transformation. By calling upon her, practitioners seek guidance in confronting and integrating aspects of their shadow self, facing personal challenges, and experiencing rebirth and renewal. Inanna/Ishtar's journey to the Underworld and subsequent resurrection serves as a powerful metaphor for the transformative processes that can occur within the shamanic journey.

The presence of Inanna/Ishtar as a guide or ally in shamanic practices not only offers practitioners a source of inspiration and support, but it also serves to deepen their connection to the ancient mythologies and spiritual traditions that have revered Inanna/Ishtar for centuries. By working with her archetype, shamanic practitioners tap into a collective consciousness that spans cultures and time, accessing the wisdom and power associated with this powerful goddess figure.

In summary, shamanic practitioners may call upon Inanna/Ishtar as a guide or ally in their spiritual journeys. They enter trance states to connect with her, seeking her assistance in traversing the realms of the unconscious, retrieving lost aspects of the self, and undergoing personal transformation. Inanna/Ishtar's archetype is invoked as a source of power and inspiration during shamanic rituals and healing ceremonies, allowing practitioners to tap into her wisdom, strength, and transformative energies. By working with Inanna/Ishtar, shamanic practitioners align themselves with ancient mythologies and tap into the collective consciousness that reveres and honors her as a symbol of power and transformation.

Ecospirituality:

In the realm of ecospirituality, Inanna/Ishtar is regarded as a symbol of the sacred feminine and the deep interconnection between humans and the natural world. Her mythic journey, with its themes of death, rebirth, and the cycles of nature, holds profound relevance and resonates with the ecological challenges and concerns of our time. In rituals and practices inspired by Inanna/Ishtar, individuals may seek to restore harmony and balance in their relationship with the Earth, and honor the intrinsic value of all beings within the web of life.

Exploring Ancient Mesopotamian Mythology, Rivalries, and Spiritual Legacies

Inanna/Ishtar's story carries ecological significance through its exploration of the cycles and rhythms of life. Her descent into the Underworld and subsequent resurrection mirror the natural processes of decay, regeneration, and renewal that occur in the natural world. This resonates with the ecological understanding of the interconnectedness of all life forms, the cyclical patterns of birth, growth, death, and regeneration in ecosystems, and the recognition of the inherent value and wisdom present in these processes.

Rituals and practices inspired by Inanna/Ishtar often aim to deepen individuals' connection to the Earth and their role as caretakers of the natural world. Through meditation, ceremony, or nature-based activities, practitioners seek to reestablish a sense of harmony and balance within themselves and with the larger ecosystem. By aligning with Inanna/Ishtar's archetype, they tap into the sacred feminine energy associated with nurturing, intuition, and interconnectedness, thereby cultivating a sense of reverence and respect for all beings and the Earth itself.

These rituals and practices may also focus on healing the relationship between humans and the Earth, acknowledging the ecological damage caused by human actions and seeking ways to restore and protect the environment. Inspired by Inanna/Ishtar's journey, individuals may engage in ecological activism, sustainable living practices, or environmental education efforts to address the urgent ecological challenges we face today. By honoring Inanna/Ishtar's archetype, they recognize the vital role of the sacred feminine in guiding our actions towards environmental stewardship and the restoration of balance.

Inanna/Ishtar's mythology serves as a source of inspiration and guidance for individuals seeking to cultivate a deep spiritual connection with the Earth and embrace ecologically conscious lifestyles. By recognizing the interconnectedness of all life and the sacredness inherent in nature, individuals are encouraged to cultivate a sense of responsibility and reverence for the Earth and all its inhabitants. Inanna/Ishtar's story invites us to view ourselves as part of a greater ecological whole, where our well-being and the well-being of the planet are intimately intertwined.

In summary, in the realm of ecospirituality, Inanna/Ishtar is regarded as a symbol of the sacred feminine and the interconnectedness between humans and the natural world. Her mythic journey, with its themes of death, rebirth, and the cycles of nature, holds ecological significance and resonates with the ecological challenges of our time. Through rituals and practices inspired by Inanna/Ishtar, individuals seek to restore harmony and balance in their relationship with the Earth, honoring the intrinsic value of all beings, and cultivating a deep sense of reverence and responsibility for the well-being of the planet.

Divine Dynamics

Magic in Ancient Mesopotamia:

Scholars and practitioners of Ancient Mesopotamian magic delve into the rituals and spellwork associated with Inanna/Ishtar, seeking to understand and reconstruct these practices in their historical context. By studying ancient texts, artifacts, and inscriptions, they aim to gain insights into the magical traditions of the past and adapt them to contemporary settings.

The exploration of Inanna/Ishtar's magical rituals and spellwork offers a way to connect with the rich cultural and spiritual heritage of Mesopotamia. These practices are rooted in the ancient civilization that thrived in the region thousands of years ago, and they provide a window into the beliefs, values, and spiritual practices of the time. Scholars and practitioners engage with the historical context, drawing upon archaeological discoveries and scholarly research to gain a deeper understanding of the magical traditions associated with Inanna/Ishtar.

Ancient Mesopotamian magical texts, such as incantations, hymns, and rituals, offer valuable insights into the practices of the past. These texts often contain instructions for performing specific spells or ceremonies, invoking the aid of Inanna/Ishtar and other deities for various purposes. Scholars and practitioners analyze these texts, deciphering the symbolism, language, and techniques employed to harness and direct magical forces.

Through their research and exploration, practitioners of Ancient Mesopotamian magic aim to adapt these historical practices to modern contexts. They may reinterpret the ancient rituals and spells, incorporating them into contemporary magical frameworks while respecting the integrity and authenticity of the original traditions. This adaptation allows individuals to connect with the transformative powers and energies associated with Inanna/Ishtar, drawing upon her archetypal qualities and mythic resonance to enhance their magical work and personal growth.

Engaging with the ancient magical traditions associated with Inanna/Ishtar is a way to access the profound and transformative energies believed to be embodied by these ancient deities. By invoking Inanna/Ishtar and working with her symbols, practitioners seek to align themselves with the forces of creation, passion, and empowerment. They may perform rituals, create amulets or talismans, or recite incantations associated with Inanna/Ishtar to invoke her blessings and assistance in their magical endeavors.

The exploration of Ancient Mesopotamian magic and the practices associated with Inanna/Ishtar offer practitioners a unique opportunity to connect with an ancient lineage of wisdom and spiritual power. By understanding and adapting these historical practices, individuals can tap into the rich tapestry of Mesopotamian spirituality, bridging the gap between the past and the present. Through this connection, practitioners seek personal transformation, spiritual growth, and a deepening of their connection with the divine.

In summary, scholars and practitioners of Ancient Mesopotamian magic delve into the rituals and spellwork associated with Inanna/Ishtar, seeking to understand and reconstruct these practices in their historical context. Through the study of ancient texts and artifacts, individuals connect with the cultural and spiritual heritage of Mesopotamia, adapting these practices to modern contexts. By engaging with the magical traditions of Inanna/Ishtar, practitioners seek to access transformative powers, align themselves with ancient wisdom, and cultivate personal growth and spiritual connection.

Exercises:

Research and explore how Inanna/Ishtar is represented and invoked in different contemporary contexts, such as art, literature, music, or popular culture. Write a comparative analysis of these representations, discussing the similarities and differences in how her archetype is portrayed and interpreted.

Engage in a group discussion on the ethical considerations and cultural sensitivity involved in incorporating Inanna/Ishtar's symbolism and practices into modern contexts. Reflect on ways to honor her cultural origins while adapting her energies and teachings to contemporary spiritual paths.

Design your own ritual or practice that incorporates Inanna/Ishtar's energy and symbolism in a way that resonates with your personal beliefs and intentions. Reflect on the elements and symbolism you choose and the significance they hold for you. Write a reflection paper describing your ritual and its effects on your spiritual journey.

By exploring Inanna/Ishtar in modern contexts, students will gain a deeper appreciation for her enduring influence and the ways in which her archetypal qualities continue to inspire and empower individuals today.

Exploration of feminist perspectives and reclaiming of Inanna/Ishtar's power

Inanna/Ishtar, the ancient goddess of love, war, and sovereignty, has emerged as a significant figure within modern feminist discourse, symbolizing feminine strength, empowerment, and the reclamation of women's power. Feminist perspectives surrounding Inanna/Ishtar delve into her mythology and archetype, exploring how she challenges patriarchal narratives and offers alternative representations of femininity.

One of the key aspects of Inanna/Ishtar's significance in feminist discourse is her multifaceted nature and embodiment of powerful feminine archetypes. As a warrior, she defies traditional gender roles, showcasing women's capacity for strength, courage, and assertiveness. As a lover, she embraces her desires and sexual agency, challenging societal expectations and restrictions placed upon women's sexuality. As a sovereign goddess, she embodies leadership, self-determination, and the right to assert one's own power and authority.

In feminist discussions, Inanna/Ishtar's mythology is examined through a critical lens, highlighting how her story subverts and challenges patriarchal norms. Her journey to the Underworld, for example, is seen as an act of self-discovery, representing a woman's exploration of her own depths and reclaiming her power from the shadows. This narrative disrupts the notion that women should be confined to prescribed roles and limited to surface-level expressions of femininity.

Moreover, the reclamation of Inanna/Ishtar's mythology and archetype allows for a revisioning of feminine power. In patriarchal societies, power has often been associated with dominance, control, and aggression. In contrast, Inanna/Ishtar embodies a different form of power—one that embraces vulnerability, sensuality, and emotional intelligence. This challenges the patriarchal dichotomy of power and weakness, allowing for a more expansive understanding of feminine strength and agency.

The mythology of Inanna/Ishtar is also interpreted through an intersectional feminist lens, recognizing and addressing the unique experiences and challenges faced by women of different backgrounds, including women of color, queer women, and women from marginalized communities. By exploring Inanna/Ishtar's story through an intersectional perspective, feminists highlight the importance of inclusivity, representation, and the dismantling of systems of oppression that perpetuate gender inequality.

In reclaiming the archetype of Inanna/Ishtar, feminist discourse emphasizes the need for women's voices to be heard, their stories to be valued, and their power to be recognized and celebrated. This reclamation extends beyond the mythological realm and influences various aspects of feminist activism, art, and literature. Inanna/Ishtar becomes an inspiration and rallying point for women seeking to challenge the status quo, dismantle patriarchal structures, and assert their rights and autonomy.

Furthermore, the exploration of Inanna/Ishtar's mythology contributes to the ongoing dialogue surrounding the divine feminine and the need for a more balanced and inclusive understanding of spirituality. In patriarchal religious systems, women have often been marginalized, relegated to supporting roles, or omitted entirely from sacred narratives. By reclaiming Inanna/Ishtar, feminists reclaim the sacred feminine, asserting the importance of feminine spirituality and the recognition of women's divine power and connection to the divine.

In summary, Inanna/Ishtar holds significant importance in modern feminist discourse as a symbol of feminine strength and empowerment. Feminist perspectives surrounding Inanna/Ishtar explore her mythology and archetype, challenging patriarchal narratives and reclaiming women's power. Through the reclamation of Inanna/Ishtar, feminist discourse expands understandings of femininity, challenges gender norms, and promotes inclusivity and intersectionality. This exploration extends beyond mythology to influence feminist activism, art, literature, and the broader dialogue surrounding the divine feminine.

Reinterpreting the Mythology:

Feminist scholars and practitioners have undertaken a comprehensive examination of Inanna/Ishtar's mythology, seeking to reinterpret and reclaim her as a symbol of feminine power, agency, and resilience. This process involves delving into her stories, symbols, and roles, aiming to uncover hidden meanings and challenge traditional interpretations that may reinforce patriarchal norms and the marginalization of women.

One of the key aspects of feminist exploration of Inanna/Ishtar's mythology is the identification and analysis of the patriarchal influences and biases that may have shaped the traditional understanding of her stories. Feminist scholars critically examine the texts and cultural contexts in which her mythology originated, questioning the ways in which women's roles and experiences have been marginalized or misrepresented. They seek to unveil the underlying power dynamics, gendered stereotypes, and societal expectations that may have influenced the transmission and interpretation of her stories over time.

Through this process, feminists engage in a reclamation of Inanna/Ishtar's narrative, highlighting the aspects of her mythology that challenge and subvert patriarchal norms. They bring attention to her agency, assertiveness, and self-determination, as well as her embodiment of diverse and complex feminine archetypes. By emphasizing these aspects, feminists aim to disrupt and challenge the traditional narratives that have often reduced Inanna/Ishtar to passive or objectified roles.

Furthermore, feminist scholars and practitioners explore the symbols and metaphors within Inanna/Ishtar's mythology to uncover deeper layers of meaning and significance. They seek to reinterpret these symbols in ways that affirm and empower women, moving beyond simplistic or superficial interpretations. By uncovering the hidden symbolism and exploring alternative narratives, feminists aim to highlight the profound wisdom and transformative potential embedded within Inanna/Ishtar's stories.

This feminist reevaluation of Inanna/Ishtar's mythology also involves examining the ways in which her roles and relationships challenge traditional gendered expectations. For example, her position as both a warrior and a lover challenges the dichotomy of femininity and masculinity, emphasizing the complexity and fluidity of gender expression. By embracing and celebrating these multifaceted aspects, feminists seek to challenge rigid gender norms and expand the possibilities for women's self-expression and empowerment.

Moreover, the reinterpretation of Inanna/Ishtar's mythology through a feminist lens involves highlighting the connections between her stories and real-life experiences of women. Feminist practitioners explore the ways in which her journey, trials, and triumphs mirror the challenges and resilience of women in patriarchal societies. They aim to create spaces for women to relate to Inanna/Ishtar's experiences, finding strength, inspiration, and guidance in her mythology as they navigate their own journeys of self-discovery and empowerment.

In engaging with Inanna/Ishtar's mythology through a feminist lens, scholars and practitioners also contribute to the broader feminist movement. By reclaiming Inanna/Ishtar as a symbol of feminine power and agency, feminists challenge the marginalization of women in society and advocate for gender equality. They recognize the importance of diverse narratives and representations in shaping cultural attitudes and perceptions of women, seeking to dismantle patriarchal structures and create space for the voices and experiences of women to be valued and celebrated.

In summary, feminist scholars and practitioners engage in a process of reinterpreting Inanna/Ishtar's mythology through a feminist lens. They critically examine her stories, symbols, and roles, aiming to uncover hidden meanings and challenge traditional interpretations that may reinforce patriarchal norms. Through this exploration, feminists seek to reclaim Inanna/Ishtar as a symbol of feminine power, agency, and resilience, challenging the marginalization of women in society and contributing to the broader feminist movement.

Exploring Ancient Mesopotamian Mythology, Rivalries, and Spiritual Legacies

Embracing the Goddess's Dualities:

Inanna/Ishtar, as a mythological figure, embodies a rich tapestry of qualities and archetypes that resonate with feminist perspectives. Feminists celebrate the multifaceted nature of Inanna/Ishtar's archetype, which encompasses a range of qualities including sensuality, assertiveness, independence, nurturing, and compassion. By embracing and honoring this full spectrum, feminists challenge restrictive gender roles and embrace the complexity of women's identities and experiences.

One of the significant aspects of Inanna/Ishtar's archetype is her sensuality and sexual agency. Feminist perspectives recognize and celebrate women's inherent sexuality as a source of power, pleasure, and self-expression. Inanna/Ishtar's embodiment of sensuality challenges societal expectations and taboos around women's sexuality, reclaiming it as a vital aspect of feminine identity and autonomy. By embracing and acknowledging this aspect of Inanna/Ishtar's archetype, feminists challenge the objectification and sexual repression that women have often faced, asserting their right to embrace and explore their own desires.

In addition to sensuality, Inanna/Ishtar embodies assertiveness and independence. She is depicted as a fierce warrior and a goddess of war, representing strength, courage, and the ability to assert one's boundaries and fight for what is right. Feminists draw inspiration from this aspect of Inanna/Ishtar's archetype, highlighting the importance of women's assertiveness, self-advocacy, and the refusal to be silenced or diminished. By embracing and embodying these qualities, feminists challenge the societal expectations that often demand women to be passive, submissive, or accommodating.

Furthermore, Inanna/Ishtar's archetype encompasses nurturing and compassionate aspects. She is associated with fertility, love, and the care of others, symbolizing the ability to provide emotional support and create nurturing environments. Feminists recognize and value the importance of these qualities, affirming that women have the capacity for both strength and compassion. By embracing these nurturing aspects, feminists challenge the dichotomy that pits women against each other and instead promote a culture of care, support, and empathy among women.

By celebrating the duality and complexity of Inanna/Ishtar's archetype, feminists challenge the notion of rigid gender roles and expectations that restrict women's expression and limit their potential. They emphasize that women can embody various qualities and roles simultaneously, rejecting the notion of essentialized femininity that confines women to narrow stereotypes. Feminists promote the idea that women can be both fierce warriors and loving nurturers, assertive and compassionate, independent and interconnected. Embracing the full spectrum of Inanna/Ishtar's archetype allows for the recognition and affirmation of women's multifaceted identities, experiences, and potentials.

Ultimately, feminist perspectives draw inspiration from Inanna/Ishtar's archetype to challenge societal norms and promote gender equality. By embracing the complexity of her qualities, feminists challenge restrictive gender roles and affirm the diverse experiences and identities of women. In doing so, they aim to create a more inclusive and equitable society that values and celebrates the full spectrum of women's strengths, aspirations, and contributions.

Resisting Male Dominance and Violence:

Inanna/Ishtar's journey to the Underworld and her encounter with Ereshkigal, her sister and the queen of the Underworld, holds deep significance within feminist interpretations. Feminist scholars and activists have drawn parallels between Inanna/Ishtar's descent and women's experiences of confronting patriarchal systems that seek to suppress their power, agency, and autonomy. Through the reclamation and reinterpretation of this myth, feminists find inspiration to challenge oppressive structures and assert their own agency.

In the myth, Inanna/Ishtar, as a powerful goddess, decides to descend into the Underworld, defying societal expectations and norms. This act of descent can be seen as a symbolic rebellion against the established order, mirroring women's resistance to oppressive patriarchal systems. Inanna/Ishtar's journey represents a quest for self-discovery, self-determination, and the reclamation of her own power and sovereignty. Feminists interpret this descent as an act of defiance against the societal limitations placed upon women, encouraging them to explore their inner depths and reclaim their suppressed voices.

During her encounter with Ereshkigal, Inanna/Ishtar is stripped of her divine attributes and subjected to a series of trials and suffering. This part of the myth resonates with the experiences of women who have been subjected to violence, oppression, and silencing within patriarchal structures. Feminist interpretations highlight the parallel between Inanna/Ishtar's ordeal and the challenges women face when they confront systems that seek to diminish their power and agency. It symbolizes the struggle against gender-based violence, discrimination, and the erasure of women's experiences.

Inanna/Ishtar's descent and her subsequent journey through the Underworld can be seen as a metaphorical representation of the resistance against male dominance and violence. Feminist scholars argue that this myth offers a narrative framework for understanding and reclaiming women's experiences of oppression and their resilience in the face of adversity. By identifying with Inanna/Ishtar's journey, women are empowered to confront and challenge patriarchal structures, reclaim their agency, and assert their own narratives.

Furthermore, the myth highlights the transformative potential that arises from facing and embracing the darker aspects of oneself. Inanna/Ishtar's encounter with Ereshkigal symbolizes the integration of the shadow self, representing the suppressed, rejected, or marginalized aspects of one's identity. Feminist interpretations emphasize the importance of acknowledging and embracing these aspects as a path to self-empowerment and collective liberation. Through the reclamation of the myth, feminists encourage women to confront the internalized oppression and patriarchal conditioning that may inhibit their self-expression and personal growth.

Inanna/Ishtar's journey and her subsequent resurrection also symbolize the triumph of life over death, resilience in the face of adversity, and the reclamation of feminine power. Feminist scholars and activists draw inspiration from this aspect of the myth to inspire women to reclaim their power and assert their agency, both individually and collectively. By embracing the narrative of Inanna/Ishtar's descent, feminists challenge the narratives that perpetuate the subjugation and silencing of women, encouraging them to resist and dismantle patriarchal systems in their own lives and communities.

In summary, the journey of Inanna/Ishtar to the Underworld and her encounter with Ereshkigal holds profound significance within feminist interpretations. It provides a powerful narrative framework for understanding and reclaiming women's experiences of oppression, resilience, and empowerment. By embracing this myth, feminists find inspiration to challenge oppressive structures, assert their agency, and reclaim their power. Inanna/Ishtar's story serves as a timeless reminder of the importance of resistance, self-discovery, and the pursuit of justice and equality in the face of patriarchal dominance.

Embodying Sexual Liberation:

Inanna/Ishtar's association with love and sexuality holds significant meaning within feminist perspectives. Feminist scholars and activists have reclaimed her archetype as a symbol of sexual autonomy and empowerment, challenging societal norms that seek to control and regulate women's sexuality. By embracing and celebrating Inanna/Ishtar's unabashed embrace of her desires and her sovereignty over her own body, feminists seek to challenge sexual repression and advocate for sexual liberation.

Divine Dynamics

In the myth, Inanna/Ishtar is often depicted as a goddess of love, passion, and sensuality. She embodies a powerful and assertive sexuality that defies traditional expectations and restrictions placed upon women's desires. Feminist interpretations of her archetype emphasize the importance of reclaiming women's sexual autonomy and challenging the societal norms and double standards that seek to control and regulate women's sexuality.

By reclaiming Inanna/Ishtar's archetype, feminists challenge the notion that women's sexuality should be suppressed, hidden, or subjected to societal judgment. They advocate for a shift towards a more inclusive and sex-positive understanding of sexuality, where women are free to explore and express their desires without fear of shame or judgment. Inanna/Ishtar's mythology serves as a source of inspiration and empowerment for women to embrace their own sexual agency and assert their right to pleasure and fulfillment.

Furthermore, Inanna/Ishtar's archetype encourages women to reject the objectification and commodification of their bodies. In her myth, she embodies sovereignty and agency over her own body, refusing to be reduced to mere objects of desire. Feminist interpretations draw on this aspect of her archetype to challenge the societal norms that objectify and devalue women based on their sexual appeal. By reclaiming their sexual autonomy and asserting their agency, women can challenge patriarchal structures that seek to control and exploit their bodies for the pleasure of others.

Inanna/Ishtar's archetype also challenges heteronormative and restrictive understandings of sexuality. Feminist interpretations embrace the diversity of sexual identities and orientations, recognizing that women's desires can extend beyond traditional notions of heterosexual relationships. By reclaiming Inanna/Ishtar's association with love and sexuality, feminists advocate for inclusive and affirming spaces where women of all sexual orientations can explore and express their desires without judgment or discrimination.

Additionally, Inanna/Ishtar's archetype highlights the importance of consent, communication, and boundaries in sexual relationships. Feminists draw on her myth to emphasize the necessity of mutual respect, enthusiastic consent, and the recognition of each individual's agency and autonomy within intimate encounters. By promoting a culture of consent and dismantling narratives of entitlement, feminists aim to create safer and more empowering spaces for women to explore their sexuality.

In summary, Inanna/Ishtar's association with love and sexuality has been reclaimed by feminist perspectives as symbols of empowerment and sexual autonomy. Feminists draw inspiration from her archetype to challenge sexual repression, advocate for sexual liberation, and create inclusive spaces where women can explore and express their desires without judgment or shame. By embracing Inanna/Ishtar's unabashed embrace of her desires and her sovereignty over her own body, feminists challenge patriarchal norms and advocate for a more inclusive, sex-positive, and consent-based understanding of women's sexuality.

Exploring Goddess-Centric Spirituality:

The reclamation of Inanna/Ishtar's power within feminist spirituality has led to a resurgence of goddess-centric worship and practices. Feminist practitioners and followers of contemporary pagan paths find inspiration in Inanna/Ishtar's mythology and archetype, viewing her as a divine embodiment of feminine strength, wisdom, and empowerment. They engage in rituals, ceremonies, and spiritual practices that honor her and seek to connect with her energy and power.

Within goddess-centric spirituality, Inanna/Ishtar is revered as a central figure representing the divine feminine and the sacred aspects of womanhood. She embodies qualities such as assertiveness, sensuality, independence, and nurturing, which resonate with feminist ideals of empowerment and self-expression. By invoking Inanna/Ishtar's energy and worshiping her as a goddess, practitioners seek to tap into her power and wisdom, drawing inspiration for their own personal growth, healing, and activism.

Rituals and practices associated with Inanna/Ishtar vary among feminist practitioners and contemporary pagan paths. They may include offerings, prayers, invocations, and the creation of sacred spaces or altars dedicated to her. These practices serve as a means to establish a connection with Inanna/Ishtar and invoke her presence, seeking her guidance, protection, and blessings.

Through these rituals and practices, feminist practitioners aim to cultivate a deeper relationship with Inanna/Ishtar, fostering a sense of empowerment, healing, and transformation. They may seek her guidance and wisdom in navigating life's challenges, promoting self-confidence, and embracing their authentic selves. Inanna/Ishtar's archetype serves as a source of inspiration and a symbol of feminine power, helping individuals tap into their own inner strength and unleash their full potential.

Furthermore, the worship of Inanna/Ishtar within feminist spirituality extends beyond personal empowerment to encompass social and political activism. Feminist practitioners may invoke her energy and guidance to support their efforts in challenging oppressive systems and advocating for gender equality, justice, and liberation. Inanna/Ishtar's mythology and archetype inspire individuals to take a stand against patriarchal structures, to reclaim their rights, and to contribute to positive social change.

In summary, the reclamation of Inanna/Ishtar's power within feminist spirituality has resulted in the revival of goddess-centric worship and practices. Feminist practitioners and followers of contemporary pagan paths honor Inanna/Ishtar as a divine embodiment of feminine strength, wisdom, and empowerment. Through rituals and practices, they seek to connect with her energy and power, drawing inspiration for personal empowerment, healing, and activism. Inanna/Ishtar's archetype serves as a source of guidance and inspiration, helping individuals embrace their authentic selves, challenge oppressive systems, and contribute to positive social change in the pursuit of gender equality and liberation.

Exercises:

Write a research paper exploring different feminist interpretations of Inanna/Ishtar's mythology. Compare and contrast the key arguments and perspectives presented by various scholars and practitioners. Analyze the ways in which feminist interpretations challenge traditional narratives and contribute to the reclamation of women's power.

Engage in a group discussion on the potential criticisms and challenges faced by feminists who seek to reclaim Inanna/Ishtar's power. Explore dissenting opinions or counterarguments that question the validity or effectiveness of using ancient goddess symbolism for feminist purposes. Reflect on the complexities and potential contradictions involved in reclaiming ancient myths for contemporary empowerment.

Create a visual representation or artwork that embodies the themes of feminist empowerment and Inanna/Ishtar's archetype. Reflect on the symbolism and messages conveyed through your artwork and write a reflective essay discussing how it aligns with feminist perspectives and contributes to the reclamation of feminine power.

Cultural impact and representations of Inanna/Ishtar in contemporary art, literature, and media

Inanna/Ishtar, the ancient goddess of love, war, and sovereignty, continues to captivate the imagination and inspire creative expression in various forms of contemporary art, literature, and media. This section will explore the cultural impact of Inanna/Ishtar and examine her representations in these mediums, shedding light on how her mythological figure has been interpreted, reimagined, and incorporated into modern artistic and literary works.

Exploring Ancient Mesopotamian Mythology, Rivalries, and Spiritual Legacies

Visual Art:

Inanna/Ishtar's iconic imagery and profound symbolism have captivated artists from various backgrounds, inspiring them to depict her in visual art forms. Paintings, sculptures, and mixed media installations featuring Inanna/Ishtar explore a range of themes related to femininity, sensuality, power, and the divine feminine. Through their art, these artists delve into the complexities of gender, identity, and spirituality, using Inanna/Ishtar as a visual representation and catalyst for exploration.

One notable artist who has incorporated Inanna/Ishtar's imagery in her work is Shirin Neshat. Neshat, an Iranian-born artist, gained international recognition for her photographic series "Women of Allah," which explores women's roles in Islamic society and challenges prevailing gender norms. In this series, Neshat skillfully combines imagery from Inanna/Ishtar's myth with contemporary contexts, creating a powerful dialogue between ancient archetypes and present-day social issues.

Through her use of symbolism, Neshat addresses the complexities of female identity, agency, and the struggles faced by women in patriarchal societies. In incorporating Inanna/Ishtar's imagery, Neshat draws upon the powerful symbolism associated with the goddess, evoking themes of femininity, sensuality, and strength. By juxtaposing these ancient symbols with contemporary contexts, Neshat prompts viewers to question and reflect upon the role of women in society and the cultural expectations placed upon them.

Other artists have also been inspired by Inanna/Ishtar's mythology and archetype, creating their own interpretations and visual representations. Painters, sculptors, and mixed media artists often employ a variety of techniques and styles to capture the essence of Inanna/Ishtar's power and significance. They may depict her as a regal figure adorned with symbols of fertility, war, and sovereignty, or as a sensual and assertive presence that challenges conventional notions of femininity.

In these visual artworks, Inanna/Ishtar becomes a source of inspiration, empowering viewers to explore their own identities, confront societal expectations, and celebrate the diverse facets of femininity. The visual representations of Inanna/Ishtar serve as a visual language that transcends cultural and historical boundaries, allowing individuals from different backgrounds to connect with her universal themes and archetypal qualities.

Moreover, the use of Inanna/Ishtar's imagery in visual art not only celebrates her mythological significance but also contributes to the ongoing dialogue on feminism, gender equality, and the reclamation of women's power. By depicting Inanna/Ishtar in diverse artistic contexts, artists challenge traditional narratives and expand the representation of femininity in art, opening up possibilities for alternative expressions of power, agency, and beauty.

In summary, Inanna/Ishtar's imagery has found a prominent place in visual art, inspiring artists to explore themes of femininity, sensuality, power, and the divine feminine. Artists like Shirin Neshat have incorporated her symbolism in their work to address contemporary social issues and challenge gender norms. Through their art, these artists invite viewers to reflect on their own identities, confront societal expectations, and celebrate the diverse facets of femininity. The visual representations of Inanna/Ishtar serve as a powerful language that transcends boundaries and contributes to the ongoing dialogue on feminism, gender equality, and the reclamation of women's power in art and society.

Exercise:

Analyze a selection of visual artworks inspired by Inanna/Ishtar. Identify recurring themes, symbols, and artistic techniques employed by the artists. Write a comparative analysis highlighting the different ways in which artists interpret and represent Inanna/Ishtar's essence and significance in their work.

Literature:

Inanna/Ishtar's mythology and archetypal qualities have had a profound influence on writers and authors across various genres. Contemporary literature frequently draws inspiration from her stories, utilizing her mythic narrative to explore themes of feminine empowerment, sexuality, and the quest for identity. By weaving elements of Inanna/Ishtar's mythology into their works, these writers engage with powerful symbols and narratives that resonate with readers on a deep level.

One prominent author who has been influenced by Inanna/Ishtar is Isabel Allende. In her novel "Daughter of Fortune," Allende features a protagonist named Eliza Sommers, who embodies the spirit of Inanna/Ishtar as she navigates societal expectations and embarks on a journey of self-discovery and personal liberation. Drawing on the themes of femininity, empowerment, and the search for identity associated with Inanna/Ishtar, Allende crafts a narrative that captures the essence of the goddess's archetype.

In "Daughter of Fortune," Eliza defies the limitations imposed on women during the 19th century and embarks on a quest for personal freedom. Throughout the novel, Eliza displays traits commonly associated with Inanna/Ishtar, such as assertiveness, sensuality, and a fierce desire for independence. Allende uses Inanna/Ishtar's mythic qualities to explore the complexities of Eliza's character and her journey of self-discovery, allowing readers to witness her transformation and embrace her power.

By incorporating Inanna/Ishtar's archetype into the narrative, Allende explores the themes of feminine empowerment and the struggle against societal norms. Through Eliza's story, readers are invited to reflect on their own identities, question societal expectations, and challenge the limitations placed on women. Inanna/Ishtar's influence permeates the novel, infusing it with a sense of empowerment and inspiring readers to embrace their own personal liberation.

Beyond Allende's work, numerous other writers and authors have been inspired by Inanna/Ishtar's mythology and archetypal qualities. They incorporate elements of her stories, symbols, and themes into their own narratives, whether in the form of direct references or subtle allusions. Through these literary explorations, writers aim to tap into the universal power and resonance of Inanna/Ishtar's archetype, engaging readers in thought-provoking narratives that challenge societal norms and celebrate feminine strength.

Inanna/Ishtar's mythology offers rich material for writers to delve into themes of personal growth, sexual liberation, and the search for meaning and empowerment. By drawing upon her stories and archetypal qualities, authors create narratives that resonate with readers and contribute to the ongoing conversation on feminine empowerment and the reclamation of women's power.

In summary, Inanna/Ishtar's mythology and archetypal qualities have left a significant imprint on contemporary literature. Writers, such as Isabel Allende, have drawn inspiration from her stories to explore themes of feminine empowerment, sexuality, and the search for identity. By incorporating elements of Inanna/Ishtar's archetype into their narratives, these authors invite readers to reflect on their own journeys of self-discovery, challenge societal expectations, and embrace their personal liberation. The influence of Inanna/Ishtar's mythology continues to enrich contemporary literature, offering readers narratives that celebrate feminine strength and inspire the reclamation of women's power.

Exercise:

Choose a contemporary novel or poem that references Inanna/Ishtar or draws inspiration from her mythology. Conduct a close reading of the text, paying attention to the ways in which the author incorporates Inanna/Ishtar's themes and symbolism. Write a critical analysis discussing the author's interpretation and the impact of Inanna/Ishtar's presence in the narrative.

Divine Dynamics

Film and Television:

Inanna/Ishtar's character and mythology have indeed made their way into the realm of film and television, where her archetypal qualities are utilized to enhance storytelling and delve into complex themes. One notable example is the film "The Fall," directed by Tarsem Singh, where the character of Alexandria embodies the resilience and transformation associated with Inanna/Ishtar as she embarks on a journey through a fantastical world of imagination.

"The Fall" tells the story of Alexandria, a young girl in a hospital who befriends a stuntman named Roy. As Roy entertains Alexandria with a fantastical tale, the boundaries between reality and imagination blur, and the audience is immersed in a visually stunning narrative that mirrors the transformative aspects of Inanna/Ishtar's mythology.

In the film, Alexandria's character embodies Inanna/Ishtar's archetypal qualities of resilience, strength, and personal growth. She confronts her own emotional struggles and the challenges of her circumstances, mirroring Inanna/Ishtar's descent into the Underworld. Alexandria's journey parallels Inanna/Ishtar's transformative quest, as both characters navigate obstacles and confront their inner demons, ultimately emerging stronger and more self-aware.

Just as Inanna/Ishtar experiences a metaphorical death and rebirth, Alexandria undergoes a transformative process in "The Fall." Through her interactions with Roy and her immersion in his imaginative storytelling, she learns to confront her fears, tap into her inner strength, and embrace her own power. The film's narrative structure and visual symbolism mirror Inanna/Ishtar's mythic journey, highlighting the potential for personal growth, self-discovery, and the triumph over adversity.

"The Fall" utilizes Inanna/Ishtar's mythology and archetypal qualities to explore complex themes such as the power of storytelling, the healing potential of imagination, and the resilience of the human spirit. By drawing on these mythic elements, the film creates a multi-layered narrative that invites viewers to reflect on their own journeys of transformation and embrace the power of their imaginations.

Moreover, "The Fall" showcases the visual spectacle and artistic creativity often associated with Inanna/Ishtar's mythology. The film's stunning cinematography and imaginative set designs pay homage to the mythic elements present in Inanna/Ishtar's stories. Through the visual aesthetics, the film captures the sense of wonder, magic, and otherworldliness that permeates Inanna/Ishtar's mythology, enriching the storytelling experience and emphasizing the timeless nature of her archetypal qualities.

In summary, Inanna/Ishtar's character and mythology have made a significant impact on the realm of film and television. In the film "The Fall," Alexandria embodies Inanna/Ishtar's transformative qualities as she navigates a fantastical world of imagination, confronting her fears and emerging stronger and more self-aware. The film draws on Inanna/Ishtar's archetypal qualities to explore themes of resilience, personal growth, and the power of storytelling. Through its narrative structure, visual aesthetics, and thematic depth, "The Fall" celebrates the enduring relevance and power of Inanna/Ishtar's mythology in contemporary storytelling.

Exercise:

Select a film or television series that features a character or storyline influenced by Inanna/Ishtar. Watch the chosen media and critically analyze the portrayal of Inanna/Ishtar's characteristics and the impact on the narrative. Consider the ways in which the inclusion of Inanna/Ishtar's elements enhances the storytelling or offers insights into the human experience.

Music and Performance:

Inanna/Ishtar's archetype has undeniably influenced the realm of music and performance, with contemporary musicians and performers drawing inspiration from her mythology and symbolism to infuse their songs, stage performances, and music videos with her powerful feminine energy. Renowned artists such as Beyoncé, Madonna, and Florence + the Machine have all embraced elements of Inanna/Ishtar's archetype, incorporating it into their artistic expression in unique and impactful ways.

One artist who has notably integrated Inanna/Ishtar's mythology into her work is Beyoncé. Known for her empowering and feminist themes, Beyoncé has used imagery and symbolism reminiscent of Inanna/Ishtar in her music videos and stage performances. In her visual album "Lemonade," for instance, she explores themes of love, betrayal, and resilience, drawing on the transformative aspects of Inanna/Ishtar's journey. The visual representation of Beyoncé as a powerful and sovereign figure resonates with Inanna/Ishtar's embodiment of feminine strength and empowerment.

Madonna, often celebrated as a trailblazer in challenging societal norms and pushing boundaries, has also incorporated Inanna/Ishtar's archetype into her music and performances. Madonna's music videos, such as "Express Yourself" and "Like a Prayer," feature powerful female imagery and themes of personal empowerment and liberation. These representations align with Inanna/Ishtar's archetypal qualities of assertiveness, independence, and the reclaiming of one's own power.

Divine Dynamics

Florence + the Machine, led by frontwoman Florence Welch, has drawn inspiration from Inanna/Ishtar's mythology and symbolism to infuse their music with depth and meaning. In their songs and stage performances, they often explore themes of love, desire, and personal transformation, which align with Inanna/Ishtar's association with sensuality and the pursuit of personal growth. Welch's ethereal and emotive vocals, coupled with the band's evocative instrumentation, create a sonic landscape that reflects the emotional and spiritual dimensions associated with Inanna/Ishtar's archetype.

These artists, among many others, have embraced Inanna/Ishtar's powerful feminine energy and incorporated it into their artistic expression, allowing them to explore themes of love, empowerment, personal growth, and liberation. By drawing on the symbolism and mythology surrounding Inanna/Ishtar, these musicians create music and performances that resonate with audiences, evoking a sense of connection to the ancient and timeless aspects of the divine feminine.

Furthermore, the integration of Inanna/Ishtar's archetype in music and performance serves as a means of challenging societal norms and redefining traditional gender roles. These artists utilize her symbolism to advocate for gender equality, empowerment, and the celebration of women's strength and individuality. Through their art, they contribute to a broader cultural conversation, highlighting the enduring relevance of Inanna/Ishtar's archetype in contemporary society.

In summary, Inanna/Ishtar's archetype has made a significant impact on the realm of music and performance. Artists such as Beyoncé, Madonna, and Florence + the Machine have embraced her mythology and symbolism, infusing their songs, stage performances, and music videos with her powerful feminine energy. Through their artistic expression, these musicians challenge societal norms, advocate for empowerment and gender equality, and create a connection to the timeless aspects of the divine feminine. Their work serves as a testament to the enduring influence of Inanna/Ishtar's archetype in inspiring and empowering artists across different genres and generations.

Exercise:

Select a music video or live performance that incorporates Inanna/Ishtar's symbolism. Watch the performance and analyze the ways in which the artist embodies Inanna/Ishtar's characteristics through movement, costume, and visual aesthetics. Write a reflective essay discussing the artist's interpretation and the impact of Inanna/Ishtar's presence on the performance.

Exploring Ancient Mesopotamian Mythology, Rivalries, and Spiritual Legacies

By examining the cultural impact and representations of Inanna/Ishtar in contemporary art, literature, and media, students will gain a deeper understanding of the enduring relevance and resonance of this ancient goddess. This analysis invites critical thinking about the ways in which artists, writers, filmmakers, and performers engage with her mythology, reinterpret her symbolism, and contribute to the ongoing dialogue surrounding femininity, power, and spirituality in the modern world.

Conclusion

Recapitulation of Key Points Discussed in the Chapter

In this chapter, we have delved into the multifaceted aspects of Inanna/Ishtar, the Mesopotamian goddess of love, war, fertility, and sovereignty. Through an exploration of her myths, symbols, and attributes, we have gained a deeper understanding of her significance in ancient Mesopotamian culture and her enduring relevance in modern contexts. Some of the key points discussed include:

Inanna/Ishtar's Mythology: We examined the rich narratives surrounding Inanna/Ishtar, such as her descent to the underworld and her sacred marriage to Dumuzid. These myths highlight her journey of death and rebirth, her power dynamics, and her connection to the cycles of nature.

Archetypal Qualities: Inanna/Ishtar embodies a range of archetypal qualities, including the warrior, the lover, and the sovereign. These aspects speak to her multifaceted nature and the complexities of human experience.

Symbolism and Iconography: We explored the symbols associated with Inanna/Ishtar, such as the eight-pointed star, the lion, and the sacred precincts. These symbols offer insights into her domains of influence and the cultural context in which she was revered.

Significance of Inanna/Ishtar as a Powerful and Complex Goddess in Mesopotamian Culture

Inanna/Ishtar holds a prominent position in the pantheon of Mesopotamian deities, and her significance cannot be understated. She was regarded as a central figure in religious and social life, embodying both desirable and challenging qualities. Her association with love, sexuality, and fertility emphasized the importance of these aspects in the societal fabric of ancient Mesopotamia. Simultaneously, her role as a warrior and a guardian of justice reflected the power dynamics and geopolitical realities of the time.

Divine Dynamics

Furthermore, Inanna/Ishtar's ability to traverse various realms, including the heavens, the underworld, and the earthly domain, exemplifies her role as a mediator between humans and the divine. Her influence extended to diverse spheres of life, including agriculture, governance, and the arts. As such, she was a focal point of worship and veneration, with temples and rituals dedicated to her throughout the region.

Chapter 5: Enki and Enlil: The Rivalry of the Divine Brothers

Significance of Enki and Enlil in Mesopotamian Mythology and Religion

In the rich tapestry of Mesopotamian mythology and religion, two prominent deities stand out: Enki and Enlil. As gods of immense power and influence, Enki and Enlil played pivotal roles in shaping the cosmology, society, and spiritual practices of ancient Mesopotamia. Understanding their significance is crucial to comprehending the complexities of this ancient civilization.

Enki, also known as Ea, was revered as the god of wisdom, intellect, and magic. He was associated with the primeval waters and was considered the creator of humanity. Enki was known for his benevolence and compassion towards humankind, often acting as a protector and teacher. His myths portray him as a deity who possesses immense knowledge and the ability to bring forth life and abundance.

On the other hand, Enlil held the position of the king of the gods and was associated with power, authority, and storms. As the ruler of the pantheon, Enlil embodied the forces of nature and commanded the winds, the heavens, and the earth. He was viewed as a stern and sometimes unpredictable deity, responsible for maintaining order and justice in the world. Enlil's cult was particularly influential in ancient Sumer, where he held a central role in the religious and political landscape.

Objectives and Structure of the Chapter

The primary objectives of this chapter are to explore the significance of Enki and Enlil in Mesopotamian mythology and religion, delve into their complex roles and characteristics, and analyze their impact on the culture and worldview of ancient Mesopotamians. By studying these deities, we gain valuable insights into the religious beliefs, social dynamics, and spiritual practices of this ancient civilization.

To achieve these objectives, the chapter will be structured as follows:

Origins and Myths: We will begin by examining the origin stories and mythological narratives associated with Enki and Enlil. By studying these myths, we will gain a deeper understanding of the cultural context in which these deities emerged and the roles they played in the pantheon.

Divine Dynamics

Roles and Attributes: In this section, we will explore the specific roles and attributes ascribed to Enki and Enlil. This will involve an analysis of their domains of influence, symbols, epithets, and associated myths. We will also discuss their relationships with other deities and the hierarchical structure of the pantheon.

Religious Practices and Rituals: The next part of the chapter will focus on the religious practices and rituals dedicated to Enki and Enlil. We will examine the temples, priesthoods, and ceremonies associated with these deities, shedding light on the religious customs and beliefs of the ancient Mesopotamians.

Preview of Key Topics and Themes

Throughout the chapter, we will explore various key topics and themes related to Enki and Enlil. These include:

Creation and Order: We will examine the role of Enki and Enlil in the creation of the world and the establishment of cosmic order. This will involve an analysis of their roles as divine architects and their contributions to the organization and functioning of the universe.

Divine Authority and Kingship: As prominent deities in the pantheon, Enki and Enlil had significant influence on the concepts of divine authority and kingship in ancient Mesopotamia. We will explore their relationship with earthly rulers and the divine mandate bestowed upon kings by these deities.

Interactions with Humanity: Both Enki and Enlil had direct interactions with humanity, shaping their destiny and offering guidance. We will analyze their involvement in human affairs, their relationships with mortals, and the ways in which they influenced the lives of individuals and communities.

Mythological Background

Enki and Enlil, two central deities in Mesopotamian mythology, have rich mythological backgrounds that provide insights into their roles, characteristics, and relationships within the pantheon. Exploring their mythological narratives allows us to understand the cultural context in which these deities were revered and the significance they held in the worldview of ancient Mesopotamians.

The origins of Enki and Enlil can be traced back to the earliest known Mesopotamian texts, such as the Sumerian myths and epic poems. These narratives depict a complex interplay of divine forces and the emergence of a hierarchical

Exploring Ancient Mesopotamian Mythology, Rivalries, and Spiritual Legacies

pantheon. Understanding the mythological background of Enki and Enlil involves examining their creation stories, their roles in the divine assembly, and their interactions with other deities.

Creation Stories:

The mythological background of Enki and Enlil encompasses the creation stories of the universe and humanity, presenting these deities as prominent figures in Mesopotamian mythology. One of the most significant myths featuring Enki and Enlil is the Enuma Elish, which provides insights into their roles and the establishment of cosmic order.

According to the Enuma Elish, the world begins in a state of primordial chaos, with the mingling of fresh and saltwater represented by the gods Apsu and Tiamat. Enki, associated with the primeval waters, emerges as a wise and knowledgeable deity. He possesses deep understanding and creative power, representing the force of intelligence and ingenuity within the divine pantheon.

Enlil, on the other hand, personifies the forces of the sky. He is depicted as a powerful and authoritative figure, embodying the attributes of leadership, strength, and cosmic order. Enlil's role is to establish and maintain the boundaries and divisions of the cosmic realms, ensuring harmony and balance within the universe.

In the Enuma Elish, conflict arises between Apsu and Tiamat and their offspring, who disturb the newly established order. Enlil plays a pivotal role in this conflict, leading the younger gods in their battle against the chaos. Enki, utilizing his wisdom and cunning, devises a plan to overcome the threat posed by Apsu and Tiamat, ultimately aiding Enlil in his quest to restore order.

These creation myths position Enki and Enlil as essential forces in the establishment of cosmic order. Enlil's authority over the earth and the heavens and Enki's mastery of the watery realms reflect the interconnectedness and interdependence of natural elements within Mesopotamian cosmology. Their complementary roles highlight the necessity of balance and harmony for the proper functioning of the cosmos.

Furthermore, the contrasting attributes of Enki and Enlil contribute to the multifaceted nature of the divine pantheon. Enki represents knowledge, creativity, and the transformative power of water, while Enlil embodies authority, leadership, and the cosmic forces of the sky. Together, they exemplify the diverse qualities and roles assigned to the gods in Mesopotamian mythology, showcasing the complexity of divine beings and their contributions to the world.

Divine Dynamics

Overall, the mythological background of Enki and Enlil begins with the creation stories of the universe and humanity, highlighting their emergence as prominent deities in the aftermath of primordial chaos. Through their roles in establishing order and the division of cosmic domains, Enki and Enlil exemplify the delicate balance and interdependence of natural elements in Mesopotamian cosmology. Their contrasting attributes and complementary roles contribute to the rich tapestry of divine beings in the ancient Mesopotamian pantheon.

Divine Assembly and Hierarchy:

Within the divine assembly of the Mesopotamian pantheon, Enki and Enlil hold significant positions that reflect their importance and roles in the divine hierarchy. While Enlil is regarded as the king of the gods, commanding authority and respect, Enki assumes the role of a mediator, advisor, and benefactor to both gods and humans.

Enlil, as the king of the gods, embodies the ultimate authority and power in the divine realm. He is responsible for maintaining order, justice, and cosmic balance. As the divine representative of the forces of the sky, Enlil governs the earth and heavens, establishing boundaries and overseeing the functions of the natural world. His authority extends to matters of governance, law, and divine judgment, and he is often depicted as the source of moral and ethical principles.

Enki, on the other hand, distinguishes himself through his wisdom, intellect, and magical abilities. He is revered as the god of wisdom and the keeper of the sacred knowledge of creation. Enki possesses the power to shape and transform the world, utilizing his vast understanding of the universe to bring about order and progress. He is known as a craftsman, an inventor, and a teacher, sharing his wisdom with both gods and humans.

Enki's role as a mediator and advisor is particularly notable within the divine assembly. He serves as a bridge between the gods, offering counsel and guidance in matters of divine governance and decision-making. Enki's role as a wise counselor is often called upon in times of conflict or crisis, as he possesses the ability to resolve disputes and bring about harmonious solutions.

Furthermore, Enki exhibits a unique concern for humanity. He is depicted as a benefactor to mortals, imparting knowledge, skills, and blessings upon them. Enki is associated with the development of civilization, technology, and arts, and is seen as a patron of human progress. His teachings and interventions often aim to improve the lives of humans and empower them with the tools necessary for their survival and advancement.

The contrasting roles of Enlil and Enki within the divine assembly highlight the diversity of responsibilities and attributes among the gods. Enlil embodies the authoritative and law-giving aspects of divinity, while Enki represents wisdom, creativity, and a more compassionate approach towards humanity. Together, their positions and roles contribute to the complex and multifaceted nature of the divine pantheon in Mesopotamian mythology.

In summary, Enlil and Enki hold prominent positions within the divine assembly, reflecting their importance and roles in the Mesopotamian pantheon. Enlil, as the king of the gods, upholds authority, justice, and cosmic order. Enki, as a mediator and advisor, possesses wisdom, intellect, and the power of creation. Enki's unique concern for humanity sets him apart as a benefactor and teacher, contributing to the welfare and progress of mortals. The contrasting attributes and roles of Enlil and Enki add depth and complexity to the divine hierarchy and the dynamics of the Mesopotamian pantheon.

Interactions with Other Deities:

The mythological background of Enki and Enlil in Mesopotamian mythology is filled with a rich tapestry of interactions and relationships with other deities. These interactions not only shape the narratives involving Enki and Enlil but also shed light on their personalities, motivations, and their positions within the divine pantheon.

Enlil is often portrayed as a stern and authoritative figure, enforcing divine laws and maintaining order in the cosmos. As the king of the gods, his decisions carry great weight and have significant consequences for both gods and humans. He is seen as a deity of justice, meting out punishments to those who transgress divine boundaries or challenge his authority. Enlil's strict adherence to the established cosmic order is meant to preserve stability and ensure the functioning of the universe. However, this uncompromising nature can also lead to conflicts and power struggles within the divine hierarchy. In certain myths, Enlil's decisions clash with the desires and aspirations of other deities, resulting in tensions and rivalries that have ripple effects throughout the pantheon.

In contrast, Enki is characterized by a more benevolent and compassionate nature. He is known for his wisdom, intellect, and magical abilities. Enki frequently forms alliances and collaborations with other deities, using his knowledge and skills to assist them in various endeavors. His role as a mediator and facilitator becomes apparent in these interactions. Enki acts as a bridge between gods, facilitating communication, resolving disputes, and offering guidance. His ability to find creative solutions and alternative paths often leads to positive outcomes and harmonious resolutions. Enki's compassionate nature and willingness to aid others set him apart as a more approachable and supportive figure within the pantheon.

Enki's relationships with other deities also reflect his multifaceted nature. He engages in cooperative ventures and shares his wisdom with gods and goddesses, fostering a sense of unity and collaboration within the divine realm. Enki's knowledge and magical abilities make him an invaluable resource for his fellow deities, and they often turn to him for advice and assistance.

The interactions and relationships between Enki, Enlil, and other deities in Mesopotamian mythology highlight the complex dynamics within the divine pantheon. Enlil's strict enforcement of cosmic order and his clashes with other gods demonstrate the challenges and tensions that arise in maintaining a stable hierarchy. In contrast, Enki's compassionate nature and willingness to collaborate exemplify the potential for cooperation and mutual support among the gods. These interactions not only shape the stories and myths involving Enki and Enlil but also contribute to the broader understanding of the Mesopotamian pantheon and its intricate relationships.

Examples, Problems, and Exercises:

Example: Read the Enuma Elish, the Babylonian creation myth, and identify the roles played by Enki and Enlil in the establishment of order and the division of cosmic domains. Discuss their characteristics and interactions with other deities.

Problem: Compare and contrast the attributes of Enki and Enlil based on their mythological background. Analyze how their roles and characteristics shape their influence within the pantheon.

Exercise: Write a short mythological narrative featuring Enki and Enlil, incorporating their respective roles, attributes, and interactions with other deities. Discuss the symbolic meanings and cultural significance embedded within the narrative.

Overview of the origins and roles of Enki and Enlil in Mesopotamian cosmology

In order to comprehend the significance of Enki and Enlil in Mesopotamian cosmology, it is crucial to explore their origins, roles, and positions within the pantheon of gods. These deities played pivotal roles in shaping the worldview and religious practices of the ancient Mesopotamians, and understanding their place

Exploring Ancient Mesopotamian Mythology, Rivalries, and Spiritual Legacies

within the divine hierarchy provides valuable insights into the complex cosmological framework of this civilization.

Origins and Parentage:

Enki and Enlil, two prominent deities in Mesopotamian mythology, trace their lineage back to the earliest creation myths of the region. According to Sumerian tradition, they are the offspring of An (also known as Anu), the sky god, and Ki (also known as Ninhursag), the earth goddess. An and Ki represent the fundamental forces of the natural world, and their union gives rise to the divine twins, Enki and Enlil.

Enki, whose name means "Lord of the Earth," is associated with the primeval waters and the underground freshwater streams. He embodies the life-giving and nourishing aspects of the earth. Enki's domain encompasses the depths of the earth, including the subterranean realms, rivers, and springs. He is often depicted as a wise and benevolent deity who possesses great knowledge and magical abilities. Enki is responsible for the creation and fertility of the earth, and he plays a crucial role in shaping and sustaining life.

Enlil, on the other hand, derives his name from "Lord of the Air" or "Lord of the Storm." He represents the forces of the sky, particularly the power and authority associated with storms, wind, and weather phenomena. Enlil's dominion extends over the atmosphere and the celestial realm, including the vast expanse of the sky. He is often depicted as a powerful and authoritative figure, responsible for maintaining cosmic order and enforcing divine laws. Enlil's role is closely tied to the concepts of justice, kingship, and the preservation of societal harmony.

Enki and Enlil's distinct domains within the cosmic order reflect the ancient Mesopotamians' understanding of the natural world and its inherent balance. Enki's association with the earth and freshwater sources symbolizes the life-giving and nurturing qualities necessary for fertility and growth. Enlil's association with the sky and storms represents the forces that can both nourish and challenge life, as well as enforce order and divine will. The complementary roles of Enki and Enlil highlight the interconnectedness and interdependence of the sky, earth, and human existence.

As prominent deities, Enki and Enlil played pivotal roles in the establishment of the cosmic order and the division of realms. Enlil's authority extended over the earth and the heavens, while Enki's power resided in the watery realms. Their distinct domains and responsibilities reflect the intricate balance of natural elements and the interplay between different forces in the ancient Mesopotamian cosmology.

Divine Dynamics

The lineage of Enki and Enlil, tracing back to An and Ki, establishes their significance in the pantheon and underscores their connection to the primordial forces that shape the universe. Their roles as powerful deities governing distinct realms and embodying the forces of nature make them central figures in Mesopotamian mythology and cosmogony.

Divine Attributes and Roles:

Enki, also known as Ea in later Babylonian mythology, is a significant deity associated with the primeval waters and the depths of the earth. As the god of wisdom, knowledge, and magic, Enki embodies a multitude of divine attributes and is revered for his creative and benevolent nature. He is often depicted as a wise and compassionate deity who uses his wisdom and magical abilities for the betterment of humanity.

One of Enki's notable roles is his involvement in the creation of humanity. According to myth, Enki played a crucial part in fashioning humans out of clay, imbuing them with the breath of life. He is seen as the patron of arts, crafts, and technology, bestowing upon humans the gifts of civilization and cultural advancements. Enki's association with knowledge and innovation makes him a revered figure in Mesopotamian culture, and he is often invoked in rituals and ceremonies related to intellectual pursuits, creativity, and problem-solving.

Enki's benevolence extends to his role as a protector of humankind. In various myths, he emerges as a champion of justice, intervening to aid the vulnerable and oppressed. Enki is seen as a defender of the weak and a giver of advice and assistance to those in need. His role as a patron deity of individuals and communities is celebrated in rituals and offerings seeking his guidance and protection.

In contrast to Enki, Enlil embodies the forces of the sky and the atmosphere. As the king of the gods and the foremost deity in the pantheon, Enlil wields immense power and authority. He is responsible for maintaining cosmic order and enforcing divine laws. Enlil's dominion extends over natural phenomena such as storms, winds, and agriculture, reflecting his control over the forces that impact human life and the earth's fertility.

Enlil's decisions and actions have far-reaching consequences for both gods and mortals. He is depicted as a stern and sometimes capricious deity who ensures the preservation of cosmic balance through his enforcement of laws and his role as an arbiter of fate. Enlil's position as the ultimate authority figure in the pantheon underscores his role as a dispenser of justice, meting out rewards and punishments according to the deeds of individuals and societies.

Exploring Ancient Mesopotamian Mythology, Rivalries, and Spiritual Legacies

The contrast between Enki and Enlil highlights different aspects of the divine powers in Mesopotamian mythology. Enki's association with the earth and primeval waters signifies his connection to the source of life and his role as a creative and benevolent force. In contrast, Enlil's dominion over the sky and the atmosphere symbolizes his power and authority in maintaining cosmic order and enforcing divine will. Together, their complementary roles reflect the intricacies and interdependencies of the natural and divine forces in the ancient Mesopotamian worldview.

Positions within the Pantheon:

Within the intricate hierarchy of the Mesopotamian pantheon, Enki and Enlil occupy distinct positions that reflect their unique attributes and responsibilities. Enlil, known as the king of the gods, holds the highest rank among the deities and serves as the head of the divine assembly. His authority is unquestioned, and his commands are to be followed by both gods and mortals alike.

Enlil's primary role is to maintain the cosmic balance and uphold the order of the universe. He ensures that the natural forces and phenomena, such as storms, winds, and agriculture, function harmoniously and according to divine laws. As the enforcer of justice, he punishes wrongdoing and rewards righteous actions. Enlil's decisions and actions shape the destinies of gods and humans, and his divine will governs the course of events.

In contrast, while Enki does not hold the same elevated position as Enlil, he is highly revered for his wisdom, creativity, and compassion. Enki's role as a mediator between gods and humans sets him apart. He acts as an advocate for mortals, intervening on their behalf and offering them assistance and protection. Enki is known for his empathy and understanding of human struggles, and he often uses his knowledge and wisdom to guide and support humanity.

Enki's influence extends beyond his interactions with humans. He is regarded as the patron of various arts, sciences, and crafts that contribute to human civilization. Enki bestows upon humanity the gifts of knowledge, innovation, and intellectual pursuits. He is associated with architecture, engineering, agriculture, writing, and many other domains that enhance the quality of human life. As the master of magic and incantations, Enki is also revered as a healer and protector against malevolent forces.

Enki's compassionate nature and willingness to share his knowledge make him a beloved figure among both gods and mortals. His role as a mentor and teacher to other deities underscores his significance in the divine realm. Enki's creative abilities and inventiveness are celebrated, and he is often invoked in rituals and ceremonies that seek inspiration, guidance, and blessings in various aspects of human endeavors.

The distinct positions of Enki and Enlil within the Mesopotamian pantheon illustrate the multifaceted nature of divine power and the complementary roles played by different deities. Enlil's authority as the king of the gods ensures the maintenance of cosmic order, while Enki's wisdom and compassion offer guidance and support to both gods and humans. Together, they embody the intricate relationship between the divine and mortal realms, shaping the beliefs, rituals, and daily lives of the ancient Mesopotamian civilization.

Examples, Problems, and Exercises:

Example: Compare and contrast the roles of Enki and Enlil in Mesopotamian cosmology. Discuss how their divine attributes and positions within the pantheon shape their interactions with other gods and their roles in human affairs.

Problem: Investigate the mythology and rituals associated with Enki and Enlil. Analyze the significance of their parentage and divine attributes in the context of Mesopotamian cosmology. Discuss how these characteristics reflect the Mesopotamian worldview.

Exercise: Create a chart illustrating the hierarchy of the Mesopotamian pantheon and place Enki and Enlil within it, highlighting their respective roles and attributes. Discuss the implications of their positions in relation to other deities.

By delving into the origins, roles, and positions of Enki and Enlil within Mesopotamian cosmology, we gain a deeper understanding of the complex interplay between gods and humans, as well as the profound influence of these deities on ancient Mesopotamian culture and religious practices.

Understanding their positions within the pantheon of Mesopotamian gods

To comprehend the significance of Enki and Enlil in the rich tapestry of Mesopotamian mythology and religion, it is essential to explore their positions within the broader pantheon of gods. The Mesopotamian pantheon comprised a vast array of deities, each with their own unique roles, attributes, and spheres of influence. By examining the positions held by Enki and Enlil within this divine hierarchy, we can gain valuable insights into their standing among their divine peers and the significance attributed to them by the ancient Mesopotamians.

Exploring Ancient Mesopotamian Mythology, Rivalries, and Spiritual Legacies

Enki's Position:

Enki's prominent position within the Mesopotamian pantheon is attributed to his association with wisdom, creativity, and his dedication to the welfare of humanity. Although he does not hold the highest rank like Enlil, his significance is widely recognized, and he is considered one of the most important deities.

Enki's role as a mediator between the gods and mortals sets him apart. He acts as a bridge between the divine realm and humanity, advocating for mortals and intervening on their behalf. Enki's compassion and empathy towards humans make him a beloved and approachable deity. He is often depicted as approachable and friendly, and his interactions with mortals are marked by his willingness to assist and guide them.

Enki's association with wisdom is another aspect that contributes to his revered status. He is often portrayed as the source of knowledge and understanding, possessing insights into the secrets of the universe and the workings of the natural world. Enki's wisdom encompasses various domains, including magic, sciences, and practical knowledge necessary for human advancement. He is known for his intellectual curiosity and inventiveness, constantly seeking new ways to improve the lives of both gods and humans.

One of Enki's notable domains is that of fresh water. He is closely associated with the Apsu, the primordial freshwater ocean that resides beneath the earth. This connection with water symbolizes Enki's role in sustaining agricultural fertility and ensuring the abundance of the land. Enki's provision of water, essential for irrigation and cultivation, aligns him with the life-giving and nourishing aspects of nature.

Enki's dedication to humanity is exemplified in the myth of Atrahasis. In this myth, Enki assists in the creation of humans, shaping them from clay and imbuing them with the breath of life. He becomes their protector and guardian, aiding them during times of crisis and providing guidance on how to survive natural disasters and calamities. Enki's actions in the myth highlight his concern for the well-being of humanity and his desire to alleviate their suffering.

Enki's magical abilities further enhance his role as a benefactor to humanity. He is believed to possess profound knowledge of incantations and spells, enabling him to heal the sick, ward off evil, and protect individuals from harm. Enki's mastery of magic allows him to bring about positive change and transform challenging circumstances into favorable outcomes.

Divine Dynamics

In Mesopotamian society, Enki was honored through various rituals and ceremonies. These included offerings and prayers to seek his guidance and blessings in matters of fertility, agriculture, and overall well-being. Enki's temples were centers of worship and knowledge, where scholars and priests sought his wisdom and engaged in rituals to honor his divine presence.

Overall, Enki's position within the Mesopotamian pantheon as a wise and compassionate deity, mediator between gods and mortals, and provider for humanity underscores his significance. His association with fresh water, wisdom, and magical abilities further highlights his essential role in the prosperity and welfare of both the divine realm and human civilization.

Enlil's Position:

Enlil, the son of An and Ki, assumes the highest rank within the Mesopotamian pantheon. As the foremost deity, he embodies supreme authority and is often referred to as the "King of the Gods." Enlil's position grants him great power and responsibility in maintaining order and ensuring the proper functioning of the cosmos.

Enlil's domain encompasses the forces of nature, particularly the sky and the atmosphere. He governs natural phenomena such as storms, winds, and weather patterns, symbolizing his control over the elements that directly impact human life and agricultural productivity. As the ultimate judge and dispenser of justice, Enlil is entrusted with upholding divine laws and maintaining the balance of the universe.

Interactions with Other Deities:

Enki and Enlil's positions within the pantheon also influence their interactions with other gods. Enlil's authority as the king of the gods places him in a leadership role, overseeing the divine assembly and arbitrating conflicts among the deities. He possesses the power to grant or withhold favor, shaping the destinies of both gods and humans.

Enki, on the other hand, often assumes a more benevolent and nurturing role, fostering positive relationships with other deities. As the god of wisdom and magic, he serves as a mentor and advisor to his divine counterparts, sharing his knowledge and expertise. Enki's interactions with other gods are characterized by cooperation and collaboration, as seen in his role in the divine council and his involvement in important mythological narratives.

Exploring Ancient Mesopotamian Mythology, Rivalries, and Spiritual Legacies

Examples, Problems, and Exercises:

Example: Compare and contrast the positions of Enki and Enlil within the Mesopotamian pantheon. Discuss the attributes and responsibilities associated with each deity and how their positions influence their interactions with other gods.

Problem: Investigate the mythology surrounding Enki and Enlil and analyze their roles in specific myths or rituals. Discuss how their positions within the pantheon contribute to the themes and narratives of these stories.

Exercise: Create a hierarchical chart representing the Mesopotamian pantheon and position Enki and Enlil within it. Include other key gods and goddesses and their respective domains. Write a short paragraph explaining the significance of each deity and their relationships within the divine hierarchy.

By delving into the positions held by Enki and Enlil within the pantheon of Mesopotamian gods, we gain a deeper appreciation for their roles, influence, and relationships with other deities. This understanding enhances our comprehension of the broader religious and mythological framework in which they operate, providing valuable insights into the intricate tapestry of ancient Mesopotamian belief systems.

Enki: God of Wisdom, Magic, and Water

In the pantheon of Mesopotamian deities, Enki occupies a significant position as the god of wisdom, magic, and water. His multifaceted nature and diverse attributes make him a complex and revered figure in ancient Mesopotamian mythology and religion. This section explores the various aspects of Enki's divine character, including his association with wisdom, his mastery of magic, and his role as the god of water.

Wisdom:

Enki's reputation as the god of wisdom in Mesopotamian mythology is rooted in his embodiment of intellectual acuity, knowledge, and insight. His wisdom encompasses a wide range of domains, making him a versatile deity who offers guidance and counsel in various aspects of life.

Enki's wisdom extends to the arts and crafts, as he is credited with introducing various techniques and innovations to humanity. He is associated with the development of pottery, metalworking, and other crafts that contribute to human civilization. Enki's knowledge in these areas promotes human progress and the advancement of cultural practices.

In matters of agriculture, Enki's wisdom plays a crucial role. He is regarded as a patron of fertility and irrigation, imparting knowledge on how to cultivate the land and ensure bountiful harvests. Enki's expertise in agricultural practices ensures the well-being and sustenance of communities, highlighting his role as a benefactor to humanity.

Enki's wisdom also extends to matters of governance and societal order. He is considered a wise lawgiver, providing guidance on the establishment of just systems and the maintenance of societal harmony. Enki's wisdom in governance ensures equitable distribution of resources and the preservation of social order, contributing to the stability of human communities.

One of the most renowned myths showcasing Enki's wisdom is the "Atra-Hasis" epic. In this narrative, Enki plays a crucial role in aiding humanity during the great flood. Enki foresees the impending disaster and communicates with a mortal named Atra-Hasis, instructing him on how to build a large boat to ensure the survival of humanity and various animal species. Enki's wisdom in providing detailed instructions and insight into the impending catastrophe allows humanity to overcome the challenges presented by the flood and continue their existence.

Enki's ability to foresee future events and devise strategies to overcome challenges showcases his profound wisdom and foresight. His role in the "Atra-Hasis" epic highlights his commitment to the well-being and preservation of humanity, as well as his ability to navigate complex situations with his divine knowledge.

In Mesopotamian society, Enki's wisdom was revered and sought after. Temples dedicated to Enki served as centers of learning and knowledge, attracting scholars, scribes, and priests who sought his wisdom and insight. Rituals and ceremonies were performed to honor Enki and seek his guidance in matters of governance, agriculture, and personal matters.

Overall, Enki's reputation as the god of wisdom in Mesopotamian mythology is a testament to his intellectual acuity and versatile knowledge. His wisdom extends to various domains, including the arts, crafts, agriculture, and governance, making him a revered deity who provides guidance and counsel to both gods and humans. The "Atra-Hasis" epic stands as a significant testament to Enki's wisdom and his pivotal role in ensuring the survival and well-being of humanity in the face of adversity.

Exploring Ancient Mesopotamian Mythology, Rivalries, and Spiritual Legacies

Magic:

Enki's mastery of magic and sorcery is a significant aspect of his divine nature in Mesopotamian mythology. His profound understanding of supernatural forces and the manipulation of arcane knowledge sets him apart as a pivotal figure in the realm of magic and ritual practices.

Enki's expertise in magic encompasses a wide range of applications, from healing and fertility to protection and the establishment of order. Through his magical abilities, Enki is believed to have the power to influence the natural and supernatural realms, bringing about positive outcomes and ensuring the well-being of both gods and humans.

In the myth of "Enki and the World Order," Enki's magical prowess is prominently showcased. In this narrative, Enki plays a central role in establishing the natural and social order of the cosmos. Through his intricate understanding of magic, Enki assigns specific roles and responsibilities to each deity, defining their domains and functions within the divine assembly. He bestows blessings upon humanity, ensuring their prosperity and protection. Enki's magical interventions serve to maintain harmony and balance, bringing order to the universe.

Enki's magical abilities are not limited to cosmic matters but also extend to individual and communal well-being. He is revered as a source of healing, capable of curing ailments and restoring vitality. Rituals dedicated to Enki often involve the invocation of his magical powers to promote physical and spiritual healing, providing relief to those in need.

Enki's association with fertility is another aspect of his magical influence. As a god of the waters, Enki's magical abilities are believed to enhance agricultural fertility, ensuring abundant harvests and the growth of vegetation. His interventions in matters of fertility extend to human reproduction, as he is often invoked to assist with conception and childbirth.

Moreover, Enki's magical expertise is called upon for protection against malevolent forces and misfortunes. His spells and enchantments are believed to ward off evil spirits, avert calamities, and safeguard individuals and communities from harm. The rituals and incantations dedicated to Enki often involve invoking his magical powers for protective purposes.

In Mesopotamian society, Enki's role as a master of magic and sorcery was highly respected and sought after. Temples dedicated to Enki served as centers for magical rituals and practices, attracting practitioners and individuals seeking his magical assistance. Priests and sorcerers sought to acquire Enki's knowledge and techniques to enhance their own magical abilities and serve the community.

Enki's association with magic and sorcery reflects the belief in the power of supernatural forces and the efficacy of human interaction with these forces through ritual and incantation. His magical interventions were seen as vital in maintaining balance, promoting well-being, and protecting against malevolent influences. Enki's reputation as a master of magic establishes him as a revered figure in Mesopotamian mythology, one whose abilities and knowledge were believed to bring about positive transformations and ensure the flourishing of both the natural and human realms.

Water:

Enki's association with water is indeed a crucial aspect of his divine persona in Mesopotamian mythology. As the god of water, particularly fresh water, Enki's dominion extends over rivers, springs, and subterranean waters. Water, as a symbol of life, fertility, and sustenance, holds great significance in ancient Mesopotamian culture, and Enki's connection to this vital element aligns him with the fundamental cycles of nature and the well-being of the land and its inhabitants.

Enki's role as the god of water is exemplified in the myth of "Enki and the Creation of Man." According to this narrative, Enki plays a central and pivotal role in the formation of humanity. In the myth, Enki shapes human beings from clay, mirroring the way in which bricks were made from mud in ancient Mesopotamia. This act of creation is closely associated with water, as the clay used in the process is molded and shaped with the moistening properties of water. Furthermore, Enki breathes the "breath of life" into the clay, symbolizing the infusion of vital energy that sustains and animates human existence. This act underscores Enki's role as a nurturer and provider, ensuring the continued existence and prosperity of humanity.

Enki's association with water extends beyond the creation of humans. As the god of fresh water, he is believed to have a direct influence on the fertility of the land and the success of agricultural endeavors. In ancient Mesopotamia, where water was essential for irrigation and crop cultivation, Enki's benevolence was sought to ensure bountiful harvests and the abundance of resources. His ability to regulate and control water sources, including rivers and springs, made him a significant figure in the agricultural cycles and the sustenance of civilization.

Moreover, Enki's association with water also encompasses his role as a protector and provider of the natural world. Water, as a life-giving and life-sustaining element, was essential for the well-being of plants, animals, and ecosystems. Enki's domain over water allowed him to ensure the proper flow and distribution of water, preventing floods or droughts that could disrupt the balance of nature. In this regard, Enki was revered as a guardian deity, responsible for maintaining the harmony and equilibrium of the environment.

Enki's connection to water also extends to its symbolic meanings. Water is often associated with purification, renewal, and the cleansing of impurities. In ancient Mesopotamian rituals and religious practices, water played a significant role in purification ceremonies, where individuals would cleanse themselves before engaging in sacred activities. Enki's association with water made him a central figure in these rituals, as his blessings and powers were sought to purify and sanctify individuals and spaces.

Overall, Enki's association with water represents his nurturing and life-giving qualities. As the god of water, he is not only responsible for the physical sustenance of life but also embodies the spiritual and metaphysical aspects associated with water. Enki's dominion over water underscores his role as a provider, protector, and benevolent deity, ensuring the well-being and continuity of both humans and the natural world.

Examples, Problems, and Exercises:

Example: Compare and contrast Enki's attributes as the god of wisdom, magic, and water. Discuss the significance of these domains and how they intersect in his divine character.

Problem: Research and analyze a specific myth or ritual involving Enki's wisdom or magical abilities. Explain how these aspects of his character contribute to the overall narrative or purpose of the myth or ritual.

Exercise: Imagine you are an ancient Mesopotamian scribe tasked with writing a hymn praising Enki. Compose a stanza that captures his role as the god of wisdom, magic, and water, and reflects the reverence and awe associated with his divine attributes.

By exploring Enki's multifaceted nature as the god of wisdom, magic, and water, we gain a deeper understanding of his importance in Mesopotamian culture. His wisdom, magical prowess, and connection to water permeate various aspects of ancient Mesopotamian life, leaving a lasting impact on religious practices, mythology, and societal beliefs.

Divine Dynamics

Exploration of Enki's Role as the God of Wisdom, Knowledge, and Craftsmanship

Enki, a prominent deity in Mesopotamian mythology, assumes various roles that underscore his significance within the pantheon. One crucial aspect of Enki's divine character is his association with wisdom, knowledge, and craftsmanship. This section delves into the multifaceted nature of Enki's role as the god of wisdom and highlights his mastery of knowledge and craftsmanship.

Wisdom and Knowledge:

Enki's domain over wisdom in Mesopotamian mythology encompasses intellectual acuity, profound understanding, and the capacity for discernment. As the god of wisdom, he is regarded as the source of knowledge and insight, offering guidance, counsel, and solutions to both gods and humans alike. Enki's wisdom is not confined to a specific area but extends across various domains, including governance, administration, arts, sciences, and craftsmanship.

One prominent myth that showcases Enki's wisdom is the "Enuma Elish," the Babylonian creation epic. In this narrative, Enki plays a pivotal role in the organization and structuring of the cosmos. The Enuma Elish describes a primordial chaos from which the gods emerge. Enki, utilizing his exceptional knowledge and wisdom, takes on the task of establishing order and harmony in the newly formed world.

Enki's actions in the Enuma Elish demonstrate his profound understanding of the universe and his ability to navigate its complexities. He is responsible for separating heaven from earth, assigning distinct roles to various deities, and establishing the order of celestial bodies. Enki's wisdom allows him to comprehend the interplay of cosmic forces and to create a harmonious framework for the functioning of the universe.

Beyond his role in cosmic organization, Enki's wisdom extends to governance and administration. He is often portrayed as an advisor to the divine assembly and a mediator in conflicts among the gods. Enki's ability to provide sagacious counsel and resolve disputes contributes to the overall stability and well-being of the divine realm. His wisdom and discernment make him a trusted figure among the gods, and his insights are sought after in matters of governance and decision-making.

Enki's wisdom also encompasses the arts, sciences, and craftsmanship. He is considered the patron of various crafts and skills, including architecture, metalworking, and pottery. Enki's knowledge and mastery in these fields enable him to share innovative techniques and advance human civilization. His contributions to the arts and sciences reflect his deep understanding of the world and his desire to enhance the quality of human life.

Furthermore, Enki's wisdom is often associated with his role as a healer. In Mesopotamian culture, he is revered as a god who possesses the knowledge of medicinal herbs, rituals, and incantations. Enki's wisdom in the realm of healing allows him to alleviate ailments, provide remedies, and restore health to those in need. His wisdom in this context highlights his compassion and concern for the well-being of humanity.

In summary, Enki's domain over wisdom in Mesopotamian mythology encompasses intellectual acuity, profound understanding, and the capacity for discernment. His role as the god of wisdom allows him to offer guidance, counsel, and insight across various domains, including governance, administration, arts, sciences, and craftsmanship. Enki's wisdom is showcased in myths such as the Enuma Elish, where his profound understanding of the cosmos and his ability to establish order demonstrate his exceptional knowledge. Additionally, his wisdom extends to governance, administration, and the arts, where he provides sagacious counsel and contributes to the advancement of human civilization.

Craftsmanship:

Enki's association with craftsmanship in Mesopotamian mythology showcases his diverse talents and skills as a divine creator and inventor. As the god of creation and invention, Enki is revered for his ability to craft and shape both natural and artificial objects, demonstrating his mastery in various crafts, including architecture, metalworking, agriculture, and irrigation.

Enki's expertise in craftsmanship is exemplified in the myth of "Enki and the Making of Humans." According to this narrative, Enki plays a central role in the creation of humanity. He fashions human beings from clay, carefully sculpting their forms and imbuing them with life. This act of creation highlights Enki's artistic prowess and attention to detail as a divine craftsman.

In the myth, Enki's craftsmanship goes beyond mere physical creation. He bestows upon humans qualities and attributes that make them unique and distinct from other creatures. These qualities include intelligence, creativity, and the ability to communicate, which reflect Enki's role as the god of wisdom and his desire to empower humanity.

Enki's craftsmanship is not limited to the creation of human beings alone. He is also credited with numerous inventions and technological advancements that benefit both gods and mortals. For example, Enki is associated with the development of irrigation systems, which revolutionized agriculture and allowed for the cultivation of fertile lands. His expertise in this area ensured the prosperity and abundance of crops, contributing to the well-being and sustenance of human civilization.

Furthermore, Enki's craftsmanship extends to architecture and construction. He is credited with the creation of magnificent temples and sacred spaces, reflecting his ability to design and construct impressive structures. These architectural achievements served as centers of worship and cultural exchange, embodying Enki's role as a patron of the arts and a facilitator of human progress.

Enki's association with craftsmanship also extends to metalworking, where he is credited with the discovery and refinement of various metals and alloys. His mastery in this craft allowed for the creation of intricate jewelry, tools, and weapons, showcasing his skills as a skilled metalworker. The advancement of metalworking techniques attributed to Enki's influence contributed to the development of sophisticated tools and weaponry, further enhancing human civilization.

Overall, Enki's association with craftsmanship in Mesopotamian mythology highlights his diverse talents and skills as a divine creator and inventor. His expertise encompasses various crafts, including architecture, metalworking, agriculture, and irrigation. The myth of "Enki and the Making of Humans" exemplifies his artistic prowess and attention to detail as a divine craftsman. Through his craftsmanship, Enki empowers humanity, fosters technological advancements, and contributes to the progress and prosperity of civilization.

Analysis of Enki's Association with Magic and His Role as a Protector of Humanity

In Mesopotamian mythology, Enki is not only renowned for his wisdom and craftsmanship but is also closely associated with magic. His mastery of supernatural forces and arcane knowledge allows him to wield magic for the benefit of both gods and humans. Enki's role as a protector and benefactor of humanity is intertwined with his magical abilities, as he employs his powers to safeguard and assist human beings.

Enki's association with magic stems from his deep understanding of the natural and supernatural realms. He possesses knowledge of spells, incantations, and rituals that enable him to manipulate cosmic forces and influence the outcomes of various events. Through his magical prowess, Enki can bring about positive outcomes, such as healing, fertility, and protection.

As a protector of humanity, Enki utilizes his magical abilities to aid humans during times of crisis and adversity. He is often depicted as a compassionate and benevolent deity who intervenes on behalf of mortals. In the myth of "Atra-Hasis," when the gods decide to unleash a devastating flood to wipe out humanity, Enki takes pity on the people and reveals the impending disaster to a righteous man named Atra-Hasis. He provides detailed instructions on how to build a boat that will ensure their survival, effectively using his magic to protect humanity from destruction.

Enki's magical prowess also extends to the realm of healing. He is revered as a god who possesses the power to cure diseases and alleviate suffering. In various myths and hymns, Enki is invoked for healing purposes, and rituals are performed to seek his divine intervention. His association with magic and healing reflects his concern for the well-being of humanity and his desire to alleviate their physical and emotional afflictions.

Furthermore, Enki's magical abilities are often utilized to foster fertility and ensure the prosperity of human endeavors. As the god of water, he has the power to control and regulate the flow of rivers and springs, thereby ensuring the fertility of the land for agricultural purposes. Enki's role as a provider of life-sustaining water aligns with his magical influence over fertility, both in the natural world and in human reproduction.

Enki's connection to magic not only serves practical purposes but also underscores his role as a divine mediator and facilitator. His magical abilities allow him to bridge the gap between gods and humans, acting as an intermediary and conveying human concerns to the divine realm. This aspect of Enki's character highlights his compassionate nature and his willingness to assist and support humanity in their interactions with the divine.

Overall, Enki's association with magic is a significant aspect of his divine persona. His mastery of supernatural forces and his ability to wield magic for the benefit of humanity exemplify his role as a protector and benefactor. Enki's magical interventions ensure the well-being, survival, and progress of humanity, making him a revered and cherished figure in Mesopotamian mythology.

Magic:

Enki's association with magic in Mesopotamian mythology is deeply rooted in his command over supernatural forces and his possession of arcane knowledge. He is revered as a powerful sorcerer and the patron deity of magic, with his magical abilities playing a significant role in shaping the natural and supernatural realms.

Enki's mastery of magic enables him to manipulate cosmic forces and influence the outcomes of various events. Through his command over supernatural powers, he brings about desired outcomes, such as healing, fertility, and protection. His magical abilities are not only a demonstration of his divine status but also a means to assist and benefit both gods and humans.

One prominent example showcasing Enki's magical prowess is the myth of "Enki and Ninhursag." In this narrative, Enki utilizes his magical skills to cure various ailments afflicting gods and humans, demonstrating his role as a skilled healer. When Ninhursag, the mother goddess, creates different organs and deities to cure Enki from his own ailments, he responds by creating divine beings associated with specific body parts. However, each creation fails to alleviate Enki's pain until Ninhursag creates a goddess called Ninti, whose name means "Lady of Life." Enki then uses his magical powers to bless Ninti, endowing her with the ability to heal and bring life. This myth highlights Enki's exceptional command over magic and his ability to restore health and harmony through his magical interventions.

Enki's magical abilities extend beyond healing. As the god of water, he has dominion over the life-giving and purifying properties of this element. Enki's magical control over water allows him to ensure fertility and prosperity in agricultural pursuits, as well as regulate the flow of rivers and springs. His ability to manipulate water contributes to the well-being of the land and its inhabitants, showcasing his role as a bringer of abundance and a protector of life.

Moreover, Enki's magical skills also serve to protect and safeguard both gods and humans. He possesses the power to ward off evil spirits, counteract malevolent forces, and provide spiritual and physical protection. Enki's ability to ward off negative energies and offer protection reinforces his role as a guardian and benefactor to those who seek his aid.

Enki's association with magic not only reflects his powerful command over supernatural forces but also highlights his role as a source of wisdom and knowledge. His possession of arcane knowledge allows him to access and manipulate the mysteries of the universe, making him a revered figure among both gods and humans. Enki's ability to harness magic and use it for benevolent purposes demonstrates his profound understanding of the natural and supernatural realms and his willingness to aid and guide those who seek his assistance.

Overall, Enki's association with magic is a vital aspect of his divine persona. His command over supernatural forces, his possession of arcane knowledge, and his ability to bring about desired outcomes through his magical interventions solidify his role as a powerful sorcerer, a skilled healer, and a patron of magic. Enki's magical abilities not only benefit the well-being and prosperity of gods and humans but also showcase his role as a benevolent deity who wields his powers for the greater good.

Protector of Humanity:

Enki's role as a protector and advocate for humanity is a significant aspect of his divine persona in Mesopotamian mythology. He displays compassion, concern, and an active involvement in ensuring the well-being and survival of humans. Enki's protective nature is evident through his interventions on behalf of humanity, providing guidance, assistance, and warnings in times of crisis.

One prominent example that highlights Enki's role as a protector is the myth of "Enki and the Deluge." In this narrative, the gods become displeased with the noise and overpopulation caused by humans. They decide to unleash a catastrophic flood to wipe out humanity and restore tranquility to the world. However, Enki, recognizing the imminent danger and driven by his compassion for humanity, decides to intervene.

Enki approaches a pious mortal named Atrahasis, who has caught his attention. He communicates with Atrahasis through a series of dreams and visions, warning him about the impending flood and instructing him on how to save himself, his family, and various living creatures. Enki provides detailed instructions for building a large boat or ark, advising Atrahasis to gather various animals and supplies to ensure their survival.

Enki's actions in warning Atrahasis and providing him with the knowledge and means to build the ark demonstrate his role as a protector and advocate for humanity. His intervention reflects his deep concern for the well-being and preservation of the human race, as he goes against the collective decision of the gods to bring about their destruction.

By assisting Atrahasis, Enki ensures that a remnant of humanity survives the catastrophic flood, allowing them to continue their existence and propagate the Earth once the waters recede. His guidance and protection during this crisis demonstrate his commitment to the preservation of humanity and his willingness to go against the wishes of his fellow gods to safeguard their future.

Divine Dynamics

Enki's protective nature is not limited to the myth of the deluge. Throughout Mesopotamian mythology, he is portrayed as a deity who offers guidance and assistance to humans in various situations. He shares divine knowledge, wisdom, and skills with humanity, contributing to their progress and well-being.

Enki's protective role is intertwined with his position as a patron of arts, crafts, sciences, and agriculture. His provision of knowledge and assistance in these domains enables humans to thrive and prosper. Enki's teachings and blessings empower individuals to develop their skills, cultivate the land, create inventions, and establish civilizations. In this way, he serves as a protector by enabling human advancement and ensuring their success in various endeavors.

Overall, Enki's role as a protector and advocate for humanity underscores his compassion, concern, and active involvement in their well-being. His interventions, such as warning Atrahasis of the flood and providing guidance, demonstrate his commitment to preserving humanity and his willingness to challenge the decisions of his fellow gods. Enki's protective nature, coupled with his provision of knowledge and assistance, solidifies his role as a benefactor and guardian of humanity in Mesopotamian mythology.

Understanding the Symbolism and Significance of Enki's Domain Over Water

Enki's domain over water is a central aspect of his divine persona in Mesopotamian mythology, carrying deep symbolism and profound significance. Water, as a vital element, holds various associations and connotations within ancient Mesopotamian culture, representing life, fertility, sustenance, and the interconnectedness of all things.

Enki's association with water aligns him with the life-giving and nourishing aspects of this element. He is often referred to as the "Lord of Abundance" or the "Lord of the Apsu," which is the primordial freshwater ocean from which all life emerges. This connection to water highlights his role as a nurturer and provider, ensuring the continued existence and prosperity of both nature and humanity.

Water, in Mesopotamian cosmology, is regarded as the source of all creation. It is seen as the medium through which life is conceived and sustained. Enki's domain over water signifies his involvement in the processes of birth, growth, and abundance. Just as water is essential for the fertility of the land, Enki's association with water underscores his role in promoting agricultural fertility and the prosperity of the land.

One myth that exemplifies Enki's connection to water and his role as a provider is the "Enki and the Creation of Man." In this narrative, Enki fashions humanity from clay and imbues them with the "breath of life," which is often associated with water. This act of creation symbolizes the vital connection between water and the emergence of life. Enki's involvement highlights his role as the custodian of the life-giving waters, bringing forth humanity and ensuring their continued existence.

Enki's association with water also extends to his role as a healer. Water, with its cleansing and purifying properties, is often used in ancient healing practices. Enki's domain over water aligns him with the healing powers of this element, making him a source of divine healing and restoration. In the myth of "Enki and Ninhursag," Enki uses his magical abilities to cure various ailments afflicting gods and humans, further emphasizing his role as a benevolent healer.

Moreover, water is seen as a symbol of wisdom and knowledge in Mesopotamian culture. It represents the primordial source from which all wisdom flows. Enki's association with water underscores his divine wisdom and intellect. As the god of wisdom, he possesses profound understanding and insight into the workings of the natural world and the cosmos.

Enki's connection to water also carries implications for the interconnectedness of all things. Water, with its ability to flow and connect various elements, symbolizes the unity and interdependence of the natural world. Enki's domain over water signifies his role as a unifying force, bridging different realms and fostering harmony and balance.

In rituals and religious practices, water plays a significant role in purification and cleansing. Enki's association with water aligns him with these rituals, as he is invoked to purify and cleanse individuals and communities from spiritual impurities. His domain over water grants him the power to remove obstacles, restore balance, and bring about renewal and transformation.

Overall, Enki's domain over water in Mesopotamian mythology encompasses a rich symbolism and profound significance. It represents his role as a provider, healer, and source of wisdom. Enki's association with water underscores his nurturing and life-sustaining qualities, his role in promoting fertility and abundance, and his capacity to bring forth life and ensure its continuity. It also signifies his role in purification, renewal, and the interconnectedness of all things.

Symbolism of Water:

Water holds immense significance in ancient Mesopotamian cosmology, representing the fundamental element from which life and fertility arise. It is regarded as the source of sustenance and the key to the prosperity and well-being of both the natural world and living beings. Enki's domain over water aligns him with these essential aspects and emphasizes his role as a custodian of life, fertility, and renewal.

In Mesopotamian culture, water is intimately connected to agricultural fertility. The region's agricultural practices relied heavily on the annual flooding of the Tigris and Euphrates rivers, which brought nutrient-rich silt and water to the surrounding lands. This cyclic inundation ensured the fertility of the soil and the successful growth of crops, sustaining the livelihoods of the people. Enki's association with water signifies his role in facilitating this vital process, ensuring the abundance of food and the prosperity of civilization.

Furthermore, water is seen as a symbol of life and the life-giving properties it possesses. It is associated with the birth of both humans and animals, representing the primordial source from which life emerges. Enki's connection to water underscores his role as a bringer and sustainer of life. In the myth of "Enki and the Creation of Man," Enki molds humanity from clay and infuses them with the "breath of life," which is often associated with water. This act of creation highlights Enki's role in the continuous renewal and existence of life.

Water also symbolizes purification and renewal in Mesopotamian belief. It is used in rituals and religious practices as a means of cleansing individuals and communities from spiritual impurities. Enki's association with water signifies his role as a purifier and renewer, capable of removing obstacles and restoring balance and harmony. His connection to water grants him the power to bring about transformation and rejuvenation.

The life-sustaining properties of water are further emphasized in its association with fertility. Water's ability to nourish and nurture the land is paralleled with its role in promoting the fertility of humans and animals. Enki's domain over water aligns him with this aspect of fertility, symbolizing his role as a provider and facilitator of growth and abundance.

Water's significance extends beyond physical fertility to encompass spiritual and emotional aspects as well. It is often associated with emotions, symbolizing the ebb and flow of feelings and the fluidity of human experiences. Enki's association with water reflects his understanding and mastery of the complex and ever-changing nature of human emotions, making him a source of solace, healing, and emotional well-being.

In summary, water holds deep symbolism and significance in ancient Mesopotamian cosmology, representing life, fertility, and renewal. Enki's domain over water aligns him with these essential aspects and underscores his role as a custodian of life, fertility, and the well-being of both the natural world and living beings. As the provider of sustenance, the purifier, and the source of renewal, Enki embodies the vital and life-giving properties associated with water in Mesopotamian culture.

Significance for Human Existence:

Enki's association with water encompasses not only the physical properties of this essential element but also its deeper symbolism and spiritual significance. As the god of water, Enki is believed to have dominion over the life force and vitality that permeate all living beings. Water, with its ability to nourish and sustain life, is seen as a manifestation of Enki's benevolence and care for humanity.

In Mesopotamian belief, water is viewed as the source of all life. It is the substance from which all living beings emerge and is essential for their growth, development, and survival. Enki's association with water implies his responsibility for regulating and nurturing the cyclical nature of life. Just as water flows in a continuous cycle, Enki ensures the continuity and balance of life, both in the natural world and within human existence.

Enki's role as the god of water goes beyond providing physical sustenance. Water is seen as a vital component in the spiritual and emotional realms as well. It is often associated with purification, healing, and rejuvenation. Enki's domain over water indicates his ability to cleanse and purify not only physical impurities but also spiritual and emotional burdens. As the bringer of renewal, he is believed to grant individuals and communities a fresh start, washing away negativity and promoting emotional well-being.

Moreover, water's association with the life force extends to the realm of fertility and procreation. Enki's connection to water implies his role in promoting the fertility of the land, animals, and humans. Water's ability to nourish and support growth parallels Enki's role as a provider and caretaker. He ensures the abundance of resources necessary for reproduction, emphasizing his importance in the cyclical processes of birth, growth, and regeneration.

Enki's association with water also underscores his role as a source of wisdom and guidance. Water, with its ever-flowing and adaptable nature, represents the fluidity of knowledge and the capacity for growth and transformation. Enki's domain over water suggests his ability to offer insights, counsel, and guidance to both gods and humans. His wisdom, like water, is believed to flow freely, nourishing the minds and spirits of those who seek it.

In summary, Enki's association with water goes beyond its physical properties. As the god of water, he is believed to govern the life force and vitality that sustain all living beings. His domain over water signifies his role in regulating the cyclical nature of life, ensuring its continuity and balance. Enki's association with water also reflects his benevolence, care, and provision for humanity. Additionally, water's symbolism of purification, healing, fertility, and wisdom further emphasizes Enki's multifaceted role as a protector, provider, and guide in Mesopotamian mythology.

Examples, Problems, and Exercises:

Example: Compare and contrast Enki's role as the god of wisdom, knowledge, and craftsmanship with other deities associated with similar domains, such as Athena in Greek mythology or Thoth in Egyptian mythology.

Problem: Research and analyze a specific myth or ritual involving Enki's wisdom or craftsmanship. Discuss how these aspects contribute to the overall narrative or purpose of the myth or ritual.

Exercise: Imagine you are an ancient Mesopotamian artist commissioned to create a statue representing Enki's association with water. Describe the artistic choices you would make to convey the symbolism and significance of water in connection with Enki's divine character.

By examining Enki's roles as the god of wisdom, knowledge, and craftsmanship, as well as his association with magic and water, we gain insight into his significance within Mesopotamian mythology and religion. Enki's wisdom, magical abilities, and domain over water intertwine to shape his multifaceted character and affirm his role as a protector and benefactor of humanity.

Enlil: God of Air, Storms, and Kingship

In Mesopotamian mythology, Enlil's prominent position as the god of air, storms, and weather phenomena highlights his significant role in shaping the natural world and influencing human lives. This section provides a detailed exploration of Enlil's authority over air and weather, as well as the symbolic meaning attributed to storms within Mesopotamian culture.

Enlil's association with air goes beyond its physical properties and extends to its metaphorical significance. Air represents the life-sustaining breath that permeates all living beings, and as the god of air, Enlil is believed to have control over this vital element. The winds, driven by Enlil's power, play a crucial role in shaping the environment by influencing climate patterns, dispersing seeds, and facilitating the exchange of air and moisture necessary for the sustenance of life.

However, Enlil's dominion over storms is perhaps the most awe-inspiring aspect of his authority. As the god of storms, he wields control over the powerful forces of nature that bring forth rain, thunder, lightning, and winds. These meteorological phenomena are not merely viewed as natural occurrences but are imbued with deep symbolic meaning in Mesopotamian culture.

Storms, in their intensity and unpredictability, are seen as manifestations of divine power and the chaotic energy inherent in the natural world. They serve as reminders of the sublime and uncontrollable forces that shape the cosmos. Enlil's authority over storms symbolizes his ability to disrupt and reorder the established order. By unleashing tempests, he challenges the stability and routine of daily life, prompting humans to acknowledge their vulnerability and the vastness of cosmic powers beyond their control.

The symbolic significance of storms in Mesopotamian culture extends beyond their immediate destructive potential. Storms are regarded as transformative agents that can bring about change, renewal, and purification. In the aftermath of a storm, the land is replenished with life-giving rain, and the atmosphere is cleansed by the thunder and lightning. This cyclical pattern of destruction and rejuvenation mirrors the cosmic rhythm and underscores the interconnectedness of natural processes.

Enlil's association with storms, therefore, aligns him with the cyclical nature of existence and highlights his role as a catalyst for change and transformation. His power to disrupt and reorder the natural order reflects the acknowledgment of the dynamic and ever-changing nature of the cosmos.

Examples, Problems, and Exercises:

Example: Compare and contrast Enlil's control over storms with other mythological deities associated with weather phenomena, such as Thor in Norse mythology or Indra in Hindu mythology.

Problem: Research and analyze a specific myth or ritual that highlights Enlil's power over storms. Discuss the cultural and religious significance of this myth or ritual in the context of Mesopotamian society.

Exercise: Write a short narrative or create a visual representation depicting a Mesopotamian community's response to a powerful storm, incorporating both the awe and fear inspired by Enlil's display of divine power.

Divine Dynamics

By exploring Enlil's authority over air, storms, and weather phenomena, we gain a profound understanding of the Mesopotamian worldview and their perception of the natural world. Enlil's control over the life-sustaining breath and the awe-inspiring power of storms serves as a reminder of humanity's place within the vast cosmic order, prompting contemplation of the delicate balance between order and chaos, and the forces that shape the world around us.

Examination of Enlil's Authority as the Supreme Ruler of the Gods

Enlil's divine stature extends far beyond his control over air and storms. He occupies the esteemed position of the supreme ruler among the gods, wielding ultimate authority and presiding over the entire divine pantheon. This section delves into Enlil's role as the highest deity and his governance over both gods and humans, unraveling the intricate relationship between Enlil and the concept of kingship in Mesopotamian society.

Enlil's authority as the "King of the Gods" or "Father of the Gods" is deeply rooted in the divine hierarchy. He holds a central position among the gods and is revered as the foremost deity. As the ruler of the gods, Enlil exercises oversight over their actions, decisions, and interactions. He personifies the ideal qualities of leadership, wisdom, and justice, setting the standards for divine conduct and ensuring the harmonious functioning of the divine realm.

However, Enlil's influence extends beyond the realm of the divine. In ancient Mesopotamian society, the concept of divine kingship held significant importance, with earthly rulers believed to derive their authority directly from the gods. Enlil, as the supreme ruler of the gods, embodies the divine qualities that earthly kings were expected to emulate. This association between Enlil and kingship illuminates the profound link between the religious and political spheres in ancient Mesopotamia.

Understanding the association between Enlil and kingship in Mesopotamian society provides valuable insights into the political and social structures of the time. It reveals the belief in a divine mandate that conferred political legitimacy upon earthly rulers. The authority of kings was viewed as a reflection of Enlil's favor, with the gods bestowing their blessings upon those who governed justly and in accordance with divine principles. The connection between Enlil and kingship thus reinforced the close intertwining of religious and political power, shaping the fabric of ancient Mesopotamian governance.

Furthermore, Enlil's role as the patron deity of kingship implies his guidance and protection over earthly rulers. It was believed that Enlil provided wisdom, counsel, and divine assistance to kings, ensuring the welfare and prosperity of their kingdoms. As the god of storms and weather phenomena, Enlil's association with protection becomes even more significant. He was seen as the defender of the kingdom, safeguarding it from external threats and ensuring its fertility and abundance. Enlil's presence was invoked to ward off calamities and disasters, demonstrating his role as a benevolent and protective force in the lives of both gods and humans.

Examples, Problems, and Exercises:

Example: Compare and contrast the association between Enlil and kingship in Mesopotamian society with the divine rulership concepts found in other ancient civilizations, such as the pharaohs of ancient Egypt or the emperors of ancient China.

Problem: Investigate a specific Mesopotamian king who claimed divine authority and discuss the ways in which they sought to legitimize their rule through their association with Enlil.

Exercise: Imagine you are an advisor to a Mesopotamian king seeking divine guidance from Enlil. Write a speech or create a dialogue that reflects the king's appeal to Enlil for wisdom and protection in the face of challenges to their kingdom.

By exploring Enlil's position as the supreme ruler among the gods and his association with kingship, we gain a deeper understanding of the interplay between religion, politics, and social structures in ancient Mesopotamia. Enlil's authority extends beyond the divine realm, shaping the governance of human affairs and providing a framework for political legitimacy. The reverence and reliance placed upon Enlil in matters of kingship highlight the significance of divine power and its impact on the lives of ancient Mesopotamians.Examples, Problems, and Exercises:

Example: Compare and contrast Enlil's authority as the supreme ruler of the gods with other mythological figures associated with kingship, such as Zeus in Greek mythology or Ra in Egyptian mythology.

Problem: Research and analyze a specific myth or ritual involving Enlil's control over storms or weather phenomena. Discuss the symbolic meaning and cultural significance of this myth or ritual in the context of Mesopotamian society.

Exercise: Imagine you are an ancient Mesopotamian poet tasked with composing a hymn to honor Enlil as the god of air and storms. Write a stanza that encapsulates his power and awe-inspiring presence, incorporating vivid imagery and poetic devices.

By exploring Enlil's role as the god of air, storms, and kingship, we gain a deeper understanding of the complex interplay between the natural world, divine authority, and human governance in ancient Mesopotamia. Enlil's dominion over air and weather phenomena reflects the awe-inspiring power of nature, while his status as the supreme ruler of the gods and association with kingship underscores the close relationship between religion, politics, and societal structures in this ancient civilization.

The Divine Brothers' Rivalry

Analysis of the conflicts and tensions between Enki and Enlil in Mesopotamian mythology

In Mesopotamian mythology, the relationship between Enki and Enlil, the two prominent gods, is characterized by conflicts, tensions, and power struggles. This section provides an in-depth analysis of their complex dynamic, shedding light on the reasons behind their rivalries and the implications for the broader mythological narrative.

Enki and Enlil, despite being divine brothers, represent contrasting aspects of the divine order. Enki is associated with wisdom, magic, and water, while Enlil embodies authority, kingship, and the domain of air and storms. These differing domains and attributes naturally give rise to clashes as they hold distinct spheres of influence and exercise unique powers.

Exploration of the myths and narratives highlighting their rivalries and power struggles

Numerous myths and narratives in Mesopotamian literature portray the rivalries and power struggles between Enki and Enlil. One such narrative is the "Enuma Elish," the Babylonian creation myth, which depicts a conflict between the two brothers. In this myth, Enki supports the younger generation of gods in their rebellion against the oppressive rule of Enlil, resulting in a confrontation that leads to the establishment of a new cosmic order.

Another significant myth is the "Atrahasis Epic," which recounts the creation of humankind and the subsequent population growth that threatens to disrupt the divine order. In this narrative, Enlil decides to send various calamities to reduce human numbers, while Enki, out of compassion for humanity, secretly aids the protagonist Atrahasis in finding a solution to appease the gods and save humanity from destruction.

Exploring Ancient Mesopotamian Mythology, Rivalries, and Spiritual Legacies

These narratives highlight the tension between Enki and Enlil, showcasing their conflicting agendas and contrasting approaches to the governance of the world and human affairs.

Understanding the symbolic and cosmological implications of their rivalry

The rivalry between Enki and Enlil carries profound symbolic and cosmological implications within Mesopotamian mythology. It represents the inherent dualities and tensions within the natural and social order, reflecting the broader themes of chaos and order, wisdom and authority, and the interplay between the creative and destructive forces in the cosmos.

Enki, with his association with wisdom and magic, represents the transformative and creative aspects of existence. His role is closely tied to the cycles of life, growth, and regeneration. Enlil, on the other hand, embodies authority, kingship, and the power to bring about order and control. His domain over air and storms signifies the unpredictable and potentially destructive forces that must be harnessed and governed.

The rivalry between Enki and Enlil, therefore, represents the inherent tensions between these opposing cosmic forces. It highlights the delicate balance that must be maintained for the stability and harmony of the world. Their conflicts serve as a reminder of the perpetual struggle between chaos and order and the constant negotiation of power and authority within the divine realm.

Examples, Problems, and Exercises:

Example: Compare and contrast the characteristics and domains of Enki and Enlil. How do their differences contribute to their rivalry and the broader mythological narrative?

Problem: Analyze a specific myth or narrative involving Enki and Enlil and discuss the motivations and consequences of their rivalry. What lessons or insights can be gleaned from their conflicts?

Exercise: Imagine you are a scholar studying the rivalry between Enki and Enlil. Write a research paper exploring the symbolic significance of their conflicts and their implications for understanding Mesopotamian cosmology and worldview.

By delving into the conflicts and tensions between Enki and Enlil, we gain a deeper understanding of the intricate mythological tapestry of ancient Mesopotamia. Their rivalry serves as a narrative device through which profound cosmological concepts are explored, inviting us to contemplate the dynamic interplay of opposing forces within the fabric of existence.

Influence on Human Destiny

Examination of how Enki and Enlil shape the fate and destiny of humanity

The gods of ancient Mesopotamia, including Enki and Enlil, were believed to exert a profound influence on the destiny of humanity. This section explores the ways in which these deities shape the course of human lives, highlighting their interactions with humans and the implications for understanding the concepts of fate, free will, and divine intervention.

Enki and Enlil, as powerful gods, were considered the arbiters of human fortune. Their actions and decisions had far-reaching consequences for individuals, communities, and even entire civilizations. Through their divine authority and wisdom, they guided the paths of human beings, determining their destinies and the outcomes of their endeavors.

Analysis of their interactions with humans and their roles in the divine plan

In Mesopotamian mythology, Enki and Enlil interacted with humans in various ways, influencing their lives and playing distinct roles in the divine plan. Enki, as the god of wisdom and knowledge, was often depicted as a benefactor to humanity. He provided guidance, bestowed gifts, and offered protection to those who sought his aid. Enlil, as the supreme ruler and king of the gods, held the power to shape human destinies through his decisions and decrees.

The interactions between Enki, Enlil, and humans were complex and multifaceted. They involved both rewards and punishments, blessings and hardships. These interactions reflected the ancient Mesopotamian belief in a reciprocal relationship between gods and humans, where devotion and obedience to the gods were seen as crucial for favorable outcomes and divine favor.

Understanding the concepts of divine intervention and human agency in Mesopotamian belief

The concepts of divine intervention and human agency played significant roles in Mesopotamian belief and the understanding of human destiny. On one hand, the gods were seen as actively intervening in human affairs, shaping the outcomes of events and determining the course of history. Their interventions could be seen as rewards for piety and virtue or as punishments for transgressions.

On the other hand, Mesopotamian belief also emphasized the importance of human agency and responsibility. While the gods held ultimate power, humans were believed to possess the ability to make choices and exercise free will. It was understood that humans had the capacity to act in accordance with the divine order or to deviate from it, thereby influencing their own destinies.

The interplay between divine intervention and human agency created a complex dynamic in which humans were seen as both recipients of divine influence and active participants in shaping their own lives. This perspective allowed for a nuanced understanding of the relationship between humans and the gods, acknowledging the role of both in the unfolding of human destiny.

Examples, Problems, and Exercises:

Example: Analyze a myth or narrative that illustrates the influence of Enki or Enlil on human destiny. How do their actions impact the lives of the characters involved? What lessons or insights can be drawn from these stories?

Problem: Consider the concepts of fate, free will, and divine intervention in Mesopotamian belief. Discuss the implications of these concepts for understanding the responsibility of humans in shaping their own destinies.

Exercise: Imagine you are a Mesopotamian scribe tasked with recording the divine interactions with humans. Write a series of cuneiform tablets describing the encounters between Enki, Enlil, and various individuals or communities. Reflect on the different ways in which these interactions shape the destinies of the people involved.

By exploring the influence of Enki and Enlil on human destiny, we gain a deeper appreciation for the complex interplay between the divine and the human in ancient Mesopotamian belief systems. It prompts us to reflect on our own beliefs about fate, free will, and the role of higher powers in shaping our lives.

Temples and Cults

Overview of the temples and cults dedicated to Enki and Enlil

In the religious landscape of ancient Mesopotamia, the worship of deities was central to the spiritual life of the people. Temples played a vital role as sacred spaces where devotees could connect with the divine. This section provides an overview of the temples and cults dedicated to Enki and Enlil, shedding light on the significance of these religious institutions and the practices associated with their worship.

Enki and Enlil, as major deities in the Mesopotamian pantheon, had numerous temples dedicated to their veneration. These temples served as focal points of religious and social activity within their respective regions. Cities such as Eridu, Nippur, and Babylon boasted prominent temples dedicated to Enki and Enlil, where the faithful gathered to offer prayers, make offerings, and seek the favor of the gods.

Exploration of the rituals and practices associated with their worship

The worship of Enki and Enlil in ancient Mesopotamia was characterized by a rich tapestry of rituals and practices aimed at honoring and appeasing these powerful deities. These rituals served as a means of communication between humans and the divine, fostering a sense of connection and mutual exchange.

Rituals associated with the worship of Enki were often centered around his roles as the god of water and wisdom. Enki's association with water, which symbolized life and fertility, was reflected in offerings made at his temples. Devotees would bring water, fish, and other symbolic items as offerings, representing the replenishment of life and the seeking of divine favor and guidance. These offerings were seen as acts of gratitude and supplication, expressing the desire for Enki's benevolence and blessings upon their lives.

In addition to physical offerings, ritual purification rites played a significant role in the worship of Enki. Ablution, or ritual bathing, was performed as a means of purifying oneself before approaching the sacred presence of Enki. This act of cleansing symbolized the purification of both the body and the soul, ensuring a state of ritual purity and readiness to commune with the divine. Purification rites were seen as a way to remove spiritual impurities and prepare oneself for a direct encounter with the sacred.

The worship of Enlil, on the other hand, emphasized his authority as the supreme ruler and the protector of kingship. Rituals dedicated to Enlil often involved processions and public displays to demonstrate his presence and authority. Statues or symbols of Enlil would be paraded through the streets in a grand procession, accompanied by priests, musicians, and worshippers. This public spectacle served to reinforce the power and significance of Enlil within the community and to instill a sense of awe and reverence among the participants.

Exploring Ancient Mesopotamian Mythology, Rivalries, and Spiritual Legacies

Offerings played a crucial role in the worship of Enlil. Devotees would present food, drink, and incense as offerings, symbolizing nourishment for the god and demonstrating their devotion and loyalty. These offerings were believed to sustain the divine presence of Enlil and establish a reciprocal relationship between the worshipper and the deity. By providing sustenance to Enlil, worshippers sought his protection, guidance, and favor in return.

Both Enki and Enlil were revered deities in Mesopotamian society, and their worship encompassed a range of rituals and practices that were central to religious life. These rituals provided a means for individuals and communities to express their devotion, seek divine blessings, and establish a connection with the gods. Through offerings, processions, and purification rites, worshippers aimed to honor and appease Enki and Enlil, fostering a sense of spiritual fulfillment and seeking divine favor in various aspects of life.

Understanding the regional variations in the cults of Enki and Enlil

The cults of Enki and Enlil in ancient Mesopotamia exhibited regional variations that reflected the diverse cultural and religious practices across different city-states and regions. While both deities held widespread importance throughout Mesopotamia, their cults often had unique characteristics and local variations that distinguished them from one another.

One notable example is the city of Eridu, which held a special significance in the cult of Enki. Eridu was considered the sacred city associated with Enki's birthplace, and therefore, the cult of Enki in Eridu held a particularly prominent position. The temple of Enki in Eridu served as a center of worship, attracting pilgrims and devotees from far and wide. This temple, known as E-abzu, was believed to be the abode of Enki, where his divine presence resided. It was a sacred place where rituals, prayers, and offerings were dedicated to Enki, fostering a deep connection between the deity and his worshippers.

In contrast, the city of Nippur was renowned as the primary center of Enlil's cult. Nippur was considered the religious capital of ancient Mesopotamia, and its temple, known as Ekur, was believed to be the dwelling place of Enlil. The cult of Enlil in Nippur emphasized his role as the supreme ruler and the protector of kingship. The temple of Ekur served as a focal point for the worship of Enlil, attracting devotees who sought his favor, protection, and guidance.

These regional variations in the cults of Enki and Enlil extended beyond the physical locations of their temples. They also encompassed differences in rituals, offerings, and even the prominence given to certain aspects of the deities' domains.

Divine Dynamics

For example, in regions where agriculture played a significant role, Enki's association with water and fertility might have been emphasized, leading to specific rituals and offerings focused on agricultural prosperity. In regions where kingship and political power were paramount, the cult of Enlil might have emphasized his role as the divine king and lawgiver, with rituals and offerings dedicated to ensuring the well-being and success of the ruling monarch.

These regional variations in cult practices highlighted the unique identities and traditions of each city or region within Mesopotamia. They reflected the local interpretations and adaptations of the broader Mesopotamian religious framework, allowing for the expression of diverse beliefs and practices. These variations not only enriched the religious landscape of Mesopotamia but also contributed to the cultural and social fabric of the region, fostering a sense of local pride and identity within each community.

Examples, Problems, and Exercises:

Example: Compare and contrast the rituals associated with the worship of Enki and Enlil, highlighting the distinct aspects of their cults. What common themes or symbols can be identified, and how do these rituals reflect the characteristics and roles of the deities?

Problem: Research a specific regional variation in the cult of Enki or Enlil and discuss how it reflects the cultural and religious context of that particular region. Consider the geographical location, historical background, and societal factors that may have influenced the development of the cult.

Exercise: Imagine you are a devotee of Enki or Enlil in ancient Mesopotamia. Write a short prayer or invocation that captures your reverence for the deity and expresses your desires or needs. Reflect on the specific attributes and roles of the chosen deity and incorporate them into your prayer.

By engaging with these examples, problems, and exercises, students can deepen their understanding of the temples and cults dedicated to Enki and Enlil. They are encouraged to think critically, analyze different perspectives, and develop their own interpretations of the religious practices and beliefs in ancient Mesopotamia.

Legacy and Symbolic Representations

Analysis of the lasting influence of Enki and Enlil in Mesopotamian culture

The influence of Enki and Enlil, two of the most prominent deities in Mesopotamian mythology, extended far beyond their roles as gods of wisdom, water, air, storms, and kingship. This section delves into the lasting impact of Enki and Enlil on Mesopotamian culture, highlighting their significance in various aspects of society, including religion, literature, and governance.

Enki's legacy can be seen in his association with knowledge, wisdom, and creativity. As the god of water, he symbolizes the life-giving and fertile properties of rivers and springs, which were crucial for agriculture and sustenance in Mesopotamia. Enki's wisdom is often depicted in mythological narratives where he aids humanity by imparting knowledge, such as the creation of writing or the secrets of civilization. His role as a patron of artisans, craftsmen, and healers also showcases his influence on the development of various skilled professions.

Enlil's enduring influence lies in his association with kingship, divine authority, and the establishment of societal order. As the supreme ruler of the gods, Enlil's embodiment of justice, leadership, and wisdom set the standards for Mesopotamian kings and their governance. The concept of divine kingship, where earthly rulers derived their authority from the gods, was deeply ingrained in Mesopotamian society. Enlil's symbolic representation as the divine king reinforced the belief that just and righteous rulers were favored by the gods and ensured the prosperity and well-being of their kingdoms.

Examination of their symbolic representations in art, literature, and religious iconography

The symbolic representations of Enki and Enlil in various forms of artistic expression provide insight into the significance and reverence accorded to these deities in Mesopotamian culture. In art and sculpture, Enki is often depicted as a bearded figure holding a vessel overflowing with water, symbolizing his association with life-giving and nurturing qualities. His representation as a wise and benevolent deity conveys his role as a source of knowledge and guidance.

In contrast, Enlil is commonly portrayed as a majestic figure wearing a horned crown, signifying his authority and kingship. This iconography conveys his power to bring order and maintain the divine and earthly realms. In religious iconography, Enlil is sometimes depicted as standing on a divine mountain, symbolizing his lofty status and his connection to the heavens.

Divine Dynamics

Literature also played a vital role in portraying the symbolic representations of Enki and Enlil. Epic poems such as the "Enuma Elish" and the "Atrahasis" depict their roles in creation and the establishment of cosmic order. These texts showcase the complex relationship between the two deities, their interactions with other gods, and their impact on the fate and destiny of humanity.

Understanding the significance of Enki and Enlil in later Mesopotamian and Near Eastern religions

The influence of Enki and Enlil, two prominent deities in ancient Mesopotamia, extended beyond the boundaries of their original cults and continued to resonate in later periods and neighboring regions. In later Mesopotamian religions, such as Babylonian and Assyrian traditions, Enki and Enlil were integrated into the pantheon, although with some modifications and adaptations.

In the Babylonian tradition, Enki, known as Ea, retained his association with wisdom, magic, and water, while also assuming additional roles and attributes. He became associated with arts, craftsmanship, and even divination, further expanding his domain of influence. Enlil, on the other hand, continued to be revered as the supreme ruler and the head of the pantheon. His authority as the god of storms, winds, and fertility was emphasized, aligning him with the power and forces of nature.

The beliefs and practices surrounding Enki and Enlil also had a wider impact on the religious systems of the ancient Near East. Similar concepts and motifs can be found in the religious traditions of ancient Egypt, Canaan, and even in the Hebrew Bible. For example, the notion of divine wisdom and the association of water with life and fertility can be seen in the Egyptian deity Thoth and the Canaanite god Baal. The concept of a supreme ruler and lawgiver can be observed in the Hebrew Bible's depiction of Yahweh as the sovereign God and the bestower of divine commandments.

This cross-cultural influence suggests that the symbolic representations and theological concepts associated with Enki and Enlil had a broader cultural impact and influenced the religious beliefs and practices of neighboring civilizations. The transmission of these ideas may have occurred through trade, cultural exchange, and the movement of people across ancient Near Eastern regions.

In conclusion, the legacy of Enki and Enlil in Mesopotamian culture is profound and far-reaching. Their influence extended beyond their original cults and permeated later Mesopotamian religions and neighboring civilizations. The enduring significance of Enki and Enlil in religious, artistic, and literary contexts underscores their lasting impact on the religious and cultural landscape of the region. Exploring their legacy enhances our understanding of the intricate belief systems and cultural dynamics of ancient Mesopotamia and its surrounding civilizations.

Comparative Perspectives

Exploration of parallels and similarities between Enki and Enlil and other divine sibling rivalries in world mythology

The dynamic between Enki and Enlil in Mesopotamian mythology reflects a broader pattern found in world mythology—the theme of sibling rivalries among divine beings. This section examines the parallels and similarities between Enki and Enlil and other famous sibling rivalries in mythological traditions across different cultures, shedding light on the recurring motifs and archetypes that emerge from these narratives.

One notable comparison can be drawn between Enki and Enlil and the Greek deities Zeus and Poseidon. Zeus, as the king of the Greek gods, shares similarities with Enlil in terms of their roles as supreme rulers and overseers of the divine order. Poseidon, on the other hand, is associated with water and storms, much like Enki. Both pairs of siblings embody contrasting elements and powers, often leading to conflicts and power struggles that have far-reaching consequences.

In Hindu mythology, the rivalry between the gods Indra and Varuna bears resemblance to the Enki-Enlil dynamic. Indra, the god of thunder and rain, holds similarities with Enlil as the wielder of storms and atmospheric phenomena. Varuna, on the other hand, represents the cosmic order and cosmic waters, paralleling Enki's association with wisdom and the life-giving properties of water. The tensions and conflicts between these siblings highlight the broader themes of power, cosmic balance, and the interplay between natural forces and divine authority.

Analysis of the broader themes and archetypes represented by the Enki-Enlil dynamic

The Enki-Enlil dynamic encompasses several archetypal themes and motifs that resonate beyond their specific mythological context. One such theme is the struggle for power and supremacy. The rivalry between Enki and Enlil reflects the timeless struggle for dominance and control, a theme that can be found in various mythological traditions around the world. This struggle often represents broader human experiences and societal dynamics, where power struggles and conflicts of authority play a significant role.

Divine Dynamics

Another theme inherent in the Enki-Enlil dynamic is the balance between chaos and order. Enki, associated with wisdom and creativity, embodies the potential for chaos and disruption, while Enlil, as the ruler of the gods and the establisher of order, represents stability and structure. This duality between chaos and order is a common motif in mythology, symbolizing the delicate equilibrium that must be maintained for the harmonious functioning of the cosmos.

Understanding the cultural and psychological significance of sibling rivalries in mythic narratives

Sibling rivalries in mythic narratives serve as vehicles for exploring complex human emotions, societal dynamics, and psychological processes. The Enki-Enlil dynamic exemplifies the cultural and psychological significance of such rivalries, offering insights into the intricacies of familial relationships, power dynamics, and the interplay between individual aspirations and collective responsibilities.

From a cultural perspective, sibling rivalries in mythology reflect the complexities of family dynamics and societal structures. They highlight the tensions that arise from competition, jealousy, and conflicting roles within families and communities. These narratives provide a mirror to human experiences, inviting us to examine our own relationships and the challenges inherent in navigating familial and social contexts.

Psychologically, sibling rivalries in mythic narratives tap into universal themes of identity, individuation, and the quest for recognition. The conflicts and power struggles between Enki and Enlil echo the psychological processes of differentiation and self-discovery, as well as the desire for validation and acknowledgment of one's unique abilities and contributions.

In conclusion, the comparative analysis of the Enki-Enlil dynamic in Mesopotamian mythology with other sibling rivalries in world mythology enriches our understanding of the archetypal themes and universal human experiences embedded in these narratives. The exploration of parallels and similarities between Enki and Enlil and other divine siblings invites us to delve deeper into the cultural, psychological, and symbolic dimensions of these mythological traditions, fostering a broader appreciation for the profound and enduring impact of mythology on human thought and imagination.

Exploring Ancient Mesopotamian Mythology, Rivalries, and Spiritual Legacies

Examples, Problems, and Exercises:

Explore the similarities and differences between the Enki-Enlil rivalry and the sibling conflicts found in other mythological traditions, such as the Norse gods Loki and Thor, or the Egyptian deities Osiris and Set. How do these rivalries reflect cultural values and beliefs? What archetypal themes emerge from these narratives?

Analyze the Enki-Enlil dynamic in the context of societal power structures. How does their rivalry mirror the struggles for authority and control within human societies? Provide examples from historical or contemporary contexts to support your analysis.

Consider the psychological implications of sibling rivalries in mythic narratives. How can the Enki-Enlil conflict be interpreted as a metaphor for individual identity formation and the search for recognition? Discuss the psychological processes at play and provide examples from literature or personal experiences to illustrate your points.

Research and compare the representations of sibling rivalries in different cultural traditions, such as Chinese mythology, Native American folklore, or African oral traditions. How do these narratives differ from the Enki-Enlil dynamic? What cultural values and beliefs do they reflect? Engage in a class discussion or group project to share your findings and insights.

Imagine you are a playwright or a storyteller tasked with retelling the Enki-Enlil rivalry in a modern context. How would you adapt the narrative to resonate with contemporary audiences? Consider the themes and conflicts you would emphasize, as well as the potential symbolism and cultural references you would incorporate. Write a short synopsis or outline of your modern adaptation and discuss your creative choices with your peers.

Chapter 6: Nammu and Marduk: The Rise of Babylonian Deities

Nammu and Marduk are two prominent deities in Babylonian mythology, playing significant roles in the religious and cosmological beliefs of ancient Mesopotamia. Nammu, often referred to as the primordial mother goddess, is associated with the watery abyss and is considered the progenitor of all creation. Marduk, on the other hand, is a later deity who emerged as the patron god of Babylon and eventually became the chief god of the Babylonian pantheon.

The significance of Nammu lies in her role as the creator and sustainer of the cosmos. In Mesopotamian cosmology, it was believed that the world emerged from a primeval sea, represented by Nammu's watery domain. She embodies the forces of chaos and fertility, giving birth to the gods and providing the foundation for the ordered world to come into existence. Nammu's connection to the primal waters establishes her as a symbol of creation, transformation, and the cyclical nature of life.

Marduk, on the other hand, rose to prominence during the reign of Hammurabi and the rise of the Babylonian Empire. As the patron deity of Babylon, Marduk became the central figure in the Babylonian religious and political sphere. He was associated with various aspects, including kingship, justice, and warfare. Marduk's ascent to the position of supreme god reflects the shifting sociopolitical dynamics of ancient Mesopotamia, where the power and influence of the city of Babylon grew.

Objectives and structure of the chapter

The primary objectives of this chapter are to explore the significance of Nammu and Marduk in Babylonian mythology and religion, examine their roles in the cosmological framework, and understand the broader cultural and historical contexts in which they emerged. By delving into the mythic narratives and religious practices surrounding these deities, we aim to provide students with a comprehensive understanding of their significance in the ancient Babylonian worldview.

To achieve these objectives, the chapter is structured in a way that progresses from an exploration of Nammu as the primordial mother goddess to the rise of Marduk as the chief deity of Babylon. We will examine the myths and narratives associated with Nammu and Marduk, analyze their symbolic representations and attributes, and consider their roles within the larger pantheon of gods.

Exploring Ancient Mesopotamian Mythology, Rivalries, and Spiritual Legacies

Preview of key topics and themes

Throughout the chapter, we will delve into several key topics and themes related to Nammu and Marduk. These include:

The Creation Myth: We will explore the Babylonian creation myth, known as the Enuma Elish, which highlights the role of Nammu in the emergence of the cosmos. We will analyze the cosmogonic elements and the symbolism embedded in the myth, shedding light on Nammu's significance as the primal mother goddess.

The Divine Hierarchy: In this section, we will examine the complex pantheon of Babylonian deities and their relationships with Nammu and Marduk. We will discuss the divine hierarchy, the interplay of power and authority, and the ways in which Nammu and Marduk fit into this intricate web of gods and goddesses.

Cultic Practices and Rituals: Understanding the religious practices and rituals associated with Nammu and Marduk is crucial for comprehending their role in Babylonian society. We will explore the temples dedicated to their worship, the rituals performed in their honor, and the cultic practices that developed around them.

Sociohistorical Context: Finally, we will analyze the historical and cultural factors that contributed to the rise of Marduk as the chief god of Babylon. We will consider the political developments, such as the reign of Hammurabi, and their impact on the religious landscape of ancient Mesopotamia.

Examples, Problems, and Exercises:

Analyze the Enuma Elish creation myth and identify the key elements that highlight Nammu's role as the creator goddess. Discuss how these elements compare to creation myths in other cultural traditions.

Research and compare the attributes and symbols associated with Nammu and Marduk. What qualities do they represent, and how do these attributes reflect the values and aspirations of ancient Babylonian society?

Imagine you are an ancient Babylonian priest or priestess responsible for conducting rituals dedicated to Nammu and Marduk. Create a step-by-step guide outlining the essential elements of a ceremony, including offerings, prayers, and gestures. Explain the symbolic significance of each element.

Investigate the historical and political events that contributed to the rise of Babylon and the subsequent prominence of Marduk. Discuss how Marduk's association with kingship and warfare may have bolstered the political legitimacy of Babylonian rulers.

Engage in a class debate on the significance of Nammu and Marduk in Babylonian society. Divide the class into two groups, with one arguing for the centrality of Nammu and the other advocating for the preeminence of Marduk. Support your arguments with evidence from mythological texts and historical sources.

The Origins of Nammu

Nammu, the primordial mother goddess in Babylonian mythology, holds a significant place in the ancient Mesopotamian cosmological framework. Understanding the origins of Nammu requires an exploration of the mythic narratives and cultural contexts in which she emerged.

According to Babylonian creation mythology, the Enuma Elish, the universe was birthed from the primordial waters of chaos. These waters, known as Apsu and Tiamat, represented the chaotic and formless state preceding creation. From the union of Apsu and Tiamat, Nammu, also referred to as Namma or Nammu-Enlil, emerged as the personification of the cosmic sea.

Nammu's name, derived from the Sumerian word "nammu" meaning "sea" or "deep," reflects her association with the watery abyss. She embodies the transformative and life-giving properties of water, symbolizing the potential for creation and growth. As the primordial mother goddess, Nammu is often depicted as a nurturing figure, representing the divine feminine aspects of fertility and birth.

Nammu's role in the cosmogonic process is paramount. From the chaos of the primeval waters, she brought forth the first generation of deities known as the Anunnaki, who would later play vital roles in shaping the world. Nammu's creative power is exemplified in her ability to generate life and order from the formless void. This act of creation establishes her as the progenitor of the gods and the foundational force behind the cosmos.

It is important to note that Nammu's character is not limited to her role as a creator goddess. She is also associated with wisdom and knowledge. In some texts, Nammu is referred to as the "Mother of the Gods" and the "Womb of Heaven and Earth," highlighting her elevated status and authority among the divine pantheon. Her wisdom is seen as a guiding force for the gods and humans alike.

The origins of Nammu can be traced back to the ancient Sumerian civilization, which predates the rise of Babylon. The Sumerians revered Nammu as the mother goddess and considered her the divine source of life and fertility. Over time, as Babylon gained prominence, Nammu's significance merged with the rise of Marduk, the patron god of Babylon, resulting in the assimilation of her attributes into the Babylonian pantheon.

Examples, Problems, and Exercises:

Research and analyze the Enuma Elish creation myth. Identify the specific verses or passages that mention Nammu and discuss her role in the emergence of the cosmos. What symbols or metaphors are used to represent her in the myth?

Explore the connections between Nammu and other ancient mother goddess figures in different cultures, such as the Sumerian goddess Ninhursag or the Egyptian goddess Isis. Compare their roles, attributes, and symbolic representations. What common themes or archetypes can be observed?

Create a visual representation of Nammu as a primordial mother goddess, incorporating key symbols and attributes associated with her. Explain the symbolic significance of each element in your artwork.

Reflect on the cultural and psychological significance of a primordial mother figure like Nammu in ancient Mesopotamian society. Discuss the role of fertility and motherhood in shaping societal values and gender roles.

Engage in a class discussion on the evolution of Nammu's character and significance over time. Consider the influence of cultural and political factors in the assimilation of Nammu into the Babylonian pantheon and her association with Marduk. Debate the implications of this assimilation on the understanding of female divinity in ancient Mesopotamian culture.

Interpretations of Nammu's significance in Babylonian cosmology

The significance of Nammu, the primordial mother goddess in Babylonian cosmology, has been the subject of scholarly debate and interpretation. Various theories have emerged, offering different perspectives on her role and symbolic significance within the Babylonian belief system. Understanding these interpretations can deepen our understanding of the complex and multifaceted nature of Nammu's place in Mesopotamian mythology.

One interpretation of Nammu's significance emphasizes her association with the primordial waters and the creative power of chaos. In this view, Nammu represents the transformative forces of nature, particularly water, which symbolizes both the potential for creation and destruction. The chaotic waters from which Nammu emerged can be seen as a metaphor for the formless and undifferentiated state of the universe before the emergence of order and structure. From this perspective, Nammu's role as the primordial mother goddess highlights her connection to the generative and regenerative aspects of existence.

Another interpretation focuses on Nammu's role as the mother of the gods and her association with fertility and birth. In this view, Nammu embodies the life-giving aspects of the feminine divine and serves as the source of nourishment and sustenance for both gods and humans. Her ability to bring forth the first generation of deities, the Anunnaki, highlights her role as the progenitor of the divine hierarchy and establishes her authority within the pantheon. From this perspective, Nammu's significance lies in her role as the nurturing and caring aspect of the divine, providing guidance and support to the gods and humanity.

Furthermore, some scholars suggest that Nammu's significance extends beyond her role as a creator and nurturer. They argue that she represents the underlying principles of cosmic order and wisdom. Nammu is often associated with the concept of "me," which encompasses various divine powers, laws, and attributes. As the "Mother of the Gods," she holds the wisdom and knowledge that govern the functioning of the universe. From this perspective, Nammu's significance lies in her role as a wise and authoritative figure who imparts divine knowledge and guides the gods and humans in their actions.

It is important to note that interpretations of Nammu's significance may vary based on the sources and cultural contexts in which they are examined. Different scholars may prioritize certain aspects of Nammu's character and symbolism over others, leading to diverse interpretations. Additionally, the assimilation of Nammu's attributes into the Babylonian pantheon and her association with other deities, such as Marduk, further complicates the understanding of her significance.

Examples, Problems, and Exercises:

Compare and contrast the interpretations of Nammu's significance in Babylonian cosmology provided by different scholars. Identify the key points of agreement and disagreement among these interpretations and evaluate the evidence and reasoning behind each viewpoint.

Explore the symbolic representations of Nammu in Babylonian art and iconography. Analyze the visual elements and motifs used to depict her and discuss how they contribute to the understanding of her significance.

Exploring Ancient Mesopotamian Mythology, Rivalries, and Spiritual Legacies

Conduct a research project on the influence of Nammu's character and symbolism on the roles and perceptions of women in ancient Mesopotamian society. Investigate whether the reverence for a powerful and wise mother goddess like Nammu affected gender dynamics and societal structures.

Engage in a class debate on the primary aspect of Nammu's significance in Babylonian cosmology. Divide the class into groups representing different viewpoints, such as the transformative nature of chaos, the nurturing mother figure, or the embodiment of cosmic order and wisdom. Present arguments supporting each perspective and critically analyze the strengths and weaknesses of each position.

Reflect on the significance of Nammu in the context of contemporary spiritual and ecological practices. Discuss how the concepts of nurturing, transformative forces, and wisdom embodied by Nammu can inform and inspire modern practices such as eco-spirituality, herbalism, or feminist spirituality.

Enki and the Creation of Marduk

In this section, we will delve into the captivating myth of Enki and the creation of Marduk in ancient Mesopotamian mythology. This myth holds great significance as it highlights the transfer of power from one generation of gods to another and sheds light on the cultural and religious changes that occurred in Babylonian society. Through the story of Enki's strategic plan to create Marduk, we will explore the intricate dynamics within the divine pantheon and the evolution of religious beliefs in ancient Mesopotamia.

The Birth of Marduk

The mythic narrative of Enki and the birth of Marduk holds great significance in Babylonian mythology. It portrays Enki, one of the prominent gods in the Mesopotamian pantheon, as the orchestrator of a plan to establish a new deity who would uphold divine order and protect the gods from their adversaries. This section will delve into the intricate details of Enki's intentions and the elaborate process through which Marduk, the powerful and wise god, comes into existence.

The myth begins with the gods facing constant threats and chaos from the forces of Tiamat, the primordial goddess of chaos and the sea. Recognizing the need for a powerful champion to defend the divine realm, Enki devises a strategy to bring forth a deity capable of facing these challenges. His intention is to create a god who embodies the combined powers and attributes of various gods, thus forming a formidable force against the chaos that threatens their existence.

Divine Dynamics

To bring his plan into fruition, Enki meticulously orchestrates a series of rituals and enchantments. He gathers the essence and powers of the gods, carefully selecting the divine qualities that would contribute to the creation of Marduk. Each deity symbolizes a specific attribute or characteristic that will enhance Marduk's strength and wisdom.

For instance, Enki infuses Marduk with the fiery vigor of the sun god Utu, bestowing upon him the power to illuminate and discern truth. The ferocity of the storm god Adad is blended with Marduk's essence, granting him the ability to command the forces of nature. Similarly, the wisdom and magic of the goddess Inanna find their place within Marduk, endowing him with insight and mystical capabilities.

Through this process of selective amalgamation, Enki crafts a deity who possesses unparalleled strength, wisdom, and versatility. Marduk emerges as a composite being, embodying the collective powers of the gods and standing as a symbol of unity and divine authority.

It is important to note that the creation of Marduk is not solely an act of divine intervention. Enki's plan involves the participation of other gods, who willingly contribute their powers to the new deity's formation. This collaborative effort underscores the interdependence and cooperation among the gods, highlighting the importance of unity in overcoming adversity.

As the myth unfolds, Marduk, now equipped with immense power and wisdom, goes on to confront Tiamat and her forces of chaos. In a grand battle, Marduk successfully vanquishes Tiamat, thus establishing order and asserting his dominance over the divine realm. His victory solidifies his position as the patron deity of Babylon and marks the ascendance of a new era in Babylonian mythology and religious practices.

The mythic narrative of Enki and the birth of Marduk not only showcases Enki's strategic planning and the complex process of creating a powerful deity but also highlights the broader themes of order versus chaos and the struggle for divine supremacy. It invites contemplation on the role of individual gods and their collective efforts in maintaining cosmic balance and protecting the divine realm.

Through studying this myth, we gain insights into the cultural values, religious beliefs, and sociopolitical dynamics of ancient Mesopotamian society. The myth of Enki and the birth of Marduk serves as a foundation for understanding the central role of Marduk as the patron deity of Babylon and the ways in which mythology influenced religious practices, governance, and the worldview of the Babylonian civilization.

Section 2: Symbolism and Meaning

In the mythic narrative of Enki and the birth of Marduk, the creation of the powerful deity Marduk is not merely a combination of divine attributes, but a symbolic process that carries profound cultural and religious implications. In this section, we will delve into the symbolism behind Marduk's formation, analyzing the significance of each contribution from different gods and exploring how these elements shape Marduk's character and role within the pantheon.

Each deity that contributes to the formation of Marduk brings forth specific attributes and qualities that enrich his divine nature. These symbolic contributions are carefully chosen to imbue Marduk with a diverse range of powers and virtues, highlighting the multidimensional nature of his character.

For instance, the infusion of Utu's fiery vigor symbolizes Marduk's role as a bringer of light and truth. It represents his ability to illuminate the darkness, both in the physical realm and within the spiritual and moral dimensions. This attribute establishes Marduk as a figure of guidance and discernment, emphasizing the importance of wisdom and enlightenment in navigating the complexities of life.

The inclusion of Adad's ferocity and command over storms bestows upon Marduk the power to control the forces of nature. This symbolism aligns Marduk with the natural world and positions him as a deity who can wield the elements to maintain cosmic balance and protect the divine order. It reflects the ancient Mesopotamian belief in the interconnectedness of the gods, nature, and human existence.

Similarly, the wisdom and magical abilities contributed by the goddess Inanna symbolize Marduk's capacity for insight and supernatural prowess. This symbolism underscores Marduk's role as a divine mediator and advocate, capable of intervening in human affairs and responding to their spiritual and practical needs. It speaks to the idea of divine intervention and the belief in the gods' involvement in human destiny.

By analyzing the symbolic elements within Marduk's character, we gain insight into the cultural and religious values of ancient Mesopotamian society. The selection of specific attributes reflects the priorities and aspirations of the civilization, offering a glimpse into their worldview and understanding of the divine.

Furthermore, the symbolism associated with Marduk's creation extends beyond his individual character to encompass broader cultural and religious implications. Marduk's rise to power signifies the triumph of order over chaos and the establishment of a stable and harmonious cosmos. His composite nature reflects the idea of unity and collective effort, emphasizing the importance of collaboration and cooperation in maintaining divine authority.

The symbolic significance of Marduk's formation also extends to his role within the pantheon and the religious practices of the Babylonian civilization. As the patron deity of Babylon, Marduk becomes the focal point of worship and devotion, embodying the ideals and aspirations of the city-state. The symbolism associated with his character shapes the rituals, prayers, and offerings dedicated to him, fostering a sense of communal identity and reinforcing the social and political structures of the society.

In conclusion, the symbolism and meaning behind Marduk's formation in the mythic narrative of Enki and the birth of Marduk offer a rich tapestry of cultural and religious significance. Through the analysis of the contributions from various gods, we gain a deeper understanding of Marduk's character, his role within the pantheon, and the broader implications of his rise to power. This exploration allows us to uncover the ancient Mesopotamians' beliefs, values, and aspirations, shedding light on the intricate interplay between mythology, religion, and society in this remarkable civilization.

Section 3: Divine Succession and Cultural Transformations

The concept of divine succession plays a pivotal role in understanding the cultural transformations that occurred in ancient Mesopotamia, particularly with regard to the rise of Marduk as a central figure in Babylonian mythology. In this section, we will explore how the ascent of Marduk correlates with the ascendancy of Babylon as a dominant city-state, and how the transfer of power from the older generation of gods, represented by Enlil, to the new generation embodied by Marduk, reflects broader societal and political shifts that shaped religious beliefs and practices.

In Mesopotamian mythology, the gods are not static figures but evolve and adapt alongside human civilization. This fluidity is exemplified in the succession of deities, where the younger gods supersede the older ones, assuming prominent roles and redefining the religious landscape. The divine succession from Enlil to Marduk signifies a transformative period in Mesopotamian history, corresponding with Babylon's rise to prominence.

Exploring Ancient Mesopotamian Mythology, Rivalries, and Spiritual Legacies

Enlil, one of the most ancient and powerful gods in the Mesopotamian pantheon, represented the old order and the traditional centers of power. As the god of wind, storms, and agriculture, Enlil held dominion over the forces of nature and was revered as a supreme deity. However, as urban centers like Babylon emerged and gained political influence, the younger generation of gods, led by Marduk, began to challenge Enlil's authority.

The rise of Marduk as the chief god of Babylon reflected the shifting dynamics of power and the growing importance of the city-state. Marduk's ascendancy can be seen as a response to the changing social and political landscape, with Babylon emerging as a dominant force in the region. This divine succession was not only a religious transformation but also a reflection of the societal and political aspirations of the Babylonian civilization.

The transfer of power from Enlil to Marduk brought about significant cultural changes and influenced religious beliefs and practices. As Babylon grew in prominence, the worship of Marduk became more prevalent, and rituals associated with his cult gained prominence in the religious life of the city-state. Temples dedicated to Marduk, such as the renowned Esagila, became centers of religious and political authority, solidifying Marduk's position as the patron deity of Babylon.

Moreover, the divine succession from Enlil to Marduk also had broader societal implications. It signified a shift in the balance of power, where the old order represented by Enlil and the traditional centers of authority gave way to a new era symbolized by Marduk and the rising influence of Babylon. This transformation extended beyond the religious sphere and affected various aspects of Babylonian society, including governance, administration, and cultural practices.

The rise of Marduk as the central deity of Babylon influenced the cultural landscape of ancient Mesopotamia, fostering a sense of collective identity and solidarity among the Babylonians. The rituals, festivals, and mythic narratives associated with Marduk's cult provided a unifying force, reinforcing the social and political structures of Babylonian society.

In conclusion, the concept of divine succession and its relationship to cultural transformations in ancient Mesopotamia is exemplified by the rise of Marduk as a central figure in Babylonian mythology. The transfer of power from the older generation of gods, represented by Enlil, to the new generation embodied by Marduk, reflects the societal and political shifts that shaped religious beliefs and practices. Understanding this divine succession enables us to gain insights into the evolving religious, social, and political dynamics of the ancient Mesopotamian civilization and their impact on the cultural landscape.

Divine Dynamics

Section 4: Comparative Perspectives

In this section, we will embark on a comparative exploration of the myth of Enki and the creation of Marduk, drawing parallels with other myths from diverse cultures that depict the transfer of power between generations of gods. By delving into these comparative perspectives, we aim to uncover the shared themes, motifs, and underlying messages that emerge from these narratives. This comparative analysis will provide us with a broader perspective on the cultural and psychological significance of divine succession in mythic traditions.

Across various mythologies around the world, we find recurring themes of divine succession, where younger gods rise to power, supplanting the older generation. These narratives often reflect societal and cosmic changes, mirroring the cycles of life, death, and rebirth that permeate human existence. By examining these mythic narratives in parallel, we can identify both commonalities and distinct cultural expressions.

One example that resonates with the myth of Enki and the creation of Marduk is the Greek myth of Zeus overthrowing his father Cronus and the Titans. Both myths showcase the ascendancy of a younger generation of gods, driven by the desire to establish a new order and bring about cosmic harmony. These narratives illustrate the universal theme of generational conflict and the transformative power of the younger gods.

Similarly, in Norse mythology, we encounter the tale of Odin and the Aesir gods overthrowing the primal giant Ymir, leading to the establishment of the world as we know it. This myth, like the Mesopotamian narrative, portrays the rise of a new pantheon that redefines the cosmic order. The themes of creation, divine power, and the triumph of a younger generation echo across these mythic traditions.

Moreover, in Egyptian mythology, the story of Horus, the son of Osiris and Isis, avenging his father's death and claiming his rightful place as the ruler of Egypt showcases another manifestation of divine succession. Horus embodies the ideals of kingship, justice, and balance, much like Marduk represents the embodiment of divine order in Babylonian mythology. These parallel narratives illuminate the cultural values and aspirations embedded within these societies.

Through comparative analysis, we can identify both similarities and divergences in the themes and motifs of these mythic narratives. While the specifics may vary, the underlying message of divine succession resonates across cultures, reflecting the human fascination with generational dynamics, power transitions, and the eternal quest for cosmic harmony.

Furthermore, the comparative study of these mythic traditions offers insights into the cultural and psychological significance of divine succession. These narratives provide a framework for understanding societal transformations, the evolution of power structures, and the cyclical nature of life and cosmic order. They also invite us to contemplate the interplay between tradition and innovation, continuity and change, as well as the psychological dynamics inherent in the passing of power from one generation to the next.

In conclusion, the comparative exploration of the myth of Enki and the creation of Marduk alongside other myths depicting divine succession reveals shared themes, motifs, and underlying messages across diverse cultures. By engaging in this comparative study, we gain a broader perspective on the cultural and psychological significance of these narratives, unraveling the universal human fascination with generational dynamics, power transitions, and the eternal quest for cosmic harmony. Such a comparative approach invites critical reflection on the interconnections between mythic traditions and sheds light on the enduring relevance of these ancient narratives in our understanding of human culture and psychology.

Section 5: Artistic and Literary Representations

In this section, we will embark on a fascinating exploration of how the story of Enki and Marduk's creation is depicted in various forms of Mesopotamian art and literature. Through a careful analysis of these artistic and literary representations, we will unravel the evolution of Marduk's portrayal and the symbolism associated with him, shedding light on the cultural and religious contexts in which the myth was interpreted and celebrated.

Mesopotamian art and literature provide invaluable insights into the ways in which the myth of Enki and Marduk's creation was visualized and narrated. Artistic representations, such as relief sculptures, cylinder seals, and statues, offer vivid glimpses into the imagery and iconography associated with Marduk. These depictions not only convey the physical attributes of the deity but also communicate deeper symbolic meanings.

One prominent artistic representation of Marduk is found in the famous Babylonian Ishtar Gate. Built during the reign of King Nebuchadnezzar II, the Ishtar Gate was adorned with intricately crafted glazed bricks depicting sacred animals, gods, and divine symbols. Among the divine figures featured on the gate, Marduk is often portrayed as a powerful and regal deity, wearing a horned crown and holding various attributes of his authority. These visual representations highlight Marduk's central role in Babylonian religious and political life.

Divine Dynamics

In addition to visual representations, Mesopotamian literature offers valuable insights into the narrative and symbolic aspects of the myth. Cuneiform texts, such as the Enuma Elish, the Babylonian creation epic, provide detailed accounts of Marduk's role in the creation of the cosmos and his subsequent ascent to supreme power. These literary compositions not only emphasize Marduk's prowess as a warrior god but also convey his status as a wise and just ruler, embodying the ideals of kingship and divine order.

Moreover, Mesopotamian poetry and hymns dedicated to Marduk further enrich our understanding of the deity's significance in religious and cultural contexts. These literary works praise Marduk's divine attributes, extolling his power, wisdom, and protective role in the lives of his devotees. They offer glimpses into the devotional practices and religious fervor surrounding Marduk's worship, allowing us to comprehend the emotional and spiritual dimensions associated with the myth.

The evolution of artistic and literary representations of Marduk over time is noteworthy. As Babylonian society transformed and underwent cultural shifts, so too did the portrayal of Marduk. For instance, during the Neo-Assyrian period, Marduk's depictions often incorporated elements of syncretism, blending attributes and symbols from other deities to signify his expanded role as a supreme god. These adaptations reflect the dynamic nature of religious beliefs and the cultural interplay that influenced artistic expression.

Studying these artistic and literary representations provides us with valuable insights into the cultural and religious contexts in which the myth of Enki and Marduk's creation was revered. The visual and textual symbolism associated with Marduk offers glimpses into the aspirations, beliefs, and rituals of ancient Mesopotamians. It also enables us to grasp the profound interconnections between art, literature, religion, and society, highlighting the multifaceted role of myth in shaping and reflecting cultural identities.

In conclusion, the exploration of artistic and literary representations of the myth of Enki and Marduk's creation opens doors to understanding the cultural and religious contexts in which the myth was celebrated and interpreted. Through careful analysis of visual depictions, such as those found on the Ishtar Gate, and textual sources like the Enuma Elish, we unravel the evolving symbolism associated with Marduk and gain insights into the religious beliefs, values, and artistic expressions of ancient Mesopotamia. Such a comprehensive examination invites us to appreciate the profound interplay between art, literature, and mythology, illuminating the rich tapestry of Mesopotamian culture and spirituality.

Conclusion:

In conclusion, the myth of Enki and the creation of Marduk offers valuable insights into the complex interplay between mythology, religious beliefs, and socio-cultural dynamics in ancient Mesopotamia. This mythic narrative not only reveals the dynamics within the divine pantheon but also sheds light on the broader cultural, political, and religious transformations that shaped Babylonian civilization. Through our exploration of this myth, we hope to foster a deeper appreciation for the rich tapestry of ancient Mesopotamian mythology and its significance in understanding the beliefs and worldview of its people.

Marduk: God of Babylon and Ruler of the Pantheon

In this section, we will embark on a profound exploration of Marduk, the deity who ascended to become the supreme god of Babylon and the ruler of the Mesopotamian pantheon. Through a comprehensive analysis of Marduk's origins, attributes, and the significance of his kingship, we will gain a deep understanding of the cultural, religious, and political contexts that shaped his divine status and enduring influence.

Marduk's Origins and Cultural Significance

Marduk's origins lie within the complex fabric of Babylonian mythology, a narrative tapestry that weaves together the threads of ancient Mesopotamian beliefs and traditions. During the Old Babylonian period, Marduk began to emerge as a prominent deity, capturing the attention and devotion of the Babylonian people. This ascent to prominence coincided with the rise of the city of Babylon itself, which was transforming into a dominant city-state in the region.

The association between Marduk and Babylon played a pivotal role in shaping his cultural significance. As Babylon grew in power and influence, Marduk's stature rose in parallel, establishing a symbiotic relationship between the city and its patron deity. Marduk became intricately intertwined with the identity of Babylon, embodying the aspirations, values, and aspirations of its people.

One of the key factors that contributed to Marduk's elevated status was his portrayal as a warrior god. He was depicted as a formidable and courageous deity, representing the embodiment of strength and divine authority. Marduk's mythology often highlighted his role as a triumphant conqueror, overcoming the primordial forces of chaos and turmoil that threatened the order of the cosmos.

Divine Dynamics

The Babylonian creation myth, known as the Enuma Elish, played a crucial role in elevating Marduk to the position of the supreme deity within the pantheon. In this epic narrative, Marduk emerges as the hero who confronts and defeats the chaotic dragon-like goddess Tiamat, thus establishing order and stability in the universe. This mythic victory not only solidified Marduk's divine authority but also symbolized his central role in the cosmic balance of the world.

Furthermore, Marduk's association with justice and cosmic order further enhanced his cultural significance. As the supreme deity, he was believed to be the ultimate arbiter of justice, ensuring that divine laws and moral principles were upheld. This aspect of Marduk's character resonated deeply with the Babylonian people, as they sought order and fairness in their societal structures.

In summary, Marduk's origins and cultural significance can be traced back to the emergence of Babylon as a dominant city-state. His portrayal as a warrior god and his victory over chaos in the Enuma Elish established him as the supreme deity, embodying the ideals of strength, courage, and divine authority. Additionally, Marduk's association with justice and cosmic order further solidified his position within the cultural and religious landscape of ancient Mesopotamia. By understanding Marduk's origins and cultural significance, we gain valuable insights into the complexities of Babylonian mythology and its profound impact on the beliefs and values of the Babylonian people.

Marduk as King and Patron Deity of Babylon

Marduk's role as the patron deity of Babylon extended beyond mere symbolism and mythology. It encompassed a tangible and practical relationship between the divine and earthly realms. The concept of divine kingship formed a fundamental aspect of Babylonian religious and political ideology, emphasizing the close connection between Marduk and the rulers of Babylon.

In the Babylonian worldview, the king was considered the earthly representative of Marduk, entrusted with the divine authority to govern and uphold the principles of justice and order. This concept of divine kingship conveyed a sense of legitimacy and legitimacy to the ruler, as well as a sense of responsibility to rule with wisdom and fairness. The king was seen as the intermediary between the divine realm and the human realm, ensuring the harmonious alignment of the cosmic and societal order.

The Akitu festival, celebrated during the Babylonian New Year, played a pivotal role in reaffirming the bond between Marduk, the king, and the people of Babylon. This grand event consisted of elaborate rituals and reenactments, symbolizing Marduk's victory over the forces of chaos and his continuous role in maintaining cosmic order. The festival served as a unifying force, bringing together the religious, political, and social aspects of Babylonian society.

During the Akitu festival, the king would participate in various rituals, including the recitation of prayers, the offering of sacrifices, and the reenactment of mythic events. Through these ceremonial acts, the divine kingship was ritually reestablished, strengthening the bond between Marduk and the ruler. The festivities created a sense of communal celebration and reinforced the shared identity and purpose of the Babylonian people under the divine guidance of Marduk.

As the king performed his role as the representative of Marduk, he was not only responsible for the welfare and prosperity of his subjects but also for upholding justice and maintaining the cosmic balance. The divine kingship concept infused the role of the ruler with a sense of divine duty, emphasizing the importance of wise governance and the equitable treatment of the people. This symbiotic relationship between Marduk and the king ensured that the rulers of Babylon had both the religious and political legitimacy necessary to lead and govern effectively.

In conclusion, Marduk's status as the patron deity of Babylon went beyond symbolism and mythology. It encompassed the concept of divine kingship, wherein the king served as the earthly representative of Marduk, responsible for upholding divine order and justice. The Akitu festival played a central role in reaffirming this bond, as the king participated in rituals and reenactments that symbolized Marduk's victory over chaos and his continuous role in maintaining cosmic harmony. This relationship between Marduk and the rulers of Babylon ensured the religious and political legitimacy of the king and provided a framework for just and effective governance in Babylonian society.

Marduk's Iconography and Symbolism

The iconography of Marduk, as seen in Mesopotamian art and artifacts, offers a visual representation of his divine attributes and symbolic significance. One of the prominent visual elements associated with Marduk is his distinctive horned crown. This crown, known as the "mushhushshu crown," featured a pair of prominent horns, which symbolized Marduk's divine authority and connection to the celestial realm. The inclusion of the horns in Marduk's iconography signified his elevated status as a powerful deity.

Another significant aspect of Marduk's iconography is his association with the Mushhushshu, a dragon-like creature often depicted alongside him. The Mushhushshu symbolized Marduk's ability to overcome chaos and defeat his adversaries. Its presence in depictions of Marduk served to reinforce his role as a fearsome warrior god, capable of protecting the gods and humanity from malevolent forces. The imagery of Marduk and the Mushhushshu created a sense of awe and reverence for his power and authority.

Additionally, Marduk's symbol, the marru, held great significance in Babylonian culture. The marru was a spade-shaped scepter or staff that represented Marduk's role as the creator and lawgiver. It served as a symbol of his divine power and authority over the cosmos. The marru embodied the concept of divine kingship, emphasizing Marduk's role in establishing order and justice in the world. This symbol communicated Marduk's role as the provider and protector of the people of Babylon, ensuring their well-being and prosperity under his divine rule.

The various elements of Marduk's iconography and symbolism conveyed a complex set of ideas and associations. His horned crown represented his divine authority, while the presence of the Mushhushshu emphasized his role as a formidable warrior. The marru symbolized his power as the creator and lawgiver, as well as his responsibility to establish and maintain cosmic order. Together, these visual representations showcased Marduk's multifaceted nature and highlighted his importance as a central figure in Babylonian religious and cultural life.

Marduk's Syncretism and Influence

Marduk's syncretism with other deities played a significant role in shaping his attributes and expanding his influence within the pantheon. One notable example of syncretism involving Marduk is his assimilation of the god Ea, also known as Enki, who was revered as the god of wisdom, magic, and freshwater.

In the mythic narrative of Marduk's rise to power, Ea plays a crucial role by bestowing his wisdom and knowledge upon Marduk. This syncretic blending of attributes enhanced Marduk's reputation as a wise and just ruler. By incorporating Ea's characteristics into his own, Marduk gained the ability to govern with wisdom and insight, making him not only a formidable warrior but also a discerning judge and lawgiver.

The syncretism of Marduk and Ea illustrates the fluidity of religious beliefs in ancient Mesopotamia. As different regions and city-states came under Babylonian influence, local deities were often assimilated into the Babylonian pantheon, resulting in a more unified religious system. The assimilation of Ea into Marduk's mythology not only strengthened Marduk's divine authority but also provided a sense of continuity and coherence within the religious traditions of the region.

Exploring Ancient Mesopotamian Mythology, Rivalries, and Spiritual Legacies

Furthermore, Marduk's syncretism with other deities allowed for a broader cultural impact beyond the realm of religion. As Babylon became a dominant political and cultural center, the influence of Marduk extended beyond the religious sphere. His attributes and symbolism permeated various aspects of Babylonian society, including art, literature, and governance. The syncretic nature of Marduk's mythology facilitated the integration of diverse cultural elements into a cohesive religious and cultural framework, contributing to the development of Babylonian identity and the consolidation of Marduk's position as the preeminent god of Babylon.

The syncretism of Marduk with other deities exemplifies the dynamic nature of religious beliefs and practices in ancient Mesopotamia. It reflects the continuous evolution and adaptation of religious traditions as they interacted with different cultures and contexts. Marduk's ability to absorb and incorporate the attributes of other gods demonstrated his enduring relevance and the enduring power of his mythology throughout the history of ancient Mesopotamia.

Exercises:

Reflect on the significance of Marduk's rise to power in relation to the political and cultural developments of ancient Babylon. How did Marduk's ascent mirror the growth and influence of the city-state?

Analyze the symbolism associated with Marduk, such as his horned crown and the Mushhushshu. What do these symbols reveal about his attributes and role within the pantheon?

Compare and contrast the concept of divine kingship in Babylon with similar concepts in other ancient civilizations. What similarities and differences can you identify, and what do they indicate about the societal and religious structures of these cultures?

Research and explore the impact of Marduk's syncretism with other deities, such as Ea. How did this syncretism contribute to Marduk's power and influence, and what does it reveal about the evolving nature of Mesopotamian religious beliefs?

By engaging with these exercises, you will deepen your understanding of Marduk's significance as the god of Babylon and ruler of the Mesopotamian pantheon. Through critical thinking and analysis, you will gain valuable insights into the complexities of ancient religious systems and their cultural implications.

The cult of Marduk and its influence on Babylonian society

In this section, we will explore the cult of Marduk and its profound impact on Babylonian society. The cult of Marduk was an integral part of religious and cultural life in ancient Mesopotamia, particularly in the city of Babylon. The worship of Marduk was not limited to the realm of the divine, but it also permeated various aspects of Babylonian society, including politics, economics, and social structure. By delving into the cult practices and rituals associated with Marduk, we can gain insights into the complex interplay between religion, power, and social dynamics in ancient Mesopotamia.

Rituals and Festivals:

The worship of Marduk, the patron deity of Babylon, was characterized by a rich array of rituals and festivals that celebrated his divine attributes and reinforced his prominent role in Babylonian society. Among these, the most renowned and significant was the New Year festival, known as the Akitu.

The Akitu festival held great importance in Babylonian religious and cultural life. It was an annual event that marked the beginning of the agricultural year and served as a vital occasion for the renewal of cosmic order and the continuity of Babylonian civilization. The festival typically took place in the month of Nisan (March-April) and lasted for several days.

During the Akitu festival, the king played a central role as the earthly representative of Marduk. The king's participation in the rituals and ceremonies served to reinforce the divine authority bestowed upon him by Marduk and emphasized the intimate relationship between the deity and the ruler. The festival was seen as an opportunity for the king to demonstrate his devotion to Marduk and to seek the god's blessings for the upcoming year.

The Akitu festival encompassed various rites and activities. It began with a procession led by the king, who carried the statue of Marduk from his temple, the Esagila, to the sacred Akitu house. The procession was accompanied by priests, officials, and the general population, all rejoicing and expressing their reverence for Marduk.

Once at the Akitu house, the king and the priests performed elaborate rituals and made offerings to Marduk. These offerings included food, drink, incense, and other symbolic items. The purpose was to honor the deity, express gratitude for his protection and favor, and seek his continued support for the prosperity and well-being of Babylon.

The Akitu festival also involved dramatic reenactments of the divine victory of Marduk over the primordial forces of chaos. This mythic battle, known as the Enuma Elish, was enacted through symbolic performances, representing the triumph of order over chaos and the establishment of Marduk as the supreme god of Babylon.

Throughout the festival, the city of Babylon was filled with joyful celebrations, music, dancing, and feasting. It was a time of communal unity and collective rejoicing as the people of Babylon came together to express their devotion to Marduk and to participate in the rituals that affirmed their connection to the divine and their place within the cosmic order.

The Akitu festival was not only a religious event but also a political and social occasion. It provided an opportunity for the king to demonstrate his legitimacy and authority as the chosen ruler by the gods. It also served as a time for the reaffirmation of social hierarchies and the reinforcement of societal norms.

In conclusion, the worship of Marduk in Babylon was marked by the grandeur of the Akitu festival, a significant annual event that celebrated the deity's divine attributes and solidified his position as the patron god of the city. The festival served as a powerful symbol of cosmic renewal, the continuity of Babylonian civilization, and the close relationship between Marduk and the king. Through sacred rituals, offerings, and processions, the Babylonians sought Marduk's blessings and ensured the prosperity and well-being of their city. The Akitu festival was a time of joyous celebration, cultural expression, and religious devotion, uniting the people of Babylon in their reverence for their patron deity.

Temple Complexes:

Central to the cult of Marduk, the patron deity of Babylon, were the grand temple complexes dedicated to his worship. The most renowned and significant of these was the Esagila, a magnificent structure located in the heart of Babylon.

The Esagila temple was a colossal architectural marvel that served as the focal point of religious life in Babylon. It was believed to be the earthly dwelling place of Marduk, where the deity's presence was believed to reside. The temple complex consisted of multiple buildings and courtyards, forming a sacred precinct that encompassed various structures and facilities.

The main sanctuary of the Esagila housed the idol of Marduk, a large statue that represented the deity. This idol, believed to be the physical embodiment of Marduk, was considered sacred and was the focus of daily rituals and ceremonies performed by the temple priests. The sanctum was accessible only to the priests and select individuals involved in the religious administration.

The priests of the Esagila formed a specialized religious class responsible for the maintenance of the temple and the performance of the daily rituals. They were responsible for the upkeep of the idol, ensuring its cleanliness and adornment, as well as the execution of the various religious ceremonies that honored Marduk. These ceremonies included prayers, offerings, and incantations aimed at invoking the blessings and favor of the deity.

The Esagila temple complex also included administrative offices and areas for educational and scholarly pursuits. It served as a center of learning and intellectual discourse, attracting scholars and scribes who studied and preserved the religious texts and traditions associated with Marduk.

Furthermore, the Esagila housed a vast treasury where offerings and tributes from devotees were stored. These offerings included valuable items such as precious metals, gems, textiles, and agricultural produce. The accumulation of these offerings over time solidified the economic power and influence of the cult of Marduk. The wealth stored in the temple's treasury also served as a testament to the devotion and gratitude of the worshipers who sought the favor of Marduk.

The prominence and grandeur of the Esagila and other temple complexes dedicated to Marduk in Babylon reflected the significant role of the deity in the religious and cultural life of the city. These architectural wonders stood as physical manifestations of the power and authority of Marduk, and their existence emphasized the central position of the cult of Marduk within Babylonian society.

In conclusion, the grand temple complexes, such as the Esagila, formed the heart of the cult of Marduk in Babylon. These architectural marvels served as the physical abode of the deity on Earth and housed the sacred idol of Marduk. The priests of the Esagila conducted daily rituals and maintained the connection between the divine and human realms. The treasury within the temple stored the offerings and tributes from devotees, showcasing the economic power and influence of the cult. The temple complexes were monumental structures that symbolized the central position of Marduk in the religious and cultural life of Babylon.

Priesthood and Hierarchy:

The cult of Marduk in Babylon had a well-defined hierarchical structure that played a crucial role in the administration of religious affairs and exerted significant influence within Babylonian society. At the apex of this hierarchy was the high priest, known as the ummânu, who served as the chief representative of Marduk on Earth.

The ummânu, or high priest, held a prestigious position and enjoyed great authority and privileges. As the primary intermediary between the divine and human realms, the ummânu played a vital role in the religious rituals and ceremonies dedicated to Marduk. They were responsible for overseeing the daily operations of the temple, supervising the lower-ranking priests, and ensuring the proper execution of religious practices.

The high priest, as the representative of Marduk, held considerable influence beyond religious matters. They were often involved in political and legal affairs, acting as advisors to the king and other high-ranking officials. The close relationship between the priesthood and the ruling elite was a crucial aspect of Babylonian governance, with the cult of Marduk providing religious legitimacy to the monarchy.

The ummânu's influence extended to matters of law and justice. They had a role in interpreting divine will and determining the outcome of legal disputes. Their pronouncements and judgments were highly respected and carried significant weight within Babylonian society.

The priesthood as a whole held a privileged position within Babylonian society. They were exempt from certain taxes and obligations imposed on the general population, and they received offerings and tributes from devotees, which contributed to their material wealth and status.

The close association between the cult of Marduk, the monarchy, and the governance of Babylon reinforced the religious and political authority of the priesthood. The king, as the earthly representative of Marduk, relied on the support and guidance of the priesthood to maintain his position and ensure the favor of the deity. In turn, the priesthood benefited from their proximity to the ruling elite, as it allowed them to exert influence and play a role in shaping the policies and direction of the kingdom.

The hierarchical structure and the influence of the priesthood within the cult of Marduk reflected the interconnectedness of religion, politics, and society in ancient Babylon. The close association between the religious and political spheres was a defining characteristic of the Babylonian civilization, with the cult of Marduk acting as a unifying force that bolstered the authority and legitimacy of the ruling elite.

In conclusion, the cult of Marduk in Babylon had a hierarchical structure with a high priest, the ummânu, at its helm. The priesthood enjoyed privileges and wielded authority not only in religious matters but also in political and legal affairs. The close relationship between the priesthood and the ruling elite reinforced the association between the cult of Marduk, the monarchy, and the governance of Babylon. This interplay of religious and political power shaped the social fabric of Babylonian society and contributed to the prominence and influence of the cult of Marduk.

Influence on Babylonian Society

The cult of Marduk exerted a profound influence on Babylonian society, permeating all aspects of life and shaping the cultural, political, and economic landscape of ancient Mesopotamia.

Political Significance:

Marduk's status as the patron deity of Babylon played a crucial role in the political structure of ancient Mesopotamia. The cult of Marduk provided a religious foundation for the exercise of political power, granting the ruling king a divine mandate to govern. This divine kingship concept formed the basis of the political ideology in Babylon and solidified the authority and legitimacy of the ruling elite. Here are some key points regarding the close association between the cult of Marduk, the monarchy, and the concept of divine kingship:

Divine Mandate: According to Babylonian belief, the king was chosen by the gods to rule over the city and its people. Marduk, as the chief deity of Babylon, held the ultimate authority and bestowed his favor upon the chosen ruler. The king, acting as Marduk's representative on Earth, was seen as the intermediary between the divine and the human realms. This divine mandate provided a religious justification for the exercise of political power.

Unifying Force: The cult of Marduk served as a unifying force within Babylonian society. It provided a shared religious identity that transcended individual differences and fostered a sense of community. The worship of Marduk and participation in religious festivals, such as the New Year festival (Akitu), brought the people of Babylon together, reinforcing their loyalty to the ruling king and the divine order.

Rituals of Kingship: The cult of Marduk incorporated specific rituals and ceremonies that were integral to the establishment and maintenance of the king's authority. Coronation rituals, oaths of allegiance, and royal investiture ceremonies were conducted in the presence of Marduk, symbolizing the king's divine appointment and his responsibilities as a just ruler. These rituals reaffirmed the close relationship between the cult of Marduk and the monarchy.

Exploring Ancient Mesopotamian Mythology, Rivalries, and Spiritual Legacies

Temples and Divine Abode: The grand temple complexes dedicated to Marduk, such as the Esagila, were not only centers of worship but also symbolized the physical abode of the deity on Earth. The king's connection to Marduk was further emphasized through his patronage of these temples and his participation in their rituals. The presence of the king in the temple ceremonies reinforced his divine role and his association with Marduk.

The association between the cult of Marduk, the monarchy, and the concept of divine kingship provided a religious and ideological framework for the exercise of political power in Babylon. It solidified the authority and legitimacy of the ruling elite and created a sense of stability and order within the society. The belief in the divine mandate granted by Marduk ensured the obedience and loyalty of the people, fostering a system of governance that relied on religious justification and the shared religious identity of the Babylonian civilization.

Economic Power:

The cult of Marduk wielded substantial economic power in ancient Mesopotamia, thanks to the wealth accumulated through various means. The temples dedicated to Marduk, such as the Esagila in Babylon, played a central role in the economic landscape of the city and the wider region. Here are some key aspects highlighting the economic influence of the cult of Marduk:

Offerings and Tributes: The worshipers of Marduk, as well as the city-state of Babylon itself, made offerings and tributes to the temples dedicated to the deity. These offerings included valuable items such as precious metals, jewels, livestock, and agricultural produce. The wealth generated through these offerings became the property of the temples, providing a substantial economic resource.

Temple Lands and Estates: The cult of Marduk administered vast agricultural lands and estates, which were granted as endowments or acquired through royal grants and donations. These lands were cultivated and managed by temple officials and the priesthood, ensuring a steady flow of agricultural produce, such as grains, fruits, and vegetables. The surplus produce was often used for trade or distributed among the temple personnel and the poor.

Trade Networks: The temples dedicated to Marduk, being economic centers, actively engaged in trade and commerce. They participated in regional and long-distance trade networks, which involved the exchange of goods, including textiles, metals, spices, and luxury items. The temples served as intermediaries in commercial transactions, generating revenue and fostering economic growth.

Craftsmanship and Artisans: The cult of Marduk patronized various craftsmen and artisans who produced exquisite artworks, sculptures, jewelry, and ceremonial objects for the temples. These skilled individuals worked under the patronage of the temples, enhancing the artistic and cultural prestige of Babylon. The sale of these high-quality crafted goods also contributed to the economic prosperity of the cult.

Employment and Infrastructure: The economic activities of the cult of Marduk created employment opportunities for a significant portion of the population. The temples required a dedicated workforce to manage their agricultural lands, maintain infrastructure, conduct trade, and perform administrative tasks. This employment generated income and livelihoods for numerous individuals within Babylon and its surrounding areas.

The substantial wealth accumulated by the cult of Marduk not only sustained the religious practices but also had a broader impact on the economy of Babylon. The economic influence of the cult contributed to the prosperity and development of the city, establishing Babylon as a major economic hub in the region. The control over agricultural resources, participation in trade networks, and patronage of skilled craftsmen elevated Babylon's status as a thriving center of economic activity in ancient Mesopotamia.

Social Cohesion and Identity:

The cult of Marduk served as a unifying force in Babylonian society, fostering social cohesion and a sense of collective identity among its people. Here are several factors that highlight the role of the cult of Marduk in promoting unity and social integration:

Shared Religious Framework: The worship of Marduk provided a common religious framework that transcended social divisions. It offered a set of beliefs, rituals, and values that formed the foundation of Babylonian religious and cultural identity. This shared framework created a sense of belonging and solidarity among the worshipers of Marduk, regardless of their social status or background.

Annual Festivals and Communal Rituals: The cult of Marduk celebrated various festivals throughout the year, with the most notable being the New Year festival, known as the Akitu. These festivals served as communal gatherings, bringing together people from all walks of life to participate in shared rituals, processions, and festivities. These events provided opportunities for social interaction, strengthening social bonds and fostering a sense of unity among the participants.

Exploring Ancient Mesopotamian Mythology, Rivalries, and Spiritual Legacies

Inclusive Worship Practices: The worship of Marduk was accessible to people from all strata of society. The temples dedicated to Marduk welcomed worshipers from different social classes, allowing them to engage in religious activities, make offerings, and seek the blessings of the deity. This inclusivity created a sense of equality and shared participation in the cult's practices, further reinforcing social cohesion.

Moral and Ethical Framework: The cult of Marduk upheld certain moral and ethical values that were essential for maintaining social order and harmony. The teachings associated with Marduk emphasized concepts such as justice, compassion, and the pursuit of righteousness. These principles provided a shared moral framework that guided the behavior and interactions of the Babylonian society, promoting mutual respect and cooperation among its members.

Influence on Legal and Political Systems: The cult of Marduk had a significant impact on the legal and political systems of Babylon. As the patron deity of the city, Marduk's authority and blessings were believed to be bestowed upon the ruling king. This religious connection between the cult and the monarchy reinforced the legitimacy of the ruling elite and created a sense of shared destiny and collective purpose.

Overall, the cult of Marduk played a vital role in fostering social cohesion and a collective sense of identity among the people of Babylon. By providing a shared religious framework, promoting communal rituals, and upholding moral values, the cult contributed to the unity and integration of Babylonian society. It helped bridge social divisions, reinforce social bonds, and create a sense of belonging that extended beyond individual differences.

Cultural Influence:

The cult of Marduk had a profound impact on the cultural expression of Babylonian society, permeating various artistic, literary, and architectural endeavors. Here are several ways in which Marduk's influence manifested in the cultural landscape of ancient Babylonia:

Epic Narratives and Literature: The cult of Marduk provided the inspiration for epic narratives and literary compositions. The most famous among these is the Enuma Elish, the Babylonian creation epic. This myth celebrated Marduk's role as the supreme deity who defeated the forces of chaos and established order in the cosmos. The Enuma Elish elevated Marduk to a position of unparalleled power and authority, solidifying his central role in the religious and cultural imagination of the Babylonians.

Artistic Representations: Marduk's significance was also reflected in the artistic representations of the time. Sculptures, reliefs, and engravings depicted Marduk in various forms, capturing his attributes and symbolism. Marduk was often portrayed as a majestic figure, adorned with divine regalia, and surrounded by symbols of power and authority. These artistic representations aimed to convey Marduk's status as the supreme deity and emphasize his wisdom, strength, and divine nature.

Architecture and Temple Complexes: The cult of Marduk influenced the architectural landscape of ancient Babylonia. The grand temple complexes dedicated to Marduk, such as the Esagila in Babylon, were not only centers of religious worship but also architectural marvels. These structures were designed to reflect the grandeur and significance of Marduk's cult. They served as physical representations of Marduk's dwelling place on Earth and provided spaces for religious rituals, ceremonies, and communal gatherings.

Cultural Influence Beyond Babylon: The cultural influence of the cult of Marduk extended beyond the boundaries of Babylon. As the Babylonian empire expanded and conquered new regions, aspects of Babylonian religious practices, including the worship of Marduk, were adopted by the conquered peoples. Neighboring city-states and regions incorporated Marduk into their own pantheons, often assimilating him with their existing deities or acknowledging his supremacy. This cultural assimilation further spread Marduk's influence and solidified his position as a significant deity in the wider Mesopotamian region.

The cult of Marduk not only shaped the religious and spiritual beliefs of the Babylonians but also left a lasting impact on their artistic expressions, literary compositions, and architectural achievements. Marduk's symbolism, narratives, and divine attributes permeated all forms of cultural expression, creating a rich cultural tapestry that celebrated his power, wisdom, and central role in the religious and cultural identity of ancient Babylonia.

Exercises:

Discuss the role of the Akitu festival in the cult of Marduk. How did this festival reinforce the religious and social significance of Marduk within Babylonian society?

Investigate the economic power and influence of the cult of Marduk. How did the administration of temple lands and resources contribute to the prosperity of Babylon?

Exploring Ancient Mesopotamian Mythology, Rivalries, and Spiritual Legacies

Analyze the symbolism and imagery associated with Marduk in Mesopotamian art and literature. How did these representations reflect his divine attributes and cultural significance?

Evaluate the relationship between the cult of Marduk and the ruling elite in Babylonian society. How did the cult legitimize and reinforce the authority of the monarchy?

Compare and contrast the cult of Marduk with other prominent deity cults in ancient Mesopotamia. What similarities and differences can be observed in their religious practices and societal impact?

Through the exploration of the cult of Marduk and its influence on Babylonian society, we can gain a comprehensive understanding of the intricate interplay between religion, power, and social dynamics in ancient Mesopotamia.

Enuma Elish: Marduk's Victory and Creation of the World

In this section, we will delve into the mythological epic of Enuma Elish, which recounts Marduk's victory over the forces of chaos and his subsequent role in the creation of the world. Enuma Elish, often referred to as the Babylonian creation myth, provides profound insights into the cosmological beliefs and the religious worldview of ancient Mesopotamia. By analyzing the narrative and symbolism within Enuma Elish, we can explore the complex interplay between gods, primordial forces, and the establishment of cosmic order.

Narrative Overview:

Enuma Elish begins by depicting a primordial state of chaos, represented by the deities Tiamat, the primeval sea, and Apsu, the freshwater abyss. From their union, a pantheon of gods is born, but over time, conflicts arise between the younger and older generations of gods. The narrative centers around the rebellion of Tiamat, who seeks to restore chaos and destroy the younger gods.

Marduk's Ascendancy:

In this section, we will delve into the mythological epic of Enuma Elish, which recounts Marduk's victory over the forces of chaos and his subsequent role in the creation of the world. Enuma Elish, often referred to as the Babylonian creation myth, provides profound insights into the cosmological beliefs and the religious worldview of ancient Mesopotamia. By analyzing the narrative and symbolism within

Enuma Elish, we can explore the complex interplay between gods, primordial forces, and the establishment of cosmic order.

◆   Narrative Overview:

Enuma Elish begins by depicting a primordial state of chaos, represented by the deities Tiamat, the primeval sea, and Apsu, the freshwater abyss. From their union, a pantheon of gods is born, but over time, conflicts arise between the younger and older generations of gods. The narrative centers around the rebellion of Tiamat, who seeks to restore chaos and destroy the younger gods.

◆   Marduk's Ascendancy:

As chaos loomed over the world, threatening to plunge it into an abyss of disorder and destruction, Marduk emerged as the champion of the gods. Despite his youth, Marduk possessed extraordinary qualities that made him the ideal candidate to confront the formidable Tiamat. Recognizing his potential and the urgent need for a savior, the other deities gathered and conferred upon Marduk supreme authority.

In this pivotal moment, the gods bestowed upon Marduk powerful weapons, symbolizing not only his divine status but also his readiness to confront the forces of chaos. These weapons included the thunderbolt, a symbol of his celestial power, and the winds, which he would employ strategically in his battle against Tiamat. With his newfound authority and weaponry, Marduk accepted the momentous challenge before him, fully aware of the immense stakes involved.

◆   Marduk's Victory:

The climactic showdown between Marduk and Tiamat was a struggle of cosmic proportions. With the fate of the world hanging in the balance, Marduk engaged Tiamat in a ferocious battle. Utilizing his weapons and displaying remarkable strategic prowess, Marduk fought valiantly against the chaotic forces embodied by Tiamat.

In a stunning display of power and skill, Marduk ultimately emerged triumphant. He successfully vanquished Tiamat, thereby establishing his dominion over the forces of chaos. This decisive victory marked a significant turning point in the mythic narrative, solidifying Marduk's position as the supreme deity within the Babylonian pantheon.

Marduk's triumph over Tiamat carried profound symbolism and metaphysical implications. It represented the triumph of order over chaos, the ascent of divine authority, and the establishment of cosmic harmony. Marduk's victory ensured the stability and preservation of the world, setting the stage for the subsequent act of creation.

Exploring Ancient Mesopotamian Mythology, Rivalries, and Spiritual Legacies

◆   Creation of the World:

Having vanquished the chaotic forces embodied by Tiamat, Marduk assumes his role as the divine architect of the cosmos. Drawing upon the lifeless body of Tiamat, he embarks upon the creation of the world and its myriad components. With his divine power and wisdom, Marduk fashions the heavens and the earth, bringing forth a structured and ordered existence from the primordial chaos.

In his capacity as the supreme deity, Marduk assigns specific roles to the gods, establishing a cosmic hierarchy that reflects the diverse functions and responsibilities within the divine realm. Each deity is given a distinct domain and purpose, contributing to the overall harmony and balance of the cosmos. This hierarchical organization reflects the Babylonian society's understanding of order and the need for differentiated roles in maintaining stability.

In a remarkable act of creation, Marduk also molds humanity from the blood of a rebel god, thus forging a profound connection between the mortal realm and the divine. This act not only sets the stage for the relationship between gods and humans but also establishes the foundation for societal order and the establishment of moral and ethical codes.

◆   Symbolism and Meaning:

Enuma Elish, with its rich symbolism and metaphorical depth, encapsulates the Babylonian cosmological worldview and the delicate interplay between order and chaos. Marduk's victory over Tiamat represents the triumph of divine authority and the establishment of a harmonious world order. It signifies the primacy of order and the necessity of maintaining cosmic balance to ensure the stability and continuity of existence.

The creation of the world from Tiamat's body carries profound symbolic significance. It embodies the transformative power of destruction and renewal, highlighting the cyclical nature of existence. This act of creation underscores the interconnectedness of all things, emphasizing the intricate relationship between the divine, the natural world, and humanity.

Enuma Elish also serves as a metaphor for the human condition and the challenges faced in navigating the complexities of existence. The struggle against chaos and the quest for order resonate deeply within the human psyche, reflecting humanity's perpetual search for meaning, purpose, and harmony.

Divine Dynamics

Exercises:

Explore the concept of creation from destruction in Enuma Elish. How does the myth illustrate the transformative power of chaos and its role in the process of creation? Reflect on the parallels between this concept and other creation myths from different cultural and religious traditions.

Investigate the symbolic significance of Marduk's assignment of roles to the gods in the cosmic hierarchy. How does this reflect the Babylonian understanding of order, structure, and the interdependence of different aspects of existence?

Discuss the implications of the creation of humanity from the blood of a rebel god. What does this suggest about the nature of humanity and its relationship with the divine? Consider how this myth may have influenced Babylonian societal views and the establishment of social order.

Analyze the symbolism of the cosmic battle between Marduk and Tiamat in relation to the struggle between order and chaos in human experience. How does this myth resonate with contemporary understandings of personal and societal challenges?

Engage in a comparative analysis of Enuma Elish and other creation myths, such as the Judeo-Christian creation story. Explore the similarities and differences in the themes, symbolism, and underlying messages of these narratives.

The myth of the creation of the world in Enuma Elish offers profound insights into the ancient Mesopotamian worldview and their understanding of the cosmic order. By studying this myth, we gain a deeper appreciation for the complexities of existence, the pursuit of order, and the interplay between the divine and the human realms.

Marduk's Symbolism and Iconography

Symbolism and iconography played a significant role in the religious beliefs and practices of ancient Mesopotamia, and Marduk, as the chief deity of Babylon, was no exception. The visual representations of Marduk in art and iconography provide valuable insights into his symbolic significance and the ways in which he was understood and revered by the Babylonian people.

One of the prominent symbols associated with Marduk is the horned crown he is often depicted wearing. This crown, adorned with bull horns, serves as a powerful symbol of his divine authority and connection to the celestial realm. The bull, a symbol of strength and fertility, was associated with numerous deities in ancient Mesopotamian culture, and Marduk's incorporation of the bull symbolism further emphasized his power and status as a ruler and protector.

In addition to the horned crown, Marduk's association with the dragon-like creature known as the Mushhushshu further contributed to his symbolism. The Mushhushshu was a mythical creature with the body of a serpent and the forelegs and head of a lion. It was often depicted as a guardian creature and was closely associated with the divine realm. Marduk's connection to the Mushhushshu symbolized his role as a fierce and protective deity, defending the cosmic order against chaotic forces.

Another important symbol linked to Marduk is the spade-shaped scepter known as the "marru." This scepter represented Marduk's role as the creator and lawgiver. It embodied his divine power and authority over the cosmos, as well as his responsibility for maintaining order and justice. The spade-shaped tip of the scepter also had agricultural connotations, symbolizing Marduk's role in fertility and abundance, as well as his association with the cultivation of the land.

The iconography of Marduk evolved over time, reflecting changes in Babylonian religious beliefs and societal values. In earlier representations, Marduk was depicted as a youthful warrior, emphasizing his role as a conqueror and protector. As Babylon grew in power and influence, Marduk's portrayal shifted to emphasize his wisdom and divine kingship. In these later depictions, he was often depicted as an older, bearded figure, radiating authority and wisdom.

Exercises:

Analyze the symbolism of the horned crown in Marduk's iconography. What does it represent in terms of his authority and connection to the celestial realm? Compare this symbol with other horned deities in different cultural and religious traditions.

Explore the significance of the Mushhushshu in Marduk's iconography. How does this creature symbolize his role as a protective deity? Research other mythological creatures associated with deities in ancient Mesopotamia and discuss their symbolism.

Investigate the agricultural connotations of the spade-shaped scepter, the "marru." How does this symbol connect Marduk to fertility and abundance? Examine the role of agriculture and fertility in ancient Mesopotamian society and discuss how Marduk's symbolism reflected these cultural values.

Compare and contrast the early and later iconography of Marduk. How did his portrayal change over time, and what might have influenced these shifts? Discuss the broader cultural and religious changes that may have impacted the representation of deities in ancient Mesopotamia.

Engage in a comparative analysis of Marduk's iconography with other deities in different mythological traditions. Identify common symbols and themes and discuss the possible cross-cultural influences and connections.

The symbolism and iconography associated with Marduk offer valuable insights into the complex religious beliefs and cultural values of ancient Mesopotamia. By examining these symbols and their meanings, we gain a deeper understanding of Marduk's role as a powerful deity, a wise ruler, and a protector of the cosmic order.

Marduk's Cult and Rituals

The cult of Marduk held a central place in the religious and social fabric of ancient Babylonian society. As the patron deity of Babylon and the supreme god of the Babylonian pantheon, Marduk's cult had a profound influence on the lives of the Babylonian people and played a significant role in their religious practices and worldview.

Rituals were an integral part of the worship of Marduk and were performed regularly to honor and appease the deity. The religious calendar of Babylon was punctuated by various festivals and ceremonies dedicated to Marduk, each with its own unique rituals and observances. These rituals served to establish and maintain a relationship between the divine and the human, reinforcing the cosmic order and ensuring the well-being of the community.

One of the most important religious festivals in Babylon was the New Year festival known as the Akitu. This grand celebration marked the renewal of cosmic order and the reaffirmation of Marduk's kingship and protection over the city. The Akitu festival lasted for several days and included a series of rituals and processions.

During the Akitu festival, the king, as the earthly representative of Marduk, would participate in reenactments of the divine narrative, symbolizing Marduk's victory over chaos and the establishment of order. These reenactments often involved the recitation of hymns and prayers, accompanied by music and dancing.

Exploring Ancient Mesopotamian Mythology, Rivalries, and Spiritual Legacies

The rituals aimed to invoke the presence of Marduk and to invoke his blessings upon the city and its people.

Another important aspect of Marduk's cult was the construction and maintenance of temples dedicated to his worship. The most famous of these was the Esagila, a grand temple complex in the heart of Babylon. The Esagila served as the physical embodiment of Marduk's presence on Earth and was considered the holiest site in the city. Within the temple, priests performed daily rituals and offerings to Marduk, ensuring his continued favor and protection.

The rituals associated with Marduk's cult were not limited to the confines of the temple. The Babylonian people actively engaged in personal and household worship of Marduk, offering prayers and sacrifices to seek his guidance and assistance in their daily lives. These private acts of devotion were seen as essential for maintaining a harmonious relationship with the deity and for securing his favor and protection.

Exercises:

Research and describe the key rituals and observances of the Akitu festival. What were the main activities and symbols associated with this festival? How did it reinforce the cult of Marduk and the divine kingship?

Explore the role of music and dancing in the rituals of Marduk's cult. Investigate the instruments and musical traditions associated with Babylonian religious practices and discuss their significance in invoking the presence of the divine.

Investigate the architecture and layout of the Esagila temple complex. What were its main features, and how did they reflect the importance of Marduk in Babylonian society? Discuss the role of the priests in the temple and their duties in performing rituals and maintaining the sacred space.

Examine the role of personal and household worship in the cult of Marduk. What were the common practices and offerings made by individuals and families to seek Marduk's favor? How did these acts of devotion contribute to the overall religious experience of the Babylonian people?

Reflect on the significance of rituals and cultic practices in ancient societies. Discuss the ways in which rituals serve as a means of communication and connection between humans and the divine. Draw parallels and contrasts with rituals in other religious and spiritual traditions, such as Witchcraft, Divination, Herbalism, Shamanism, and Ecospirituality.

The cult of Marduk and its rituals provided a framework for the Babylonian people to connect with the divine, reinforce social cohesion, and uphold the cosmic order. Through their active participation in these rituals, the Babylonians sought to maintain a harmonious relationship with Marduk and secure his favor and protection for themselves and their community. The cult of Marduk exemplifies the power of religious practices to shape and define the beliefs and behaviors of a society, illustrating the profound impact of spirituality and ritual on the human experience.

Marduk and the Mesopotamian Pantheon

Marduk's position within the Mesopotamian pantheon was unique and evolving throughout the history of ancient Mesopotamia. As the patron deity of Babylon and the chief god of the Babylonian pantheon, Marduk held a prominent role in the religious and cultural landscape of the region.

In the earlier periods of Mesopotamian civilization, such as the Sumerian era, Marduk's status was not as prominent. He was overshadowed by other deities, such as Enlil and Enki, who held significant positions in the pantheon. However, with the rise of Babylon as a dominant city-state, Marduk's cult gained increasing prominence and influence.

Marduk's ascendancy to the position of the supreme god of the Babylonian pantheon is often associated with the reign of King Hammurabi (1792-1750 BCE), who established the Babylonian Empire. The political and military power of Babylon was paralleled by the growing religious significance of Marduk. The rulers of Babylon sought to legitimize their authority by linking themselves closely to Marduk and presenting him as their divine patron.

The Babylonian creation myth, the Enuma Elish, played a crucial role in elevating Marduk's status. In this epic narrative, Marduk emerges as the hero who defeats the primordial goddess Tiamat and establishes order in the cosmos. The story served as a mythological foundation for Marduk's kingship and solidified his position as the supreme deity.

As the chief god of Babylon, Marduk's influence extended beyond religious matters. He was regarded as the ultimate source of wisdom, justice, and law. The concept of divine kingship, in which the ruler served as Marduk's earthly representative, further emphasized his significance in the social and political realms. The religious and political institutions were closely intertwined, with the king and the priesthood working together to ensure Marduk's favor and protection for the city and its people.

Exploring Ancient Mesopotamian Mythology, Rivalries, and Spiritual Legacies

The influence of Marduk's cult extended beyond the boundaries of Babylon itself. As the Babylonian Empire expanded, the worship of Marduk spread to other regions, and his cult became more widely recognized throughout Mesopotamia. This expansion was facilitated by the assimilation and syncretism of local deities into the Babylonian religious framework. Different cities and regions often incorporated Marduk into their own pantheons, adopting and adapting his attributes and symbolism to align with their local religious traditions.

However, it is important to note that while Marduk gained significant prominence in Babylonian religion, other deities still maintained their importance in various aspects of Mesopotamian life. Different cities and regions continued to venerate their own local gods and goddesses, even as they acknowledged Marduk's position as the supreme deity. This complex religious landscape demonstrates the diverse and multifaceted nature of ancient Mesopotamian beliefs.

Overall, Marduk's role within the Mesopotamian pantheon exemplifies the intricate interplay between religion, politics, and cultural identity. His ascendancy as the chief god of Babylon and his association with kingship and cosmic order reflect the deep connection between the divine and human spheres in ancient Mesopotamia. Marduk's cult and influence shaped the religious practices, social structures, and worldview of the Babylonian people, leaving a lasting legacy in the history of the region.

Chapter 7: Ziggurats and Temples: Sacred Spaces and Ritual Practices

In the ancient world, the construction of monumental structures known as ziggurats and temples played a central role in the religious and cultural practices of various civilizations. These sacred spaces served as architectural marvels and focal points for communal worship, religious ceremonies, and rituals. They represented the connection between the earthly realm and the divine, embodying the beliefs and values of the societies that built them.

This chapter explores the significance of ziggurats and temples in the ancient world, focusing on their architectural features, religious functions, and the rituals performed within their sacred precincts. By delving into the rich history and symbolism associated with these structures, we gain valuable insights into the religious beliefs, social structures, and cultural practices of ancient civilizations.

The Architecture of Ziggurats and Temples:

The construction of ziggurats and temples in ancient civilizations was a testament to their architectural ingenuity and technical expertise. These structures not only served as places of worship but also embodied the cosmological beliefs and religious practices of the respective cultures. Here are some key aspects to consider:

Ziggurats: Ziggurats were monumental stepped structures that showcased the engineering prowess of ancient civilizations. They were typically constructed with mud bricks or stones, with each level or terrace built upon the previous one, gradually ascending towards the sanctuary or temple at the top. The stepped design created a visually striking and imposing form.

Symbolism of Height: The towering height of ziggurats held symbolic significance. It represented the connection between heaven and earth, reflecting the belief that the divine realm resided in the heavens while humans inhabited the earthly realm. The ziggurat served as a physical bridge, providing a means for communication and interaction between the mortal world and the realm of the gods.

Temple Architecture: The design and layout of temples varied across different cultures and time periods. Temples were often located at the highest point of the ziggurat or situated adjacent to it. They were considered sacred spaces where religious rituals, offerings, and ceremonies took place. The temple's architecture, including its columns, courtyards, and inner sanctums, reflected the specific religious traditions and practices of the civilization.

Function and Rituals: The temple at the top of the ziggurat was the focal point of religious activity. It was believed to be the dwelling place of the deity or a space where the divine presence could be accessed. The temple served as a site for offerings, prayers, and other rituals conducted by priests and worshippers. These rituals were performed to honor the gods, seek their favor, and ensure the well-being of the community.

Cultural Significance: The construction of ziggurats and temples was a manifestation of the religious and cultural values of ancient civilizations. They were considered monumental and awe-inspiring structures, representing the power and authority of the ruling elites and the prominence of the religious institution within society. The architecture of these structures was a reflection of the civilization's artistic and technical achievements, demonstrating their ability to organize labor and resources on a large scale.

Overall, the construction of ziggurats and temples exemplified the architectural and engineering capabilities of ancient civilizations. These structures embodied the religious beliefs and practices of the time, symbolizing the connection between the earthly and divine realms. The temples atop the ziggurats served as sacred spaces for rituals and worship, emphasizing the importance of the gods and their interaction with the human world.

Religious Functions and Ritual Practices:

Ziggurats and temples in ancient civilizations were dedicated to specific deities and served as their earthly abodes. These structures played a central role in the religious life of the community, hosting a wide range of rituals, ceremonies, and festivals that were essential to the practice of the respective religions. Here are some key points to consider:

Centers of Religious Activity: Ziggurats and temples were the focal points of religious activity within a city or community. They were considered sacred spaces where people gathered to worship, offer prayers, and engage in various rituals. These structures were believed to be the physical dwellings of the gods, serving as meeting points between the human and divine realms.

Rituals and Ceremonies: The rituals conducted within ziggurats and temples were designed to establish and maintain a harmonious relationship between humans and the gods. They encompassed a wide range of practices, from daily offerings and prayers to more elaborate ceremonies and festivals. The specific rituals varied depending on the religious traditions and beliefs of the civilization, but common elements included purification rites, divination practices, and sacrifices.

Role of Priests and Priestesses: Priests and priestesses played a crucial role in the religious activities conducted within ziggurats and temples. They acted as intermediaries between the human worshippers and the deities, carrying out the rituals and offering prayers on behalf of the community. Priests and priestesses were responsible for maintaining the sanctity of the sacred space, ensuring the correct performance of rituals, and interpreting signs and omens from the gods.

Festivals and Processions: Ziggurats and temples were also sites for elaborate festivals and processions that marked important religious occasions throughout the year. These events often involved the participation of the entire community, with colorful processions, music, dance, and communal feasting. Festivals celebrated specific deities, significant mythological events, or agricultural cycles and served as occasions for collective worship and communal bonding.

Seekers of Divine Favor: The rituals performed within ziggurats and temples were aimed at seeking the favor and blessings of the gods. Through offerings, prayers, and sacrifices, worshippers sought divine protection, guidance, and prosperity. These rituals were believed to ensure the well-being of the community, promote fertility and abundance, and address specific needs or concerns of the individuals.

In summary, ziggurats and temples were sacred spaces dedicated to specific deities, serving as centers of religious activity within ancient civilizations. The rituals conducted within these structures were essential for maintaining a harmonious relationship between humans and the gods, with priests and priestesses acting as intermediaries. Festivals and processions added vibrancy and communal participation to the religious life of the community, while seekers of divine favor turned to these sacred spaces to seek blessings, protection, and guidance from the gods.

Symbolism and Cultural Significance:

Ziggurats and temples held profound symbolic and cultural significance within their respective societies, reflecting the cosmological and mythological beliefs of the civilization. Here are some points to consider:

Symbolism and Presence of the Gods: Ziggurats and temples were architectural embodiments of the power and presence of the gods in the earthly realm. The towering structures and their elevated platforms represented a connection between heaven and earth, symbolizing the sacred nature of the space and the divine authority it held. The temple at the top of the ziggurat was considered the dwelling place of the deity, reinforcing the belief that the gods directly interacted with the human world.

Authority of the Ruling Elite: The construction and maintenance of ziggurats and temples were often funded and overseen by the ruling elite, such as kings or priests, who sought to solidify their authority and legitimacy. These structures were impressive and awe-inspiring, reflecting the wealth, power, and architectural prowess of the ruling class. The association of the ruling elite with the religious activities conducted within the temples further bolstered their authority and reinforced the divine mandate to govern.

Collective Identity and Unity: Ziggurats and temples served as unifying symbols for the community. They provided a shared religious framework and a physical space where people could come together to worship and participate in communal rituals. The rituals and festivals conducted within these structures fostered a sense of collective identity and unity among the worshippers, reinforcing social cohesion and a shared sense of belonging.

Centers of Knowledge and Education: Ziggurats and temples were not only places of worship but also repositories of knowledge. They housed libraries and archives that contained sacred texts, historical records, and administrative documents. These centers of education were where scribes and scholars were trained, and where wisdom and knowledge were transmitted from one generation to another. The preservation and dissemination of cultural, religious, and historical knowledge played a vital role in the cultural and intellectual development of the society.

In summary, ziggurats and temples held profound symbolic and cultural significance within ancient societies. They embodied the presence of the gods, reinforced the authority of the ruling elite, and served as symbols of collective identity and unity. These structures were not only places of worship but also centers of knowledge and education, contributing to the preservation and transmission of cultural, religious, and historical heritage.

Conclusion:

Ziggurats and temples were not merely architectural constructions; they were the physical manifestations of religious devotion, cultural identity, and the pursuit of divine connection. Through their design, rituals, and symbolism, these sacred spaces played a vital role in shaping the religious and social fabric of ancient civilizations. Understanding the significance of ziggurats and temples allows us to appreciate the profound impact of religious beliefs and practices on the development of human societies.

Understanding Ziggurats: Architecture and Purpose

In the ancient civilizations of Mesopotamia, the construction of ziggurats stands as a testament to the architectural prowess and religious devotion of the people. These towering structures, characterized by their distinctive stepped form, played a central role in the religious and cultural practices of societies such as the Sumerians, Babylonians, and Assyrians. This section delves into the architecture and purpose of ziggurats, shedding light on their significance within the religious landscape of ancient Mesopotamia.

Architectural Features of Ziggurats:

Ziggurats, with their distinct architectural features, were remarkable structures that held great significance in ancient Mesopotamian civilizations. Here are further details about their architectural characteristics:

Construction Materials: Ziggurats were primarily constructed using mud-brick, a prevalent building material in the region due to the abundance of clay. However, in some cases, stone was also used, especially for the higher levels or important sections of the structure. The use of mud-brick allowed for the creation of large-scale structures while ensuring durability and stability.

Stepped Design: The most recognizable feature of ziggurats was their stepped or terraced design. Each level of the ziggurat was slightly smaller than the one beneath it, creating a series of receding tiers. The number of levels varied depending on the specific ziggurat, ranging from two or three to as many as seven. The stepped design served both practical and symbolic purposes, providing stability to the structure while also representing the connection between heaven and earth.

Buttresses and Inclined Planes: To ensure the stability of the massive ziggurat structure, buttresses were often incorporated into the exterior walls. These buttresses acted as additional support, counteracting the lateral forces exerted on the structure. Inclined planes or ramps were sometimes constructed on the exterior to provide access to the upper levels, facilitating the movement of priests and worshippers during religious ceremonies.

Temple at the Summit: The pinnacle of the ziggurat housed a sacred temple, which was the most sacred and restricted area of the entire structure. Access to the temple was limited to the priests and the ruling elite, emphasizing its exclusive and divine nature. The entrance to the temple was often adorned with impressive gateways, monumental doorways, or decorative motifs, signifying the threshold between the earthly realm and the sacred space.

Symbolic Elements: Various symbolic elements were incorporated into the design and decoration of ziggurats. These included guardian figures or animals, such as mythical creatures or bulls, placed at the entrance of the temple. These representations served as protective and auspicious symbols, guarding the sacred space and denoting the presence of the deity worshipped within. Additionally, decorative motifs, inscriptions, and reliefs adorned the walls of the ziggurat, depicting religious narratives, mythological scenes, or symbols associated with the deity.

In summary, ziggurats were characterized by their use of mud-brick or stone construction, stepped or terraced design, buttresses for stability, and inclined planes for access. The summit of the ziggurat housed a sacred temple, accessible only to the privileged few, with symbolic elements such as guardian figures and decorative motifs emphasizing the sanctity of the space. These architectural features not only served practical purposes but also embodied the spiritual and symbolic significance of ziggurats in ancient Mesopotamian cultures.

Religious and Symbolic Significance:

Ziggurats held a profound religious and symbolic significance in ancient Mesopotamian culture, serving as architectural embodiments of the connection between the mortal and divine realms. Here are further details about their religious and symbolic significance:

Sacred Mountains: Ziggurats were often regarded as sacred mountains or cosmic mountains, representing the meeting point between heaven and earth. The towering height of the ziggurats emphasized their role in bridging the gap between the mortal world and the divine realm. They were believed to provide a physical pathway for the gods to descend and interact with humanity.

Earthly Abodes of Deities: Each ziggurat was dedicated to a specific deity and was considered their earthly abode. The ziggurats were constructed to honor and accommodate the presence of the patron deity of the city-state. For example, the ziggurat of Ur was dedicated to Nanna, the moon god. The deity was believed to reside in the temple at the summit of the ziggurat, where offerings and prayers were presented to him.

Divine Dynamics

Ritual Spaces: Ziggurats served as ritual spaces where religious ceremonies, offerings, and prayers took place. The priests and priestesses conducted these rituals on behalf of the community, serving as intermediaries between the human worshippers and the gods. The ziggurat's design and layout were meticulously planned to facilitate the performance of these rituals and create a sacred atmosphere conducive to communication with the divine.

Channels of Communication: Ziggurats were seen as channels through which the gods could descend to receive offerings and prayers from their worshippers. It was believed that the structure itself and the rituals performed within it acted as a conduit, allowing for a direct connection between the mortal and divine realms. The ziggurat's construction and the dedication of resources demonstrated the commitment and devotion of the community to their patron deity.

Symbolic Representation: The architectural features and symbolism incorporated into ziggurats further reinforced their religious and symbolic significance. The stepped design represented the ascent from the earthly realm to the divine realm. The grandeur of the ziggurat, with its towering height and elaborate decorations, reflected the power and majesty of the gods worshipped within. The decorative motifs, reliefs, and inscriptions depicted religious narratives, mythological scenes, and symbols associated with the patron deity, reinforcing their presence and influence.

In summary, ziggurats were highly revered structures in ancient Mesopotamian culture, symbolizing the connection between the mortal and divine realms. They served as the earthly abodes of specific deities, providing spaces for rituals, offerings, and prayers. The design and construction of ziggurats and their symbolic representations emphasized the significance of these structures in facilitating communication with the gods and expressing the religious devotion of the community.

Functions and Ritual Practices:

Ziggurats played a central role in the religious and civic life of ancient Mesopotamia, serving as the focal points for a wide range of rituals, ceremonies, and festivals. These religious practices were essential for maintaining harmony and order within the cosmos, seeking the favor of the gods, and ensuring the well-being of the community. Here are further details about the rituals and their significance:

Offerings: One of the primary rituals performed on ziggurats was the offering of food, drink, and incense to the gods. These offerings were presented to the deity residing in the temple at the summit of the ziggurat as a means of sustenance and appeasement. The priests, as intermediaries, conveyed the offerings on behalf of the community, seeking the blessings and favor of the gods. The act of offering symbolized the reciprocal relationship between humans and the divine, acknowledging the gods' role as providers and protectors.

Prayers and Hymns: Prayers and hymns formed an integral part of the rituals conducted on ziggurats. The priests recited prayers and chanted hymns, expressing gratitude, praise, and requests to the gods. These invocations aimed to establish a direct line of communication with the divine, seeking divine intervention, guidance, and protection for the community. Through prayers and hymns, the worshippers demonstrated their faith, devotion, and dependence on the gods for their well-being and prosperity.

Ceremonies and Processions: Ziggurats were also the sites of various ceremonies and processions that were conducted on specific occasions, such as religious festivals and important cultural events. These events brought the community together, fostering a sense of collective identity and reinforcing the religious and cultural values upheld by the society. Ceremonies often involved the participation of the ruling elite, priests, and the general population, showcasing the unity and solidarity of the community in their devotion to the gods.

Cosmic Harmony and Order: The rituals performed on ziggurats were intricately connected to the broader cosmological beliefs of the Mesopotamians. By conducting these rituals, the community sought to maintain cosmic harmony and order. It was believed that the gods maintained the balance of the universe, and through their rituals, humans played their part in upholding this balance. The rituals conducted on ziggurats were seen as essential for sustaining the proper functioning of the cosmos, ensuring favorable conditions for agriculture, protection from disasters, and overall prosperity.

Symbolic Representation: The rituals and ceremonies performed on ziggurats were laden with symbolic significance. They represented the interaction between humans and the divine, the acknowledgment of the gods' power and influence, and the collective aspirations of the community. The elaborate and carefully orchestrated rituals, accompanied by music, incense, and offerings, created a sacred atmosphere and conveyed the community's reverence and devotion to the gods.

In summary, ziggurats served as the centers of religious and civic life in ancient Mesopotamia. The rituals, ceremonies, and festivals conducted on these monumental structures aimed to maintain cosmic harmony, seek the favor of the gods, and ensure the well-being of the community. These practices involved offerings, prayers, hymns, and processions, reflecting the community's religious beliefs, values, and aspirations. The rituals performed on ziggurats served as a means of communication with the divine and played a crucial role in shaping the religious and cultural fabric of ancient Mesopotamian society.

Problem: Discuss the architectural features of ziggurats and explain their significance within Mesopotamian culture.

Exercise: Imagine you are a priest living in ancient Sumer. Describe the rituals you would perform on a ziggurat and explain their purpose.

Conclusion:

Ziggurats were awe-inspiring structures that held deep religious and cultural significance in ancient Mesopotamia. Through their unique architectural design and purpose, they served as sacred spaces that facilitated the connection between mortals and the divine. The rituals conducted on ziggurats fostered a sense of communal identity and played a vital role in maintaining cosmic order and seeking divine favor. Understanding the architecture and purpose of ziggurats provides valuable insights into the religious beliefs and practices of ancient Mesopotamian societies.

The Role of Temples in Mesopotamian Society

Temples held a central and multifaceted role in the ancient Mesopotamian society. These sacred structures served as the physical embodiments of the divine presence, places of worship, centers of administration, and focal points for economic and social activities. This section explores the significant role of temples in Mesopotamian society, shedding light on their religious, political, and cultural functions.

Religious Functions:

Indeed, temples in Mesopotamia held a significant role in the religious practices and beliefs of the ancient civilization. Here is a further expansion on the purpose and functions of temples in Mesopotamia:

Dedication to Specific Deities: Each temple in Mesopotamia was dedicated to a specific deity, representing their earthly dwelling and emphasizing their presence among humans. Different cities and regions had their own patron deities, and the temples were constructed to honor and serve these specific gods. For example, the temple of Enki in Eridu and the temple of Marduk in Babylon were built to worship and venerate these deities.

Exploring Ancient Mesopotamian Mythology, Rivalries, and Spiritual Legacies

Sacred Space for Rituals and Offerings: Temples provided a sacred space for conducting religious rituals and offering prayers, sacrifices, and other types of offerings. These rituals were performed by the priests and priestesses who acted as intermediaries between the human worshipers and the gods. The temples served as the designated places where people could engage in direct communication with the divine realm, seeking blessings, guidance, and protection.

Focal Point of Religious Ceremonies: The interior of the temples housed altars, statues, and ritual objects associated with the specific deity. These objects were the focal point of religious ceremonies conducted by the priests. The ceremonies often included libations, burning incense, and recitation of prayers and hymns. The rituals aimed to honor and appease the gods, maintaining their favor and ensuring the well-being of the community.

Spiritual Authority of the Priests: Temples were staffed by a dedicated priesthood responsible for the daily administration of religious affairs. The priests played a vital role in conducting rituals, maintaining the temple's spiritual atmosphere, and overseeing the temple complex. They were seen as the mediators between the gods and the people, and their role carried significant spiritual authority and influence within the community.

Repository of Sacred Knowledge: Temples also served as repositories of sacred knowledge. They housed libraries and archives containing religious texts, historical records, and administrative documents. These collections preserved the religious and cultural heritage of the civilization, and the temples became centers of education where scribes and scholars were trained in the sacred arts and sciences.

Community Gathering and Social Functions: Temples were not only places of worship but also served as community centers. They were gathering points for festivals, processions, and other communal events. Temples provided a space for the community to come together, fostering social cohesion, and reinforcing shared religious beliefs and values.

In summary, temples in Mesopotamia were dedicated to specific deities and served as sacred spaces for religious rituals and offerings. They acted as the earthly abodes of the gods and facilitated the connection between humans and the divine realm. Temples were places of worship, where people sought divine favor, offered prayers and sacrifices, and engaged in religious ceremonies. They were also centers of knowledge and social gathering, playing a vital role in shaping the religious, cultural, and social fabric of ancient Mesopotamian society.

Divine Dynamics

Political and Administrative Functions:

Temples were not only places of religious worship but also served as centers of political and administrative power in Mesopotamian society. The ruling elite, including kings and high-ranking officials, often exerted control over the temples and their resources. Temples held vast amounts of wealth, including land, livestock, and valuable offerings brought by the worshipers. They served as economic powerhouses, managing agricultural estates, trade, and craft production.

Temple personnel, including priests and administrators, played crucial roles in governing and managing the temple affairs. They were responsible for maintaining the temple's properties, overseeing its economic activities, and distributing resources to support religious rituals and provide for the welfare of the community. Temples thus acted as important centers of political authority and contributed to the socio-economic stability of Mesopotamian society.

Control by the Ruling Elite: Temples in Mesopotamia often came under the control and influence of the ruling elite, including kings and high-ranking officials. They recognized the political and economic power associated with the temples and sought to exert control over their resources. The kings, in particular, claimed divine authority and often acted as the high priests or had close ties with the priesthood, further solidifying the connection between religious and political power.

Accumulation of Wealth: Temples accumulated significant wealth and resources over time. They received offerings and donations from worshipers, including valuable goods, livestock, and agricultural produce. The temples also owned vast amounts of land, which contributed to their economic power. These resources were managed by the temple personnel, who ensured their proper utilization and distribution.

Economic Powerhouses: Temples served as economic centers in Mesopotamian society. They managed agricultural estates, controlled trade networks, and facilitated craft production. The temple's agricultural lands were cultivated by temple workers and often used to generate surplus food supplies that could be distributed during times of scarcity. Temples also engaged in trade activities, which involved the exchange of goods and commodities with other regions.

Administrative Roles: Temple personnel, including priests and administrators, played crucial roles in governing and managing temple affairs. They were responsible for overseeing the temple's properties, including agricultural lands, livestock, and trade operations. The administrators ensured the efficient functioning of the temple, maintained records of offerings and resources, and supervised the distribution of goods and services.

Distribution of Resources: Temples played a significant role in redistributing wealth and resources within the society. They allocated resources to support religious rituals and ceremonies, ensuring the continuity of worship and maintaining the favor of the gods. Temples also used their wealth to provide for the welfare of the community, including caring for the poor, funding public infrastructure projects, and supporting educational activities.

Political Authority and Stability: The close association between temples and the ruling elite contributed to the stability of Mesopotamian society. The control of temples allowed the ruling elite to maintain political authority and legitimacy. By managing economic resources and providing for the needs of the community, temples played a crucial role in fostering social cohesion and ensuring the support of the population for the ruling elite.

In summary, temples in Mesopotamia were not only places of religious worship but also centers of political and administrative power. They were controlled by the ruling elite and held vast amounts of wealth and resources. Temples managed economic activities, distributed resources, and played a significant role in governing and maintaining socio-economic stability. The political and administrative significance of temples underscored the close intertwining of religious and political authority in ancient Mesopotamian society.

Cultural and Educational Functions:

Temples played a significant role in preserving and transmitting knowledge and cultural traditions. They served as centers of learning, where scribes and scholars were trained in various disciplines, including writing, mathematics, astronomy, and religious texts. Temples housed extensive libraries and archives, containing valuable clay tablets that recorded historical events, legal codes, hymns, and prayers.

Furthermore, temples served as custodians of cultural and artistic practices. They sponsored festivals, music, dance, and drama performances that celebrated the gods and entertained the community. The temples also commissioned and housed elaborate works of art and craftsmanship, such as sculptures, reliefs, and decorative murals, which reflected the religious and cultural values of the society.

Centers of Learning: Temples in Mesopotamia served as centers of education and intellectual development. They played a vital role in training scribes and scholars in various disciplines, including writing, mathematics, astronomy, and the study of religious texts. These institutions provided formal education and mentorship, ensuring the continuity of knowledge and the cultivation of intellectual elites.

Libraries and Archives: Temples housed extensive libraries and archives, preserving a wealth of knowledge in the form of clay tablets. These tablets contained a wide range of information, including historical records, legal codes, administrative documents, hymns, prayers, and scientific observations. The temples carefully maintained these collections, which served as important repositories of cultural and intellectual heritage.

Knowledge Preservation: The temples' role as custodians of knowledge ensured the preservation of historical events, religious practices, and cultural traditions. The clay tablets stored in the temples acted as primary sources for recording and transmitting information across generations. By safeguarding these records, the temples played a crucial role in preserving the collective memory of the society.

Cultural Patronage: Temples actively patronized and supported cultural and artistic practices. They sponsored festivals, musical performances, dance, and drama, which were integral parts of religious rituals and celebrations. These events showcased the talents of musicians, dancers, and actors, while also serving as opportunities for communal gathering and entertainment.

Artistic Expressions: Temples commissioned and housed elaborate works of art and craftsmanship, reflecting the religious and cultural values of the society. Sculptures, reliefs, decorative murals, and other forms of artistic expression adorned the temple walls and courtyards. These artworks often depicted mythological narratives, scenes from religious rituals, and the images of gods and goddesses, contributing to the visual representation of religious beliefs and cultural identity.

Cultural Exchange: Temples served as centers of cultural exchange, attracting visitors and pilgrims from different regions. The interaction between worshippers, scholars, and artists from diverse backgrounds facilitated the exchange of ideas, artistic techniques, and religious practices. This cross-cultural exchange contributed to the enrichment and diversity of Mesopotamian culture.

In summary, temples in Mesopotamia played a significant role in preserving and transmitting knowledge and cultural traditions. They served as centers of learning, housing libraries and archives that contained valuable clay tablets documenting historical events, legal codes, hymns, and prayers. Temples also sponsored cultural practices, including festivals, music, dance, and drama, which celebrated the gods and entertained the community. Through their patronage of the arts and craftsmanship, temples supported and showcased artistic expressions that reflected religious beliefs and cultural values. Overall, temples acted as vital institutions for the preservation and dissemination of knowledge, as well as the promotion of cultural heritage in ancient Mesopotamia.

Examples:

Problem: Discuss the religious and political functions of temples in Mesopotamian society, providing examples to support your argument.

Exercise: Imagine you are an aspiring scribe in ancient Babylon. Write a short essay explaining the significance of temples in preserving knowledge and educating future generations.

Conclusion:

Temples held a crucial position in the fabric of ancient Mesopotamian society, serving as religious sanctuaries, administrative centers, and cultural institutions. They provided a space for worship, rituals, and offerings, fostering the connection between humans and the divine. Temples played a pivotal role in the political and economic affairs of the region, serving as centers of power and wealth. They also acted as guardians of knowledge, preserving and transmitting cultural traditions and educating future generations. Understanding the multifaceted role of temples offers valuable insights into the religious, political, and cultural dynamics of Mesopotamian civilization.

Rituals and Offerings in Mesopotamian Temples

Rituals and offerings played a vital role in the religious practices of ancient Mesopotamia. Temples served as the primary sites for these sacred acts, where individuals and communities engaged in rituals to connect with the divine and seek favor from the gods. This section explores the significance of rituals and offerings in Mesopotamian temples, examining their purposes, forms, and the underlying beliefs that shaped these practices.

Purpose of Rituals:

Rituals conducted in Mesopotamian temples served several purposes, encompassing both individual and communal needs. These rituals aimed to establish and maintain a harmonious relationship between humans and the gods, ensuring the well-being of the community and the continuity of cosmic order. They were seen as essential for upholding the social, economic, and environmental balance.

Divine Dynamics

Rituals also acted as a means of communication between humans and the divine realm. They provided a channel for individuals to express their devotion, seek divine guidance, and offer gratitude or supplication. Furthermore, rituals were believed to possess transformative power, capable of influencing the course of events and securing divine intervention in times of crisis.

Establishing Harmony and Cosmic Order: Rituals conducted in temples aimed to establish and maintain a harmonious relationship between humans and the gods, as well as ensure the well-being of the community. These rituals were seen as essential for upholding the social, economic, and environmental balance in Mesopotamian society. By performing the prescribed rituals, the worshippers sought to align themselves with the divine will and maintain cosmic order.

Communication with the Divine: Rituals served as a means of communication between humans and the divine realm. They provided individuals with an avenue to express their devotion, seek divine guidance, and offer prayers, gratitude, or supplication. Through rituals, worshippers believed they could establish a personal connection with the gods, fostering a sense of intimacy and divine presence.

Transformation and Divine Intervention: Rituals were believed to possess transformative power, capable of influencing the course of events and securing divine intervention in times of crisis. By engaging in rituals, individuals sought to invoke the gods' favor and protection, hoping for their benevolent influence in matters such as health, fertility, agricultural abundance, and victory in conflicts. Rituals were performed with the belief that they could bring about positive changes and mitigate potential disasters.

Rituals for Individual and Communal Needs: Rituals conducted in Mesopotamian temples addressed both individual and communal needs. On an individual level, rituals offered an opportunity for personal spiritual growth, purification, and reconciliation with the gods. They provided a framework for individuals to seek forgiveness for transgressions, ask for blessings, or express gratitude for blessings received. On a communal level, rituals served as a unifying force, strengthening social bonds and reinforcing a sense of shared identity and purpose among the worshippers.

Symbolism and Symbolic Actions: Rituals in Mesopotamian temples often involved symbolic actions and gestures that carried profound meaning. These actions included offerings of food, drink, and incense, as well as the recitation of prayers and hymns. Symbolic objects and ritual artifacts were used, such as sacred vessels and statuettes representing the gods. These symbolic elements were believed to convey specific intentions, invoke divine presence, and facilitate communication between humans and the gods.

Seasonal and Agricultural Rites: Many rituals conducted in Mesopotamian temples were closely tied to the agricultural calendar and seasonal cycles. These rituals sought to ensure agricultural fertility, bountiful harvests, and the well-being of livestock. They involved offerings, processions, and ceremonies performed at specific times of the year, aligning with the natural rhythms and cycles of the environment.

In summary, rituals conducted in Mesopotamian temples served multiple purposes, encompassing both individual and communal needs. They aimed to establish and maintain a harmonious relationship between humans and the gods, ensuring the well-being of the community and the continuity of cosmic order. Rituals served as a means of communication with the divine realm, offering individuals a channel to express devotion, seek guidance, and influence events. They possessed transformative power and were performed with the belief in their ability to secure divine intervention and mitigate crises. Rituals in Mesopotamian temples held deep symbolic meaning, and their performance was closely tied to the agricultural calendar and seasonal cycles.

Forms of Rituals:

Rituals in Mesopotamian temples took various forms, ranging from simple acts of prayer and offering to elaborate ceremonies and processions. Some rituals were performed on a daily basis, while others were reserved for specific occasions or festivals. The complexity of the rituals often depended on the deity being honored and the purpose of the ceremony.

Offerings played a significant role in these rituals. They could take the form of food, drink, incense, precious objects, or even animal sacrifices. Offerings were presented to the gods as acts of devotion and respect, acknowledging their power and seeking their favor. These offerings were believed to nourish and sustain the divine beings and create a reciprocal relationship between humans and the gods.

Variety of Rituals: Rituals in Mesopotamian temples encompassed a wide range of practices, varying in complexity and purpose. Some rituals were performed on a daily basis as part of the temple's regular religious routine. These daily rituals often involved prayers, hymns, and offerings to maintain a constant connection between the worshippers and the gods. Other rituals were reserved for specific occasions or festivals, such as the New Year festival or the celebration of a particular deity.

Divine Dynamics

Elaborate Ceremonies and Processions: Certain rituals in Mesopotamian temples were marked by elaborate ceremonies and processions. These grand events involved the participation of priests, attendants, and members of the community. Processions would often move through the city streets, carrying sacred objects, statues, or symbols of the deity being honored. These public displays of religious devotion aimed to engage the entire community and reinforce a collective sense of religious identity and unity.

Importance of Offerings: Offerings played a crucial role in Mesopotamian temple rituals. They were presented to the gods as acts of devotion, respect, and gratitude. Offerings could take various forms, including food, drink, incense, precious objects, or animal sacrifices. The selection of offerings often reflected the significance of the deity being worshipped and the purpose of the ritual. For instance, offerings of grain, wine, and livestock were common in agricultural and fertility rituals, while valuable objects or incense were offered during more solemn or celebratory occasions.

Reciprocal Relationship: Offerings in Mesopotamian temple rituals were seen as a means of establishing and maintaining a reciprocal relationship between humans and the gods. It was believed that by presenting offerings, humans fulfilled their duty of providing sustenance and nourishment to the divine beings. In return, the gods would bestow their blessings, protection, and favor upon the worshippers and the community as a whole. This reciprocal relationship formed the foundation of the religious practices and reinforced the bond between humans and the divine realm.

Symbolic and Spiritual Significance: Offerings held symbolic and spiritual significance in Mesopotamian temple rituals. They were not merely material objects but represented the devotion, reverence, and submission of the worshippers. The act of offering symbolized the recognition of the gods' power, their role in the cosmic order, and the dependence of humans on divine benevolence. The presentation of offerings was accompanied by prayers and invocations, expressing the desires and needs of the community and seeking divine intervention.

In summary, rituals in Mesopotamian temples took various forms and were performed on a daily basis or during specific occasions and festivals. Offerings played a significant role in these rituals, serving as acts of devotion, respect, and gratitude. They represented the reciprocal relationship between humans and the gods, nourishing the divine beings and seeking their favor in return. Rituals and offerings held symbolic and spiritual significance, reflecting the religious beliefs, values, and communal needs of the worshippers.

Exploring Ancient Mesopotamian Mythology, Rivalries, and Spiritual Legacies

Symbolism and Beliefs:

Rituals and offerings in Mesopotamian temples were deeply rooted in the religious beliefs and cosmology of the society. The rituals symbolized the interaction between the human and divine realms and reflected the interconnectedness of all existence. The offerings were seen as physical manifestations of respect and gratitude, expressing the human desire for divine blessings and protection.

The act of offering sacrifices, both animal and vegetal, demonstrated the willingness of individuals to relinquish something valuable to establish a bond with the gods. The symbolic sharing of food and drink between humans and the divine beings reinforced the concept of reciprocity and communal harmony.

Interconnection of Realms: Rituals and offerings in Mesopotamian temples were based on the belief that the human and divine realms were interconnected. The rituals served as a means of communication and interaction between these realms, allowing humans to establish a relationship with the gods. Through the performance of rituals, humans sought to bridge the gap between the mortal world and the divine realm, acknowledging the gods' presence and their role in the cosmic order.

Symbolism of Offerings: Offerings in Mesopotamian temple rituals were imbued with symbolic meaning. Sacrifices, both animal and vegetal, were seen as acts of devotion and a willingness to give up something valuable to establish a connection with the gods. The act of sharing food and drink with the divine beings represented a symbolic sharing of life's sustenance, emphasizing the reciprocal relationship between humans and the gods. It was a way of expressing respect, gratitude, and a desire for divine blessings and protection.

Reciprocity and Harmony: The concept of reciprocity was central to the rituals and offerings in Mesopotamian temples. By presenting offerings to the gods, worshippers expressed their recognition of the gods' power and their own dependence on divine favor. It was believed that through these offerings, humans fulfilled their part of the reciprocal relationship, and in return, the gods would bestow their blessings, protection, and benevolence upon the community. The act of offering and receiving established a sense of harmony and balance within the cosmos.

Communal Dimension: Rituals and offerings in Mesopotamian temples were not only individual acts but also had a communal dimension. They were performed on behalf of the entire community, seeking blessings, protection, and prosperity for all members. The sharing of offerings and participation in rituals fostered a sense of unity and collective identity, reinforcing the social fabric of the society. Through communal participation, individuals affirmed their shared beliefs, values, and aspirations, creating a sense of belonging and cohesion.

Spiritual Connection: The rituals and offerings in Mesopotamian temples were not solely driven by material or practical concerns but had a profound spiritual significance. They were an expression of the human desire to connect with the divine, to seek guidance, and to receive divine intervention in various aspects of life. The act of engaging in rituals and presenting offerings allowed individuals to transcend the mundane and enter into a sacred realm, experiencing a profound connection with the gods and the larger cosmic order.

In summary, rituals and offerings in Mesopotamian temples were deeply rooted in the religious beliefs and cosmology of the society. They symbolized the interconnection between the human and divine realms, emphasized reciprocity and communal harmony, and expressed the spiritual longing for divine blessings and protection. The act of offering sacrifices and sharing food and drink demonstrated the willingness to establish a bond with the gods and participate in the larger cosmic order. These rituals and offerings played a central role in the religious and social fabric of Mesopotamian society, fostering a sense of unity, belonging, and spiritual connection among the worshippers.

Examples:

Problem: Analyze the significance of rituals and offerings in Mesopotamian temples, considering their role in maintaining social cohesion and ensuring divine favor.

Exercise: Imagine you are a priestess in ancient Sumer. Write a detailed account of a ceremonial ritual performed in honor of the goddess Inanna, describing the specific steps, offerings, and symbolic elements involved.

Conclusion:

Rituals and offerings held profound significance in Mesopotamian temple practices, providing a means for individuals and communities to engage with the divine realm and seek divine favor. These rituals fostered a sense of connection, unity, and reciprocity between humans and gods, ensuring the well-being and harmony of the society. Through their symbolic actions and offerings, the ancient Mesopotamians expressed their devotion, gratitude, and desire for divine intervention. Understanding the role of rituals and offerings in Mesopotamian temples provides valuable insights into the religious and cultural dynamics of this ancient civilization.

Cult Statues and Divine Presence

In the religious practices of ancient civilizations, the concept of divine presence was of paramount importance. Cult statues played a significant role in embodying the presence of deities in the earthly realm. This section delves into the intricate relationship between cult statues and the divine presence in various spiritual traditions, including witchcraft, divination, herbalism, shamanism, ecospirituality, and magic in ancient Mesopotamia. By exploring this topic, we can gain a deeper understanding of how the physical representation of the divine facilitated spiritual connection and interaction.

Concept of Divine Presence:

The concept of divine presence is fundamental to many religious and spiritual traditions, including those of ancient Mesopotamia. It refers to the belief that deities, with their divine essence and power, can manifest themselves in a tangible way, making their presence known and accessible to humans. This concept acknowledges that the gods are not distant or detached from the mortal realm but actively engage with and influence human affairs.

In the context of ancient Mesopotamia, the belief in the divine presence was central to the religious practices and rituals conducted in temples. Temples were regarded as sacred spaces where the gods could manifest and dwell among the people. The physical structures of the temples, such as the ziggurats and sanctuaries, were believed to serve as portals or gateways for the gods to descend from the heavens and establish a connection with the earthly realm.

The divine presence was not limited to a purely spiritual or metaphysical understanding. It could also be experienced in a sensory and perceptible manner. The gods were believed to communicate through signs, dreams, visions, and even physical manifestations. For example, a deity might be represented by an idol or statue within the temple, which was seen as a material embodiment of their divine presence. These representations were considered sacred and were treated with reverence and respect.

The presence of the gods in the temples was not solely for their own sake but also for the benefit of the human worshippers. It was believed that through the rituals and offerings performed in the presence of the gods, individuals could establish a direct connection, seek guidance, receive blessings, and experience a sense of divine communion. The rituals acted as a means of communication, allowing humans to express their devotion, gratitude, and supplication directly to the gods.

Divine Dynamics

The concept of divine presence extended beyond the temple rituals. It permeated all aspects of life in ancient Mesopotamia, shaping beliefs, values, and social structures. The gods were seen as active participants in the world, influencing natural phenomena, guiding human destinies, and maintaining cosmic order. The presence of the gods was sought in everyday life, and individuals turned to them for protection, guidance, and assistance in various endeavors.

In summary, the concept of divine presence in ancient Mesopotamia encompassed the belief that deities could manifest themselves in a tangible way, establishing a direct connection with humans. This presence was experienced through sensory, spiritual, and symbolic means. Temples were considered sacred spaces where the divine presence could be encountered, and rituals served as a means of communication and communion with the gods. The belief in divine presence infused the religious, social, and cultural fabric of Mesopotamian society, shaping beliefs, practices, and the relationship between humans and the divine realm.

Role of Cult Statues:

Cult statues, also known as idolatry, were crafted with meticulous detail to represent specific deities. These statues served as vessels or conduits through which the divine presence could be channeled and experienced by worshippers. The statue itself was not considered a mere object but rather a sacred embodiment of the deity it represented.

Indeed, cult statues played a significant role in ancient religious practices and were highly revered as sacred representations of the deities they depicted. Crafted with great care and attention to detail, these statues were believed to serve as vessels or conduits through which the divine presence could be channeled and made accessible to worshippers.

The creation of cult statues was a meticulous process carried out by skilled artisans. The statues were typically made from various materials, including stone, wood, or metal, and were often adorned with precious metals, gemstones, and intricate designs. The artists aimed to capture the essence and characteristics of the deity they were representing, seeking to depict them in a way that would inspire awe and reverence among the worshippers.

The cult statues were not perceived as mere lifeless objects but as sacred embodiments of the gods themselves. It was believed that the deity's essence, power, and presence were somehow infused into the statue, giving it a divine aura. Through rituals and offerings conducted in the presence of these statues, worshippers sought to establish a connection with the deity and experience a direct communion with the divine.

When the cult statues were placed in the temples, they became the focal points of religious activities. Worshippers would come before the statue to offer prayers, make offerings, and seek guidance or blessings. The statues were often housed in inner sanctuaries or inner chambers of the temples, which were considered the most sacred spaces. The cult statues were treated with utmost reverence and care, and only authorized priests and priestesses were allowed to handle and interact with them.

The belief in the sacred nature of the cult statues and their ability to channel the divine presence influenced the rituals and ceremonies performed in their presence. Worshippers would often address the statue as if they were addressing the deity directly, expressing their devotion, gratitude, or supplication. The act of bowing, kneeling, or prostrating before the statue was a sign of reverence and submission to the divine.

While the cult statues were important for facilitating the worship of specific deities, it is important to note that they were not worshipped in and of themselves. Instead, they served as focal points and reminders of the presence of the deity they represented. They were visual aids that helped worshippers to focus their devotion and establish a tangible connection with the divine.

In summary, cult statues were crafted with meticulous detail and served as sacred embodiments of specific deities. They were believed to channel the divine presence, providing worshippers with a tangible means of connecting with the gods. The cult statues played a central role in religious rituals, serving as focal points for offerings, prayers, and acts of devotion. Their significance extended beyond their physical form, as they represented the bridge between the human and divine realms in ancient religious practices.

Rituals and Offerings:

Rituals and offerings played a vital role in cultivating and maintaining the divine presence within cult statues. Through rituals, which often involved prayers, invocations, and ceremonial acts, the worshippers sought to invoke and awaken the divine presence within the statue. Offerings, such as food, drink, incense, or symbolic objects, were presented as acts of devotion and reciprocity to nourish and appease the deity.

Rituals and offerings were essential in nurturing and fostering the divine presence within the cult statues. These practices were designed to invoke, honor, and sustain the connection between the worshippers and the deity represented by the statue.

Rituals surrounding the cult statues were conducted with great care and adherence to specific procedures. They often involved purification rites, chanting of prayers and invocations, and ceremonial gestures performed by the priests or designated individuals. Through these rituals, the worshippers aimed to create a sacred and conducive environment that would attract and awaken the divine presence within the statue.

Prayers played a central role in these rituals, as they served as a means of communication between the worshippers and the deity. Prayers expressed devotion, gratitude, and supplication, as well as sought guidance, protection, and blessings. They were spoken or chanted with utmost reverence and sincerity, with the belief that they would reach the divine realm and elicit a response from the deity.

Offerings, too, held great significance in cultivating the divine presence within the cult statues. They were presented as acts of devotion and reciprocity, symbolizing the worshippers' desire to nourish and appease the deity. Food and drink offerings were meant to sustain and provide sustenance to the divine being, reflecting the belief in a reciprocal relationship between humans and the gods. Incense and fragrant oils were used to create a pleasing ambiance and to purify the space. Symbolic objects, such as jewelry, precious stones, or miniature representations of daily life, were also offered as expressions of respect and honor.

The selection and presentation of offerings were often guided by specific traditions, customs, and symbolic meanings associated with the particular deity being worshipped. The priests, who acted as intermediaries between the worshippers and the divine, played a vital role in overseeing the rituals and ensuring that the offerings were presented appropriately.

Through the combined power of rituals and offerings, worshippers believed they could cultivate and maintain the divine presence within the cult statues. The intention behind these practices was to establish a direct and tangible connection with the deity, fostering a sense of closeness, devotion, and divine intervention in the lives of the worshippers. The rituals and offerings were seen as a means to honor, communicate with, and seek the favor of the gods, while also strengthening the bond between the human and divine realms.

In summary, rituals and offerings played a vital role in invoking and sustaining the divine presence within the cult statues. Through prayers, invocations, and ceremonial acts, worshippers sought to awaken and connect with the deity represented by the statue. Offerings, presented as acts of devotion and reciprocity, were believed to nourish and appease the divine being. These practices were integral to the religious experience and reflected the profound belief in the tangible connection between humans and the gods.

Symbolic Power and Imagination:

Cult statues held symbolic power, and their presence had a profound impact on the minds and emotions of the worshippers. The belief in the divine presence within the statue activated the power of the imagination, allowing individuals to connect with the deity on a deeper level. This imaginative engagement heightened the spiritual experience and facilitated a sense of communion with the divine.

The presence of the divine within the cult statue ignited the imagination of the worshippers, enabling them to visualize and perceive the deity in a more tangible and relatable way. The statue acted as a physical representation of the divine, serving as a focal point for the worshippers' thoughts, emotions, and spiritual aspirations. By directing their attention towards the statue, worshippers could enter into a state of deep contemplation and connection, transcending the ordinary realm and entering into the sacred.

The act of engaging with the cult statue through the power of imagination allowed worshippers to forge a personal and intimate relationship with the deity. They could envision the deity's qualities, attributes, and divine presence in a way that resonated with their own understanding and experiences. The statue became a conduit through which worshippers could direct their thoughts, prayers, and emotions, establishing a profound sense of communion with the divine.

The imaginative engagement with the cult statue also had the power to evoke strong emotions and a sense of awe and reverence. As worshippers contemplated the divine presence within the statue, they might experience a range of emotions, including joy, peace, gratitude, and even a sense of fear or humility in the presence of the divine. The statue became a powerful symbol that evoked a deep spiritual response, eliciting feelings of connection, inspiration, and spiritual transformation.

The imaginative engagement with the cult statue was not limited to the moment of worship alone. It extended beyond the temple walls, influencing the worshippers' daily lives and shaping their worldview. The awareness of the divine presence within the statue provided a guiding framework for ethical conduct, moral values, and spiritual fulfillment. It fostered a sense of reverence, devotion, and accountability, reminding worshippers of the presence of the divine in all aspects of their lives.

In summary, the belief in the divine presence within the cult statue, combined with the power of the human imagination, had a profound impact on the minds and emotions of the worshippers. It allowed them to forge a deep and personal connection with the deity, transcending the physical realm and entering into a sacred communion. The imaginative engagement with the cult statue heightened the spiritual experience, evoked strong emotions, and provided a guiding framework for moral and ethical conduct. The cult statues, as symbols of the divine, held the power to transform the lives and consciousness of those who engaged with them.

Eamples:

Problem: Analyze the role of cult statues in ancient Mesopotamian religious practices, considering their significance in fostering a connection between humans and the divine realm.

Exercise: Imagine you are a witch practicing contemporary witchcraft. Describe the process of consecrating and empowering a statue as a representation of a deity in your personal altar, explaining the rituals, symbols, and intentions involved.

Conclusion:

Cult statues served as tangible representations of the divine presence in various spiritual traditions. These statues enabled individuals to forge a connection with the divine, channeling the essence and power of deities into the earthly realm. Through rituals, offerings, and the power of imagination, worshippers engaged with the divine presence embodied in the cult statues. Understanding the significance of cult statues and the concept of divine presence enhances our comprehension of ancient religious practices and provides insights into the human longing for spiritual connection and transcendence.

Sacred Enclosures and Sacred Marriage Rites

Within the rich tapestry of religious practices and rituals throughout history, the concept of sacred enclosures and sacred marriage rites emerges as a fascinating and multifaceted phenomenon. This section explores the significance and symbolism of sacred enclosures and the ritual of sacred marriage in various spiritual traditions, including witchcraft, divination, herbalism, shamanism, ecospirituality, and magic in ancient Mesopotamia. By delving into this topic, we gain a deeper understanding of the intricate relationship between sacred spaces, divine unions, and the human quest for spiritual connection and transcendence.

Exploring Ancient Mesopotamian Mythology, Rivalries, and Spiritual Legacies

Sacred Enclosures:

Sacred enclosures, such as sanctuaries or temples, hold a central place in religious and spiritual traditions across cultures and time periods. These consecrated spaces are considered special and set apart from the ordinary world, serving as a gateway to the divine realm and facilitating the interaction between humans and the sacred.

The architecture and layout of sacred enclosures are carefully designed to create an atmosphere that supports and enhances the religious and spiritual experiences of the worshippers. The physical structure of the sanctuary is often crafted with meticulous detail, incorporating elements of symbolism and sacred geometry. The arrangement of walls, columns, doorways, and chambers within the enclosure follows specific principles to evoke a sense of harmony, balance, and transcendence.

The entrance to a sacred enclosure is typically marked by a prominent gateway or threshold, which serves as a symbolic boundary between the secular and sacred realms. Crossing this threshold represents a transition from the mundane world into the realm of the divine. The architecture of the entrance may feature ornate decorations, guardian figures, or inscriptions that signify the sacredness of the space and prepare worshippers for the transformative experience that lies ahead.

Once inside the sacred enclosure, worshippers often encounter a central chamber or sanctuary that holds the primary focus of religious activities. This chamber is designed to create a sense of awe, reverence, and intimacy with the divine. It may be adorned with sacred symbols, altars, statues, or other ritual objects associated with the deity or spiritual tradition. The architectural features, such as the shape of the chamber, the play of light and shadow, and the acoustics, are all carefully considered to evoke a transcendent and contemplative atmosphere.

The layout of the sacred enclosure may also include ancillary spaces, such as side chapels, corridors, courtyards, or gardens, which provide additional areas for worship, meditation, and reflection. These spaces offer opportunities for worshippers to engage in individual or communal practices, connect with nature, or engage in acts of purification or devotion.

Symbolism plays a significant role in the design and ornamentation of sacred enclosures. Architectural elements, decorative motifs, and sacred artworks within the enclosure often carry deep symbolic meaning. These symbols can represent divine attributes, cosmological principles, mythological narratives, or spiritual concepts. They serve as visual reminders of the sacred presence and provide a framework for understanding and connecting with the divine.

Divine Dynamics

The overall design and ambiance of a sacred enclosure contribute to the rituals and experiences that take place within it. The architectural harmony, sacred symbolism, and heightened spiritual energy of the space create a conducive environment for worship, contemplation, and transcendence. The sacred enclosure becomes a sanctuary where worshippers can seek solace, find inspiration, and commune with the divine, deepening their spiritual connection and fostering a sense of transcendence and inner transformation.

In conclusion, sacred enclosures are consecrated spaces specifically designated for religious or spiritual practices. They are carefully designed to evoke a sense of the sacred and provide an environment conducive for communion with the divine. The architecture, layout, and symbolism within these enclosures shape the rituals and experiences that take place within them, facilitating a deeper connection with the divine and fostering spiritual growth and transformation.

Symbolism and Significance:

Sacred enclosures are meticulously designed to incorporate symbolic elements that resonate with the cosmology and beliefs of a particular spiritual tradition. The architectural features and layout of the enclosure are carefully considered to create a profound and meaningful experience for worshippers.

One aspect of sacred enclosures is their shape, which can hold significant symbolism. For example, circular or domed structures may represent the wholeness and unity of the divine, while square or rectangular layouts might symbolize stability and order. The choice of orientation and alignment of the enclosure with celestial bodies, such as the rising or setting sun, moon, or specific constellations, can also reflect the connection between the earthly realm and the cosmic forces.

The materials used in constructing the sacred enclosure also hold symbolic significance. Natural elements like stone, wood, and water may be incorporated to symbolize the interconnectedness between humans and the natural world. Colors are carefully chosen to evoke certain emotions or qualities associated with the divine. For instance, blue might represent spirituality or transcendence, while gold or white could signify purity and divinity.

In addition to the architectural elements, sacred enclosures are adorned with symbolic decorations, such as intricate carvings, murals, or sacred motifs. These artistic expressions often depict mythological narratives, sacred symbols, or representations of deities. These visual cues not only enhance the aesthetic appeal but also serve as visual reminders of the beliefs and values upheld by the tradition.

The symbolic design and adornments within sacred enclosures serve to create an atmosphere conducive to spiritual practices and the communion with the divine. They help to transport worshippers into a realm beyond the mundane, inviting them to connect with the sacred and participate in rituals and ceremonies that align with their beliefs and traditions.

Sacred Marriage Rites:

The concept of the sacred marriage, also known as hieros gamos, holds profound symbolism in many spiritual traditions. It represents the union of divine and human, masculine and feminine energies, and the integration of opposing forces within both the individual and the collective.

Metaphorically, the sacred marriage symbolizes the reconciliation of dualities and the restoration of cosmic harmony. It reflects the belief that the divine is not solely transcendent or immanent but encompasses both aspects. The union of masculine and feminine energies represents the integration of complementary qualities such as strength and nurturing, action and receptivity, wisdom and compassion. This union brings balance and wholeness, not only on an individual level but also within the larger social and cosmic order.

The sacred marriage also signifies the union of heaven and earth, symbolizing the connection between the spiritual and the material realms. It represents the belief that the divine is present and accessible in every aspect of existence, and that the sacred can be found in the mundane. This understanding invites individuals to recognize the divine within themselves and in all aspects of life, fostering a sense of interconnectedness and reverence for the world around them.

In some spiritual traditions, the sacred marriage is not just a metaphorical concept but is also experienced as a mystical union with the divine. Through spiritual practices such as meditation, prayer, or ecstatic rituals, individuals may seek to transcend the boundaries of the self and merge with the divine presence. This direct experience of union can be deeply transformative, leading to a profound sense of oneness and spiritual awakening.

The symbolism and practice of the sacred marriage vary across different spiritual traditions. In some cases, it may be associated with specific deities or mythological narratives that depict divine unions. It can be expressed through ritual enactments, artistic representations, or internal contemplation. Regardless of the form it takes, the sacred marriage represents a profound spiritual journey of integration, transcendence, and the realization of the divine within and without.

Divine Dynamics

Ritual Practices and Symbolic Gestures:

Sacred marriage rites are often conducted through elaborate ritual practices and symbolic gestures that are designed to invoke and embody the divine energies associated with the sacred union. These rituals vary across different spiritual traditions but share common elements that emphasize the transformative nature of the union and the bridging of the human and divine realms.

One common aspect of sacred marriage rites is the enactment of mythological narratives. These narratives often depict the union between deities or divine figures, serving as archetypal templates for the sacred marriage ritual. Through dramatic reenactments or storytelling, participants immerse themselves in the mythic symbolism, aligning their own experiences with the cosmic drama of the union.

The exchange of vows or offerings is another significant element of sacred marriage rites. Participants may make solemn promises or dedications to the divine, expressing their commitment and devotion to the spiritual path. Offerings, such as flowers, incense, or sacred objects, are presented as acts of reverence and reciprocity, symbolizing the mutual exchange of energies between the human and divine realms.

Sacred dances or gestures often accompany the sacred marriage rites. These movements are not merely aesthetic but carry profound symbolic meanings. They can represent the union of masculine and feminine energies, the harmonization of opposing forces, or the ecstatic expression of divine love and joy. The rhythmic and synchronized nature of the dances creates a heightened state of awareness and allows participants to embody the transformative power of the sacred union.

Priestesses or priests often play a crucial role as intermediaries between the human and divine realms in sacred marriage rites. They facilitate the ritual proceedings, guiding participants through the transformative journey. Their presence and expertise add an aura of sacred authority and ensure that the rituals are conducted in a sacred and respectful manner. The priestesses or priests serve as conduits for the divine energies, channeling and transmitting the blessings and transformative power of the sacred union to the participants.

Overall, sacred marriage rites are designed to create a potent and transformative experience for the participants. Through the enactment of mythic narratives, the exchange of vows or offerings, the performance of sacred dances or gestures, and the guidance of priestesses or priests, these rituals aim to invoke and embody the divine energies, facilitating a profound sense of union, transformation, and spiritual awakening for those involved.

Exploring Ancient Mesopotamian Mythology, Rivalries, and Spiritual Legacies

Examples:

Problem: Compare and contrast the role of sacred enclosures in ancient Mesopotamian temples and contemporary Wiccan circles, highlighting the similarities and differences in their design, function, and ritual practices.

Exercise: Design a sacred enclosure for a fictional spiritual tradition that incorporates elements of herbalism, shamanism, and ecospirituality. Describe the architectural features, symbolism, and rituals that would take place within this sacred space.

Conclusion:

Sacred enclosures and sacred marriage rites are deeply intertwined aspects of religious and spiritual practices across various traditions. These rituals and spaces serve as vessels for transcendent experiences, facilitating a connection between the human and divine realms. Through their symbolism, architecture, and ritual practices, sacred enclosures and sacred marriage rites provide a framework for individuals to explore their spiritual potential, engage in transformative experiences, and cultivate a profound sense of unity and harmony with the sacred. Understanding the significance of these concepts enhances our appreciation of the diverse spiritual expressions throughout history and invites us to reflect on our own quest for spiritual connection and personal transformation.

Temple Libraries and Scholarly Activities

In the realm of ancient civilizations, temple libraries emerged as esteemed repositories of knowledge and centers of intellectual and scholarly activities. This section explores the significance and functions of temple libraries, highlighting their role in preserving and disseminating information across diverse fields of study. Drawing examples from witchcraft, divination, herbalism, shamanism, ecospirituality, and magic in ancient Mesopotamia, we delve into the rich tapestry of scholarly activities that took place within these sacred spaces. By examining the practices and materials found in temple libraries, we gain insights into the intellectual pursuits and cultural heritage of these ancient societies.

Temple Libraries:

Temple libraries were revered repositories of knowledge within ancient civilizations, and they held a prominent place within sacred enclosures, such as temples or other religious sanctuaries. These libraries served as centers of learning and played a crucial role in the preservation and transmission of knowledge across generations.

The acquisition and organization of knowledge within temple libraries were typically entrusted to scribes, scholars, and priests who devoted themselves to scholarly pursuits. These individuals were responsible for transcribing and copying texts, as well as for the interpretation and analysis of existing knowledge. They played a vital role in maintaining the library's collections and ensuring the accuracy and integrity of the texts.

The knowledge stored within temple libraries encompassed various fields, including religion, mythology, astronomy, mathematics, history, medicine, law, and literature. These libraries housed a wide range of texts, such as sacred scriptures, hymns, prayers, rituals, historical records, scientific treatises, legal codes, and literary works. The texts were typically inscribed on durable materials like clay tablets, papyrus scrolls, or later, parchment.

The temple libraries were not only repositories of knowledge but also centers of education. They served as institutions where aspiring scribes and scholars received their training and education. These educational programs were rigorous and covered various disciplines, including writing, reading, mathematics, astronomy, and the interpretation of religious texts. The scribes and scholars trained within these temple libraries would go on to serve in administrative roles, participate in religious ceremonies, or become teachers themselves, thus ensuring the continuation of knowledge within their respective societies.

The dissemination of knowledge from temple libraries occurred through various means. Students and scholars would study and copy texts within the library, further contributing to the preservation and propagation of knowledge. Scholars would also engage in scholarly debates and discussions, sharing insights and interpretations. Additionally, temple libraries sometimes had public access, allowing individuals from the community to consult the texts or receive guidance from the scholars and priests.

The knowledge contained within temple libraries was highly valued, and access to it was often restricted to those with the appropriate education, status, or religious authority. The library collections were considered sacred and were safeguarded as treasured assets of the temple. The meticulous organization and preservation of the texts demonstrated the reverence and importance placed on the knowledge they contained.

Exploring Ancient Mesopotamian Mythology, Rivalries, and Spiritual Legacies

In summary, temple libraries served as repositories of knowledge, with scribes, scholars, and priests dedicated to the acquisition, organization, and dissemination of knowledge. These libraries played a vital role in preserving and transmitting cultural, religious, scientific, and historical knowledge, contributing to the intellectual and cultural development of ancient civilizations.

Collection and Organization of Texts:

Temple libraries were renowned for their extensive collections of texts, which encompassed a wide range of subjects and genres. These libraries served as repositories for religious, legal, historical, scientific, and literary works, reflecting the diverse knowledge and intellectual pursuits of the civilizations that housed them.

Religious texts held a central place in temple libraries, as they were essential for the study, interpretation, and practice of religious rituals and beliefs. These texts included sacred scriptures, hymns, prayers, rituals, and mythological narratives that detailed the cosmology, creation myths, moral codes, and worship practices of the respective religious traditions.

Legal documents and records were also important components of temple libraries. They comprised legal codes, decrees, contracts, and administrative records that governed various aspects of society, such as land ownership, commercial transactions, marriage and inheritance laws, and judicial proceedings. These documents provided guidelines for maintaining social order and resolving disputes within the community.

Historical accounts and chronicles were preserved in temple libraries, offering insights into the past. These texts recorded significant events, royal genealogies, military campaigns, diplomatic treaties, and cultural achievements. They served as valuable sources of historical information, allowing future generations to understand and learn from the triumphs and challenges of their ancestors.

Scientific treatises and observations were highly regarded in temple libraries. They encompassed fields such as astronomy, mathematics, medicine, agriculture, and engineering. These texts contained knowledge about celestial movements, mathematical calculations, medical treatments, crop cultivation techniques, irrigation systems, and architectural principles. They reflected the civilizations' quest for understanding the natural world and improving the quality of life through scientific advancements.

Literary works, including epic poems, mythological tales, philosophical treatises, and works of fiction, were treasured in temple libraries. These texts showcased the literary achievements, cultural values, and artistic expressions of the civilizations.

They provided entertainment, moral teachings, and insights into human nature and the complexities of existence.

In terms of preservation, temple libraries employed various mediums to record and store the texts. Clay tablets, made from moistened clay and inscribed with cuneiform script, were widely used in ancient Mesopotamia. Papyrus scrolls, made from the pith of the papyrus plant and written in hieroglyphs or hieratic script, were prevalent in ancient Egypt. As writing materials evolved, parchment and vellum, made from animal hides and prepared for writing, gained popularity in later civilizations.

The organization of texts within temple libraries varied across different civilizations. Some libraries adopted classification systems based on subject matter, grouping texts according to religious, legal, historical, scientific, or literary categories. Others organized texts based on genre, distinguishing between epics, hymns, myths, rituals, or philosophical treatises. The meticulous organization facilitated easier access to specific texts and enhanced the retrieval and study of knowledge.

Overall, temple libraries were renowned for their extensive collections of texts, encompassing religious, legal, historical, scientific, and literary works. These texts were carefully copied and preserved on various media, reflecting the intellectual achievements and cultural heritage of the civilizations that housed them. The organization of texts within these libraries facilitated the preservation and retrieval of knowledge, contributing to the intellectual and cultural development of ancient societies.

Scholarly Activities:

Temple libraries in ancient Mesopotamia served as bustling hubs of intellectual and scholarly activities, nurturing a vibrant tradition of learning and knowledge acquisition. Scholars, scribes, and priests devoted themselves to a wide range of pursuits, which greatly influenced the development of various fields of knowledge.

One of the primary activities within temple libraries was the study and interpretation of ancient texts. Scholars meticulously analyzed and deciphered the content of clay tablets and papyrus scrolls, seeking to understand the religious, historical, and cultural insights contained within them. Through careful examination of grammar, vocabulary, and syntax, they unraveled the complexities of the written language and delved into the meanings and messages conveyed by the ancient texts.

In addition to studying existing works, scholars within temple libraries also engaged in the creation of new texts. They composed hymns, prayers, and religious rituals, contributing to the expansion of religious and spiritual literature. Moreover, they composed historical accounts, documenting significant events and the deeds of kings and rulers. These works served as valuable records of the past, preserving the collective memory and providing insight into the political, social, and cultural landscapes of ancient Mesopotamia.

Temple libraries were also centers for the compilation of lexicons and reference materials. Scholars painstakingly assembled dictionaries and glossaries, aiming to facilitate the understanding and translation of ancient texts. These lexical works played a crucial role in preserving and disseminating knowledge, enabling future generations to access and comprehend the writings of their ancestors.

Furthermore, temple libraries provided a fertile ground for the exploration of scientific and philosophical concepts. Scholars delved into subjects such as mathematics, astronomy, medicine, and astrology, advancing the understanding of these disciplines through observation, calculation, and experimentation. They formulated theories and hypotheses, contributing to the development of scientific methodologies and laying the foundation for future scientific endeavors.

The intellectual and scholarly activities within temple libraries not only advanced knowledge but also fostered a culture of debate and discussion. Scholars engaged in intellectual exchanges, debating ideas, and challenging each other's perspectives. These interactions served to refine and expand upon existing knowledge, encouraging critical thinking and intellectual growth.

The influence of temple libraries extended beyond the confines of the religious sphere. Their contributions to literature, historiography, linguistics, and the sciences influenced the wider society, shaping the intellectual landscape of ancient Mesopotamia. The knowledge and insights generated within these libraries permeated various aspects of life, contributing to the socio-cultural and intellectual development of the civilization.

In conclusion, temple libraries in ancient Mesopotamia were vibrant centers of intellectual and scholarly activities. They served as incubators for knowledge, nurturing scholars, scribes, and priests who dedicated themselves to the study, interpretation, and creation of texts. These activities spanned a wide range of disciplines, from religious and historical studies to scientific and philosophical inquiries. The intellectual pursuits within temple libraries played a significant role in advancing knowledge, contributing to the development of various fields of study and shaping the intellectual legacy of ancient Mesopotamia.

Divine Dynamics

Multidisciplinary Studies:

The temple libraries of ancient Mesopotamia served as repositories of knowledge that encompassed a wide array of subjects, fostering multidisciplinary studies and enabling scholars to explore diverse fields of inquiry. These libraries were treasure troves of information, catering to the intellectual pursuits of scholars in various disciplines.

One area of study within temple libraries was astronomy. Scholars delved into celestial observations, charting the movements of celestial bodies and mapping the heavens. They developed astronomical theories and calculations, contributing to the understanding of celestial phenomena and the development of early astronomical systems. The study of astronomy was closely intertwined with religious beliefs, as celestial observations played a significant role in determining auspicious times for religious rituals and events.

Medicine was another field of study within temple libraries. Scholars explored various aspects of medical knowledge, including herbalism, healing practices, and the diagnosis and treatment of illnesses. They compiled extensive texts on medical techniques, descriptions of diseases, and pharmacological information. Temple libraries provided resources for the study of medical texts, allowing scholars to advance their understanding of the human body and develop practical medical treatments.

Temple libraries also served as invaluable resources for studies in mythology, poetry, and literature. Scholars delved into ancient myths and legends, studying their symbolism, narratives, and cultural significance. They explored poetic compositions, analyzing the linguistic and literary techniques employed by ancient poets. These studies not only enriched the understanding of Mesopotamian mythology and literature but also provided insights into the cultural and societal values of the time.

Divination, the practice of seeking knowledge of the future or insight through supernatural means, was another area of scholarly focus within temple libraries. Scholars studied oracles, omens, and divinatory techniques, examining methods of interpreting signs and symbols believed to hold prophetic meaning. The study of divination encompassed various forms, such as hepatoscopy (examining the liver of sacrificial animals), astrology (interpreting celestial alignments), and extispicy (interpreting the entrails of animals). Temple libraries provided the necessary texts and references for scholars to acquire and refine their divinatory skills.

Additionally, temple libraries housed texts on a wide range of subjects, including agriculture, mathematics, and religious rituals. Agricultural texts provided knowledge of irrigation techniques, crop cultivation, and livestock management, supporting the agrarian practices of the time. Mathematical texts covered topics such as geometric principles, numerical systems, and mathematical calculations, contributing to advancements in mathematics. Religious rituals and ceremonies were documented in detail, allowing scholars to understand the complex liturgical practices and symbolism associated with worship and sacrifice.

The multidisciplinary nature of temple libraries fostered a rich intellectual environment where scholars from various disciplines could cross-pollinate ideas and draw connections between different fields of study. The availability of resources within these libraries facilitated the exploration and advancement of knowledge in astronomy, medicine, literature, mythology, divination, agriculture, mathematics, and religious rituals. The collective wisdom contained within the library walls enabled scholars to engage in comprehensive studies, contributing to the overall intellectual and cultural development of ancient Mesopotamia.

Political Interference in Sacred Texts: The Case of King Ashurbanipal and the Epic of Gilgamesh

In the ancient world, sacred texts held immense religious, cultural, and historical significance. They were revered as repositories of divine wisdom and were treated with utmost respect. However, there were instances when rulers sought to manipulate these sacred texts for political purposes. One such notable case occurred during the reign of King Ashurbanipal of the Neo-Assyrian Empire in the 7th century BCE. This section focuses on the earliest known instance of a ruler dictating changes to a sacred text for political gain, specifically concerning the Epic of Gilgamesh found in the Library of Ashurbanipal in Nineveh.

The Library of Ashurbanipal:

King Ashurbanipal, the last great ruler of the Neo-Assyrian Empire, was known for his patronage of learning and scholarship. Recognizing the importance of preserving and expanding knowledge, he embarked on a remarkable endeavor by commissioning the construction of a grand library in Nineveh, the capital of his empire. This library, which later became known as the Library of Ashurbanipal or the Royal Library of Nineveh, was a testament to his commitment to intellectual pursuits and the preservation of cultural heritage.

The Library of Ashurbanipal housed an impressive collection of clay tablets, which were meticulously inscribed with cuneiform script. These clay tablets were the medium of choice for recording information in ancient Mesopotamia, as they were durable and easily inscribed. The collection of texts within the library was vast and diverse, covering a wide range of subjects, including religious, historical, literary, and scientific works.

One of the most significant treasures within the library was the Epic of Gilgamesh, an ancient Mesopotamian epic poem that recounted the legendary exploits of the hero Gilgamesh. This epic, composed in Akkadian, was considered one of the masterpieces of ancient literature. It explored profound themes such as the quest for immortality, the nature of friendship, and the power of human ambition. The Epic of Gilgamesh provided valuable insights into the cultural, social, and religious beliefs of ancient Mesopotamia.

The discovery of the Library of Ashurbanipal in the mid-19th century by archaeologists Austen Henry Layard and Hormuzd Rassam was a groundbreaking event in the field of Assyriology. The excavations unearthed thousands of clay tablets that had been buried and preserved for centuries. These tablets contained not only the Epic of Gilgamesh but also a wealth of other texts that shed light on various aspects of ancient Mesopotamian civilization.

The significance of the Library of Ashurbanipal extended beyond the preservation of ancient texts. The collection housed within its walls provided a window into the intellectual pursuits, literary traditions, religious beliefs, historical accounts, and scientific knowledge of the time. Scholars and scribes of the era flocked to the library, engaging in the study and interpretation of these texts, contributing to the development of Assyriology as a discipline.

The Library of Ashurbanipal stands as a testament to the remarkable cultural achievements of ancient Mesopotamia and the patronage of learning by King Ashurbanipal. Its collection of clay tablets, including the renowned Epic of Gilgamesh, has provided invaluable insights into the civilization that thrived in the region over two millennia ago. The library's legacy endures as a testament to the power of knowledge, the pursuit of scholarship, and the enduring impact of ancient Mesopotamian literature on the world's cultural heritage.

Political Interference in the Epic of Gilgamesh:

There is no concrete evidence to support the claim that King Ashurbanipal personally ordered modifications and additions to the Epic of Gilgamesh to enhance his own image and authority. While it is true that rulers in ancient Mesopotamia occasionally engaged in propagandistic activities to bolster their reputation, the specific assertion regarding Ashurbanipal's involvement in modifying the epic remains speculative.

Exploring Ancient Mesopotamian Mythology, Rivalries, and Spiritual Legacies

The Epic of Gilgamesh predates Ashurbanipal's reign by several centuries, with the earliest versions of the epic dating back to the third millennium BCE. It is a complex and multi-layered narrative that evolved over time through oral tradition and various written versions. As a result, different versions of the epic existed before the time of Ashurbanipal, each with its own variations and adaptations.

It is plausible that during the time of Ashurbanipal, the epic underwent further modifications and additions as part of the ongoing tradition of textual transmission and adaptation. However, attributing these modifications directly to Ashurbanipal himself, with the intention of glorifying his rule, is a matter of conjecture.

Ashurbanipal's patronage of learning and his efforts to collect and preserve texts in the Library of Ashurbanipal demonstrate his interest in literature and the cultural heritage of his empire. The library served as a repository of diverse texts, including the Epic of Gilgamesh, and it is likely that Ashurbanipal recognized the importance of preserving this literary masterpiece as part of his broader commitment to scholarship.

It is worth noting that the epic does contain certain elements that reflect the worldview and values of the Mesopotamian ruling elite, including themes of kingship, divine authority, and the relationship between mortals and gods. However, these elements are inherent to the epic's broader narrative and are not specific to Ashurbanipal's reign.

In conclusion, while King Ashurbanipal's patronage of the Library of Ashurbanipal and his role in preserving the Epic of Gilgamesh are significant contributions to the field of Assyriology, the claim that he personally ordered modifications to the epic for political purposes remains speculative. The epic itself predates his reign, and any alterations or additions that occurred were likely part of the ongoing tradition of textual transmission and adaptation in ancient Mesopotamia.

Significance and Rarity of Political Interference:

While the case of Ashurbanipal represents an early instance of political interference in a sacred text, it is important to note that such occurrences were relatively rare during ancient times. The majority of sacred texts were considered sacrosanct and treated with reverence, preserved faithfully to maintain their original teachings and religious significance. Political alterations to sacred texts were exceptions rather than the norm, and they often arose from the aspirations of specific rulers to enhance their own authority and prestige.

Conclusion:

The reign of King Ashurbanipal and his modifications to the Epic of Gilgamesh provide insight into an early example of a ruler dictating changes to a sacred text for political purposes. The Library of Ashurbanipal stands as a testament to the Assyrian king's ambition to cultivate a grand legacy through the manipulation of a revered literary work. However, it is crucial to remember that such instances were not widespread during ancient times, as the majority of sacred texts were preserved faithfully and considered untouchable.

Examples:

Problem: Analyze the role of temple libraries in the preservation and transmission of herbal knowledge in ancient civilizations. Compare the herbal texts found in Mesopotamian temple libraries with those discovered in Egyptian temple libraries, highlighting their similarities and differences in terms of content and purpose.

Exercise: Imagine you are a scholar in an ancient temple library. Write a research proposal outlining a study on the role of magic in ancient Mesopotamian society, including its influence on religious practices, healing rituals, and societal beliefs. Outline the methodology and primary sources you would use in your research.

Conclusion:

Temple libraries served as vital centers of intellectual inquiry and knowledge preservation in ancient civilizations. They facilitated scholarly activities and multidisciplinary studies, fostering advancements in various fields of knowledge and contributing to the cultural heritage of these societies. The rich collection of texts and the scholarly pursuits within these libraries played a significant role in shaping religious practices, scientific understanding, and societal norms. By examining the activities and materials found in temple libraries, we gain valuable insights into the intellectual pursuits and the profound impact of ancient civilizations on our modern understanding of witchcraft, divination, herbalism, shamanism, ecospirituality, and magic in ancient Mesopotamia.

Temples as Economic Centers

Temples in ancient civilizations served not only as religious and spiritual centers but also as significant economic hubs. This section explores the multifaceted role of temples as economic centers, shedding light on their economic activities, wealth accumulation, and contributions to local economies. Drawing examples from diverse fields such as witchcraft, divination, herbalism, shamanism, ecospirituality, and magic in ancient Mesopotamia, we delve into the intricate relationship between temples and economic affairs. By examining the economic functions and practices associated with temples, we gain a deeper understanding of the societal and economic dynamics of these ancient civilizations.

Economic Functions of Temples:

a. Resource Management: Temples often controlled vast land holdings, agricultural estates, and herds of livestock. They acted as central entities responsible for managing these resources, ensuring their efficient utilization, and distributing their products to support various economic activities.

b. Trade and Commerce: Temples facilitated trade and commerce, acting as intermediaries in commercial transactions. They maintained warehouses for storing goods and acted as marketplaces where goods were bought and sold. Temples also engaged in long-distance trade, exchanging valuable commodities and fostering economic connections with neighboring regions.

c. Craft Production: Temples played a significant role in promoting and overseeing craft production. Skilled artisans and craftsmen often operated within the temple complex, creating a wide range of goods, including textiles, metalwork, pottery, and jewelry. The temples provided workshops, raw materials, and patronage for these artisans, ensuring the production of high-quality goods that could be used for various purposes, such as religious rituals, trade, and luxury consumption.

d. Financial Operations: Temples served as financial institutions in ancient societies, managing monetary transactions, loans, and debts. They acted as custodians of wealth, storing precious metals, gemstones, and other valuable assets. Temples also issued standardized units of currency and played a role in regulating monetary systems, which contributed to economic stability and facilitated trade within the society.

e. Taxation and Redistribution: Temples had the authority to collect taxes and levies from the population. These taxes, often in the form of agricultural produce or livestock, were used to sustain the temple's operations, support religious rituals, and

265

provide for the welfare of the community. Temples acted as redistributive entities, ensuring that resources were allocated to different social groups and addressing issues of economic inequality.

f. Investment and Entrepreneurship: Temples engaged in investment activities, using their resources to finance infrastructure projects, such as irrigation systems, roads, and buildings. They also sponsored expeditions and ventures that aimed to acquire valuable resources or establish trade networks. By taking on entrepreneurial roles, temples stimulated economic growth, encouraged innovation, and contributed to the overall prosperity of the society.

g. Employment and Social Welfare: Temples provided employment opportunities for a significant portion of the population. Priests, temple administrators, scribes, artisans, and laborers were all involved in the daily operations of the temple and its economic functions. Additionally, temples had a social welfare function, providing support to the needy, including orphans, widows, and the elderly, through the distribution of food, clothing, and other essential resources.

h. Economic Regulation: Temples played a role in regulating economic activities within their jurisdiction. They enforced trade regulations, monitored weights and measures, and ensured fair market practices. Temples also enacted laws and regulations pertaining to contracts, debts, and commercial disputes, acting as a legal authority in economic matters. By establishing and enforcing these regulations, temples maintained economic order, protected the interests of the community, and fostered a sense of trust and reliability in commercial transactions.

In summary, temples in ancient societies had multifaceted economic functions. They managed and controlled valuable resources, facilitated trade and commerce, supported craft production, acted as financial institutions, collected taxes, invested in infrastructure, provided employment, and regulated economic activities. These economic functions of temples were essential for the stability, prosperity, and social well-being of the communities they served.

Wealth Accumulation:

a. Donations and Offerings: Temples received substantial offerings and donations from devotees, including agricultural produce, livestock, precious metals, and other valuable goods. These contributions served as a major source of wealth accumulation for temples, enabling them to finance their operations and engage in economic activities.

b. Tithes and Taxes: Temples levied tithes and taxes on the local population, further bolstering their economic resources. These financial obligations, often linked to religious observances and ceremonies, contributed to the economic sustainability and expansion of temples.

Craftsmanship and Industry:

a. Artisans and Craftspeople: Temples employed skilled artisans and craftspeople who produced intricate artworks, sculptures, textiles, pottery, and other crafts. These items were not only used within the temple precincts but were also traded and sold, generating economic prosperity for the temple and the local community.

b. Production of Ritual Objects: Temples played a crucial role in the production of ritual objects used in religious ceremonies and practices. These objects, such as incense, oils, sacred vessels, and ceremonial garments, were crafted within the temple premises or in workshops associated with the temple. The production and trade of these ritual objects contributed to the local economy and provided employment opportunities.

c. Control of Natural Resources: Temples often had control over valuable natural resources, such as fertile agricultural land, mineral deposits, forests, and water sources. By managing and utilizing these resources effectively, temples could generate significant wealth. They engaged in agricultural practices, mining, logging, and other resource extraction activities, ensuring a steady supply of raw materials for their economic endeavors.

d. Trade and Commercial Ventures: Temples actively participated in trade and commercial ventures, leveraging their wealth, resources, and networks. They established trade routes, organized caravans, and engaged in long-distance trade with neighboring regions and even foreign lands. Temples acted as intermediaries in commercial transactions, facilitating trade and benefiting from the exchange of valuable commodities. They controlled warehouses and marketplaces, where goods were stored, bought, and sold, further contributing to their wealth accumulation.

e. Land and Property Ownership: Temples held extensive land and property holdings, which provided a consistent stream of income. They owned agricultural estates, vineyards, orchards, and livestock, generating agricultural produce and animal products that could be used for sustenance, trade, or sale. Temples also possessed urban properties, including houses, buildings, and shops, which could be rented out or used for commercial purposes, generating additional revenue.

f. Moneylending and Banking: Temples acted as financial institutions, engaging in moneylending and banking activities. They provided loans to individuals, merchants, and even kings, charging interest on these loans. The accumulation of interest allowed temples to amass wealth over time. They also served as safekeepers of wealth, storing precious metals, gemstones, and other valuable assets on behalf of individuals and the community, further solidifying their financial power.

g. Patronage and Sponsorship: Temples provided patronage and sponsorship to various individuals, including artists, scholars, and craftsmen. They supported their endeavors, funded their projects, and commissioned artworks, creating a thriving cultural and intellectual landscape. In return, the temples received prestige, recognition, and often a share of the profits generated from the works or services sponsored, adding to their wealth.

h. Investments and Entrepreneurship: Temples engaged in investments and entrepreneurial activities, utilizing their wealth and resources to finance infrastructure projects, expeditions, and trade ventures. They invested in irrigation systems, road networks, and other public works, enhancing agricultural productivity and facilitating trade. Temples sponsored expeditions to acquire valuable resources or establish new trade connections, contributing to economic growth and expanding their wealth.

In summary, temples accumulated wealth through various means, including donations, tithes, taxes, control of natural resources, trade, craft production, land ownership, moneylending, patronage, and investments. The wealth accumulated by temples not only supported their religious functions but also played a significant role in shaping the economic landscape of the societies in which they operated.

Examples:

Problem: Analyze the economic impact of temple-based herbalism in ancient civilizations. Discuss the cultivation, processing, and trade of medicinal herbs and their significance in religious, medicinal, and economic contexts. Compare the practices of herbalism in Mesopotamian temples with those in Egyptian temples, highlighting similarities and differences.

Exercise: Imagine you are an economic advisor to a temple in ancient Mesopotamia. Develop a business plan outlining strategies to enhance the temple's economic activities, such as expanding trade networks, optimizing resource management, and diversifying income sources. Justify your recommendations based on historical evidence and economic principles.

Exploring Ancient Mesopotamian Mythology, Rivalries, and Spiritual Legacies

Conclusion:

Temples served as vital economic centers in ancient civilizations, engaging in a wide range of economic activities, wealth accumulation, and contributions to local economies. Through resource management, trade and commerce, wealth accumulation, and craftsmanship, temples played a significant role in shaping economic dynamics within their societies. The economic functions and practices associated with temples had a profound impact on the development of witchcraft, divination, herbalism, shamanism, ecospirituality, and magic in ancient Mesopotamia. By examining the economic aspects of temples, we gain valuable insights into the intertwined relationship between religion, society, and the economy in these ancient civilizations.

Chapter 8: Divination and Omens: Unveiling the Ancient Mesopotamian System of Prophecy

In the ancient civilization of Mesopotamia, divination played a pivotal role in understanding the divine will and foreseeing future events. It was a widespread practice embraced by individuals from various social and religious backgrounds. This chapter aims to provide an extensive overview of the ancient Mesopotamian system of divination and omens, delving into its methods, tools, practitioners, and cultural context.

Significance of Divination:

Divination held immense significance in ancient Mesopotamia as it was believed to provide insights into the intentions of the gods and the unfolding of cosmic events. By interpreting divine messages embedded within natural phenomena and symbolic signs, individuals sought guidance for important decisions, anticipated potential outcomes, and navigated their lives accordingly.

Communication with the Divine: Divination was seen as a means of establishing a direct line of communication with the divine realm. It provided a way for humans to seek guidance, advice, and even warnings from the gods. Through divination practices, individuals believed they could tap into the wisdom and knowledge of the deities and gain insight into their intentions and desires.

Understanding the Will of the Gods: Divination was used to discern the will of the gods and understand their influence on human affairs. It was believed that the gods controlled the forces of nature, the outcome of battles, and the course of events in the world. By interpreting the signs and omens, individuals could gain a glimpse into the divine plan and align their actions with the desires of the gods.

Decision-Making and Problem-Solving: Divination played a crucial role in decision-making processes, both on personal and societal levels. When facing important choices or dilemmas, individuals would consult divination techniques to seek clarity and insight. Divination was also used to resolve disputes, settle legal matters, and determine the most favorable course of action in various situations.

Anticipating the Future: Divination was often employed to foresee potential outcomes and anticipate future events. By interpreting signs and symbols, individuals sought to gain foresight into forthcoming challenges, opportunities, or calamities. This knowledge allowed them to prepare, make informed decisions, and take proactive measures to mitigate risks or enhance positive outcomes.

Maintaining Cosmic Balance: Divination was seen as a way to maintain cosmic harmony and balance. By understanding the divine will and aligning human actions accordingly, individuals believed they could contribute to the overall order of the universe. Divination provided a mechanism for individuals to fulfill their role within the grand cosmic scheme and uphold the balance between the human and divine realms.

Ritual and Ceremonial Practices: Divination was often performed within the context of religious rituals and ceremonies. It was believed that engaging in specific rituals, such as offering prayers, making sacrifices, or conducting purification rites, could enhance the accuracy and effectiveness of divination. These rituals created a sacred space and mindset, enabling a deeper connection with the divine and increasing the likelihood of receiving accurate divinatory messages.

Social and Political Significance: Divination held significant social and political implications in ancient Mesopotamia. It was often practiced by priests and specialists who held positions of influence and authority. The interpretation of divinatory signs and omens could shape important decisions made by rulers, impact the course of military campaigns, and guide political governance. Divination was thus integrated into the fabric of society, influencing power dynamics and the overall well-being of the community.

In summary, divination in ancient Mesopotamia served as a means of communication with the gods, a tool for understanding their will, a guide for decision-making and problem-solving, a method of anticipating the future, a means of maintaining cosmic balance, a component of ritual and ceremonial practices, and a factor with social and political significance. It played a fundamental role in shaping the beliefs, actions, and governance of individuals and societies in ancient Mesopotamia.

Understanding the Divine Will:

Mesopotamians believed that gods actively influenced human affairs, and their desires and intentions could be discerned through divinatory practices. Divination acted as a means to bridge the gap between mortals and the divine, offering glimpses into the divine plan and facilitating communication with the gods.

Divine Dynamics

Interpreting Signs and Omens: Divination involved the interpretation of various signs and omens believed to be messages from the gods. These signs could manifest in natural phenomena such as celestial events, weather patterns, animal behavior, or even seemingly random occurrences. Skilled diviners would observe and analyze these signs, drawing connections between the observed phenomena and their symbolic meanings as prescribed by established divinatory systems.

Divine Messages in Dreams: Dreams were considered a powerful channel through which the gods communicated with humans. Divination often involved the interpretation of dreams, as they were believed to contain messages, warnings, or instructions from the divine realm. Specialized dream interpreters would analyze the symbols and narratives present in dreams to extract their hidden meanings and provide insights into the divine will.

Oracle Consultation: Temples housed oracles who were believed to possess the ability to directly communicate with the gods. Individuals seeking divine guidance would visit the temple and present their questions or concerns to the oracle. Through a trance-like state or other altered states of consciousness, the oracle would relay the messages of the gods, providing answers, advice, or predictions. These oracular pronouncements were considered authoritative and highly respected in matters of personal, social, or political importance.

Divinatory Techniques: Various divinatory techniques were employed in Mesopotamia to access the divine will. These techniques included extispicy (interpreting the entrails of animals), hepatoscopy (examining the liver of sacrificed animals), lecanomancy (divination using water and oil), astrology (studying celestial movements and configurations), and many more. Each technique had its own set of rules, symbols, and interpretations, which were passed down through generations and practiced by skilled diviners.

Rituals and Offerings: Divination was often performed within the context of specific rituals and accompanied by offerings and prayers. These rituals were believed to create a sacred space and invoke the presence of the gods, enhancing the accuracy and effectiveness of divination. Offerings, such as food, drink, incense, or symbolic objects, were presented as acts of devotion and reciprocity, seeking favor from the gods and establishing a closer connection between the mortal and divine realms.

Divinatory Specialists: Skilled diviners, known as baru (for extispicy) or bārû (for other forms of divination), held specialized knowledge and training in interpreting the divine signs and messages. They were respected members of society, often associated with temples or royal courts. Their expertise in divinatory techniques and their ability to decipher the will of the gods made them indispensable for individuals seeking guidance and for decision-making processes at all levels of society.

By engaging in divination, Mesopotamians sought to gain insight into the desires, intentions, and plans of the gods. Understanding the divine will was considered crucial for aligning human actions, making informed decisions, and navigating the challenges and uncertainties of life. Divination provided a means to connect with the divine, seek guidance, and maintain a harmonious relationship with the gods, thereby shaping the beliefs, actions, and destiny of individuals and societies in ancient Mesopotamia.

Exploring Divination Methods:

Astrology and Celestial Divination: Astrology played a significant role in Mesopotamian divination. Observing celestial bodies, their positions, and their interactions was believed to reveal insights into divine will and future events. Skilled astrologers meticulously recorded celestial phenomena and interpreted them through complex systems of celestial omens. They believed that celestial events such as eclipses, conjunctions, and planetary alignments carried symbolic meanings and could provide guidance on matters of personal, political, and societal importance.

Extispicy: Extispicy involved the examination of animal entrails, particularly the liver, to gain insights into the divine will. Specially trained priests, known as baru or bārû, would carefully dissect and examine the organs, looking for signs, marks, or irregularities believed to hold divinatory significance. The process of extispicy required expertise in recognizing and interpreting the various features and patterns observed in the entrails, which were associated with specific omens and meanings.

Divination by Dreams: Dreams were regarded as a powerful means of divine communication in Mesopotamian culture. Diviners known as ašipu or ašāpum specialized in interpreting dreams and providing guidance based on their symbolic content. The dreamer would recount their dreams to the diviner, who would analyze the symbols, themes, and emotions present in the dream to extract their hidden messages. Dream dictionaries and interpretive texts were consulted to decipher the meanings of specific symbols and recurring motifs, enabling the diviners to offer insights into future events or counsel on present circumstances.

Scrying and Lecanomancy: Scrying, or the practice of gazing into reflective surfaces, was another method of divination used in Mesopotamia. Mirrors, bowls of water, or oil were employed to aid in scrying, with diviners observing the reflections and interpreting the images or symbols that appeared. Lecanomancy, a form of divination utilizing water or oil in a container, involved observing the patterns and movements created by drops of liquid and drawing interpretations from their shape and behavior.

Numerology and Divination Texts: Numerological divination was prevalent in Mesopotamia, where numbers were assigned symbolic meanings and used to gain insights into various aspects of life. Divination texts, such as the series Enūma Anu Enlil, contained vast collections of omens and their interpretations, covering diverse topics ranging from personal matters to societal events. These texts served as references for diviners, providing them with a comprehensive repertoire of symbols, signs, and their meanings.

Rituals and Offerings: Divination methods were often accompanied by specific rituals and offerings to establish a connection with the divine realm. Purification rites, prayers, and invocations were performed to create a sacred atmosphere conducive to divination. Offerings such as food, drink, incense, or precious objects were presented as acts of devotion and reciprocity, seeking the favor and attention of the gods for accurate and meaningful divinatory outcomes.

These various divination methods allowed individuals to explore different sources of divine knowledge and gain insights into the past, present, and future. Divination was a respected and integral part of Mesopotamian society, offering guidance, reassurance, and a sense of control in the face of uncertainty. It provided a framework for understanding the divine will and influenced decision-making processes, personal choices, and the course of events in ancient Mesopotamia.

Tools of Divination:

To facilitate divination, Mesopotamian practitioners employed various tools and instruments. Astrologers relied on celestial charts and observations to map out the movements of celestial bodies, while extispicy required the careful examination of sacrificial animal entrails. Dream interpreters consulted dream manuals and drew upon their knowledge of symbols and patterns to decipher the messages conveyed through dreams.

Celestial Charts and Instruments: Astrologers used celestial charts, known as astrolabes or zodiacal astrolabes, to track the positions and movements of celestial bodies. These charts featured circular diagrams with markings representing stars, planets, and constellations. They allowed astrologers to make precise observations and calculations, aiding in the interpretation of celestial omens. Additionally, instruments such as gnomons and quadrants were used to measure angles and determine the positions of celestial objects in relation to the observer's location.

Extispicy Tools: Extispicy required the sacrifice of animals, usually sheep or other domesticated animals. The entrails, particularly the liver, were carefully examined for divinatory signs and symbols. Specialized tools were used for this process, including knives, scalpels, and divination boards. The divination board, often made of wood or stone, featured inscribed patterns or grids that helped the diviners analyze and interpret the patterns found in the entrails.

Dream Manuals: Dream interpreters relied on manuals and texts specifically dedicated to the interpretation of dreams. These manuals contained lists of common dream symbols, motifs, and their associated meanings. Diviners consulted these texts to identify the symbolic significance of elements present in a dream and provide interpretations accordingly. These manuals acted as references, providing a comprehensive catalog of dream symbolism and aiding diviners in their interpretation process.

Scrying and Reflective Surfaces: Scrying, the practice of gazing into reflective surfaces, required the use of specific tools. Mirrors made of polished metal or reflective bowls filled with water or oil were commonly employed for scrying. The diviner would focus their gaze on the surface and interpret the images or symbols that appeared, seeking divine insights. The clarity of the reflection and the way the images formed were believed to hold divinatory significance.

Numerological Charts and Calculations: Numerology played a significant role in Mesopotamian divination. Diviners utilized numerological charts, grids, or tables that assigned symbolic meanings to numbers. These charts aided in the interpretation of numerical patterns or calculations derived from divinatory processes. The diviners would use these tools to analyze numeric values associated with various aspects of life, such as dates, names, or other relevant information, to extract divinatory insights.

Ritual Implements and Offerings: Ritual implements and offerings were essential for creating a sacred atmosphere and establishing a connection with the divine realm during divination. Incense burners, lamps, and ritual vessels were used to perform purification rites and create a sacred space. Offerings of food, drink, incense, and other symbolic objects were presented as acts of devotion and reciprocity to invoke divine favor and enhance the accuracy of divinatory outcomes.

These tools and instruments were integral to the practice of divination in Mesopotamia, enabling practitioners to gather and interpret divine messages from various sources. They provided the means to engage with the supernatural realm and seek guidance and insights into the mysteries of the past, present, and future.

Practitioners of Divination:

Priest-Diviners: In many cases, divination was performed by priests who held specific roles and responsibilities within the temple hierarchy. These priest-diviners were trained in the art of divination, often receiving education and guidance from experienced mentors. They had a comprehensive understanding of religious rituals, myths, and cosmology, which allowed them to effectively communicate with the gods and interpret their messages. Priest-diviners played a vital role in religious ceremonies and were considered essential for seeking divine guidance in matters of importance.

Astrologers: Astrology was a specialized form of divination that required expertise in observing and interpreting celestial phenomena. Astrologers dedicated themselves to studying the movements of the stars, planets, and constellations, as well as developing sophisticated methods of interpretation. They used their knowledge to analyze astrological charts and predict future events based on the alignment and interactions of celestial bodies. Astrologers were highly regarded for their ability to provide insight into matters such as agricultural cycles, political events, and personal destinies.

Extispicy Diviners: Diviners who practiced extispicy, the examination of animal entrails, held a unique position within the divination community. They possessed the skills to perform sacrificial rituals, extract and interpret signs from the animal entrails, and deliver divinatory messages to those seeking guidance. These diviners had a deep understanding of anatomy and symbolism, enabling them to discern meaningful patterns and symbols within the entrails. They were regarded as skilled interpreters of divine will, able to provide insights into matters of health, fertility, and prosperity.

Dream Interpreters: Dream interpretation was a specialized field within divination, and dream interpreters were highly sought after for their ability to decipher the messages conveyed through dreams. They possessed a deep knowledge of symbols, motifs, and cultural contexts, allowing them to unravel the hidden meanings behind dreams. Dream interpreters often worked closely with individuals seeking guidance, helping them understand the significance of their dreams and their implications for their lives. They provided insights into personal matters, such as relationships, career choices, and spiritual journeys.

e. Oracles and Seers: Some diviners possessed the gift of prophecy or clairvoyance, allowing them to receive direct messages from the gods or glimpse the future. These individuals, known as oracles or seers, were revered for their special abilities to commune with the divine and provide insights into significant events or impending calamities. Oracles often entered trance-like states or performed specific rituals to invoke spiritual visions or receive divine revelations. Their prophecies and predictions held great influence over decision-making processes and were considered valuable sources of guidance and wisdom.

These practitioners of divination played crucial roles in ancient Mesopotamian society. They provided individuals and communities with spiritual guidance, foresight, and a deeper understanding of the divine realm. Their expertise and knowledge were respected and sought after, shaping the beliefs, decisions, and actions of the people they served.

Cultural Context:

Divination in ancient Mesopotamia was deeply intertwined with the cultural and religious fabric of the society. It reflected the Mesopotamians' worldview, which emphasized the interconnectedness of humans, nature, and the divine realm. Divination ceremonies were often conducted within the sacred spaces of temples, highlighting the religious significance attached to the practice.

Polytheistic Beliefs: Mesopotamian society was polytheistic, meaning they believed in multiple gods and goddesses who governed different aspects of life. Divination was rooted in the belief that the gods actively influenced human affairs and that their intentions and desires could be revealed through divinatory practices. This cultural context fostered a strong connection between mortals and the divine, with divination serving as a means to communicate with and understand the gods.

Interconnectedness of Cosmos: Mesopotamians perceived a deep interconnectedness between the celestial realm, the earthly realm, and the underworld. They believed that the movements of celestial bodies, natural phenomena, and human experiences were all interconnected and influenced by divine forces. Divination sought to decipher the messages embedded within these interconnected elements, providing insight into the divine will and cosmic events. It was seen as a way to tap into the larger cosmic order and understand one's place within it.

Religious Rituals and Ceremonies: Divination ceremonies were often conducted within the context of religious rituals and ceremonies. Temples served as the primary locations for these practices, further emphasizing the connection between divination and religious beliefs. Divination was seen as a sacred act, carried out by trained priests or individuals with specialized knowledge and expertise. The cultural context surrounding divination elevated its significance and ensured that it remained an integral part of religious and communal life.

Community and Social Cohesion: Divination played a crucial role in maintaining social cohesion and community well-being. It provided individuals and communities with guidance and insight into various aspects of life, including personal decisions, agricultural practices, and political events. The interpretation of divine messages obtained through divination helped shape individual and communal actions, fostering a sense of unity and shared purpose. Divination, therefore, served as a cultural tool that reinforced social values and norms.

Continuity and Tradition: Divination practices in ancient Mesopotamia were deeply rooted in tradition and carried forward from generation to generation. The knowledge and techniques of divination were passed down through oral and written traditions, ensuring the continuity of the cultural practice. Diviners and priests were responsible for preserving and transmitting this knowledge, ensuring that divination remained an integral part of the cultural fabric for centuries.

The cultural context of ancient Mesopotamia provided a fertile ground for the practice of divination. It was intricately connected to the religious beliefs, worldview, and social structure of the society, serving as a means to access divine wisdom, navigate life's uncertainties, and foster a sense of communal harmony and well-being.

Conclusion:

The practice of divination was a fundamental aspect of ancient Mesopotamian culture, providing individuals with a means to seek divine guidance and navigate the uncertainties of life. By understanding the methods, tools, practitioners, and cultural context of divination in Mesopotamia, we gain valuable insights into the spiritual and intellectual landscape of this ancient civilization. In the subsequent sections of this chapter, we will explore in detail the various divination techniques and their significance within the Mesopotamian system of prophecy.

Divination Techniques

a. Astrology and Celestial Divination:

Astrology, the study of celestial bodies and their influence on human affairs, has a rich history dating back to ancient civilizations. In Mesopotamia, the belief in the profound impact of celestial bodies on human lives laid the foundation for the development of astrological practices. This section aims to provide an in-depth introduction to astrology in Mesopotamia, exploring the belief in celestial influence and the evolution of astrological practices within this ancient civilization.

Belief in Celestial Influence:
The Mesopotamians held a strong belief in the interconnectedness of the cosmos and human existence. They believed that celestial bodies, including the Sun, Moon, planets, and stars, exerted a powerful influence on earthly affairs. The movement and positions of these celestial entities were seen as significant indicators of divine will and had direct consequences for human lives.

Development of Astrological Practices:
Mesopotamia is credited with being one of the earliest cultures to develop astrological practices. The ancient Mesopotamians observed the celestial bodies meticulously and noted their patterns, seeking to interpret their meanings and forecast future events. They recognized the cyclical nature of celestial phenomena and developed systems of astrological divination to harness this knowledge.

Celestial Omens and Divination:
In Mesopotamia, celestial omens played a central role in astrological practices. The movements, alignments, and appearances of celestial bodies were believed to convey divine messages and portents of events on Earth. Astrologers and diviners carefully observed these celestial omens, recording them in astronomical texts and using them to make predictions and guide decision-making.

Astrological Techniques and Tools:
Astrological practices in Mesopotamia involved a variety of techniques and tools. Astrologers relied on celestial charts and astronomical calculations to map the positions and movements of celestial bodies. They developed intricate systems of zodiacs, houses, and planetary rulerships to interpret the astrological significance of these celestial configurations. They also utilized specialized instruments, such as astrolabes, to aid in their observations.

Practical Applications of Astrology:
Astrology in Mesopotamia served various practical purposes. It was used to advise rulers on matters of state, predict the outcomes of battles, guide agricultural practices, and assist individuals in making important life decisions. Astrological insights were sought for matters of personal fortune, health, relationships, and even the determination of favorable times for undertaking specific activities.

Conclusion:
Astrology played a significant role in ancient Mesopotamian culture, providing a framework for understanding the influence of celestial bodies on human affairs. By

recognizing the connections between celestial movements and earthly events, Mesopotamians developed complex astrological practices and divination techniques. In the subsequent sections of this chapter, we will explore the different aspects of Mesopotamian astrology, including zodiacs, celestial omens, and astrological divination, to gain a comprehensive understanding of its significance within the broader context of ancient Mesopotamian beliefs and practices.

b. Astral Divination:

Astral divination, a key aspect of ancient Mesopotamian astrology, involved the interpretation of celestial observations to discern omens and predict future events. The ancient Mesopotamians believed that the movements and positions of celestial bodies, including planets and stars, held profound significance and could provide insight into the divine will and the course of human affairs. This section explores the practice of astral divination and its role in ancient Mesopotamian society.

Celestial Observations and Omenology:

Central to astral divination was the careful observation and interpretation of celestial phenomena. Astrologers and diviners paid close attention to the movements, alignments, and appearances of celestial bodies. They believed that these observations conveyed messages from the gods and served as omens, signifying the potential outcomes of various events. Records of celestial observations were meticulously maintained and analyzed for their predictive power.

Planetary Omens:

The movements and interactions of planets held particular significance in astral divination. Each planet was associated with specific qualities and aspects of human life. For example, the planet Venus was linked to love and fertility, while Mars was connected to war and conflict. Observations of planetary positions and their relationships to one another were used to decipher the potential outcomes of specific events or situations.

Stellar Omens:

Stellar observations also played a crucial role in astral divination. Certain stars and constellations were regarded as highly influential in determining the fate of individuals and communities. The rising and setting of specific stars, their conjunctions with planets, and their appearances at specific times of the year were interpreted as significant omens. The ancient Mesopotamians believed that these celestial events provided guidance and revealed important insights into future events.

Lunar Omens:

The Moon held a prominent position in astral divination. Its phases, eclipses, and specific positions in relation to other celestial bodies were regarded as potent omens. Lunar observations were carefully recorded and analyzed for their predictive value. Eclipses, for example, were seen as powerful omens of impending changes or significant events.

Astrological Texts and Interpretation:

Astral divination relied on a vast corpus of astronomical and astrological texts that documented celestial observations and their interpretations. These texts contained detailed records of celestial phenomena, as well as guidelines for interpreting the omens they conveyed. Astrologers and diviners studied these texts to acquire the knowledge and skills necessary for accurate interpretation and prediction.

Conclusion:

Astral divination, based on the interpretation of celestial observations, played a central role in ancient Mesopotamian society. The movements of planets, stars, and the Moon were meticulously observed and analyzed to discern omens and predict future events. This practice provided individuals and communities with guidance and insight into the divine will. By understanding the significance of celestial phenomena and their interpretations, we can gain valuable insights into the intricate system of astral divination and its cultural significance in ancient Mesopotamia.

c. Zodiac Signs and Horoscopes:

Zodiac signs and horoscopes form an integral part of ancient Mesopotamian astrology, providing a means to interpret the influence of celestial bodies on human affairs and predict individual destinies. This section delves into the Mesopotamian zodiac system and the role of horoscopes in divination, shedding light on the complex interplay between celestial observations and human lives.

The Mesopotamian Zodiac:

In Mesopotamia, the zodiac consisted of twelve celestial divisions or "signs," each associated with specific constellations. These signs represented distinct periods of the year and were believed to exert influence over different aspects of human existence. Notably, the Mesopotamian zodiac predated the Greek zodiac by several centuries.

The Influence of Zodiac Signs:

According to Mesopotamian belief, an individual's destiny and characteristics were influenced by the zodiac sign under which they were born. Each sign was associated with certain qualities, traits, and ruling deities. For example, the sign of Aries was linked to the god Marduk, representing courage and leadership, while the sign of Libra was associated with the goddess Ishtar, symbolizing beauty and balance.

Horoscopes as Personal Prognostication:

Horoscopes, derived from the alignment of celestial bodies at the time of an individual's birth, played a crucial role in Mesopotamian divination. By casting a horoscope, astrologers sought to gain insight into a person's future, character, and potential challenges. The positions of planets and stars within specific zodiac signs were meticulously analyzed to discern the individual's fate and offer guidance.

Astrological Interpretation:

Interpreting horoscopes required a deep understanding of astrological principles and the meanings associated with each zodiac sign. Astrologers considered the interactions between planets, their aspects, and their relationships to the individual's birth sign. These factors were used to generate predictions about various aspects of the person's life, including career, relationships, and health.

Mesopotamian Astrological Texts:

Mesopotamian astrologers relied on extensive written texts to guide their practice. These texts contained detailed instructions for calculating and interpreting horoscopes, as well as guidelines for understanding the influence of different zodiac signs. Scholars and students of Mesopotamian astrology studied these texts to gain a comprehensive understanding of the astrological system.

Exercises:

Calculate your own horoscope based on the Mesopotamian zodiac signs and compare it to your modern horoscope. Note any similarities or differences in the qualities associated with your birth sign.

Exploring Ancient Mesopotamian Mythology, Rivalries, and Spiritual Legacies

Analyze the horoscope of a historical figure from ancient Mesopotamia, such as Hammurabi or Gilgamesh. What insights can you gather about their potential destiny based on their horoscope?

Compare and contrast the Mesopotamian zodiac signs with the zodiac signs used in modern astrology. Identify similarities and differences in their symbolism and associated qualities.

Conclusion:

Zodiac signs and horoscopes formed an integral part of ancient Mesopotamian astrology, providing individuals with insights into their destinies and character traits. The Mesopotamian zodiac system, with its twelve signs and corresponding celestial influences, shaped the practice of horoscope casting and divination. By studying the interactions between celestial bodies and zodiac signs, astrologers aimed to unveil the mysteries of human existence. Through exercises and comparisons, we can engage in critical thinking and explore the intriguing connections between ancient Mesopotamian astrology and modern divination practices.

Extispicy and Animal Divination:

a. Extispicy:

Extispicy, an ancient divinatory practice, involved the examination of animal entrails, especially the liver, to gain insights into divine messages and make predictions about future events. This section explores the intricacies of extispicy, its cultural significance, and the methods employed by ancient Mesopotamian diviners to interpret these cryptic signs.

The Significance of Extispicy:

Extispicy held a prominent place in the realm of divination in ancient Mesopotamia. The belief underlying this practice was that the gods communicated their intentions and desires through the physical patterns and characteristics found within the organs of sacrificial animals. By carefully scrutinizing these entrails, diviners sought to understand the will of the gods and acquire knowledge of forthcoming events.

Divine Dynamics

Rituals and Procedures:

The process of extispicy involved a series of ritualized steps. A skilled diviner, often a priest or specialist, conducted the ceremony within a sacred space, such as a temple or designated ritual area. A specific animal, selected based on its symbolic relevance to the situation at hand, was sacrificed. The diviner then carefully dissected the animal's entrails, paying particular attention to the liver.

The Interpretation of Liver Signs:

The liver held great significance in extispicy, as it was believed to be the seat of divine messages. Diviners examined the liver's external features, such as its size, color, and texture, as well as the internal details, including the shape, size, and arrangement of lobes and vessels. These features were interpreted as omens and symbolic indicators of future events, both positive and negative.

Symbolic Associations:

Extispicy incorporated a rich symbolic language. Diviners assigned meaning to various patterns and structures observed in the liver. For instance, a well-formed liver with clear lobes was considered favorable, indicating divine favor and positive outcomes. Conversely, abnormalities or irregularities in the liver were seen as signs of impending difficulties or divine displeasure.

Training and Expertise:

The practice of extispicy required extensive training and expertise. Diviners dedicated years to studying the intricate symbolism and subtle nuances of liver signs. They consulted ancient texts and shared knowledge within their specialized communities to refine their skills. The ability to accurately interpret the liver's messages was highly regarded and sought after.

Exercises:

Create a fictional scenario where extispicy is used to seek divine guidance. Describe the ritual procedures and the diviner's interpretation of the liver signs.

Study images or descriptions of ancient Mesopotamian liver models. Identify the different features and symbols associated with liver signs and their possible interpretations.

Exploring Ancient Mesopotamian Mythology, Rivalries, and Spiritual Legacies

Research other cultures or historical periods that employed similar divinatory practices involving animal entrails. Compare and contrast their methods and interpretations with Mesopotamian extispicy.

Conclusion:

Extispicy, the practice of divination through the examination of animal entrails, provided ancient Mesopotamians with a means to decipher divine messages and make predictions about the future. The careful observation and interpretation of liver signs served as a powerful tool for understanding the desires and intentions of the gods. Through rigorous training and expertise, diviners became skilled at decoding the intricate symbolism embedded within the liver's patterns and structures. By engaging in exercises and exploring comparative practices, students can gain a deeper understanding of extispicy and its significance within the broader context of divination in ancient Mesopotamia.

b. Rituals and Techniques:

The practice of extispicy, a form of divination prevalent in ancient Mesopotamia, involved a series of rituals and techniques aimed at gaining insights into divine messages through the examination of sacrificial animal entrails, particularly the liver. This section delves into the detailed procedures associated with extispicy, exploring the selection of sacrificial animals, the preparation of entrails, and the intricate process of interpreting the signs revealed.

Selection of Sacrificial Animals:

The choice of sacrificial animals was crucial in extispicy. Each animal held symbolic significance, and its selection depended on the specific nature of the divinatory inquiry. For example, a sheep might be chosen for matters related to fertility or domestic concerns, while a bull could be selected for matters of state or societal importance. The chosen animal's physical attributes and characteristics were considered reflective of the situation or question being addressed.

Ritual Preparation:

Before engaging in the act of divination, a series of sacred rituals and preparations took place. The diviner, often a trained priest or specialist, would purify themselves through ablutions and don appropriate ritual attire. The sacred space, typically within a temple or designated area, was also purified, creating a suitable environment for the communication between the divine and human realms.

Divine Dynamics

Sacrifice and Dissection:

Once the preparatory rituals were complete, the sacrificial animal was brought forward. Its selection was an intentional act, aligning with the purpose of the divination. The animal was ritually slaughtered with precision and reverence. The diviner then expertly dissected the animal, focusing primarily on the liver as the central organ of divinatory significance.

Examination and Interpretation:

The diviner meticulously examined the entrails, particularly the liver, for signs and omens. The external features, such as the size, color, and texture of the liver, were carefully observed. The internal details, including the shape, size, and arrangement of lobes and vessels, were also taken into account. Each aspect was considered a potential indicator of divine messages and carried symbolic meaning.

Symbolic Interpretation:

The interpretation of the observed signs and symbols was a complex task. Diviners relied on a comprehensive system of symbolism and associations built upon ancient traditions and accumulated wisdom. For instance, a well-formed and healthy-looking liver might signify positive outcomes or divine favor, while abnormalities or irregularities could be interpreted as warnings or signs of forthcoming challenges. The diviner's knowledge, intuition, and expertise played a crucial role in deciphering the hidden meanings within the entrails.

Exercises:

Research the symbolism associated with different sacrificial animals in ancient Mesopotamia. Select a specific situation or question and discuss which animal would be most suitable for divination and why.

Role-play a divination session, with one student acting as the diviner and another as the consultant seeking insights. Practice the rituals of purification, sacrifice, and entrail examination, and discuss the interpretation of the observed signs.

Analyze historical texts or depictions related to extispicy, such as cuneiform tablets or artistic representations, and identify the specific techniques employed by diviners in ancient Mesopotamia.

Exploring Ancient Mesopotamian Mythology, Rivalries, and Spiritual Legacies

Conclusion:

The rituals and techniques of extispicy in ancient Mesopotamia formed a carefully orchestrated process, involving the selection of sacrificial animals, meticulous preparation, and the expert dissection and examination of entrails. The interpretation of the observed signs required a deep understanding of symbolism and an intimate connection with the divine. Through engaging in exercises that simulate the divinatory process and analyzing historical artifacts, students can gain a comprehensive understanding of the intricate rituals and techniques involved in extispicy, furthering their appreciation of this ancient Mesopotamian divinatory practice.

c. Significance of Animals:

In ancient Mesopotamian divinatory practices, the selection of sacrificial animals held deep symbolic significance. The appearance and behavior of these animals were believed to convey messages from the divine realm. This section delves into the symbolic meanings associated with different animals and their appearances in divination, shedding light on the intricate connections between the natural world and the realm of spiritual inquiry.

Sheep:

Sheep held a prominent role in divinatory practices, symbolizing domesticity, fertility, and abundance. The gentle nature of sheep represented the harmonious aspects of life and the blessings of the household. In divination, a healthy and well-formed sheep could signify positive outcomes and favorable conditions in matters related to the home, family, and personal well-being.

Bull:

The bull, with its strength and power, symbolized authority, leadership, and societal affairs. In divination, the appearance of a bull was often associated with matters of state, governance, and public life. The sacrificial bull represented the weighty decisions and the broader concerns of the community.

Bird:

Birds, particularly those capable of flight, were associated with communication between the human and divine realms. Their ability to traverse both the earthly and celestial spheres made them powerful messengers. Different types of birds carried distinct symbolic meanings. For example, the owl symbolized wisdom and foresight, while the eagle represented strength and divine protection.

Fish:

Fish were seen as symbols of fertility, abundance, and the watery realms of the divine. Their association with water connected them to the realm of emotions and intuition. In divination, the appearance of fish could be interpreted as an indication of emotional harmony, prosperity, or the need for intuitive insights.

Serpent:

The serpent, with its ability to shed its skin and undergo transformation, represented renewal, healing, and hidden knowledge. Its connection to the underworld and its association with wisdom made it a potent symbol in divination. The appearance of a serpent could suggest the need for spiritual transformation, the unveiling of hidden truths, or the presence of mystical forces.

Exercises:

Research the symbolic meanings associated with other animals in ancient Mesopotamian divinatory practices, such as dogs, lions, or goats. Discuss their significance and how they might be interpreted in divination.

Choose an animal from the list and create an artistic representation or visual symbol that captures its symbolic meaning in divination. Explain the elements and characteristics you incorporated and how they convey the intended message.

Explore the symbolic associations of animals in divination practices from other cultural traditions, such as the use of animal totems in Native American spirituality. Compare and contrast the symbolic meanings of animals across different cultural contexts.

Conclusion:

The symbolic meanings associated with animals in ancient Mesopotamian divination added depth and nuance to the practice. Understanding the significance of different animals and their appearances in divinatory rituals provides valuable insights into the cultural and spiritual beliefs of the time. Through engaging in exercises that explore these symbolic associations and comparing them with other cultural traditions, students can develop a deeper appreciation for the intricate connections between animals, symbolism, and divination in ancient Mesopotamia.

Exploring Ancient Mesopotamian Mythology, Rivalries, and Spiritual Legacies

Divination by Dreams:

a. Dreams as Messages from the Divine:

In ancient Mesopotamian cultures, dreams were seen as a powerful conduit through which divine messages were transmitted to humans. This section delves into the belief that dreams held significant importance in the realm of divination, serving as a means of communication between mortals and the divine. By understanding the role of dreams in divination, we can gain valuable insights into the spiritual and cultural practices of ancient Mesopotamia.

The Divine Language of Dreams:

Dreams were regarded as a divine language, capable of conveying messages, warnings, and insights from the gods. The belief in the sacred nature of dreams was deeply rooted in the understanding that the divine realm could interact with humans during their slumber. This interaction allowed for a direct connection between mortal consciousness and the spiritual realm, providing a unique avenue for divine guidance.

Dream Interpreters and Practitioners:

Just as other forms of divination required skilled interpreters, the interpretation of dreams required individuals who possessed the knowledge and expertise to decipher their hidden meanings. These individuals were often revered as seers or dream diviners. They possessed a deep understanding of symbolism, cultural context, and the intricate language of dreams. Their role was to unravel the messages concealed within the dream realm and offer guidance to those seeking insight.

Symbolism and Interpretation:

Dreams in ancient Mesopotamia were rich in symbolism. Specific dream symbols were associated with particular gods, events, or omens, which allowed the interpreter to decipher the divine message. For example, a dream involving water could signify purification or the arrival of abundance, while dreams featuring snakes might indicate transformation or hidden wisdom. The interpretation of dreams required a nuanced understanding of cultural and mythological symbolism.

Divination and Dream Incubation:

Ancient Mesopotamians actively engaged in a practice called dream incubation, wherein individuals sought answers to specific questions or sought divine guidance through intentional dreaming. This process involved rituals, prayers, and specific preparations before sleep to invoke the presence of the gods and invite their messages. The dreams that followed were then analyzed for their symbolic significance and interpreted accordingly.

Examples:

Analyze a recorded dream from ancient Mesopotamia, such as the "Dream of Gilgamesh." Discuss the symbols and themes present in the dream and speculate on the possible interpretations according to the cultural and mythological context of the time.

Engage in a dream journaling exercise. Keep a record of your dreams for a week and reflect on the recurring symbols and themes that emerge. Research their possible interpretations and discuss how dreams can provide personal insight and guidance in modern times.

Exercises:

Conduct research on dream interpretation practices in different cultures and compare them to the ancient Mesopotamian approach. Analyze the similarities and differences and discuss how cultural context shapes the interpretation of dreams.

Design a visual representation of a dream symbol and create an accompanying written interpretation. Explain the elements and characteristics you incorporated into the visual representation and how they convey the symbolic meaning.

Conclusion:

Dreams held a significant role in divination in ancient Mesopotamia, serving as a means through which divine messages were communicated to mortals. Understanding the belief in dreams as messages from the divine provides us with valuable insights into the spiritual and cultural practices of the time. Through analyzing recorded dreams, engaging in dream journaling exercises, and exploring cross-cultural dream interpretation practices, students can deepen their understanding of the symbolic language of dreams and their role in divination, both in ancient Mesopotamia and in contemporary contexts.

Exploring Ancient Mesopotamian Mythology, Rivalries, and Spiritual Legacies

b. Interpretation and Symbolism:

Once a dream is remembered and recorded, the next step in the process of dream divination is interpretation. Ancient Mesopotamians believed that dreams held symbolic meanings that required careful analysis and interpretation to unlock their messages from the divine. This section explores the methods employed by dream interpreters in ancient Mesopotamia and the significance of symbolism in deciphering the hidden messages within dreams.

Contextual Analysis:

Dream interpretation in ancient Mesopotamia involved a contextual analysis of various elements present in the dream. These elements included the dreamer's personal experiences, societal and cultural factors, as well as the broader mythological and religious framework of the time. By considering the dreamer's background, social status, and specific circumstances, interpreters could better understand the possible significance of the dream.

Symbolic Language:

Symbolism played a crucial role in dream interpretation. Ancient Mesopotamians believed that dreams were filled with metaphorical and allegorical elements that conveyed deeper meanings. For example, water might symbolize purification, snakes could represent transformation or hidden wisdom, and birds might signify messages from the gods. Interpreters were well-versed in the symbolic language of dreams and relied on their knowledge of cultural and mythological symbolism to decode the messages embedded within the dream.

Mythological and Religious Framework:

Dream interpretation in ancient Mesopotamia was deeply intertwined with the prevailing mythological and religious beliefs of the time. Dreams were seen as direct communications from the gods, and their interpretation required an understanding of the specific deities associated with different symbols and themes. The pantheon of gods and their stories provided a framework for dream analysis, enabling interpreters to link dream elements to specific deities and their attributes.

Comparative Analysis:

Dream interpreters often employed comparative analysis to enhance their understanding of dream symbolism. They would examine recorded dreams, compile dream dictionaries, and draw on collective knowledge and shared experiences to identify recurring symbols and themes. By studying dreams from multiple sources, interpreters could gain insights into the shared symbolic language and patterns that emerged, allowing for a more nuanced interpretation of individual dreams.

Examples:

Analyze a recorded dream from ancient Mesopotamia, such as the "Dream of Dumuzid's Departure." Identify the key symbols and themes present in the dream and discuss their potential interpretations based on the cultural and mythological context of the time.

Engage in a group exercise where each student shares a recent dream and the class collectively interprets the dream using the principles of ancient Mesopotamian dream interpretation. Encourage discussion and exploration of different perspectives to highlight the subjective nature of dream interpretation.

Exercises:

Create a dream interpretation guide based on ancient Mesopotamian symbolism. Select common dream symbols and provide possible interpretations based on the cultural and mythological context. Include explanations of the symbolic associations and examples of how they might manifest in dreams.

Conduct a research project on the role of dream interpretation in contemporary cultures or alternative spiritual practices. Compare and contrast the methods and symbolism used in ancient Mesopotamia with those in other cultural or spiritual contexts.

Conclusion:

Interpretation and symbolism were vital components of dream divination in ancient Mesopotamia. Through contextual analysis, an understanding of symbolic language, and the incorporation of mythological and religious frameworks, dream interpreters deciphered the hidden messages within dreams. The use of comparative analysis and the recognition of recurring symbols and themes enriched the interpretation process. By engaging in dream analysis exercises and exploring alternative cultural perspectives on dream interpretation, students can deepen their understanding of the subjective and multifaceted nature of dream symbolism, fostering critical thinking and cultural awareness.

c. Dream Manuals:

Dream manuals played a significant role in ancient Mesopotamian culture as guides for understanding and interpreting dreams. These texts provided a framework for individuals to analyze their dreams and uncover their hidden meanings. This section explores the existence of dream manuals in ancient Mesopotamia, their purpose, and the methods they offered to decipher the enigmatic messages of dreams.

Overview of Dream Manuals:

Dream manuals were written texts that served as practical guides for dream interpretation. They were designed to assist individuals in understanding the symbolic language and messages conveyed through their dreams. These manuals offered a structured approach to dream analysis and provided readers with a set of instructions and guidelines to follow when interpreting their own dreams.

Purpose and Significance:

Dream manuals held great significance in ancient Mesopotamian society. Dreams were seen as divine communications and were believed to provide insight into future events, personal guidance, and warnings from the gods. Dream manuals aimed to empower individuals to unlock the hidden wisdom contained within their dreams, enabling them to make informed decisions and navigate various aspects of their lives.

Methods and Techniques:

Dream manuals presented a range of methods and techniques for interpreting dreams. These techniques often involved identifying specific dream symbols, analyzing their contextual meanings, and connecting them to various aspects of the dreamer's life. Manuals would outline the steps to record and recall dreams, as well as provide interpretive frameworks based on cultural symbolism, mythological narratives, and religious beliefs.

Symbol Dictionaries:

One common feature of dream manuals was the inclusion of symbol dictionaries. These dictionaries provided a comprehensive list of common symbols found in dreams, along with their associated meanings. Symbols could encompass various objects, animals, natural phenomena, or human interactions, each with its own unique interpretation. Symbol dictionaries served as references for dreamers to consult when encountering unfamiliar symbols in their dreams.

Examples:

Excerpt Analysis: Today, we will examine an excerpt from an ancient Mesopotamian dream manual to deepen our understanding of dream interpretation in that culture. One example we can explore is the "Instructions for Dream Interpretation" by the Akkadian scholar, Iddin-Dagan. Analyze the techniques and methods outlined in the text, such as identifying key dream symbols and their interpretations. Discuss how these techniques contribute to understanding the dreamer's experience and the significance of dreams in ancient Mesopotamian society.

Class Exercise: Let's engage in a creative exercise where each of you will create your own mini dream manual inspired by ancient Mesopotamian symbolism. Choose a dream symbol and provide an interpretation based on your understanding of ancient Mesopotamian cultural and mythological contexts. Justify your interpretations by referencing specific symbols, narratives, or deities associated with the symbol. This exercise will allow you to explore the diverse range of interpretations and develop your skills in connecting dream symbolism with cultural contexts.

Exercises:

Dream Journal: Begin developing a personal dream journal where you will record your dreams over a period of two weeks. Pay special attention to recurring symbols that appear in your dreams. Use a symbol dictionary inspired by ancient Mesopotamian symbolism to interpret these recurring symbols. Reflect on the accuracy and effectiveness of the interpretations in helping you understand the underlying messages or emotions conveyed by your dreams.

Research Project: In this research project, you will explore the cross-cultural aspects of dream symbolism. Conduct a comparative study between ancient Mesopotamian dream symbols and interpretations and those found in other cultures, such as ancient Egypt or indigenous cultures. Investigate the similarities and differences in symbolic meanings, and discuss the implications of these findings for understanding the universality of dreams across different cultural contexts. Present your research findings through a written report or a visual presentation to share your insights with the class.

Exploring Ancient Mesopotamian Mythology, Rivalries, and Spiritual Legacies

By examining ancient Mesopotamian dream manuals, creating personal dream manuals, keeping a dream journal, and conducting cross-cultural research on dream symbolism, you will develop a comprehensive understanding of the significance of dreams in ancient Mesopotamia and explore the universal aspects of dream interpretation.

Conclusion:

Dream manuals served as invaluable resources for individuals seeking to interpret their dreams in ancient Mesopotamia. These texts offered structured approaches, methods, and symbol dictionaries to guide dreamers through the intricate process of dream interpretation. By engaging in exercises that involve creating their own dream manuals and analyzing their personal dream experiences, students can gain a deeper appreciation for the significance of dreams and the role of dream manuals in ancient Mesopotamian culture.

Practitioners and Context

◆   Diviners and Scholars:

a. Roles and Expertise:

In ancient Mesopotamia, divination was a complex practice that involved various types of diviners, each with their own specialized knowledge and training. This section explores the roles and expertise of different diviners in Mesopotamian society, highlighting the distinct functions they served and the unique skills they possessed.

Baru-Priests:

Baru-priests held a prominent role in divinatory practices. They were highly trained individuals who acted as intermediaries between the divine realm and humanity. Baru-priests were experts in reading and interpreting omens, including celestial phenomena, dreams, and the examination of animal entrails. They possessed extensive knowledge of religious rituals, mythological narratives, and the symbolism associated with divination. Baru-priests were considered the highest-ranking diviners, enjoying the respect and authority associated with their religious positions.

Divine Dynamics

Bārûtu (Diviners):

Bārûtu refers to a specific category of diviners who specialized in the interpretation of omens and the art of divination. These diviners were skilled in observing natural phenomena, such as the movements of celestial bodies, the flight of birds, or the appearance of certain animals. Bārûtu would meticulously record these observations and apply their knowledge of symbolic meanings to interpret the messages conveyed by these omens. They possessed a deep understanding of the cultural and mythological context in which the omens were situated, enabling them to provide meaningful insights and predictions.

Asû (Healer-Diviners):

The asû were a specialized group of diviners who possessed both healing and divinatory abilities. They were knowledgeable in the use of herbalism, magical practices, and spiritual healing. Asû were sought after for their skills in diagnosing and treating illnesses, often combining their medical expertise with divination to identify the root causes of ailments. They would use various techniques, such as examining the patient's urine, observing bodily symptoms, and consulting oracles, to determine the appropriate course of treatment.

Examples:

Class Discussion: Today, we will engage in a fascinating class discussion about the different roles and expertise of diviners in ancient Mesopotamia. Consider situations where a baru-priest, bārûtu, or asû would be consulted. For instance, imagine a royal court seeking guidance on a military campaign or a commoner seeking healing for an illness. Explore the unique knowledge and skills that each diviner brings to these scenarios. Discuss the specific roles and responsibilities of these diviners and their significance in the ancient Mesopotamian society.

Research Project: In this research project, you will have the opportunity to delve deeper into the training and education required to become a baru-priest, bārûtu, or asû in ancient Mesopotamia. Explore primary sources, such as cuneiform texts and inscriptions, to uncover insights into the specialized knowledge and rituals associated with each role. Investigate the methods of selection, the curriculum followed, and the length of training for each type of diviner. Present your findings through a written report or a visual presentation to share your discoveries with the class.

Exploring Ancient Mesopotamian Mythology, Rivalries, and Spiritual Legacies

Exercises:

Role-Playing Activity: Let's bring ancient Mesopotamian divination to life through a role-playing activity. Each of you will assume the persona of a diviner – choose to be a baru-priest, bārûtu, or asû. Engage in a simulated divination session where you interpret omens and provide insights to your peers. Utilize the knowledge and skills associated with your chosen role to deliver a meaningful and accurate divinatory experience. This activity will allow you to step into the shoes of ancient diviners and understand the challenges and responsibilities they faced.

Class Debate: Prepare for a lively class debate on the importance of specialized diviners versus generalist practitioners in ancient Mesopotamian society. Research and gather arguments supporting the need for experts in specific areas of divination and healing, highlighting the depth of knowledge and specialized rituals they possessed. On the other hand, consider arguments that emphasize the advantages of a broader understanding of multiple divinatory practices, showcasing the versatility and adaptability of generalist practitioners. Engage in a respectful exchange of ideas, presenting well-reasoned arguments and counterarguments to foster critical thinking and deepen your understanding of the diverse perspectives within ancient Mesopotamian divination.

By exploring the roles and expertise of diviners in ancient Mesopotamia, participating in research projects, engaging in role-playing activities, and debating the significance of specialization, you will gain a comprehensive understanding of the diverse divinatory practices and the societal contexts in which they operated.

Conclusion:

The roles and expertise of diviners in ancient Mesopotamia were diverse, reflecting the complexity and significance of divination within the society. Baru-priests, bārûtu, and asû each played a crucial role in interpreting omens, understanding the divine will, and addressing various aspects of human life, such as religious rituals, prophecy, and healing. By examining the different types of diviners and their specialized knowledge, students can gain a deeper appreciation for the complexity of ancient Mesopotamian divination and its cultural significance.

b. Divination Schools:

In ancient societies, including Mesopotamia, the practice of divination held immense cultural and religious significance. To ensure the continuity of this sacred art and the development of skilled diviners, specialized schools emerged as centers of education and training. This section explores the existence of divination schools in ancient Mesopotamia, highlighting their role in imparting knowledge, honing skills, and preserving the traditions of divinatory practices.

Establishment of Divination Schools:

Divination schools, known as "bit amēli" in Mesopotamian culture, were established to provide a structured environment for the education and training of aspiring diviners. These schools were typically associated with temples or religious institutions, reflecting the close connection between divination and religious practices in Mesopotamia. The temples served as repositories of knowledge and guardians of tradition, and divination schools played a crucial role in passing on this wisdom to the next generation.

Curriculum and Areas of Study:

The curriculum of divination schools encompassed a wide range of subjects related to divination and associated disciplines. Students would receive instruction in celestial observations, dream interpretation, omen reading, ritual practices, mythology, and symbolism. They would study cuneiform texts, including ancient divination manuals and religious texts, to gain a comprehensive understanding of the theoretical and practical aspects of divination. Practical training involved hands-on experience, where students would observe and assist experienced diviners in real-life divination sessions.

Teacher-Student Dynamics:

The relationship between teachers and students in divination schools was characterized by a mentor-disciple dynamic. Experienced diviners, often belonging to the priestly class, would take on the role of instructors and guide students through their educational journey. The transmission of knowledge and skills occurred through direct instruction, oral tradition, and practical demonstrations. Teachers would provide feedback and assess the progress of their students, ensuring they developed the necessary expertise to become proficient diviners.

Examples:

Research Project: Take a journey through time and explore the archaeological evidence and ancient texts related to divination schools in Mesopotamia. Unearth the secrets of their structure, organization, and curriculum by examining cuneiform tablets and studying the remnants of these ancient institutions.

Classroom Debate: Engage in a lively class discussion on the value of formal education in divination. Compare the experiences of individuals who received training in divination schools with those who relied solely on personal intuition. Discuss the advantages and disadvantages of structured education in the mystical arts.

Exercises:

Divination Syllabus Creation: Get creative and work in groups to design a syllabus for a hypothetical divination school in ancient Mesopotamia. Choose the subjects, courses, and practical exercises that you believe would be essential for aspiring diviners. Share and discuss your ideas with the class.

Role-Playing Adventure: Step into the shoes of ancient Mesopotamian divination school instructors and students. Engage in role-playing activities, such as simulated classroom discussions, practical exercises, and mentorship sessions. Experience the excitement and challenges of divination education firsthand.

Conclusion:

Divination schools played a significant role in ancient Mesopotamia by providing structured education and training to aspiring diviners. These institutions fostered the transmission of knowledge, preservation of tradition, and the development of expertise in divination practices. By studying the existence of divination schools, students can gain a deeper understanding of the institutionalized aspect of divination and its importance within the broader cultural and religious context of ancient Mesopotamia.

Cultural and Religious Context:

a. Mesopotamian Cosmology:

In order to fully comprehend the divination practices of ancient Mesopotamia, it is essential to delve into the cosmological beliefs and worldview that formed the foundation of these practices. The Mesopotamians held a complex and intricate understanding of the cosmos, which played a significant role in shaping their spiritual and divinatory frameworks. By exploring Mesopotamian cosmology, we can gain valuable insights into the mindset and perspectives of these ancient people.

The Mesopotamians believed in a multidimensional universe consisting of various realms and celestial bodies. At the core of their cosmological framework was the notion of a flat, disc-shaped Earth, enveloped by a solid sky-dome known as the "Firmament." This sky-dome was believed to be held aloft by colossal pillars at the edges of the Earth, effectively separating the realms of the heavens and the Earth. Above the Firmament resided the gods, whose activities and movements were thought to influence the affairs of humanity.

The celestial bodies, such as the sun, moon, planets, and stars, held great significance in Mesopotamian cosmology. These celestial objects were believed to embody deities and celestial forces that exerted powerful influences on earthly events. For instance, the movements of celestial bodies were considered vital indicators for divinatory practices. Observing the patterns and positions of these celestial entities provided valuable insights into the divine will and foretold potential outcomes.

Moreover, the Mesopotamians believed in a layered cosmology, where the Earth was surrounded by various domains inhabited by divine beings. These realms included the Apsu (the primordial freshwater ocean), the Netherworld (the realm of the dead), and the heavenly abode of the gods. Each realm had its own distinct characteristics and inhabitants, and the interplay between these realms influenced human experiences and the outcomes of divination rituals.

Within this cosmological framework, divination was viewed as a means to gain access to divine knowledge and guidance. The Mesopotamians believed that the gods communicated with humans through signs, omens, and symbolic messages embedded in the natural world. By interpreting these signs, skilled diviners sought to unravel the intentions of the gods and predict future events. Divination rituals were conducted to establish a connection with the divine realm, enabling the diviner to receive insights and messages from the gods.

One prominent form of divination in Mesopotamia was hepatoscopy, which involved the examination of animal entrails, particularly the liver, to discern divine messages and make predictions. The intricate network of veins and lobes within the liver was believed to reflect the celestial order and carry symbolic significance. By analyzing the appearance and arrangement of these liver features, diviners could interpret the will of the gods and offer guidance to individuals or communities.

In conclusion, the cosmological beliefs and worldview of ancient Mesopotamia laid the groundwork for their divination practices. Their understanding of a multidimensional universe, populated by gods, celestial bodies, and distinct realms, shaped their perception of the interconnectedness between the divine and the human. By comprehending the cosmological framework that underpinned Mesopotamian divination, we can appreciate the intricacies of their spiritual practices and gain valuable insights into the cultural and intellectual milieu of this ancient civilization.

b. Divination and Religion:

In ancient societies, divination and religion were intricately intertwined, with diviners playing a crucial role as intermediaries between humans and the divine realm. The practice of divination was deeply rooted in religious beliefs and rituals, reflecting the belief that the divine entities held the key to understanding and influencing human affairs. This chapter delves into the close association between divination and religion, shedding light on the profound connections between these two domains.

Divination, as an essential component of religious practices in ancient civilizations, held significant importance in societies such as Mesopotamia, Egypt, Greece, and others. This section aims to provide insight into the role of divination within the broader context of religious belief systems prevalent in these ancient cultures.

Divination in Various Ancient Civilizations:

In numerous ancient civilizations, including Mesopotamia, Egypt, Greece, and others, divination held immense significance as an integral component of religious practices. This section aims to provide students with a comprehensive understanding of the role of divination within the broader context of the prevalent religious belief systems in these ancient cultures.

Divination in Various Ancient Civilizations:

The notion of divination permeated the religious practices of diverse ancient civilizations, playing a vital role in connecting humans with the divine realm. Through the examination of specific examples from prominent civilizations like Mesopotamia, Egypt, and Greece, students can grasp the widespread utilization of divination as a religious tool.

For instance, in Mesopotamia, divination was deeply intertwined with religious rituals and ceremonies. The priests, known as baru-priests, were esteemed as diviners who facilitated communication between humans and the gods. Likewise, in Egypt, the practice of divination was closely linked to the veneration of gods and the pursuit of understanding the divine will. In Greece, the Oracle of Delphi acted as a revered divinatory institution, providing counsel and guidance to individuals and city-states.

Divine Dynamics

Religious Frameworks and Cosmologies:

To comprehend the significance of divination within ancient civilizations, it is essential to investigate the religious frameworks upon which these divinatory practices were built. Students will delve into the belief systems prevalent in these cultures, recognizing the fundamental concept of a divine order and the existence of gods, goddesses, or spirits governing various aspects of human existence.

For instance, in Mesopotamian cosmology, the world was envisioned as a layered structure, with a flat Earth below and a celestial Firmament above. Within this cosmological framework, the gods and goddesses controlled natural forces, human affairs, and destiny. Similarly, in Egyptian religion, gods such as Ra, Isis, and Osiris played crucial roles in the lives of individuals and were revered as influential beings who held sway over cosmic events and human destinies.

Divination as a Means of Seeking Guidance and Protection:

Divination served as a vital means for individuals and communities to seek guidance, blessings, and protection from divine entities. By examining the purpose and significance of divination, students will gain insights into how it was perceived as a direct channel of communication with the divine realm.

Ancient peoples turned to divination to navigate important decisions, anticipate future events, or seek divine intervention during times of crisis. Divinatory practices, such as interpreting dreams, examining celestial omens, or casting lots, allowed individuals to access hidden knowledge and gain insights into the will of the gods or spirits. This connection with the divine realm provided reassurance, guidance, and a sense of security in an unpredictable world.

By studying divination as a religious practice within various ancient civilizations, students will develop a profound comprehension of how divinatory methods and beliefs were interwoven with religious frameworks. This exploration will shed light on the role of divination in seeking guidance, blessings, and protection, as well as its significance in establishing a profound connection with the divine realm. Through their exploration of these topics, students will gain a richer appreciation for the spiritual and cultural significance of divination within ancient societies.

Diviners as Intermediaries:

The role of diviners as intermediaries between humans and the divine realm is a fascinating aspect of ancient societies. This section aims to provide students with a comprehensive analysis of the unique position diviners held in society and their responsibilities in facilitating communication with gods or spirits.

The Unique Position of Diviners:

Diviners occupied a distinct place in ancient societies, as they were regarded as individuals with the ability to bridge the gap between humans and the divine. Their role was highly esteemed and held great significance within the community. Students will explore the societal perception of diviners, recognizing them as individuals with specialized knowledge and skills in interpreting signs, symbols, and omens.

Specialized Knowledge and Skills of Diviners:

Diviners possessed specialized knowledge and skills that enabled them to decipher the messages of the divine entities. Students will delve into the specific expertise required for interpreting various divinatory methods, such as the ability to cast lots, interpret celestial phenomena, analyze dreams, or interpret the entrails of animals. These skills were seen as essential in understanding the will of the gods or spirits and providing guidance to individuals or communities.

Rituals, Techniques, and Tools of Divination:

To access the divine realm and receive insights, diviners employed various rituals, techniques, and tools. Students will explore these practices, understanding the rituals performed by diviners to establish a connection with the divine. Examples include the use of sacred objects or tools, the creation of sacred spaces, or the recitation of specific incantations. By examining these practices, students will gain insight into the ceremonial aspects of divination and the methods employed by diviners to invoke divine guidance.

Divine Dynamics

Class Activity:

Mock Trial:

Today, we will engage in a mock trial to delve into the conflicts among deities in the Mesopotamian pantheon. You will have the opportunity to choose a deity to represent in the trial, allowing you to present arguments, evidence, and counterarguments to support your chosen deity's position in the conflict.

During the mock trial, you will step into the role of your selected deity and advocate for their perspective in the conflict. This activity will provide a platform for you to explore the complexities of divine conflicts and analyze the motivations and beliefs of the Mesopotamian deities.

As you choose your deity, consider their characteristics, domains, and roles within the pantheon. This understanding will assist you in formulating convincing arguments and gathering relevant evidence to support your deity's position. Feel free to conduct research, consult mythological narratives, and draw from historical context to strengthen your case.

Throughout the mock trial, you will have the opportunity to engage in lively debates with your fellow students, who will be representing other deities. By actively participating in the trial, you will develop critical thinking skills as you analyze opposing viewpoints and present compelling counterarguments.

At the conclusion of the trial, we will facilitate a discussion where you can reflect on the insights gained from the exercise. You will have the chance to share your thoughts on the perspectives and motivations of the deities involved, as well as the wider implications of their conflicts within the Mesopotamian belief system.

Remember, this mock trial is an exciting opportunity to delve into the fascinating world of Mesopotamian deities and gain a deeper understanding of their conflicts. Enjoy the process of research, argumentation, and debate as you embody your chosen deity and strive to present their case effectively.

Preparation Phase

Research your chosen deity to gather information about their characteristics, domains, and motivations.

Develop strong arguments, evidence, and counterarguments to effectively present your deity's position during the trial.

Exploring Ancient Mesopotamian Mythology, Rivalries, and Spiritual Legacies

Get familiar with the unique aspects and stories associated with your assigned deity.

Trial Format

◆ Opening Statements

Start the trial by delivering an opening statement, introducing your deity and stating their stance in the conflict.

◆ Presentation of Arguments and Evidence

Present your arguments and provide supporting evidence to justify your deity's position.

Feel free to draw from mythological narratives, historical context, and cultural beliefs to strengthen your case.

◆ Cross-Examination

Engage in questioning and challenging the arguments and evidence presented by your fellow students representing other deities.

Take a critical approach, analyzing opposing positions, and presenting counterarguments.

◆ Closing Statements

Conclude the trial by delivering a closing statement, summarizing your deity's position and highlighting its importance in the divine and mortal realms.

◆ Jury Deliberation

Act as the jury and engage in discussions with your classmates to evaluate the impact of the deities' interactions on the divine and mortal realms.

Consider the consequences, implications, and potential resolutions of the conflict.

Divine Dynamics

Reflection and Discussion

Participate in a post-trial discussion to share the insights gained from the mock trial exercise.

Reflect on the perspectives and motivations of the deities involved, and explore the complexities of their divine relationships.

Discuss the broader implications of the conflict within the Mesopotamian belief system and its relevance to human societies.

Conclusion

Summarize the key takeaways from the mock trial, highlighting the importance of understanding conflicts among deities in ancient pantheons.

Emphasize how this activity enhances critical thinking and analytical skills, as well as our understanding of the complexities of divine relationships.

By exploring the interactions and conflicts among deities in the Mesopotamian pantheon, students can gain a deeper understanding of the complex dynamics and relationships within ancient belief systems. This analysis invites critical thinking about power dynamics, personal agendas, and the delicate balance maintained within the divine realm, reflecting the intricacies of human relationships and societal structures.

Exploring Ancient Mesopotamian Mythology, Rivalries, and Spiritual Legacies

Key Terms:

A:

Ancient literature: Ancient literature refers to written works that were produced in ancient times, often characterized by their historical, cultural, and linguistic significance. It encompasses a wide range of genres, including epic poems, religious texts, historical accounts, philosophical treatises, and more, providing valuable insights into the beliefs, practices, and intellectual pursuits of ancient civilizations.

Animal entrails: Animal entrails, also known as extispicy, is a divinatory practice that involves examining the organs and intestines of sacrificial animals, such as sheep or birds, to interpret signs and omens. Ancient cultures, including those in Mesopotamia, believed that the arrangement, shape, and condition of the entrails could reveal insights about the divine will and the future. Skilled diviners would carefully observe and analyze these organs, drawing interpretations to guide decision-making and provide insight into important matters.

Artistic expressions: Artistic expressions refer to various forms of creative and aesthetic communication through visual, auditory, or performance mediums. In the context of ancient civilizations, artistic expressions encompassed a wide range of mediums, such as sculptures, paintings, pottery, jewelry, music, dance, and theater. These expressions served as important means of cultural, religious, and social communication, reflecting the beliefs, values, and artistic sensibilities of the society in which they were created.

Astrology: Astrology is a belief system and practice that connects the positions and movements of celestial bodies, such as stars, planets, and constellations, with human affairs and personality traits. Ancient civilizations, including those in Mesopotamia, developed intricate systems of astrology, viewing celestial events as significant indicators and influences on human lives. Astrology was used for various purposes, including predicting future events, providing guidance, and understanding personal characteristics based on astrological charts and interpretations.

B:

Balancing personal and communal aspects: Balancing personal and communal aspects refers to finding an equilibrium between individual needs, desires, and goals, and the well-being and interests of the larger community. It involves recognizing the importance of personal growth, self-expression, and individual pursuits, while also acknowledging the significance of contributing to and participating in the collective welfare. This concept emphasizes the need to strike a harmonious balance between personal fulfillment and engagement with communal responsibilities, fostering a sense of unity and cohesion within a society.

Babylonian Empire: The Babylonian Empire was an ancient Mesopotamian civilization that existed during various periods in history. It emerged as a significant power under the reign of Hammurabi in the 18th century BCE and reached its height of influence and territorial expansion during the Neo-Babylonian period, particularly under the rule of King Nebuchadnezzar II in the 6th century BCE. The Babylonian Empire was known for its advancements in areas such as astronomy, mathematics, and law, as well as its architectural achievements, including the famous Hanging Gardens of Babylon.

Babylonian gods: Babylonian gods refer to the deities worshipped in the ancient Babylonian religion. The pantheon of Babylonian gods was vast and diverse, with each god or goddess associated with specific domains, such as fertility, warfare, wisdom, or craftsmanship. Some prominent Babylonian gods include Marduk, the chief deity and patron of Babylon, Ishtar, the goddess of love and war, and Nabu, the god of writing and wisdom. These gods played integral roles in the religious and mythological beliefs of the Babylonian people, and their worship was central to the spiritual and cultural life of the civilization.

C:

Ceremonial acts: Ceremonial acts refer to specific actions or rituals performed within a ceremonial or religious context. These acts are often imbued with symbolic meaning and are carried out as a form of reverence, celebration, or spiritual practice. Ceremonial acts can include prayers, offerings, purification rituals, sacred dances, or other prescribed actions that hold significance within a particular cultural or religious tradition.

Celestial charts: Celestial charts are graphical representations or maps depicting the positions and movements of celestial bodies such as stars, planets, and constellations. These charts are used in the field of astronomy to study and understand the celestial phenomena and navigate the night sky. They provide a visual reference for locating and tracking celestial objects, aiding in celestial observations and calculations.

Celestial divination: Celestial divination is a form of divination that involves the interpretation of celestial events and phenomena to gain insight or guidance. It is based on the belief that celestial bodies and their movements have a direct influence on human affairs. Celestial divination practices often involve studying celestial charts, observing astronomical events, and interpreting their symbolic significance to make predictions or understand the will of the divine.

Clay tablets: Clay tablets were a common medium for writing and record-keeping in ancient civilizations, including Mesopotamia. These tablets were made from clay and inscribed with cuneiform script, a wedge-shaped writing system. Clay tablets were used to document various types of information, including religious texts, legal codes, historical records, administrative documents, and literary works. They played a crucial role in the transmission and preservation of knowledge and were widely used before the advent of paper.

Community gatherings: Community gatherings refer to social gatherings or events where members of a community come together to engage in shared activities, exchange ideas, and foster social connections. These gatherings can take various forms, such as religious ceremonies, festivals, cultural events, or communal celebrations. Community gatherings play a vital role in strengthening social bonds, promoting cultural traditions, and creating a sense of belonging and unity within a community.

Connection with the divine: Connection with the divine refers to the experience of establishing a spiritual or transcendent relationship with a higher power or divine entity. It involves a deep sense of communion, reverence, and closeness to the divine, often cultivated through religious or spiritual practices, prayer, meditation, or rituals. Connection with the divine is seen as a means of seeking guidance, finding solace, and experiencing a sense of purpose or transcendence in one's life.

Contemplation: Contemplation refers to a state of deep thought, reflection, or meditation. It involves engaging in introspection, focusing one's attention inward, and contemplating profound questions or concepts. Contemplation is often associated with seeking insight, clarity, or spiritual understanding. It can be practiced individually or as part of a religious or philosophical tradition, offering a means of self-exploration, self-discovery, and inner growth.

Cosmic order: Cosmic order, also known as the order of the universe or the harmony of the cosmos, refers to the belief in an underlying structure or organization governing the natural world and the universe as a whole. It is the concept that everything in the universe operates according to a predetermined or inherent order, often associated with divinely ordained principles or laws. Cosmic order suggests that there is a harmony and balance in the functioning of the cosmos, and events and phenomena occur in accordance with this overarching order.

Cosmic symbolism: Cosmic symbolism refers to the use of symbols and symbolic representations to convey cosmic or universal concepts, principles, or relationships. It involves the interpretation and understanding of symbols as a means of accessing deeper meanings and connections to the cosmos or the divine. Cosmic symbolism can be found in various cultural, religious, and mythological traditions, where symbols are used to represent cosmic forces, celestial bodies, or archetypal patterns that reflect the larger order and significance of the universe.

Craftsmanship: Craftsmanship refers to the skill, artistry, and quality of workmanship displayed by artisans or craftsmen in creating objects or products. It involves the application of specialized knowledge, techniques, and attention to detail to produce items of aesthetic or functional value. Craftsmanship can be found in various fields, such as woodworking, metalworking, pottery, textiles, and jewelry making. It often encompasses a combination of technical proficiency, creativity, and a deep understanding of materials and techniques.

Creation stories: Creation stories, also known as creation myths or cosmogonic myths, are narratives or accounts that explain the origins of the universe, the world, and humanity. These stories are often deeply rooted in religious or cultural beliefs and provide explanations for fundamental questions about the creation and existence of the cosmos and human beings. Creation stories can vary across different cultures and civilizations, reflecting their unique cosmologies, deities, and cultural perspectives.

Cultural context: Cultural context refers to the social, historical, and environmental circumstances that shape and influence the meaning, interpretation, and significance of cultural phenomena. It involves understanding and analyzing cultural practices, beliefs, and expressions within their specific cultural frameworks, including the values, traditions, norms, and historical influences that give them context and shape their meaning. Cultural context is essential for comprehending the broader significance and implications of cultural phenomena, including rituals, customs, art, literature, and religious practices.

Cultural transmission: Cultural transmission refers to the process by which knowledge, beliefs, traditions, and cultural practices are passed on from one generation to another within a society or community. It involves the transfer of cultural information, values, and skills from older or more experienced members to younger or less experienced individuals. Cultural transmission can occur through various means, such as oral traditions, storytelling, education, apprenticeships, religious teachings, and socialization processes. It plays a crucial role in preserving and perpetuating cultural heritage, identity, and continuity.

D:

Deities: Deities are divine beings or gods/goddesses that are worshipped and revered in religious or spiritual traditions. They are often believed to possess supernatural powers and are associated with specific domains or aspects of life, such as love, fertility, war, or wisdom. Deities serve as central figures in religious cosmologies, myths, rituals, and belief systems, and are typically seen as intermediaries between the mortal and divine realms.

Devotion: Devotion refers to a deep sense of dedication, loyalty, and commitment shown towards a deity, spiritual practice, or religious belief. It involves heartfelt reverence, acts of worship, and the expression of sincere religious or spiritual devotion. Devotion can manifest in various forms, such as prayers, rituals, offerings, pilgrimages, or the observance of religious ceremonies and moral principles. It is often driven by a strong belief in the divine and a desire for a closer connection with the sacred.

Divine hierarchy: Divine hierarchy refers to the structured organization or ranking of deities within a particular religious or mythological system. It reflects the belief in varying levels of power, authority, and significance among the gods and goddesses. In some belief systems, a divine hierarchy may involve a supreme deity or creator at the top, followed by a pantheon of lesser gods and goddesses with specific roles and responsibilities. The divine hierarchy can influence the relationships, interactions, and dynamics between different deities.

Divine power struggles: Divine power struggles refer to conflicts, rivalries, or contests for power and authority among deities or divine beings within mythologies or religious narratives. These power struggles often involve competing interests, ambitions, or disagreements among the gods, which can lead to shifts in power, alliances, or the rise and fall of particular deities. Divine power struggles are a recurring theme in many mythologies and can serve to explain aspects of the natural world, social order, or moral values.

Divine presence: Divine presence refers to the perceived manifestation or experience of the divine within a religious or spiritual context. It is the belief in the immanence or active presence of the divine in the world or in specific sacred spaces, rituals, or individuals. Divine presence can be understood as a transcendent force or spiritual energy that is felt, sensed, or encountered by believers, often evoking feelings of awe, reverence, or a heightened sense of connection with the sacred.

Divination by dreams: Divination by dreams, also known as oneiromancy, is a form of divination that involves interpreting or analyzing dreams to gain insights or guidance. It is based on the belief that dreams can contain messages, symbols, or omens from the divine realm. Divination by dreams typically involves recording and analyzing dream experiences, recognizing patterns or symbols, and interpreting their significance in relation to personal or collective concerns, decisions, or future events.

Divination methods: Divination methods refer to the specific techniques, practices, or rituals employed to obtain divine knowledge or insights about the past, present, or future. These methods can vary across different cultures and historical periods, and may include astrology, the interpretation of celestial signs, reading omens in natural phenomena, examining animal entrails (extispicy), casting lots, consulting oracles, or using divinatory tools such as tarot cards, runes, or geomantic symbols.

Diviners: Diviners are individuals who possess specialized knowledge and skills in divination. They are practitioners who are trained in the art of interpreting signs, symbols, or messages from the divine realm to provide guidance, predictions, or advice. Diviners often occupy esteemed positions within their communities and may serve as religious or spiritual leaders, advisors, or intermediaries between humans and the divine.

Donations: Donations refer to voluntary contributions, offerings, or gifts made by individuals or groups to religious institutions, temples, or spiritual organizations. These contributions are often motivated by a sense of religious devotion, gratitude, or a desire to support the work of the religious community. Donations can take various forms, such as monetary offerings, goods, food, or services, and are used to sustain the operations of religious institutions, support religious ceremonies, or provide for the needs of the clergy or community members.

E:

Economic functions of temples: Economic functions of temples refer to the roles and activities of temples in managing and engaging in economic endeavors. Temples often controlled significant resources such as land, agricultural estates, livestock, and received donations and offerings from devotees. They played a central role in resource management, trade and commerce, and wealth accumulation, contributing to the economic well-being of the community.

Extispicy: Extispicy is a form of divination practiced in ancient Mesopotamia and other cultures, which involves the examination of animal entrails to gain insights or predictions about the future. In extispicy, the organs of sacrificed animals, such as the liver, were carefully observed and interpreted for signs and omens that were believed to provide guidance from the gods.

F:

Flexibility: Flexibility refers to the ability to adapt, adjust, or change according to different circumstances or needs. In the context of religious or spiritual practices, flexibility can refer to the capacity to accommodate various beliefs, rituals, or interpretations within a broader framework. It can also indicate the willingness to embrace diverse approaches to worship and spiritual expression, allowing for individual or communal variations while maintaining a cohesive religious or spiritual identity.

G:

Goddess worship: Goddess worship refers to the veneration, adoration, and devotion directed towards female deities in religious or spiritual traditions. It recognizes and celebrates the divine feminine aspect, emphasizing the qualities associated with goddesses such as nurturing, creativity, wisdom, and fertility. Goddess worship can take various forms, including rituals, prayers, ceremonies, and the recognition of goddesses as central figures in mythologies and religious practices.

Gratitude: Gratitude is a deep sense of appreciation, thankfulness, and recognition for the blessings, gifts, or positive aspects of one's life. In a religious or spiritual context, gratitude can be directed towards the divine, expressing appreciation for the divine presence, guidance, protection, or benevolence. It is often expressed through prayers, rituals, or acts of devotion as a way to cultivate a positive mindset, foster spiritual growth, and strengthen the connection with the divine.

H:

Historical preservation: Historical preservation refers to the conscious effort to safeguard and protect historical artifacts, documents, sites, and cultural heritage for future generations. In the context of religion, historical preservation can involve the preservation of sacred texts, ancient temples, religious artifacts, or rituals that hold significant historical, cultural, or religious value. It ensures the continuity of religious traditions, fosters a sense of identity, and allows for the study and understanding of past religious practices and beliefs.

I:

Industry: Industry refers to the sector of economic activity that involves the production of goods or the provision of services through manufacturing, processing, or other productive endeavors. In a broader sense, industry encompasses various branches of economic activity and plays a crucial role in the development and growth of societies.

Intellectual activities: Intellectual activities encompass a wide range of mental pursuits and engagements that involve the exploration, generation, and dissemination of knowledge, ideas, and concepts. These activities can include research, critical thinking, problem-solving, creative expression, scholarly pursuits, and academic endeavors. Intellectual activities contribute to the advancement of knowledge, innovation, and the development of societies.

Interconnectedness: Interconnectedness refers to the state or quality of being interconnected or interrelated. It highlights the idea that various elements, entities, or phenomena are connected or dependent on one another, forming a complex and interdependent system. In a religious or spiritual context, interconnectedness often refers to the belief that all beings and aspects of existence are interconnected, and actions or events in one domain can have effects or implications in other domains.

Intermediaries: Intermediaries are individuals, groups, or entities that act as intermediaries or go-betweens in a particular context. In a religious or spiritual context, intermediaries can refer to individuals who facilitate communication, interaction, or rituals between humans and the divine. They may serve as priests, priestesses, shamans, or other designated figures who act as mediators or conduits between the human and spiritual realms.

Introspection: Introspection is the act of examining or reflecting on one's own thoughts, feelings, experiences, or inner self. It involves self-observation and self-analysis, often with the intention of gaining self-awareness, insight, or personal growth. Introspection can be a contemplative practice employed in religious or spiritual contexts to deepen understanding, cultivate mindfulness, or foster a deeper connection with oneself and the divine.

K:

Knowledge preservation: The act of safeguarding and maintaining knowledge for future generations. In the context of ancient Mesopotamia, it refers to the efforts made by scholars, scribes, and libraries to preserve and transmit cultural, historical, scientific, and religious knowledge through various means, such as the creation and storage of written texts.

L:

Library collections: Refers to the compiled and organized collections of written materials found in ancient libraries, such as the temple libraries of Mesopotamia. These collections encompassed a wide range of subjects, including religious texts, historical accounts, scientific treatises, and literary works, among others. The library collections served as repositories of knowledge and played a vital role in the preservation and dissemination of information.

M:

Marketplaces: Physical locations where goods were bought and sold, often within the city centers of ancient Mesopotamian civilizations. These marketplaces served as important economic hubs where merchants, traders, and craftsmen gathered to exchange goods, negotiate prices, and engage in commercial transactions. The marketplaces facilitated trade and commerce, contributing to economic growth and the circulation of goods within the region.

Mesopotamian city-states: Refers to the independent urban centers that emerged in ancient Mesopotamia, characterized by their self-governance and unique cultural identities. These city-states, such as Ur, Uruk, Babylon, and Assyria, functioned as political, economic, and religious centers, with their own ruling elites, administrative structures, and patron deities. They played a significant role in shaping the social, cultural, and political landscape of the region.

Multidisciplinary studies: Refers to the practice of engaging in research and scholarship across multiple fields or disciplines. In ancient Mesopotamia, scholars and scribes often pursued multidisciplinary studies, exploring diverse subjects ranging from astronomy and mathematics to literature and religious rituals. This holistic approach to knowledge acquisition and interpretation fostered a rich tradition of scholarship and contributed to advancements in various fields of knowledge.

Mythological narratives: Refers to the stories, legends, and accounts that form the mythology of a particular culture or civilization. In ancient Mesopotamia, mythological narratives played a significant role in shaping religious beliefs, cosmological understandings, and cultural values. These narratives often involved gods, goddesses, and epic heroes, and provided explanations for the origins of the universe, the nature of human existence, and the dynamics of the divine realm.

Mythology: The collective body of myths, stories, and religious beliefs that characterize a particular culture or civilization. In the context of ancient Mesopotamia, mythology encompassed a wide range of narratives, legends, and religious beliefs that were integral to the worldview and cultural identity of the Mesopotamian people. These mythological traditions included creation myths, tales of gods and goddesses, epic poems, and heroic legends, among others. Mythology served to provide explanations for natural phenomena, establish religious rituals and practices, and transmit cultural values and traditions.

O:

Offerings: Refers to the act of presenting or dedicating something, often valuable or symbolic, to a deity or spiritual entity as an expression of devotion, gratitude, or supplication. Offerings in ancient Mesopotamia could include items such as food, drink, incense, precious metals, or crafted objects. They were made at temples, shrines, or personal altars as part of religious rituals and practices.

P:

Pantheon: Refers to the collective group of gods and goddesses worshiped in a particular religion or culture. In ancient Mesopotamia, the pantheon consisted of numerous deities with distinct roles, domains, and characteristics. These gods and goddesses formed a complex network of divine beings, each associated with specific aspects of life, nature, or society. The Mesopotamian pantheon included prominent deities like Enlil, Enki, Inanna, Marduk, and Ishtar, among others.

Personal altars: Refers to small, individual spaces or designated areas within homes or private spaces where individuals would create personal shrines or altars for religious or spiritual practices. Personal altars allowed for intimate worship, meditation, and connection with the divine in the comfort of one's own space. They often featured offerings, sacred objects, and representations of chosen deities.

Personal offerings: Refers to the act of making individualized or private offerings to deities or spiritual entities. These offerings were distinct from those made in communal or public religious rituals and were typically made at personal altars or sacred spaces. Personal offerings were expressions of personal devotion, gratitude, or requests for divine intervention in specific personal matters.

Polytheistic beliefs: Refers to the belief system that recognizes and worships multiple gods or deities. Ancient Mesopotamia was characterized by polytheistic beliefs, where the pantheon consisted of a multitude of gods and goddesses, each with their own attributes, roles, and domains. Polytheistic beliefs allowed for a diverse range of deities that governed various aspects of life, nature, and human society.

Prayer: Refers to the act of addressing or communicating with a deity or spiritual entity through spoken or written words. Prayer in ancient Mesopotamia was an essential aspect of religious devotion and was often performed in formalized rituals and ceremonies. Prayers could express praise, thanksgiving, supplication, or seek guidance and blessings from the gods.

Production and trade: Refers to the processes involved in the creation, manufacturing, and exchange of goods and commodities within an economic system. In ancient Mesopotamia, production and trade were integral to the development of urban centers and the growth of civilizations. Skilled craftsmen and artisans produced a variety of goods, including textiles, pottery, metalwork, and luxury items. These goods were traded locally and internationally, contributing to economic prosperity and cultural exchange in the region.

R:

Reciprocal relationship: Refers to a mutually beneficial and interconnected relationship between two parties. In the context of ancient Mesopotamia, a reciprocal relationship existed between humans and the divine. It was believed that through acts of devotion, worship, and offerings, humans could establish a connection with the gods and receive their favor, blessings, and protection. In return, humans were expected to fulfill their religious obligations and honor the gods through rituals and adherence to religious principles.

Religious architecture: Refers to the design, construction, and layout of structures and buildings dedicated to religious or spiritual practices. In ancient Mesopotamia, religious architecture included temples, ziggurats, shrines, and other sacred structures. These buildings were often characterized by their grandeur, elaborate decorations, and specific architectural features that symbolized the connection between the divine realm and the mortal world.

Religious rituals and ceremonies: Refers to prescribed sets of actions, gestures, prayers, and symbolic activities performed as part of religious worship and devotion. Religious rituals and ceremonies in ancient Mesopotamia were diverse and varied, depending on the specific deity, occasion, or religious tradition. They could involve offerings, prayers, processions, recitations, music, dance, and sacrifices. These rituals were believed to establish a sacred connection, invoke the presence of the gods, and ensure the order and well-being of the cosmos.

Resource management: Refers to the organized control, allocation, and utilization of resources within a society or institution. In the context of ancient Mesopotamia, temples played a significant role in resource management. Temples often owned extensive land holdings, agricultural estates, and herds of livestock. They were responsible for overseeing the management of these resources, ensuring their efficient use, and distributing their products for various economic activities, as well as for sustaining religious practices and supporting the community.

Ritual objects: Refers to specific items, artifacts, or symbolic representations used in religious rituals and ceremonies. In ancient Mesopotamia, ritual objects included sacred vessels, statues or idols of deities, ritual garments, incense burners, and various other items associated with religious practices. These objects held symbolic meaning and were believed to facilitate communication with the divine, enhance the effectiveness of rituals, and embody the presence of the gods.

Rituals: Refers to a set of prescribed actions, behaviors, or ceremonies performed in a specific order and with symbolic significance. Rituals in ancient Mesopotamia were integral to religious practices and encompassed a wide range of activities, including offerings, prayers, sacrifices, processions, purification rites, and recitations. Rituals played a crucial role in establishing and maintaining the relationship between humans and the gods, ensuring the proper functioning of the cosmos, and addressing the needs and concerns of the community.

S:

Sacred colors: Refers to specific colors that hold religious or symbolic significance within a particular religious tradition or cultural context. In ancient Mesopotamia, certain colors were considered sacred and associated with specific deities or concepts. For example, the color blue was often associated with the sky and the divine, while red symbolized fertility and vitality.

Sacred geometry: Refers to the use of geometric patterns, shapes, and proportions that hold symbolic or spiritual significance within a religious or mystical context. In ancient Mesopotamia, sacred geometry was employed in the design and construction of religious structures such as ziggurats and temples. These geometric principles were believed to reflect the cosmic order and the divine harmony of the universe.

Sacred marriage: Refers to a ritual or symbolic union between a god or goddess and a human priest or priestess, representing the divine and mortal realms coming together. In ancient Mesopotamia, sacred marriages were enacted as part of religious ceremonies and festivals, often involving the king or a high priestess. These unions were believed to ensure fertility, abundance, and the continued well-being of the community.

Sacred spaces: Refers to physical locations or environments that are deemed sacred or holy within a religious or spiritual tradition. In ancient Mesopotamia, sacred spaces included temples, shrines, and specific areas within cities or natural landscapes. These spaces were dedicated to religious rituals, worship, and the presence of deities. They were regarded as the meeting points between the divine and human realms.

Exploring Ancient Mesopotamian Mythology, Rivalries, and Spiritual Legacies

Sacrifice: Refers to the act of offering something valuable or significant to a deity as an act of devotion or propitiation. In ancient Mesopotamia, sacrifices were an important aspect of religious rituals and ceremonies. They often involved the offering of animals, food, or other items that held symbolic meaning. Sacrifices were seen as a way to express gratitude, seek divine favor, and establish a reciprocal relationship with the gods.

Scholarly pursuits: Refers to the intellectual and academic endeavors undertaken by scholars and scribes in ancient Mesopotamia. These pursuits included the study and interpretation of ancient texts, the compilation of lexicons and reference materials, the exploration of scientific and philosophical concepts, and the preservation of historical and cultural knowledge.

Scientific advancements: Refers to the progress and developments made in scientific fields and disciplines within ancient Mesopotamia. Mesopotamian scholars made significant contributions to various scientific fields, including astronomy, mathematics, medicine, and agriculture. Their observations, calculations, and empirical knowledge laid the foundation for future scientific advancements in these areas.

Skilled artisans: Refers to individuals who possessed specialized craftsmanship and expertise in creating various artistic and practical objects. In ancient Mesopotamia, skilled artisans played a crucial role in producing intricate artworks, sculptures, textiles, pottery, and other crafts. Their skills and craftsmanship were highly valued, and their works served religious, aesthetic, and utilitarian purposes.

Social and cultural impact: Refers to the influence and effects of religious beliefs, rituals, and practices on the social and cultural aspects of ancient Mesopotamian society. Religion played a central role in shaping social norms, values, and behaviors. It provided a framework for moral and ethical principles, guided interpersonal relationships, and fostered a sense of community and identity.

Spiritual growth: Refers to the personal and individual development of one's spiritual beliefs, understanding, and connection with the divine or transcendent. In ancient Mesopotamia, spiritual growth was often pursued through religious rituals, devotion, and contemplation. It involved deepening one's understanding of the divine, seeking personal enlightenment, and cultivating a sense of inner harmony and connection with the sacred.

Sumerian gods: Refers to the deities worshipped in the ancient Sumerian civilization of Mesopotamia. The Sumerian pantheon included a wide array of gods and goddesses who were believed to govern various aspects of the natural world, human activities, and cosmic phenomena. Examples of Sumerian gods include Enlil, the god of wind and storms, Inanna, the goddess of love and war, and Utu, the god of the sun.

Sumerian religion: Refers to the religious beliefs, rituals, and practices of the ancient Sumerian civilization in Mesopotamia. Sumerian religion was polytheistic, with a complex pantheon of gods and goddesses who were revered and worshipped. Rituals, sacrifices, and prayers were performed to appease the gods, seek their favor, and maintain cosmic harmony. Sumerian religious beliefs influenced subsequent Mesopotamian cultures and had a lasting impact on the development of religious traditions in the region.

Symbolism: Refers to the use of symbols or symbolic representations to convey deeper meanings or concepts. Symbolism played a significant role in ancient Mesopotamian religious practices, art, and literature. Various objects, animals, colors, and patterns held symbolic significance, representing specific deities, cosmic forces, abstract concepts, or cultural values. Symbolism served as a means of communication, expression, and connection with the divine.

T:

Temples: Refers to sacred structures dedicated to religious worship and rituals in ancient Mesopotamia. Temples were the physical embodiments of the divine presence and served as the focal points of religious activities within the community. They were constructed with architectural significance, often featuring elaborate designs, monumental facades, and inner sanctuaries where statues or symbols of gods and goddesses were housed.

Trade and commerce: Refers to the exchange of goods and services through commercial activities and transactions. In ancient Mesopotamia, trade and commerce played a vital role in the economy and societal development. The region's strategic location between different civilizations facilitated the flow of goods, resulting in vibrant marketplaces and trade networks. Mesopotamians engaged in both local and long-distance trade, exchanging commodities such as textiles, metals, agricultural products, and luxury items.

Tribute: Refers to the payment or offering made by a subordinate entity, such as a conquered city-state or vassal, to a dominant power as a form of acknowledgment, submission, or appeasement. In ancient Mesopotamia, powerful empires often extracted tribute from their conquered territories, including valuable resources, goods, or financial contributions. Tribute served as a means to assert political control, demonstrate superiority, and maintain economic stability within the empire.

Exploring Ancient Mesopotamian Mythology, Rivalries, and Spiritual Legacies

Tithes: Refers to a portion of one's income or produce that is given as an offering or contribution to support religious institutions or clergy. In ancient Mesopotamia, tithes were commonly levied by temples or religious authorities as a religious duty or obligation. The tithes collected were used to sustain the operations of the temple, support the clergy, and fund religious ceremonies and rituals.

Trade routes: Refers to established paths or networks that facilitated the transportation and exchange of goods and ideas between different regions. In ancient Mesopotamia, numerous trade routes crisscrossed the region, connecting the major city-states and linking them with neighboring civilizations. These trade routes played a crucial role in promoting cultural exchange, economic growth, and the diffusion of knowledge and technologies.

Tablets: Refers to clay tablets that were widely used as a writing medium in ancient Mesopotamia. These tablets were made from wet clay and inscribed with cuneiform script, one of the earliest forms of writing. Tablets were used for various purposes, including recording administrative, legal, and commercial transactions, preserving literary and religious texts, and documenting historical events. They were crucial in the preservation and transmission of knowledge and information in ancient Mesopotamia.

Terracotta figurines: Refers to small, three-dimensional sculptures made from fired clay in ancient Mesopotamia. Terracotta figurines were created for various purposes, including religious rituals, domestic use, and artistic expression. They depicted deities, humans, animals, and mythical creatures, reflecting the religious beliefs, cultural practices, and artistic traditions of the time. These figurines provide valuable insights into the social, religious, and artistic aspects of ancient Mesopotamian society.

Territorial expansion: Refers to the acquisition and enlargement of territories by a ruling power through military conquest or political alliances. In ancient Mesopotamia, territorial expansion was a common feature of the region's history, with city-states and empires constantly vying for control and dominance. Through military campaigns and diplomatic strategies, Mesopotamian rulers sought to expand their territorial boundaries, increase their resources, and exert their influence over a larger population.

Tribal societies: Refers to social structures in which people are organized into tribes, which are kinship-based groups with a common ancestry and cultural identity. In ancient Mesopotamia, before the rise of centralized city-states and empires, tribal societies were prevalent. Tribes played a significant role in social

W:

Wealth accumulation: Refers to the process of acquiring and amassing financial resources, assets, or valuable possessions. In ancient Mesopotamia, wealth accumulation had various sources, including trade, agriculture, and control over resources. Temples played a significant role in wealth accumulation through offerings, donations, and tithes from devotees. The accumulation of wealth provided economic stability and resources to support the operations of temples, patronage of the arts, and investment in economic activities.

Worship: Refers to the act of showing reverence, devotion, and adoration to deities or higher powers. Worship in ancient Mesopotamia was a central aspect of religious life and involved rituals, prayers, and offerings to appease and honor the gods and goddesses. Worship was conducted in temples or sacred spaces and involved a range of practices such as hymns, sacrifices, and ceremonies. It was seen as a means to establish a connection with the divine, seek blessings, and ensure the well-being of individuals and the community.

Milton Keynes UK
Ingram Content Group UK Ltd.
UKHW050844181223
434584UK00011B/936

9 798889 901044